The American
Search for
Mideast Peace

The American
Search for
Mideast Peace

DAN TSCHIRGI

PRAEGER

New York
Westport, Connecticut
London

Copyright Acknowledgment

Grateful acknowledgment is made to Oxford University Press for permission to base the maps appearing in this book on ones found in Michael Brecher's *Decisions in Israel's Foreign Policy* (London: Oxford University Press, 1974).

Library of Congress Cataloging-in-Publication Data

Tschirgi, Dan.
  The American search for Mideast peace.
  Bibliography: p.
  Includes index.
  1. Jewish-Arab relations—1967–1973. 2. Jewish-Arab
relations—1973– . 3. Israel-Arab conflicts.
4. United States—Foreign relations—Israel. 5. Israel—
Foreign relations—United States. 6. United States—
Foreign relations—1945– . I. Title.
DS119.7.T745 1989   327.7305694   88–25481
ISBN 0–275–92583–8 (alk. paper)

First published in 1989

Praeger Publishers, One Madison Avenue, New York, NY   10010
A division of Greenwood Press, Inc.

Printed in the United States of America

The paper used in this book complies with the
Permanent Paper Standard issued by the National
Information Standards Organization (Z39.48—1984).

10   9   8   7   6   5   4   3   2   1

For Necla, Mark, and John,
and for
Donald and Bobbie Webster,
who really are "teachers of teachers"

CONTENTS

PREFACE

So much literature has been generated by the American effort to promote peace between Arabs and Israelis that a reader should approach any new work on the topic by first asking what contribution it hopes to make. The present volume aims essentially at stocktaking. Its purpose, by synthesizing and interpreting—and therefore, one hopes, putting into the form of an intelligible panorama—the large amount of information that can be gleaned from personal accounts, partisan critiques, government documents, and the public record, is to portray and explain the current state of the U.S. search for Mideast peace.

Certainly, it seems time for this to be done. Two decades mark a sufficient passage of time to make stocktaking legitimate, all the more since most of the literature on the subject was produced simultaneously with the events chronicled here. As always under such circumstances, memoirs, reports, polemics, and analyses are swayed as much by the heat of recent and ongoing controversy as by pressing hopes and fears for the future. The utility, perhaps the luxury, of stocktaking is that some of the heat is reduced while earlier projections are possibly viewed retrospectively with more objectivity.

An even more important reason for putting the American search for Mideast peace into perspective at this time is the turn of events that occurred while the following pages were at the press and which gave birth to the *Postscript* at the book's end. With the United States now having agreed to speak directly to the Palestine Liberation Organization for the first time since 1975, a true crossroads may have been reached. Stocktaking seems not only advisable but necessary.

The analysis that unfolds below does not present a happy picture. It begins by identifying the hope for Middle East peace that gripped Washington in 1967, proceeds via an examination of steps that cumulatively undermined that goal, and concludes that both the normative and structural aspects of peace as Washington envisaged it in 1967 have been placed in serious jeopardy by the late 1980s. It also suggests that recent incipient signs of possible U.S. willingness to come to terms with Palestinian nationalism may constitute the final hope for a peaceful resolution of the Arab-Israeli problem.

The work is divided into five chapters which are, in turn, subdivided into various subsections. The four substantive chapters, as indicated by their titles, reflect stages in the progression of early U.S. hopes for peace. While the search for peace has involved far too many international actors for shortcomings to be blamed on any one party, the focus here is on the United States. Thus, the effort to understand Washington's approach to peacemaking seeks to uncover political dynamics arising from and affecting the American context of policymaking.

Chapter One examines the Johnson administration, and presents both a background to U.S. involvement with the issue of Palestine prior to 1967 and an overview of developments after that date. Chapters Two through Four follow, in more detailed and chronological form, the intricacies of the approaches taken by the administrations of Richard Nixon, Gerald Ford, Jimmy Carter, and Ronald Reagan. Chapter Five tries to suggest the nature of the underlying dynamics that have shaped two decades of the American search for Mideast peace and examines their implications for the future.

Any book is the product of many participants, although the author justifiably retains sole responsibility for all shortcomings. Without the support of several institutions, I could neither have begun nor finished this work. Among those which must be mentioned are the Center for International and Strategic Affairs of the University of California, Los Angeles, which administered a travel and research grant enabling me to spend time in Israel; the Harry S. Truman Institute for Peace Research at the Hebrew University of Jerusalem, which provided living and working space for an extended period and ready access to documents and individuals whom I would only with great difficulty have otherwise tapped; La Universidad de las Americas, Puebla, in Puebla, Mexico, which provided initial support for this study; and the American University in Cairo, where my colleagues have been more than flexible in helping me find the time required for the project's conclusion.

Many friends facilitated my work, sometimes in ways that I alone appreciate. Bennett Ramberg, Edy Kaufman, Michael Intrilligator, Geri Harrison, Teresa Austria, Ali Dessouki, Gloria Meza Casana, Hanan Mikhail Ashrawi, Shlomo and Ghulda Ilya, Rosemarie Jalbert and Margot Neuberg all have my thanks, and an acknowledgement that my ideas do not at all necessarily coincide with theirs. Don and Bobbie Webster, of Pilgrim Place in Claremont, California, not only generously provided needed research funds but also even more necessary encouragement by their faith in this project.

Two graduate students at the American University in Cairo were particularly helpful. Mr. Ashraf Mohsen put in long and thoughtful hours on a variety of assignments whose fruits appear in the following chapters. Ms. Leila Hassanein provided indispensible aid and inexhaustable patience as well as a happy skill in reproducing maps for a cantankerous professor.

Above all, I thank my wife and colleague, Necla, whose good sense, equally good humor, and even better critical powers helped keep things in perspective.

Körle Yatan, Şaşı Kalkar
("Who Lies With the Blind, Arises Cross-eyed")

Turkish Proverb

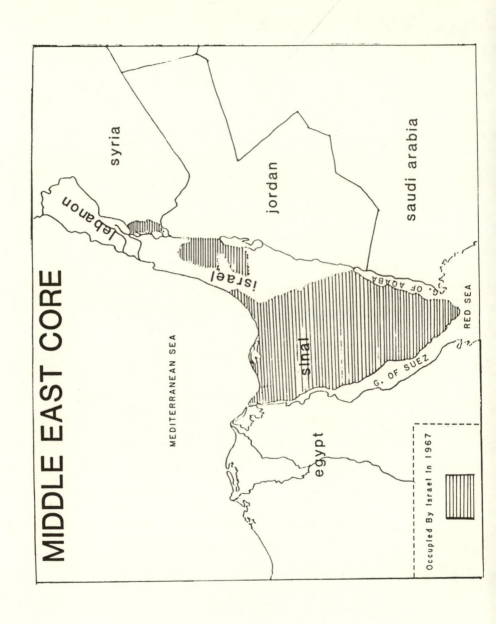

MIDDLE EAST CORE

syria

lebanon

jordan

saudi arabia

israel

sinai

G. OF AQABA

G. OF SUEZ

RED SEA

MEDITERRANEAN SEA

egypt

Occupied By Israel In 1967

1

MAKING OF AN OBJECTIVE

> ...boundaries cannot and should not reflect the weight of military conquest.
>
> Lyndon B. Johnson

The American search for Mideast peace dates from 1967. In that year, Israel's resounding victory over its bordering Arab enemies seemed to offer Washington an opportunity to push strongly for a final resolution of the conflict that for decades had complicated, and which threatened eventually to undermine, the U.S. position in the Middle East.

It fell to the administration of Lyndon Baines Johnson to settle on a new U.S. stategy for dealing with the Arab–Israeli problem. While the Johnson administration initially underestimated the major difficulties that would be encountered, it quickly enough discerned their broad outlines. Over the next two decades, all administrations would find that approaches glowing with pristine abstract logic were in practice roughly treated by the the hard reality of the needs and ambitions of other actors in the Middle East. By the time Johnson left office in early 1969, Washington had already significantly modified its original peacemaking efforts.

However, it is impossible to understand developments in U.S. policy under Johnson and subsequent presidents without first looking at two earlier phases in Washington's handling of the Arab–Israeli issue. For in the Middle East the past seems indeed to be the prelude to the future.

BACKGROUND: STAGES IN THE U.S. APPROACH TO ARAB–ZIONIST TENSIONS

From the beginning of its reluctant involvement in the struggle for Palestine, the United States has consistently declared itself in favor of a peaceful resolution of Arab–Zionist tensions in the Middle East. Yet, for most of the past fifty years this stated preference was not a sustained objective of operational policy. Not until 1967 did Washington give priority to working toward a definitive and peaceful solution.

That decision marked a new stage in active American involvement in the clash between Arab and Jewish nationalisms. Two earlier phases, the first occupying the decade between 1939 and Israel's creation in 1948 and the other the nineteen years between 1948 and 1967, differed from each other in many ways. Still, they shared a singular common feature: during both periods U.S. policy was fundamentally geared to shielding Washington from the need to adopt a precise position toward the central issue that divided Arabs and Jews; whether one, or somehow both, of the peoples claiming Palestine would achieve unquestionable political dominance in that ancient land.

Franklin Delano Roosevelt was the first U.S. president to become ensnared in the uncomfortable political thicket formed by the competing claims on Palestine. It was 1939 and World War II loomed ominously on the horizon. Feeling forsaken by Great Britain, which held the mandate for Palestine under a pledge to further the establishment of a Jewish national homeland in that country, Zionists turned to the United States in hope of achieving a Jewish state by enlisting Washington's aid against London's growing recalcitrance. Over the next several years, Zionists constructed a strong bedrock of organized support within the American body politic.

Roosevelt was soon caught between the increasing domestic political weight of American Zionism and foreign policy considerations that lent importance to the cultivation of ties with the Arab world. During the early years of World War II, the president's hesitation over supporting the Zionist cause was fueled mainly by the requirements of Allied military strategy. With Axis forces in North Africa and the Eastern Mediterranean, Washington believed that Arab goodwill was vital to the defense of the Middle East. When the Allies swung to the offensive after 1943, military considerations continued to lend importance to the preservation of Middle East tranquility. However, by the war's closing months, the administration's reluctance to embark on a pro-Zionist policy rested increasingly on its perception of long-term strategic, political, and economic U.S. interests. These basic objectives crystallized rapidly after the war and, together with the commitment to Israel's existence after 1948, have continued to define the underlying purpose of U.S. involvement in the Middle East. They include: limiting the growth of Soviet influence in the region; promoting and expanding the U.S. political and economic presence in the region; and securing the strategic capability to guarantee continued Western access to Middle East oil. In coping with the conflicting international and domestic pressures generated by the Palestine struggle, Roosevelt lapsed into well-calculated indecision. As noted by Secretary of State Cordell Hull, the president frequently adopted the simple expedient of passing out contradictory promises to Arabs and Zionists. When Roosevelt died in the spring of 1945, the United States held no clear position on the basic question of Palestine's ultimate political disposition.[1]

The issue posed even greater problems for Harry S. Truman. Lacking the protective aura of prestige and popularity acquired by Roosevelt during twelve years in office, Truman was more vulnerable to domestic pressures for a pro-Zionist policy. These were inevitably heightened at the end of the war by revelations of the enormity of Hitler's anti-semitic campaign and by the plight of thousands of homeless Jews languishing in European displaced-persons camps.

However, if the domestic horn of Washington's Palestine dilemma was sharpened when Truman took office, the same was true of the international considerations that caused Roosevelt to balk at the prospect of aligning the United States with Zionism. The prompt disintegration of the wartime alliance against the Axis soon metamorphisized into the outset of the "Cold War." The Middle East's geographic importance, as well as the commercial and military importance of its plentiful oilfields—qualities that Americans had grown to appreciate during the war—assumed added strategic significance. In short, the long-range strategic, economic, and political interests that the Roosevelt administration had perceived rapidly crystallized during Truman's first years in office. The concomitant of these interests—the necessity of securing the Arab world's friendship—could not be ignored.

Using rather different tactics, Truman sought to emulate Roosevelt's policy of avoiding a clearcut position on Palestine's political future. Despite imaginative efforts along these lines, the president's room for maneuver was ultimately undercut by the string of tentative, contradictory, and vague commitments he assumed during his first three years in office. In the end, U.S. policy was characterized by wild swings and about-faces. These included Washington's leading role in securing the UN General Assembly's resolution of November 29, 1947 that recommended Palestine's partition into Arab and Jewish states, the abrupt reversal of U.S. support for the resolution several weeks later, and Truman's subsequent de facto recognition of the newly proclaimed state of Israel, even while

American diplomats worked under orders to find some other solution. The denouement was aptly characterized by Nadev Safran as "an undignified spectacle of United States inconsistency."[2]

The outcome also carried a general lesson. For despite Washington's futile attempts to remain aloof from Palestine's affairs, both the Roosevelt and Truman administrations had generally held that war between Jews and Arabs in that country would be harmful to the best interests of the United States. Yet the circumstances that led to the outbreak of that war in 1948 were to a great extent produced by the very tactics through which Washington sought to disassociate itself from Palestine's political future. The lesson was that in the absence of a concrete and specific objective related to the points of contention between Arab and Jews, the United States was apt to find not only that power—whether defined in terms of military and economic resources or moral suasion—could be nullified, but also that its own policies could further unwanted results.[3]

The immediate results of the 1948 Arab–Israeli war did not prove as harmful to the United States as Washington had feared. Soviet hopes of becoming directly involved in the region by participating in a suggested UN peacekeeping effort were successfully frustrated. Arab regimes, although embittered by the U.S. role in the Jewish state's creation, had no intention of permitting Palestine to be the crucible of their relations with the United States. Nonetheless, the war did plunge the Middle East into an enduring crisis. Israel emerged from the fray controlling considerably more territory than envisaged by the UN partition resolution. Jerusalem, rather than internationalized, as called for by the UN plan, was divided between Israel and Jordan. The Palestinian state never materialized. Gaza came under Egyptian suzerainty, while the West Bank was taken by Jordan. After 1949, a state of war technically existed between Israel and its Arab neighbors. Egypt, Jordan, Syria, and Lebanon were therefore separated from Israel by armistice lines rather than legal borders.

What became known in the Arab world as "the disaster" fell most heavily upon the Palestinian Arabs. Unstable at best, chaotic at worst—and forced to develop under the repressive conditions of the mandate—Palestinian political life had failed to produce a strong organizational infrastructure.[4] The 1948 maelstrom was a crushing blow. Over 750,000 destitute refugees welled up from the wreckage. Some were to live under the wary eyes of Egyptian or Jordanian officials in Gaza or the West Bank. Thousands more scattered to Syria, Lebanon, and beyond. There remained in the Jewish state some 160,000 Arabs who settled into a second-class existence under watchful Israeli rule.

From Washington's vantage point, the outcome of the first Arab–Israeli War appeared to offer an opportunity to pursue long-term U.S.

objectives in the Middle East without being hindered by the intractable clash of nationalisms in Palestine. With the demise of the Palestinian community as a political actor, it was believed that no clash of vital interests now necessarily divided Israel from the surrounding Arab states. Time—for hurts to heal, for passions to subside—seemed to be the essential requirement for the development of Middle East peace. This led to the conclusion that Arab–Israeli tensions would eventually abate to a point permitting the diplomatic resolution of outstanding issues. In turn, this indicated the advisability of stabilizing the Middle East by preventing, or at least limiting, conflict between Israel and the Arab world. With Arab opinion infuriated by the 1948 defeat and inflamed by the Palestinian's plight, initial U.S. efforts to promote regional stability focused on refugee relief.[5]

This policy was as much an effort to provide tangible evidence of a continuing desire for Arab friendship as it was an attempt to contain a highly volatile source of Arab–Israeli friction. However, the most important element of the American search for Mideast stability was found in the "territorial integrity" formula enshrined in the 1950 Tripartite Declaration."

Issued jointly with Great Britain and France, the declaration sought to promote Middle East tranquility by pledging the Western powers to limit arms transfers to the region and to support impartially the territorial integrity of all Middle Eastern states.[6] As an attempt at "great power" coordination in the Middle East, the venture was a resounding failure. Within two years, French officials were making no secret of their determination to act unilaterally in the realm of arms transfers. In 1954, France entered into its first major arms agreement with Israel—inaugurating a relationship that until 1967 would make Paris that country's primary weapons supplier. A year later, the young revolutionary Egyptian regime of Gamal Abdel Nasser concluded the first arms agreement between an Arab state and the Soviet Bloc. The Middle East arms race was on, and the Tripartite Declaration's provisions on arms transfers were rendered meaningless.

Nor did the declaration's support for territorial integrity fare much better.[7] In 1956, Great Britain and France joined Israel in invading Egypt.

Still, despite its inapplicability to Western policy as a whole, the Tripartite Declaration's stress on "territorial integrity" provided the cornerstone of the U.S. approach to the Arab–Israeli problem, until 1967. The proclaimed impartiality commitment, to uphold the territorial integrity of all states in the region, together with the implication that violators of the sacrosanct principle would be punished and victims succored, in effect sought to dichotomize U.S. relations with the Middle East. On the one hand, the stand assured Israel of U.S. support for its continued existence. On the other, it attempted to convey to Arab states the readiness of the United States to react against aggressive actions by Israel. In Washington's view the approach seemed not only balanced but also a credible deterrent to renewed major fighting in the Middle East.

The strategy yielded mixed results. On the one hand, the growth of U.S. influence in the Middle East prior to 1967 owed much to Washington's efforts to open a new chapter in U.S.–Arab relations based on the "territorial integrity" formula, the high point of which was marked by the Eisenhower administration's opposition to the Israeli–French–British invasion of Egypt in 1956. Ten years after Israel's creation, the emergence of the United States as the principle great power in the Middle East seemed a solid tribute to the effectiveness of its post–1948 approach to the Arab–Israeli conflict.

However, from the perspective of a more distant vantage point it is now evident that the successful containment of the Middle East problem yielded diminishing political returns. If the United States quickly became the major external actor in the Middle East, it also increasingly became a political lightning rod for tensions between the West and the post-World War II generation of Arab nationalist regimes. While ties with such countries as Saudi Arabia, Lebanon, Libya, Tunisia, Morocco, and Jordan generally bolstered U.S. influence in the Arab world, relations with self-declared progressive states were beset by suspicion and discord—although until 1967 no Arab government seemed anxious to risk alienating the United States completely.

No single cause underlay the vicissitudes of U.S. relations with the leading exponents of Arab nationalism, which by the late 1950s included Egypt, Syria, and Iraq. Inter-Arab rivalries, the foment of modernizing efforts amid fundamental questions of national identity, the rise of Third World "positive neutralism", and an historically derived mistrust of Western intentions all helped generate tension between Washington and governments bent on seeking a new order in the Arab world. However, it is equally true that each of these sources of friction was exacerbated and complicated by the smoldering confrontation between Israel and the Arabs.

The decade that followed the Suez War amply demonstrated the detrimental impact of the unresolved Palestine conflict. Despite the facade of a relatively stable impasse between the Arab states and Israel, the issue merged with global and regional political currents to form the volatile admixture that eventually culminated in war. Under the circumstances, Washington's ability to project a principled neutrality toward the Arab–Israeli quarrel was increasingly undermined.

U.S. fears that the conflict would provide an avenue for Soviet penetration of the Middle East had been heightened in 1955, when Nasser reacted to the refusal of Western countries to sell arms to Egypt by concluding a deal with Czechoslovakia. They seemed to be confirmed in later years as the Soviet Union built on the Czech arms deal to become a direct supplier of weapons to Egypt, Syria, and Iraq.

Afraid of jeopardizing relations with the Arabs, but fearing that a destabilizing arms imbalance was in the making, the United States secretly encouraged West Germany to enter into a major arms agreement with Israel in 1961. However, a year later, with Nasser embroiled in the Yemen war, Washington agreed to sell defensive Hawk anti-aircraft missiles to Israel as well as to supply limited amounts of arms to Jordan and Saudi Arabia.

In 1963, Egypt received first-generation Soviet weapons. Although Israel still enjoyed military superiority, Washington came under increasing pressure to provide the Jewish state with more arms. The decision to do so was communicated to Arab leaders in 1965. Noting that established U.S. policy was to avoid becoming "a major supplier of arms" to the Middle East, the State Department argued that this had not prevented Washington from occasionally engaging in "selective sales":

[E]xceptions to our general policy have been based on careful case by case examinations and a determination that such a sale would not be a destabilizing factor. The United States has made over the years repeated quiet efforts to encourage limitations on arms buildups in this area. Until those bear fruit, however, the United States cannot be indifferent to the potentially destabilizing effect of massive Soviet sales of arms to the area.[8]

Although cast in subdued terms, this statement foreshadowed a major policy shift. In mid–1966, Israeli Prime Minister Levi Eshkol announced that the United States had pledged to preserve the Middle East balance of power, a development he hailed as "a revolution in American thinking."[9]

The change both reflected and furthered tensions between the United States and progressive Arab nationalists. It also implied the possibility of an accelerated arms race between those regimes and Israel. This prospect seemed even more likely after the 1966 rise to power in Syria of the radical left wing of the Ba'ath party and Washington's decision at the end of that year to demonstrate displeasure with Nasser's regime by ending grain shipments to Egypt.

By the beginning of 1967, then, the U.S. hope of preserving a modicum of stability in the Middle East while remaining aloof from the Arab–Israeli problem was clearly threatened. In itself, the confluence of global and regional politics was steadily eroding the utility of the territorial integrity formula as a basis for U.S. policy. Yet, the formula's ultimate demise cannot be attributed solely to external factors. For its original employment rested on four basic assumptions, three of which were disproved by the outbreak of the 1967 war.

The first of these unfortunate premises was that the Arab world would accept the commitment to territorial integrity as proof of U.S. impartiality toward the Arab–Israeli conflict. Neither the memory of what Arabs saw as American diplomatic treachery prior to 1948, nor the subsequent growth of a close relationship between the United States and Israel, nor the obviously pro-Israel bent of U.S. public opinion, permitted this.

A second assumption was that animosity between Arabs and Israelis would—if contained—diminish sufficiently to permit true regional peace. This did not happen. Washington occasionally tried to interest Israel and the Arab states in functional accords aimed at securing economic benefits, eliminating the Palestinian refugee problem, and, eventually, producing peace. None succeeded. All failed because the political climate, it seemed, was not yet "right."[10] However, rather than improve, the climate worsened. Constraining manifestations of hostility did not contain enmity, a clear sign of which was the development by 1965 of heightened Palestinian political consciousness and the emergence of an organized and militant Palestinian national movement.

Washington also assumed that its stand on territorial integrity was a credible deterrent. However, in the cycle of raid and counter-raid that by 1967 was daily fare along the lines dividing Israel from its neighbors, tensions escalated to the point that "aggression" became almost impossible to define. In the context of Arab threats against Israel's existence and Israeli threats to overthrow hostile Arab regimes, the distinction between the act and intention of territorial violation all but disappeared. When on June 5, 1967, Israel launched devastating attacks on Egypt, the region's territorial policeman was left with no statute to uphold and no villain to subdue.

The final assumption underlying the U.S. approach to the Arab–Israeli problem in the period between Israel's creation and 1967 was that the Palestinian Arab people did not constitute, and would not become, a political actor in the dynamics of the Arab–Israeli confrontation. Although that notion had never gone unchallenged by Arab spokesmen, the 1967 War did not in itself validate their point. Indeed, despite the ritualistic rhetoric on behalf of Palestinian national rights that regularly emanated from the Arab world after 1948, the years after 1967 would show that no major Arab regime was fully prepared to see the Palestinians determine their own future.

When Washington discarded its frayed policy of containment, it continued to see both the problem and solution as lying within the existing regional Middle East state system. While the outbreak of the 1967 war had signalled the bankruptcy of the erstwhile U.S. approach, the scope and extent of Israel's victory was held to offer an unprecedented opportunity to achieve definitive Arab–Israeli peace.

SETTING DIRECTIONS: THE 1967 CRISIS

By 1967, Lyndon Johnson's main international concern was the slogging war in Vietnam. Some 400 thousand U.S. troops were committed to the conflict, domestic opposition was flowing in the streets, and South Vietnam's security still remained elusive. Yet it was the Middle East, rather than Southeast Asia, that Johnson most feared as a trouble spot. In the president's view, the implicit danger of "every border incident" in that tense region was not "merely war between Israelis and Arabs but an ultimate confrontation between the Soviet Union and the United States and its NATO allies."[11]

The situation that Johnson faced in the spring of 1967 promised to become far more than a border incident. It arose from a volatile combination of forces that over the past few years had rendered the Middle East ripe for an explosion. In addition to the corrosive effects of the perennial Arab–Israeli problem, regional discord found major sources in rivalries that split the Arab world into competing camps. The aborted movements toward Arab unity of the past decade left "progressive" regimes as divided among themselves as they were from "conservative" Arab governments. These divisions enhanced the role of anti-Israel posturing as the touchstone of Arab legitimacy. Adding to the flammable mixture was the completion and inauguration in 1963/64 of an Israeli project for irrigating parts of the Negev Desert with water diverted from the Jordan River.[12]

During 1965, a variety of newly active Palestinian guerrilla groups took the field against Israel. Coupled with the rise to power of radical Ba'athists in Syria, this portended a further escalation of regional friction. By the fall of 1966, attacks against Israeli targets increased noticeably. Openly supported by Syria's new leaders, the guerrillas continued to harass Israel throughout the closing months of the year.[13]

As tensions mounted, Cairo and Damascus put aside a long-standing quarrel, re-established diplomatic relations, and concluded an agreement committing Egypt to Syria's defense in the event of an Israeli attack. Several days later, Israel launched a massive raid against the West Bank town of Es Samu. Although the UN Security Council, with U.S. concurrence, condemned the attack, Israel argued that its borders were being penetrated from Jordan as well as Syria.

The Es Samu raid provoked a torrent of inter-Arab quarrelling. Riots broke out on the West Bank as the population demanded arms and charged King Hussein with unwillingness to face the Israeli enemy. Cairo's influential newspaper, *Al Ahram*, accused the monarch of colluding with Israel to prevent Palestinian guerrillas from operating against the Jewish state.[14] The Syrian government took a similar position. Jordan countered with charges that Egypt and Syria were attempting to destabilize its regime, and Hussein denounced Nasser for engaging in blustery harangues while hiding behind the UN peacekeeping force that had been stationed in the Sinai since 1956. The political climate steadily worsened. Sporadic firing broke out on the Syrian-Israeli frontier in mid-November 1966. At the end of the month an Israeli warplane shot down two Egyptian MIG–19s over the Sinai. The new year was greeted by hostilities along the Syrian border. During February and March, Palestinian guerrillas struck at Israel almost daily, prompting Israeli Chief of Staff Yitzhak Rabin to warn that action was contemplated against countries harboring them. Israel emerged victorious from a major air battle on April 7, shooting down six Syrian MIGs.[15]

The Israeli government made various threatening statements against Syria, including an announcement on May 13 that Israel "would choose the time, the place and the means to counter the aggressor."[16] The crisis escalated when the Soviet Union informed Cairo and Damascus that Israeli troops were massing on the Syrian border. Although Israel denied the charge and UN observers affirmed that no unusual military movements had occurred, the Arabs claimed to believe that an Israeli move against Syria was imminent.

Whether Nasser acted on the basis of misinformation, or whether he was attempting a byzantine ploy of brinksmanship for political purposes, or whether he had simply decided to go to war, remains a moot question. Tied to Syria by the November defense agreement, and stung by doubts cast on his commitment to the Palestine cause, he now embarked on a series of actions that led the Arabs to disaster.

On May 16, Egypt declared a state of emergency and requested the removal of UN peacekeeping forces from the Sinai. A week later, after the UN had not only complied with this request but had also withdrawn its forces from the entry to the Gulf of Aqaba at the Straits of Tiran, Nasser declared that waterway closed to Israeli shipping. In the meantime, Israel and Egypt called up military reserves, Nasser sent thousands of troops into the Sinai, and Iraq and Kuwait ordered general mobilizations.

Pressed by the immediate threat of war, Hussein rushed to mend relations with the Arab world. On May 25, Jordan granted permission for Saudi Arabian and Iraqi forces to enter the country where their aid in its defense required. Five days later, the king suddenly appeared at an airbase near Cairo to sign an Egyptian–Jordanian mutual defense agreement (which was later extended to include Iraq). Although relations between Jordan and Egypt had been suspended since February, Nasser praised the agreement as an affirmation that "Arabs, no matter how divided they may be, forget everything when the issue is that of Arab destiny."[17]

Israel struck on the morning of June 5 . Within hours Egypt's air force was virtually destroyed on the ground, while those of Syria and Jordan suffered heavily. Six days later, the war was over.

As the spring crisis mounted to its climax, Washington reacted on two levels. On the one, in keeping with the strategy pursued for nearly two decades, the United States sought to stem the drift to war. On the other, certain that war would end in a quick, decisive Israeli victory, the Johnson administration was intrigued by the prospect of exploiting the outcome to bring the Arab–Israeli conflict to an end. By late May, Washington was sending conflicting signals to the Israelis.[18]

Johnson formally and publicly defined Washington's position on May 23:

To the leaders of all the nations in the Near East, I wish to say what three Presidents have said before—that the United States is firmly committed to the support of the political independence and territorial integrity of all the nations of the area.

The United States strongly opposes aggression by anyone in the area, in any form, overt or clandestine. This has been the policy of the United States led by four Presidents—President Truman, President Eisenhower, President Kennedy, and myself—as well as the policy of both of our political parties.[19]

By this time, the president had been in private contact with the Israelis, the Soviets, and the Egyptians. Convinced that the closure of the Straits of Tiran violated Israel's right to free passage, which the United States had been pledged to support since 1956, the administration nonetheless continued to urge Jerusalem to refrain from war. "Israel," Johnson carefully informed Foreign Minister Abba Eban on May 26, "will not be alone unless it decides to go it alone." In the meantime, Washington tried to muster international pressure, including a multinational flotilla, to reassert the right of free passage through the Straits of Tiran.

Contacts with the Soviet Union also were aimed at preventing the outbreak of war. Writing to Premier Kosygin, Johnson pointed out that a Middle East conflict could bring their two countries "into difficulties which I am confident neither of us seeks." He urged a joint effort "to use our influence to the full in the cause of moderation."[20]

A similar message calling for restraint was sent to Nasser. The U.S. president proposed a variety of specific measures to reduce the immediate possibility of war, including a mutual pullback of Israeli and Egyptian troops from the border region and a temporary UN presence in sensitive areas, particularly at Sharm el-Sheikh on the Strait of Tiran. Johnson also suggested that the United States would embark on a major effort to find peaceful solutions to "old problems" once the immediate crisis abated.[21]

Nasser's reply was given in a public speech. Whatever the Egyptian leader's ultimate aims may have been, his words accurately reflected the anger and frustration generated in the Arab world by the Palestine problem:

We note that there is a great deal of talk about peace these days.... If there is a true desire for peace, we say that we also work for peace. But does peace mean that we should ignore the right of the Palestinian people because of the lapse of time? They speak of a "UN presence in the region for the sake of peace." Does "UN presence in the region for peace" mean that we should close our eyes to everything? The United Nations adopted a number of resolutions in favor of the Palestinian people. Israel implemented none of these.... This brought no reaction from the United States. Today, U.S. Senators, members of the House of Representatives, the press, and the entire world speak in favor of Israel. But nothing is said in favor of the Arabs.... The peace talk is heard only when Israel is in danger. But when Arab rights and the rights of the Palestinian people are lost, no one speaks about peace, rights, or anything. Therefore, it is clear that an alliance exists between the Western powers—chiefly represented by the United States and Britain—and Israel.[22]

Nasser was wrong. Unlike what had transpired in 1956, in 1967 he did not face an "alliance" between major Western powers and Israel. Yet, despite its efforts to prevent the outbreak of hostilities, the United States seems to have fallen into an increasingly ambivalent attitude toward the crisis. Jon Kimche claims that as the crisis progressed, "Israelis were . . . informed on two distinct levels of the American position." Johnson's public and private communications urging restraint contrasted with signals from the CIA and Pentagon—where it was not doubted that Israel would emerge victorious from the looming conflict—that seemed intended to encourage Israel to seize the war option.[23]

Strong, but not conclusive, evidence also indicates that by early June the administration took active steps to ensure as speedy and total an Israeli victory as possible. Stephen Green's 1984 book, *Taking Sides*, contains a detailed story of covert U.S. military involvement in the 1967 war. The account, based on interviews with an unnamed former Air Force officer who claims to have been a participant, describes a scheme that brought a group of sophisticated U.S. Air Force photo reconnaissance planes and their crews from a base in Germany, along with military technicians stationed in Britain, first to Spain and then to a secret airfield in the Negev Desert. According to Green, the U.S. unit reached Israel on the night of June 4 and participated in military operations throughout the war.[24]

In any case, once hostilities began, there was no disguising U.S. sympathies. Despite an initial State Department claim of official neutrality, Washington clearly supported Israel. Near the end of the war, when the Soviet Union charged Israel with violating a cease-fire on the Syrian front and threatened to take "necessary actions, including military," the United States demonstrated its readiness to resist Soviet involvement. Talk of possible Soviet intervention ceased after a prompt and dramatic repositioning of elements of the Sixth Fleet.

When the shooting stopped on June 11, Israeli forces occupied over 26,000 square miles of territory previously controlled by Egypt, Syria, or Jordan. Egypt, having been pushed from the Sinai Peninsula across the Suez Canal, suffered the greatest territorial loss—nearly 24,000 square miles (including the Gaza Strip). The bulk of that area was inhospitable desert. Although the region contained oil and some mineral deposits, its importance was primarily strategic. Israel's advance to the Canal and down to the mouth of the Gulf of Aqaba gained several important advantages for the Jewish state and created concomitant difficulties for the regime in Cairo. Not only did Israel dominate the Strait of Tiran and the Suez Canal, but—more importantly—Israeli ground forces and artillery were also within easy striking distance of major Egyptian population centers. Furthermore, in the event of renewed hostilities, Israel's airforce could look forward to meeting resistance only to the west of the Canal.

In the north, Israel occupied Syria's Golan Heights. Though relatively small (443 square miles), the region was also strategically valuable. It was from these hills that Syrian guns had shelled Israeli settlements and forces below. By gaining control of the area, Israel both eliminated that danger and gained a position from which mechanized and infantry units might easily move against Damascus.

Jordan was relieved of the West Bank. All things considered, this was potentially the most serious territorial amputation suffered by the defeated regimes. Although only slightly more than 2000 square miles were involved, the West Bank not only included Jerusalem and other sites precious for both emotional reasons and tourism, but was also heavily agricultural. After the war, observers raised serious doubts about the Hashemite Kingdom's viability should it remain shorn of the West Bank for any length of time.

Israelis welcomed the West Bank's capture for a variety of reasons. Economic and strategic considerations were certainly present. Above all, however, Israelis were attracted to the region because of its religious and historical connection to the Jewish people.

Territory was not all the Arabs lost in the brief June War. Arms, men, and prestige also figured in the bill. Prestige, of course, was not abundant in the Arab world on June 11, 1967. Although Arab leaders may have feared the consequences, all Arab capitals had ostentatiously distinguished themselves by cheering the growing possibility of war during the final days before June 5. By the eleventh, there was nothing to cheer. There was wreckage—the shattered remains of fanciful slogans, thousands of equally shattered cadavers, and an estimated total loss of $1.5 billion of military equipment.[25]

Washington promptly concluded that if this debris was to provide the foundation for resolving the basic sources of Arab–Israeli friction, it would be necessary to promote an arrangement based on five principles. As expressed by President Johnson on June 19, these included: the right of every nation in the region to live and to have that right respected by its neighbors; the respect by all of maritime rights; the curtailment of the Middle East arms race; justice for "the refugees"; and respect for the "political independence and territorial integrity" of all states in the area.[26]

The last principle was no mere reaffirmation of the old territorial integrity formula. Johnson referred to the previous demarcation lines between Israel and the Arab states as "only fragile and violated truce lines." In the future, he said, there must be "recognized and secure boundaries and other arrangements that will give ... security against terror, destruction and war."

In light of later developments, it was significant that Johnson's June 19 speech did not cite direct negotiations between Arabs and Israelis as an essential principle of peace. Yet, he evidently preferred that approach:

Clearly the parties to the conflict must be the parties to the peace. Sooner or later it is they who must make a settlement in the area. It is hard to see how it is possible for nations to live together if they cannot learn to reason together.

The president touched on two other points that were basic to the U.S. view of peace. First, he presented the five principles as interrelated parts of a total package, arguing that "there must be progress toward all of them if there is to be progress toward any." Second, while holding the Arabs, and particularly Nasser, responsible for the war, he indicated that the burden of peace should fall on Arabs and Israelis alike. A clear admonition to Israel went to the root of Washington's new approach:

No nation would be true to the United Nations' Charter or to its own interests if it should permit military success to blind it to the fact that its neighbors have rights and interests of their own. . . .

In Washington's view, the possibility of ending the Middle East problem through the exchange of occupied territory for political concessions would entail a process involving only sovereign states. The Palestinian question was perceived as a humanitarian issue whose political dimension was limited to its capacity to irritate relations between Israel and the Arab states. The president's call for "justice for the refugees" implied the necessity of humanitarian measures agreed upon by the latter two parties. The Palestinians themselves were to be objects of, rather than subjects in, Middle East peacemaking.

It was evident that the success of the postwar U.S. approach to the Arab–Israeli conflict depended on several requirements being met. First, it was necessary that Israel's retention of the occupied areas be ensured until the conclusion of peace. Arab states had to be denied any realistic ambition of removing the occupation through isolated political or military gains. On the other hand, it was also necessary that the Arabs not regard a settlement simply as a dictated peace. This implied that Arab governments must not despair of regaining the bulk of their lost lands through political concessions. A third requirement was that all parties to the conflict understand that Washington's commitment to a resolution did not diminish, but rather reinforced, its support of Israel's security. There would be no question of the United States simply forcing Israel back to its strategically vulnerable pre-June confines. The occupation of Arab lands would end only in the context of peace.

Finally, it was necessary that a bartering process be initiated between Israel and the Arab states. This not only implied that Israel must be willing to use the occupied territories as currency for attaining peace but also that the bargaining process itself would ultimately have to achieve harmony between possible territorial adjustments on behalf of Israeli security and the amount of land that could be taken with Arab consent.

The administration would almost immediately find that its efforts to construct an active policy capable of simultaneously meeting these requirements could be severely complicated by the reactions of other major actors in the Middle East. During the ensuing years, all Washington policymakers would confront the same truth.

THE SOVIET UNION

A decade after the end of World War II, the Czech arms deal not only signalled Egypt's turn to Eastern Bloc arsenals but also symbolized the collapse of Western ambitions to exclude the Soviet Union from the Middle East. In a broad historical sense, the legacy of Western imperial involvement in the region offered Moscow an opportunity to capitalize politically on Arab resentment. More specifically, Soviet diplomacy after 1948 was able to exploit Arab anger over the French presence in Algeria, the West's early rejection of the neutralist philosophy proclaimed by Third World leaders at Bandung in 1955, and—above all—the tensions and fears generated by the Arab–Israeli conflict.[27]

Following the West's refusal to finance the Aswan Dam and the ensuing Anglo–French–Israeli invasion of Egypt in 1956, Soviet influence received further impetus in centers of Arab nationalism. By 1957, the Soviet Union, no longer feeling the need of an East Bloc figleaf, was not only supplying arms directly to the Nasser regime but also providing intensive training programs for the Egyptian military. In that same year, the Syrian government publicly acknowledged that it too had established an arms link with the Soviets. Two years later, following the overthrow of Iraq's Hashemite monarchy, the Soviet Union began providing arms to Baghdad as well.[28]

Thus, within five years of Moscow's first major foray into the Arab arms market Egypt, Syria, and Iraq were focal points of Soviet influence in the Middle East. The cultivation of Moscow's position continued to depend largely, but not completely, on the Soviet role as arms purveyor. Cairo, Damascus, and Baghdad also benefited from significant amounts of developmental aid and rising levels of trade with the Soviet Union and its East Bloc allies.[29]

Still, burgeoning links to friendly Arab states did not lead to a simple patron-client relationship. On the one hand, the differing strands of Nasserist and Ba'athist Pan Arabism that emerged in Egypt, Syria, and Iraq shared a common antipathy to any sort of foreign control. On the other, none was ideologically compatible with Soviet Marxism. For their part, Soviet leaders tempered their enthusiasm for Arab friendship by noting the Arab world's potential instability and by distrusting the continued preference of Arab elites for Western technology and culture.[30]

By 1967, Soviet policymakers nonetheless had solid grounds for satisfaction. Ties with the Arab world had been nurtured on a pragmatic basis that avoided serious discord over ideological questions—and which often proceeded at the expense of local communist groups. The potential for extending Soviet influence seemed enhanced in 1966 by the emergence of a radical regime in Syria and the growth of Egyptian dependency on Soviet wheat at the end of that year.

This prospect was jeopardized by Israel's stunning 1967 victory. Soviet arms and instruction had not helped Arab armies stave off humiliating defeat. Moscow's prestige was also undermined by the political clumsiness it displayed on the eve of the war and its caution during the conflict. Arabs were not likely to forget that Soviet encouragement of Nasser's militant posturing had helped propel events beyond control. Nor would they forget that Moscow's own posturing at the end of the war had been quickly and easily countered by a simple redeployment of U.S. naval units. Faced with the consequences of their disaster, it seemed likely that Arabs would question the value of Soviet friendship.

Although some Soviet ambassadors in the Middle East reportedly urged a reduced commitment to the losing Arab regimes, the Soviet leadership decided that quick action was necessary to shore up Moscow's tattered credibility. In late June and early July, President Nicolai Podgorny led a delegation to Cairo, Damascus, and Baghdad. He promised prompt replacement of recently lost arms. At almost the same time, Premier Alexis Kosygin addressed a special emergency session of the UN General Assembly, condemning Israel's "aggression" and demanding war reparations for the Arabs. Kosygin's statements came on the heels of unsuccessful Soviet efforts to have the Security Council charge Israel with aggression and call for its complete withdrawal from all occupied Arab territory.[31]

Soviet actions were more impressive than promises or oratory. The drive to rebuild Arab forces was started immediately. During the summer and fall of 1967, Soviet advisors and technicians were rushed to Egypt and Syria. Military hardware accompanied them. By November, approximately eighty percent of Arab losses had reportedly been replaced. Within a year of the defeat, Egypt's airforce was virtually restored to its prewar strength and Syria's arsenals had been replenished.[32]

In subsequent years, the Soviet Union would continue trying to consolidate and expand its influence in the Middle East by offering friendly Arab actors arms supplies and political support for key demands upon Israel. Yet, despite the increasing quantities and sophistication of the weapons involved, and notwithstanding Moscow's emergence as the Arabs' chief international advocate, no consistent or cohesive "Soviet–Arab" approach to the Middle East developed. This was largely due to three pheonmena: the Arab governments' jealous guardianship of their sovereign prerogatives; Moscow's fear that Arab miscalculation could plunge it into unwanted confrontation with the United States; and—at bottom—the inability of the Soviet Union and the Arabs to settle on a common set of objectives.

These were not discrete, but rather interrelated, sources of friction. While welcoming Soviet arms and political support, neither Egypt nor Syria would grant the Soviet Union formal rights to maintain military bases on their soil. When, as in Egypt's case by the early 1970s, the Soviets' privileged use of military facilities threatened to evolve into de facto establishment of bases, the result was a backlash that ultimately helped produce fundamental changes in Cairo's policy. By the same token, Syria and Egypt carefully guarded against Soviet penetration of their decision-making processes.[33]

Aware of the limitations on its influence, Moscow remained sensitive to the danger of being catapulted into an unwanted conflict with the United States. The caution this engendered was manifested in Soviet arms transfer policies, which were designed to enhance Arab defensive, rather than offensive, military capabilities.[34] In turn, this caused Arabs to resent what was seen as Moscow's unilateral imposition of limits on their options for dealing with Israel.

Strains in Soviet–Arab relations fundamentally stemmed from the absence of common political objectives. While the Arab world was united in its desire to recover the territories lost in the June War, there was no Arab consensus on either the tactics through which this might be accomplished or the ultimate political configuration to be sought in the Middle East. This was partly a reflection of inter-Arab differences, which in themselves precluded a cohesive Soviet–Arab political outlook on the nature of final objectives vis-à-vis Israel and how best these might be attained. However, it also stemmed from the failure of individual Arab regimes to take unambiguous positions on questions of ends and means.[35]

On the other hand, it was impossible for those beyond the Kremlin's walls to determine clearly and conclusively what constituted Soviet objectives in the Middle East. It was, of course, plain enough that Moscow hoped to increase its influence in the region by drawing closer to the Arabs in their post–1967 hour of need. What remained murky were the nature and limits of this broad goal.

The issue could not be clarified by reference to either Soviet pronouncements or actions. Soon dropping demands for Israel's unilateral withdrawal and payment of war reparations in favor of a call for a negotiated settlement, Moscow adopted a multifaceted approach that lent itself to various interpretations. As proclaimed by official spokesmen, the essence of the Soviet position was that a settlement should uphold both the return of all occupied lands to Arab control as well as Israel's right to exist. In the years after the June War, all parties, including the Arabs, found reason to doubt that this description accurately reflected Soviet priorities in the Middle East.

As early as August 1967, Mohammed Hassanein Heikal, Nasser's confidant and the editor of the influential daily *Al-Ahram*, warned that the Arab world should not take for granted the existence of an identity of interests with the Soviet Union:

[W]e must realize that there are limits on what the Soviet Union can give.

The Soviet Union is a state which takes an interest in world affairs. The USSR and the USA are perhaps the only two powers which have the potentialities to take such a world interest and are capable of doing so . . . the USSR's plans cover the surface of the globe as well as outer space. This does not make her interests limited to our demands. Furthermore, our plans, which are dictated by our independent stand, do not necessarily harmonize with her plans, at least in some fields.[36]

Early recognition of distinct Soviet and Arab objectives blossomed into a suspicion that Soviet policy in the Middle East was not only restrained by the demands of superpower relations but also designed to perpetuate Arab dependency. In 1972, Heikal used his popular column to survey a variety of reasons for the growing belief that the USSR was not so much interested in promoting a settlement as in perpetuating a state of "no war, no peace." Although claiming not to share that view, he did not shy from discussing it at length.[37]

As Nasser's successor, Anwar Sadat required little encouragement to suspect Soviet intentions. Increasingly convinced that Moscow hoped to use the spirit of "detente" to prolong the Middle East impasse while enjoying tacit U.S. approval for the consolidation of a sphere of influence in the Arab world, Sadat launched a policy reversal that by 1976 eliminated the Soviet presence in Egypt.

U.S. and Israeli policymaking also proceeded in the light of uncertainty over Soviet aims. In 1967, Moscow severed diplomatic relations with Israel to protest Jerusalem's rejection of a cease-fire on the Syrian front. Yet, the USSR not only consistently upheld the Jewish state's right to exist but also urged Arab governments and the Palestine Liberation Organization to do the same in the context of a political settlement.

Rather than finding comfort in the Soviet position, most Israelis were alarmed by the seeming contradition between Moscow's declared acceptance of Israel's legitmacy and other aspects of its policy. Among these were the Soviet Union's refusal to initiate the resumption of diplomatic relations, the frequency and vehemence of its outcries against Zionist ideology, and, of course, its support of hostile Arab regimes and organizations.[38]

Israelis generally responded to Soviet ambiguity by concluding that no necessary limits existed to Moscow's readiness to win Arab support at Israel's expense. Israeli Foreign Minister Abba Eban's 1968 comment accurately described his country's consistent reaction to Soviet peace proposals: "Israel regards and will regard with severe suspicion any Soviet plan by virtue of it being Soviet."[39]

Washington never doubted that Moscow's aim was to increase its influence in the Middle East. Yet, U.S. observers were unable to agree whether Soviet policy was composed of limited tactical steps designed to exploit opportunities as they arose or, on the other hand, of fully interrelated parts of a strategic design for global predominance. Defining the relationship between the Soviet approach to the Arab–Israeli problem and Soviet policies on other issues affecting the broader Middle East area remained a central U.S. concern. The rise of Soviet influence in Ethiopia after 1976, the development of Soviet relations with South Yemen throughout the 1970s, the Soviet reaction to the 1979 fall of Iran's Pahlavi dynasty, and the Soviet invasion of Afghanistan at the end of that year all impinged on U.S. appraisals of Soviet policy toward the Arab–Israeli conflict.

Yet no amount of interest, concern, and analysis could produce a definitive clarification of Soviet objectives in the Middle East. By the 1980s, observers were far from achieving "anything resembling a consensus concerning the underlying sources of Soviet policies."[40]

Interpretations in Washington fluctuated over the years. Each administration faced anew, and often on multiple occasions, the question of whether U.S. interests would be served or undermined by seeking active Soviet participation in the search for peace. Each had to consider the range of answers offered by respected analysts, of whom some agreed fully with Walter Laqeuer's conclusion that:

the long-term aim of the Soviet Union is to turn the Middle East into a sphere of influence from which other powers are *excluded*. This target is to be achieved by consolidating and strengthening past gains, by the replacement of the present rulers by others more closely identified with Soviet policies, and ultimately by the transformation of these regimes into political coalitions dominated by the communists or other trustworthy elements.[41]

Others tended to support the view offered by Seth Tillman:

On the basis of events and performance, a plausible case can be made that, until and unless the global power equation changes greatly, Soviet aims in the Middle East, at least in practice, do not exceed the attainment of equality of influence or perhaps a kind of condominium with the United States.[42]

ARAB GOVERNMENTS AND PALESTINIANS

The Arab world's reaction to Israel's 1967 victory was fundamentally ambiguous. While voicing eagerness for "another round," Arab spokesmen hinted at a willingness to abandon the decades-old struggle. It was quickly evident that no single "Arab position" existed. The gap between militant and relatively moderate preferences not only divided the Arab world but also lent ambivalence to the approaches of individual Arab actors.

Militancy found sources in the humiliation suffered by the Arab world's leaders and the shocked outrage that swept its population in the wake of the defeat. On June 9, less than twenty-four hours after Egypt accepted a cease-fire, Gamal Abdul Nasser assumed responsibility for the debacle and offered his resignation from public life, all the while praising Arab determination to pursue the struggle against Israel. An outpouring of popular sentiment across Egypt and the Arab world immediately provided grounds for Nasser to withdraw the resignation.

Almost simultaneously, the Damascus regime was covering its embarrassingly poor showing with inflexible vows of enduring hostility toward the Jewish state. Jordan also staunchly loosed a few verbal barrages supporting the vision of unyielding resistance.

Not surprisingly, the war brought U.S.–Arab relations to a new low. Following early Egyptian and Jordanian claims that U.S. and British warplanes were actively aiding Israel, various Arab countries, including Egypt, Iraq, Syria, Yemen, and the Sudan, severed diplomatic relations with Washington. Although Saudi Arabia, Kuwait, Libya, and the Persian Gulf sheikhdoms did not cut diplomatic ties, oil shipments to the United States and Britain were suspended.

These reactions were not as harsh as they seemed at first glance, nor did they signal unanimity over the adoption of strong measures against the West. The embargo failed to prevent Arab petroleum from reaching British or U.S. ports after trans-shipment from other destinations. Moreover, within four weeks, Saudi Arabia and Kuwait were raising alarmed complaints that the embargo threatened serious damage to their economies. Jordan, in addition to other dislocations caused by the war, now had to cope with the sudden influx of some 200,000 new Palestinian refugees. Amman carefully avoided a break with the United States. Even Nasser did not delay long before publicly backtracking from earlier pledges to continue military struggle. Of the confrontation states, only Syria—whose leaders called for a prolonged "war of popular liberation"—seemed fully committed to militant policies by the end of the summer. The dominant tenor was captured by King Hussein shortly after the war, when in an address to the United Nations he managed to combine in the same breath threats of renewed hostilities with an obvious preference for a peaceful settlement:

It is apparent that we have not yet learned well enough how to use weapons of modern warfare. But we shall if we have to. The battle which began on June 5 will then become a long war.[43]

Days later, the king implied that Arabs would accept Israel's legitimacy as the price of peace. It was not, he told reporters, Jordan's responsibility to find a solution to the Arab–Israeli dispute, but for "the world" to do so. If the international community called for Arab recognition of Israel, he hoped "the Arab World would be able to face the question."

Shortly afterward, Gamal Abdel Nasser openly injected a large dose of ambiguity into Egypt's posture. Speaking at Cairo University, he stated that Egypt would never close the door to a "political solution" but added that if forced to resort to military means, Egyptians would prove "no less determined than the people of Vietnam." Soon afterward, Yugoslavia's Marshall Tito emerged from a tete-à-tete with Nasser to report having found a definite readiness for a "political solution."[44]

From this point on Nasser no longer spoke simply of protracted war against the Jewish state. On the other hand, neither Nasser, nor Hussein, nor any other Arab leader, articulated a clear bargaining position. Hussein's vague hint that recognition of Israel's right to exist might be the Arab contribution to a political settlement did not constitute a firm Jordanian—and much less an overall Arab—stand. Nasser's call for a "political solution" left shrouded in mystery the extent of Egyptian willingness to abandon opposition to Israel's existence.

At the end of August 1967, a summit conference in Khartoum was unable to forge a common Arab position. Unwilling to modify its call for a popular war of liberation, Syria did not attend. An Iraqi demand for continued application of the oil embargo was overridden, with Jordan and Egypt agreeing to the measure's termination in return for substantial subsidies from the oil producers.

The conference's final resolution tried to provide a semblance of unity by combining the distinct strands of Arab reaction to the June War. However, it only succeeded in underscoring the prevailing uncertainty over how to proceed under the burden of defeat. A seemingly rigid policy framework—"no peace with Israel, no recognition of Israel, no negotiations with it, and insistence on the rights of the Palestinian people in their own country"—was immediately undercut by a decision to utilize international diplomacy to recover the recently occupied territories. The Arab leaders at Khartoum were hardly unaware that any political settlement achieved through international diplomacy would at minimum entail termination of the state of war with Israel and acceptance of that state's right to exist.[45]

It was a measure of the blow suffered by the Arab world that hints of moderation were so quickly adopted as a standard part of Arab diplomatic baggage. For thirty years, the possibility of acknowledging Israel's legitimacy, and therefore accepting the permanent loss of part of Palestine, had been virtually unmentionable in the Arab world. To suggest the contrary—whatever conditions might be attached to the suggestion—was not an easy step, for it not only flew in the face of three decades of rhetoric, but also inevitably heightened inter-Arab divisions.

Months after the Khartoum Conference, Egypt and Jordan accepted Security Council Resolution 242. By doing so, they moved closer to defining conditions for accepting Israel's right to exist: the return of all Arab lands occupied in 1967, and a resolution of the Palestinian refugee problem. Not until 1974 would Syria follow suit. Less than a decade later, the Palestine Liberation Organization would find itself torn asunder over the possibility of acknowledging Israel's permanence and legitimacy.

Although frequently generating flashpoints of tension, differences over the prospect of coming to terms with the Jewish state were slow to produce a complete rupture in Arab ranks. The underlying reason for this was that for more than a decade after the June War, all Arab actors were united in insisting that Israel's control over the occupied areas must be totally removed. That stand carried far-reaching implications, for it placed the Arabs collectively in opposition to Israel's unspecified, but real, territorial claims as well as to suggestions emanating from any quarter for limited territorial adjustments in the interest of Israeli security. At the same time, the demand for the return of all occupied lands gave militants both in the Arab world and in Israel an effective veto over progress toward any political settlement. Much of the international diplomacy that focused on the Middle East after the June War, and not a little of the bloodshed in the region, were linked to efforts to realize, or modify, or render irrelevant, Arab insistence on the full restoration of territory.

Although the United States and Israel differed from the outset over the final disposition of occupied territories, Washington consistently chose to avoid a confrontation over the issue. Instead, U.S. peacemaking strategy initially focused on trying to dilute the unified Arab position by encouraging Egyptian and Jordanian interest in separate settlements involving minor territorial alterations. By the early 1970s this approach seemed to have foundered on the rocks of Arab and Israeli recalcitrance. Convinced that any concession leading to a settlement on Arab terms would benefit the Soviet Union, Washington abandoned its active pursuit of peace in order to further a stalemate that threatened to tighten Israel's hold on its expanded domain.

Anwar Sadat shattered the impasse by going to war in 1973. Although Sadat overcame Washington's diplomatic inertia, he did not achieve an unqualified political victory. Over the next few years he would rapidly loosen, then for all practical purposes fully sever, the link between Egyptian and broader Arab demands.

That vital concession underlay the success of U.S. efforts to further the Egyptian–Israeli peace concluded in 1979. By then, however, the passage of time had ushered in circumstances that raised serious questions as to whether the state-to-state dynamics that ultimately worked so fruitfully between Israel and Egypt could be repeated. Syria, having seen no reasonable hope of regaining the lost Golan Heights through diplomatic means, had seized the opportunity of bolstering its political leverage by intervening in Lebanon, thereby helping to complicate immeasurably the already complex Middle East scene. Jordan had relinquished, perhaps temporarily, its claimed right to determine the West Bank's future. Above all, there were the Palestinians, who through the agency of the PLO had re-emerged as a significant political actor in the Arab–Israeli problem.

The resurgence of militant Palestinian nationalism was visible across the Middle East by the mid–1960s. The trauma of displacement that shattered the Palestinian national movement in 1948, and which during the 1950s led most Palestinian activists to seek political salvation in one or another form of Pan Arabism, had yielded to the growing conviction that Palestinians must galvanize, rather than merely rely upon, the broader Arab struggle against Israel. Frustrated by the failure of Pan Arabism to move beyond verbal commitments to Arab unity, Palestinians increasingly concluded that they must take the lead in the conflict.

Arab regimes were uncomfortable with the prospect of an independent, militant Palestinian national movement. Under Egyptian leadership, an effort to bring Palestinian militancy under control was made at an Arab summit conference in early 1964. The conclave laid the basis for establishing the Palestine Liberation Organization. Ahmed Shukairy, a member of a distinguished Palestinian family from Acre who had served as a diplomat for various Arab governments and the Arab League, was designated as the group's organizer.

Palestinian restlessness was not allayed. Although Palestine's liberation was declared the PLO's ultimate goal, the organization was not conceived of primarily as a military body. Instead, its essential purpose was political. The PLO would be the manifestation of the Palestinian demand for national self-determination. Neither this, nor plans for a regular fighting force (the Palestine Liberation Army) satisified Palestinian eagerness for an actively militant policy against Israel. Convinced that the time was ripe for launching a sustained guerilla war against the Jewish state, many Palestinian leaders saw Shukairy's organization as not only out of touch with the refugee masses but also as the tame creature of its government sponsors.[46]

Symptomatic of the groundswell of Palestinian activism was the fate of the Arab National Movement (ANM), a clandestine Arab nationalist organization founded in 1951 by George Habash, a young Christian Palestinian just out of medical school. Originally committed to a moralistic program calling for a united Arab state and the elimination of Zionism and imperialism from the Middle East, the ANM achieved considerable organizational success. By the early 1960s, its branches extended throughout the Arab World. However, by 1964 the organization was buffeted by growing doubts over the political effectiveness of Pan Arabist ideologies. Abandoning its hitherto strictly centralized structure, the ANM granted constituent units far greater automony—a process that allowed Habash to attract the bulk of the organization's most active Palestinian members to a new body that became known as the National Front for the Liberation of Palestine (NFLP). This group, while still decidely Pan-Arabist in orientation, immediately set about waging a guerrilla campaign against Israel. The first mission assigned to its military strike force, the "Vengeance Youth," was carried out in November 1964.[47]

Other Palestinian guerrilla groups were formed in the months that followed. Two of these appear to have been linked to Ahmed Jabril, a Palestinian who had served in the Syrian Army. One of the Jabril groups, the Palestinian Liberation Front (PLF) began operating in 1966. The other, known as the Heroes of the Return, first saw action at about the same time.

In the meantime, at the outset of 1965, the organization that was destined to rise swiftly to the leadership of the Palestinian national movement inaugurated its own struggle against Israel. This was the Palestine Liberation Movement, which quickly and irrevocably became known as Fateh. Unlike Habash's ANM offshoot or Jabril's creations, Fateh eschewed Pan-Arabist ideology. Its founders were displaced Palestinians who came together in the early 1950s in Cairo, or later in Kuwait. They not only shared a determination to see Palestine restored to the control of its original Arab inhabitants but also a conviction that Palestinians must accord priority to that national aim. They therefore placed Palestinian nationalism above all else. Their movement sought to accommodate different ideological tendencies as well as to avoid involvement in inter-Arab political rivalries. In short, Fateh hoped to cultivate the support of all Arab regimes by threatening none.

The devastating outcome of the 1967 war seemed to confirm leftwing Pan-Arabist claims that existing Arab regimes were incapable of mustering the total dedication required for victory over Israel. Relatively conservative Pan-Arabist leaders such as George Habash now found it possible to integrate Palestinian nationalist feelings with a radical Marxist-Leninist worldview.[48] It was a perspective that perforce linked the ultimate satisfaction of Palestinian demands to social and political revolution in the Arab world. In contrast, Fateh remained determined to pursue purely Palestinian national ends.

The June War created a favorable climate for the growth of established guerrilla groups and the proliferation of new ones. Public opinion throughout the Arab world rallied to the support of the *fedayeen* (self-sacrificers), whose exploits were seen as retrieving the Arabs' tarnished honor. Arab governments were in no position to stand against the burgeoning resistance movement's popularity. Initially, at least, they also saw the guerrillas as a useful—indeed the only—instrument for applying military pressure against Israel.

Fateh proved more successful than other Palestinian groups in establishing a broadly-based support system. By 1970, its funding sources had been diversified to include not only private Palestinian donors but also regimes as distinct as those of Libya, Syria, Kuwait, Saudi Arabia, and Algeria.

Fateh's nationalist appeal and regular strikes against Israeli targets also soon made it the largest and most prestigious Palestinian resistance group. This was particularly true after March 1968, when Fateh fighters stood their ground against a massive Israeli assault on a guerrilla base situated in the Jordanian town of Karameh. Although the much larger Israeli force technically won the encounter, it met unexpectedly stiff resistance. Rather than melt away, the guerrillas had chosen to meet the attack.

The military outcome was relatively unimportant, compared with the legend that was born. "Karameh" became synonymous with the vision of unending sacrifice against superior odds, of generation after generation fighting, falling, and passing the Kaleshnikov on to its successors. Even King Hussein was caught up by the euphoria. "We shall all be *Fedayeen* soon," he declared. The electric effect of the battle brought thousands of eager young recruits to Fateh and other guerrilla groups. Funds and pledges of support poured in from around the Arab world.[49]

In 1968, Yassir Arafat became known as Fateh's chief spokesman. A year later, with Ahmed Shukairy having lost the leadership of the PLO at the end of 1967, Arafat was elected chairman of the PLO Executive Committee. Shortly afterward, Fateh members and supporters gained control of the Palestine National Council, the quasi-legislative organ that claimed to legitimize the PLO as representative of the Palestinian people.

In the meantime, radical Pan-Arabist Palestinian factions came together in early 1968 to form the Popular Front for the Liberation of Palestine (PFLP). Headed by George Habash, the PFLP united the ANM's Palestinian section, the PLF, and the Heroes of the Return. Ideological and personal clashes soon produced various PFLP offshoots. The more important of these were Naif Hawatmeh's Popular Democratic Front for the Liberation of Palestine, known after 1974 simply as the Democratic Front for the Liberation of Palestine (DFLP); Ahmed Jibril's PFLP-General Command (A); and the PFLP-General Command (B) led by another former army officer, Ahmed Za'rur. Unlike Fateh, these groups were ideologically inclined to temper their focus on Palestine by pursuing their objectives, where possible, through intervention in Arab politics.

In their eagerness to provide channels for Palestinian activism, and so gain influence over the resistance movement as a whole, Arab regimes furthered the proliferation of guerrilla organizations. The most enduring and important officially sponsored Palestinian group was Saiqa, whose formation under Syrian auspices had been decided upon in 1966.

After winning preeminence within the PLO in 1969, Fateh still had to consolidate its leadership over the organization's diverse and independent-minded constituent groups. The degree of success achieved by Arafat and his Fateh cohorts stemmed largely from their patient, pragmatic approach to intra-Palestinian politics and the broad formulation of their final objective. After 1967, that goal was phrased as securing the Palestinians' right to return to Palestine and the establishment there of a secular, democratic state. Michael Hudson has pointed out the convenience of this formula as a means of reconciling divergent tendencies within the national movement:

It was simple and yet ambiguous enough to attract diverse and conflicting elements. As interpreted by the Fateh and PLO leadership, it differed little from the traditionalist and liberal-bourgeois Palestinian and Arab nationalist appeals of the Mandate era.

But, Hudson points out, to others, notably in the PFLP and the PDFLP, it symbolized a radical populist ideological stand:

[a] perspective whose most salient attributes were secularism, participation and social justice in the context of national liberation revolution.[50]

Although Fateh was never able to impose its will consistently or completely on all Palestinian groups within the Palestinian resistance movement, its program and leadership became solidly entrenched as those of the mainstream PLO. Never wavering from its focus on Palestinianism, Fateh nonetheless led the PLO on a course that over the years marked a changing emphasis in goals as well as a concurrent shift from military to political tactics.

After the 1973 Arab–Israeli war, the PLO officially adopted a program calling for the establishment of a "national authority" in any part of Palestine liberated from Israeli control. Although the measure was qualified by insistence that any such "national authority" would only mark a phase in the ultimate establishment of a secular democratic state in all Palestine, PLO diplomacy increasingly focused on the objective of a Palestinian state comprising the West Bank and Gaza Strip.[51] By the mid–1980s PLO leaders had made plain their willingness to accept Israel's existence in exchange for similar U.S. recognition of the Palestinians' right to statehood. The PLO had also accepted the principle that a Palestinian ministate should exist in some form of association with Jordan.

During the 1970s, and particularly after 1974, the PLO sought to project itself as a responsible, far-sighted political movement rather than as a mere guerrilla force capable of pursuing objectives only through violence. While armed struggle, including attacks against civilian targets in Israel, was not abandoned, the PLO distanced itself from terrorist activities in other areas. By the early 1980s the organization had established an extensive international network that allowed it to maintain offices throughout the world. In 1981, its representative in Moscow was granted diplomatic status, culminating a process that began in 1973 when the Soviet Union stopped considering the Palestinian issue as a "refugee problem" and supported the goal of Palestinian statehood.[52]

In the meantime, after being accorded observer status at the UN General Assembly in 1974, the PLO repeatedly and successfully worked for the passage of pro-Palestinian resolutions by a variety of UN agencies. PLO diplomacy was similarly successful in mustering the support of regional organizations such as the European Community and the Non-Aligned Movement.

As welcome as all this may have been to PLO leaders, the organization's attainment of a "respectable" presence in the international forum did little in itself to further its purpose. The crucible of efforts to create a Palestinian state still remained in the Middle East. While the PLO managed to encourage a dynamic Palestinian national consciousness through a variety of educational, social and political activities aimed primarily at the refugee masses, and although it was widely recognized as the sole representative of the Palestinian people, the organization faced a constant dilemma. The truth of the perceptive analysis offered by Fuad Jabber in the early 1970s remains unchanged:

The record suggests that only a strong Resistance movement, with a solid base of mass political support, reasonably smooth relations with host governments, and an effective military arm capable of independent action against its enemies, can continue to uphold [such gains]. But these prerequisites, though all essential, are in the final account mutually exclusive—and therein lies the Palestinians' basic dilemma. A guerrilla movement with a substantial popular base, an activist social-political program, and a viable military force would present an intolerable challenge and threat to the existing political systems in Jordan, Lebanon, and Syria, and is therefore bound to clash with the central authorities.[53]

Notwithstanding the PLO/Fateh leadership's philosophy of non-intervention in the domestic politics of Arab states, the logic of the dilemma embroiled the organization in fateful struggles with the Jordanian regime in 1970/71, and with Lebanese and Syrian forces after 1976. Ironically, the PLO's troubles with Damascus would eventually demonstrate that clashes with Arab regimes could be prompted as much by Palestinian moderation as by Palestinian militancy.

Washington was unprepared for the renewed entry of the Palestinian people as an active participant in the Arab–Israeli conflict. The Johnson administration's vision of equitable peace in the Middle East acknowledged the necessity of somehow resolving the Palestinian refugee plight on a just basis—but this, at most, implied some combination of repatriation to Israel or Israeli-controlled Palestine, compensation and measures to integrate the dispersed refugees into their host societies. It did not allow for the possibility of altering the existing regional system in the Middle East by creating a Palestinian state.

Pushed by the frustrating dynamics of its search for Mideast peace, Washington slowly, reluctantly, and ambiguously broadened its limited view of the Palestinian issue. In official U.S. parlance, allusions to the "refugee" problem metamorphisized first into references to "legitimate Palestinian interests," then changed to "Palestinian rights," then to the need for "full autonomy" for West Bank and Gaza Palestinians, and, finally, to the support for some form of "self-government" for Palestinians in the context of Jordanian–Israeli peace.[54]

In the years after 1967, U.S. relations with the PLO were generally antagonistic—but they were also complex and sometimes contradictory. Repelled by Palestinian terrorism, and distrusting the PLO as a radicalizing influence in the Middle East, Washington never accepted the organization or its leadership as the legitimate voice of the Palestinians. Yet, instances of positive contact did occur. Thus Washington considered it advisable to flirt briefly with the PLO immediately after the 1973 Arab–Israeli war—not, to be sure, with a view to incorporating the organization into the search for peace, but rather to gain a respite from its activities.[55] Still later, indirect contacts between PLO and the United States were instrumental in effecting cease-fire and security arrangements in Lebanon.

In the meantime—in 1975—Washington agreed with Israel not to negotiate with or recognize the PLO until the organization accepted Israel's right to exist. Indirect contacts were nonetheless maintained. U.S. Ambassador to the United Nations Andrew Young lost his position in 1979 for exceeding the authorized limits of intercourse by informally discussing with a PLO official the possibility of a package deal in which Israel's legitimacy and the Palestinians' right to self determination would be simultaneously upheld. Nonetheless, the question of whether grounds for a PLO–U.S. rapprochement existed continued to be occasionally addressed by both sides, frequently through the arcane medium of "signals" in the world press.

Arafat and his colleagues made no secret of their desire to open a dialogue with the United States. Yet they rejected unilateral acceptance of the Security Council resolutions (242, and, after 1973, 338) that became the symbolic touchstone of acceptance of Israel's legitimate status as a sovereign state. That step, the PLO leaders ultimately argued, could only be taken concurrently with U.S. recognition of the Palestinians' right to statehood and the PLO's role as the legitimate representative of the Palestinian people. By the late 1980s, the impasse showed little sign of weakening. Under these circumstances, despite the clear post–1967 trend toward the moderation of Palestinian goals and methods, the PLO remained technically wedded to the provisions of its charter, which—as amended in 1968—still called for the liberation of Palestine and implied the expulsion of all Jews who arrived in the country after 1948.[56]

ISRAEL

Israeli reaction to the June War was dominated by two emotions: exultation and relief. Neither was difficult to understand. Although Israeli leaders and U.S. intelligence experts may have confidently expected the Arab defeat, the downhill slide to war reminded most Israelis of the worst of Jewish experience. Little effort is required to appreciate the impact on Israel's public of then-PLO leader Ahmed Shukairy's bombast. Speaking in Amman on the eve of the war, Shukairy was quoted as saying that if Israel fell, surviving Jews would be returned to their native lands—then, chillingly adding his estimation that "none will survive."[57]

Exultation, of course, was linked to relief over the defeat of what was perceived as a concerted Arab effort to exterminate the Jewish state. Yet the emotion also sprang from far more complex sources than the immediate joy of military success. For in the extent of Israel's victory, and particularly in the newly conquered territories, Israelis of all stripes found hope that the Jewish state's long-term aims might be realized. The problem, as would soon become all too clear, was the lack of consensus over just what constituted Israel's goals.

This necessarily implied a corresponding lack of agreement over the significance of the recently acquired lands. Some Israelis, from the beginning a minority, argued that most, if not all, occupied territories—usually excepting East Jerusalem—should be returned to Arab control in exchange for a political settlement.[58] Others, whether basing themselves on pragmatic security concerns or consummatory religious-nationalist values, argued for preserving Israeli control over the newly acquired lands at all costs. Between these extremes, a variety of views on Israel's objectives and the role of the territories in their attainment competed for public support.

Underlying these differences was the question of the Jewish state's ultimate purpose, an issue that had never been fully resolved since Theodore Herzl founded the modern Zionist Movement near the end of the nineteenth century. As conceived by that flamboyant personality, Zionism postulated a pragmatic, secular solution to the Jewish people's lack of a national state, a condition that in Herzl's view forced Jews into an abnormal existence.

But while Herzl granted priority to statehood, rather than to any particular geographic location (and therefore considered a variety of possible sites), he soon found that only Palestine could serve as the focal point of Jewish nationalism. Thus, from its earliest days modern Zionism linked the Jewish future firmly to Palestine. This common foundation did not, however, preclude a diversity of outlooks—from the secular and pragmatic to the religious and the mystically nationalistic—within the movement. In the interval between Herzl's death and the establishment of Israel, the president of the Jewish Theological Seminary, Solomon Schecter, described Zionism as:

[A]n ideal and as such indefinable . . . [Zionism] is . . . subject to various interpretations and susceptive to different aspects. It may appear to one as the rebirth of national Jewish consciousness, to another as a religious revival, while to a third it may present itself as a path leading to the goal of Jewish culture; and to a fourth it may be the last and only solution to the Jewish problem.[59]

This indefinable ideal achieved a working relationship among its various adherents prior to 1948, but neither before nor after that date managed to harmonize their diverse outlooks completely. Joined in consensus over the goal of Jewish statehood, Zionism's several streams retained not only different, but in some cases incompatible, interpretations of Israel's meaning, objectives, and—in the broadest sense—limits.

For the first thirty years of its existence, Israel was led by secularists who grouped toward the left of the country's political spectrum in various shades of progressive liberal, socialist, and Marxist orientations. In their frame of reference, Israel's "normalizing" impact on Jewish life was essentially the same phenomenon that made the sovereign political identities of other nations a "normal" feature of modern life.[60]

On the other hand, religiously motivated Zionist currents tended to see Israel as manifesting the Jews' unique connection with the Divinity. The state was the special instrument of God's will, and its policies, both domestic and foreign, were therefore bound by sacred limits.[61]

A third broad category of outlooks on Israel's ultimate significance was that of ultra-nationalists who, although by no means necessarily religious, generally shared with religious Zionists the fervor and rigidity characteristic of attitudes based on consummatory values. One ultra-nationalist strand traced its intellectual and organizational origins to the romantic nationalism of Vladimir Jabotinski, who in 1935 broke with the World Zionist Organization to found the revisionist New Zionist Organization.[62] Jabotinski's creation stressed blood, race, and land while extolling military power. After 1967, ultra-nationalism rapidly developed another strand that combined mystic postulates with theories of aggressive political action. In their jointly held conviction that the ultimate expression of the Jewish people's reality required the ingathering of all Jews in all of the "Land of Israel," the distinct currents of ultra-nationalism found an ideological bedrock upon which to construct a potent political force.

These trends—secularist, religious, and ultra-nationalist—constituted neither absolute divisions nor the totality of competing views of Israel. They were, however, the major inclinations within the Israeli ideological spectrum that struggled to define the significance of the 1967 victory over the Arabs. Differences existed within each tendency, and similarities existed among certain elements within diverse categories. Yet, as politically significant orientations, they exerted a basic influence on the formulation of Israel's post–1967 policies.

While distinct attitudes toward the Jewish state's raison d'etre helped diversify Israelis' policy preferences after the June War, so too did the relatively more immediate issue of Israel's security needs. Israelis generally agreed that the war's outcome offered the prospect of enhancing the state's long-term security. However, it was unclear what this implied. Was maximum space in itself the best guarantor of safety, or were other, perhaps more complex, arrangements better suited to the task? Were the latter view taken, what combination of space and other arrangements was preferable, and just what sorts of "other" measures should be sought? Moreover, the entire relationship between space and security was complicated—as well as directly linked to the issue of ultimate purpose—by demography. Over one million Arabs had come under Israel's control as a result of the war. Given the Palestinians' traditionally higher birthrate, the permanent incorporation into Israel of any significant portion of the conquered lands could simultaneously threaten Israel's security, its democratic system, and its Jewishness.

These considerations quickly affected Israel's complex ideological and political panorama. Questions surrounding the country's future in the occupied territories swirled and merged with vital intensity, creating new alignments and antagonisms among various outspoken groups.

The most striking early development in ideological admixture was the rapid growth of an extra-parliamentary group known as the Land of Israel Movement. Formed in the summer of 1967, the Movement demanded the retention of all recently occupied lands. This stand immediately attracted many influential adherents, not only including religious Zionists and mystic-nationalists but also prominent secular-leftists who now concluded that Israel's security required significant territorial expansion.[63]

While the Land of Israel Movement expounded a position that won support from a broad cross-section of the Israeli public, its members generally did not commit themselves to settling the newly acquired territories. That form of activism fell to Gush Emunim, another extra-parliamentary group that appeared on the Israeli political scene in 1974. Although the Gush also enlisted secular as well as religiously motivated members, its ideology was firmly rooted in a messianic vision. Israel's creation, and the major steps that led to the state's establishment, were taken as visible signs of God's plan for humanity's redemption.[64] So too was the extended territory that came under the Jewish state's control in 1967. Holding that "the Jewish people and the Land of Israel in its entirety are one," Gush Emunim adherents vehemently opposed any abandonment of the occupied areas. By the same token, the Gush faith-ful—while generally not advocating steps to extend Israel's frontiers beyond the limits reached in 1967—believed that the unity of land and people would probably require further wars to bring all Eretz Israel under Jewish control.[65]

With the rise to power of Menachem Begin's strongly nationalistic Likud Government in 1977, Gush Emunim found its interest in massive Jewish settlement of the West Bank reflected in national policy. However, when the Begin government later agreed to the return of the Sinai to Egypt, the Gush stood in opposition. Many Gush members subsequently joined the extreme rightist Techiyah Party, a Likud offshoot formed in reaction to the Sinai withdrawal.[66]

More than a decade after its founding, Gush Emunim seemed destined to remain part of Israel's socio-political landscape. By then, its record was mixed. Certainly, it had not secured the extent of Jewish settlement it hoped to see in the West Bank. Yet it had gained significance, as both a manifestation and cause of the growth of popular commitment to the in-corporation into Israel of occupied territories. By the mid–1980s, some students of Israeli society not only concluded that the Gush constituted but the tip of a cultural "iceberg" resting on "a broader religious subculture," but also that its outlook was "becoming the dominant ideology in Israel."[67]

The ultimate validity of that contention remains to be seen. However, there is no doubt that the Land of Israel Movement and Gush Emunim were parts of a trend that after 1967 led to growing links between Israel and the occupied territories. Such bonds progressively appeared to un-dermine the possibility that the occupied lands might serve as currency for establishing peace between Israel and the Arab world.

Extraparliamentary movements opposing large-scale retention of the occupied territories attracted far less support than groups calling for ex-pansionist policies. Shortly after the 1967 War, an amalgam of distinct groups known as the "Peace Movement" developed in reaction to the Land of Israel Movement. It gathered under its umbrella various orga-nizations committed to the return to Arab control of the bulk of the oc-cupied territories in exchange for peace. Its members tended to be secular and politically leftwing. Academics from the Hebrew University of Jerusalem figured prominently in the Movement. Following Anwar Sadat's 1977 visit to Jerusalem, a group known as Peace Now moved to cen-ter stage as the main voice in Israel calling for the barter of territory for peace.

Unlike the Land of Israel Movement or Gush Emunim, Israeli peace groups generally had few direct links to the governments that sat in Jerusalem after 1967. They were also distinguished from their pro-expansionist extra-parliamentary counterparts by a deeper difference: while the latter shared a clear territorial vision, peace groups shared only the conviction that the bulk of occupied territories should revert to the Arabs in the context of peace. They never moved beyond this general outlook to an explicit consensus on either the limits of Israeli territorial flexibility or the nature of political concessions to be demanded of the Arabs. Nonetheless, by virtue of persistent criticism of the growing influence of expansionist sentiment, peace groups attained high visibility in the Israeli forum.

Although extra-parliamentary divisions reflected the range of major contrasts in articulate Israeli public opinion, the formulation of official policy was conducted within narrower limits. Every government that sat in Jerusalem after 1967 found it expedient to avoid adopting a clear position on ultimate territorial aims. Yet, in regard to those occupied areas that had formed part of mandated Palestine—the West Bank and Gaza—all demonstrated more interest in creating a significant and permanent Israeli presence than in considering their return to Arab control in exchange for peace.

The first government to confront the task of defining Israel's objectives after the 1967 war had been formed only days before the victory. It was a National Unity government led by Levi Eshkol and including all Knesset groups except the Communists. As leader of the moderately socialist Mapai (Labor) Party, which had dominated Israeli politics since the state's founding, Eshkol had served as prime minister and defense minister since 1963.

On the eve of the war, Eshkol came under rising public pressure to expand the ruling coalition, which was led by Mapai in close association with the unorthodox Marxist, Ahdut Ha'avoda. His reluctance to do so derived only in part from a natural inclination to resist sharing authority in a moment of crisis. It was also an understandable outgrowth of the deep blend of personal and ideological quarrels that characterized Israel's domestic politics.

It particularly galled Eshkol that the drive for an enlarged government centered on calls for the ministry of defense to be given to Moshe Dayan. Eshkol's ire was compounded by Dayan's association with David Ben Gurion. Although Ben Gurion was recognized as Israel's senior statesman, he had bolted from Mapai to found his own party, Rafi, after losing a power struggle with Eshkol in 1965. Dayan, a charismatic war hero capable of capturing the public imagination in ways totally beyond the rather drab Eshkol's power, was an acknowledged protégé of Ben Gurion.[68]

Eshkol finally gave in on June 1, 1967. With the Communists excluded, Mapam—a small party more to the left than Mapai or Ahdut Ha'avoda— occupied one end of the Government of National Unity's political spectrum. At the other end was Gahal, a partnership formed of the right-of-center Liberal Party and Herut, the extreme rightist parliamentary group led by the former guerrilla leader Menachem Begin. Rafi, ideologically indistinguishable from Mapai, was represented by Moshe Dayan

Map 1.1

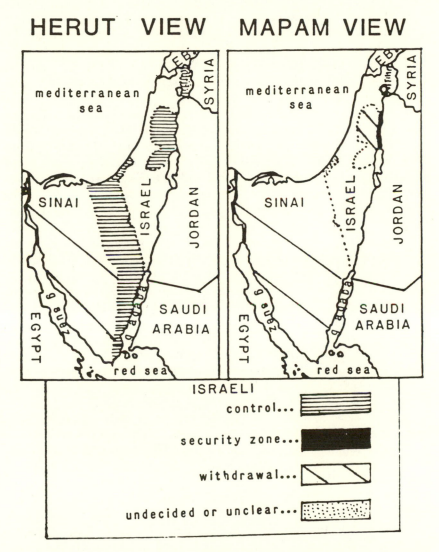

HERUT VIEW   MAPAM VIEW

as minister of defense. Representatives of the National Religious Party
and the Independent Liberals completed the cabinet's make-up.[69]

Apart from being united over the retention of East Jerusalem, the
composite government was deeply divided over the policy to be adopted
toward the territories acquired as a result of the war. At one extreme,
Herut openly advocated annexation of the West Bank and Gaza and the
retention of the Golan Heights and much of the Sinai Peninsula. At the
other, Mapam preferred to see Israel withdraw from most of the ter-

ritories in the context of a political settlement. The National Religious Party, Mapai's perennial associate in governing coalitions, exhibited a hefty territorial appetite, and a significant portion of its leadership favored the maximalist stand taken by the Land of Israel Movement.[70]

Nor did Mapai, Ahdut Ha'avoda, and Rafi—despite their merging in early 1968 to form the Israel Labor Party—settle on a single stand. In time, widely publicized, and competing, territorial proposals became associated with Ahdut Ha'avoda leader Yigal Allon and erstwhile Rafi luminary Moshe Dayan. Neither was very precise, and each implied significant territorial aggrandizement. The Allon Plan advocated Israeli control of most of the Golan Heights, the Gaza Strip, and a large, but not fully specified, slice of the Sinai. It called for Israel to have a territorial foothold along the Jordan River valley that would serve as a "security belt." The plan suggested that a diminished portion of the pre–1967 West Bank area would be allowed to federate with Jordan or opt for independence.[71]

Dayan's proposal was rather similar. It too envisaged Israeli control over much of the Golan, all of Gaza, and a part of the Sinai (being both more explicit and ambitious than Allon's plan in this last respect). The West Bank, with modifications in its pre-war boundaries, was to be returned to Jordan—with a proviso establishing the right of Israelis to settle anywhere in the area and providing for the prompt construction of four or five Jewish towns near major Arab population centers. The Jordan River would become Israel's "security frontier."[72]

Mapai's 1969 election platform was more notable for vagueness than precision when referring to the occupied territories. In what became known as the "Oral Law" formula, the future of the greater part of the Sinai and the West Bank, as well as approximately half the Golan region, was left undecided. It did, however, specify that Israel would control the Golan Heights, a corridor linking the Negev with Sharm el-Sheikh, and the Gaza Strip. It also specified that the Jordan River would be Israel's security frontier.[73]

None of these plans ever received the Israeli government's imprimatur. Officially, although the pattern of Israeli settlement construction in the occupied lands until 1976 indicated that the Labor Alignment was in practice adhering to the course suggested by the Allon Plan, each remained no more than preferences of factions, or of factions within factions. Indeed, the war had hardly ended when it became apparent that any effort to forge a formal agreement on territorial dispositions would topple the government and plunge Israel into a protracted political struggle.

Under these circumstances, cabinet crises became regular features of the Government of National Unity. The outspoken Moshe Dayan her-

Map 1.2

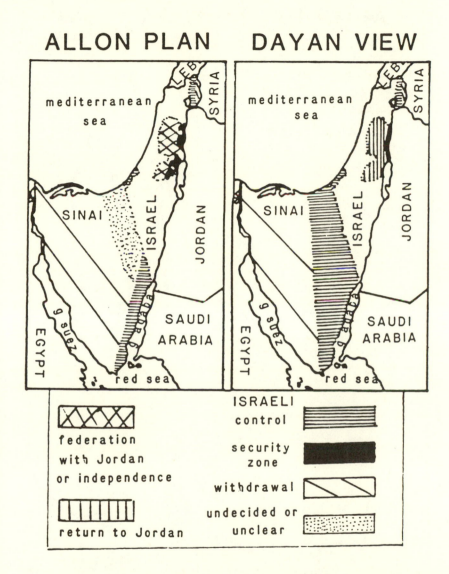

alded the pattern prior to the war's end by indicating on June 9 that
Israel would never relinquish the West Bank, the Gaza Strip, or Jerusalem.[74] Speaking to the Knesset three days later, Levi Eshkol contra-
dicted the defense minister and stated that no decisions had been taken
regarding the occupied territories.

Public differences of this sort plagued the Government of National

Map 1.3

LABOR PARTY "ORAL LAW"

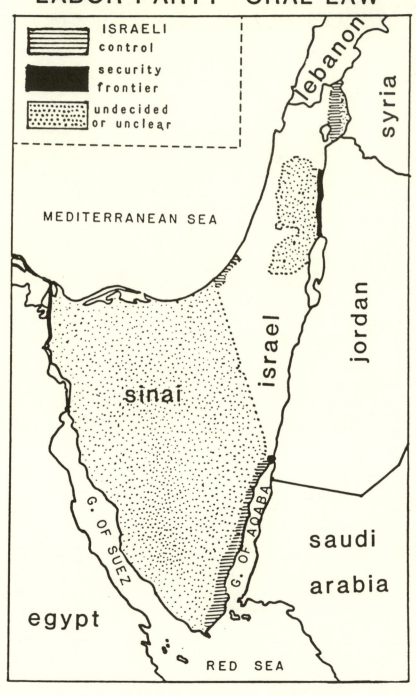

Legend:
- ISRAELI control
- security frontier
- undecided or unclear

MEDITERRANEAN SEA

lebanon

syria

israel

jordan

sinai

G. OF SUEZ

G. OF AQABA

saudi arabia

egypt

RED SEA

Unity throughout the three years of its existence. In 1969, while Foreign Minister Abba Eban continued to insist that Arabs would be surprised by Israel's generosity if they engaged in direct negotiations with the Jewish state, Dayan was offering this explanation of Israeli policy:

The primary goal of the path we are following is to create a new map, to create new borders—the end of the struggle, will be brought in the final analysis by the inclusive fact of a Jewish state here whose strength and importance will be such that it will be impossible to destroy it and it will be necessary to live with it.[75]

Nonetheless, internal differences over the ultimate disposition of occupied land did not prevent Israel's government from quickly agreeing on several important basic positions. Among these were the insistence that Israel would under no circumstances return to its pre-war frontiers, that a final settlement could be arrived at only through direct negotiations with the concerned Arab governments, and the rejection of reliance to any significant degree on external guarantees of any settlement that might eventually be reached. Each of these points emerged forcefully in the comments of Israeli spokesmen in Jerusalem and at the United Nations as well as through a variety of actions taken by the government soon after the war.

A final, very significant, area of agreement within the Israeli government was not stressed so strongly in political oratory, although it was hardly hidden in practice. This was found in an overall consensus on the principle of Israel's right to absorb lands occupied during the war. What divided Israel's leading factions was not the principle itself but preferences over the extent and timing of its application.

Thus, the outpouring of emotion that accompanied the conquest of East Jerusalem was rapidly followed by official action. On June 27, 1967, the Knesset approved measures that not only amounted to the de facto annexation of the city but also considerably expanded its borders into what had formerly been Jordanian-controlled territory.

More steps altering conditions in the territories were soon forthcoming. In mid-July, Israel announced its intention to exploit captured Egyptian oil wells in the Sinai. Days later, Jerusalem approved the establishment of the first Israeli settlements on the Golan Heights. In late September, the cabinet unveiled plans for more settlements near Hebron and on the northwest shore of the Dead Sea. Nine months later, the minister of housing revealed that eighteen settlements had been constructed in the occupied territories: ten in the Golan Heights, three on the West Bank, and five in the Sinai.[76]

The internal differences that seemed to prevent Israel from specifying the all-important territorial dimension of the peace it sought with the Arab World did little to retard what was soon known as "creeping annexation." The process was fueled by the stalemate created by the refusal of Arab governments to negotiate directly with Israel, a step that in their view would constitute a priori recognition of the Jewish state, and Israel's insistence that direct negotiations were the only avenue to a settlement. Golda Meir, who succeeded Eshkol as prime minister in 1969, gave the most succinct statement of Jerusalem's postwar policy. Israel, she stated, would only draw borders when the Arabs "were ready to receive the map from our hands."[77] The Labor-dominated governments that ruled Israel for the first decade after the 1967 war neither specified territorial aims nor stemmed the proliferation of settlements in the occupied lands. However, the consolidation of Israel's position in the occupied territories was pursued more energetically once Menachem Begin—who led the rightist Likud coalition after the Gahal joined three other groups in 1973—came to power in 1977.[78]

The switch to high gear is readily apparent in Ann Lesch's finding that of the sixty-two settlements in existence less than a year after Begin became prime minister, fully thirty-three were founded in 1977 or early 1978. Shortly before Likud entered into an uneasy coalition government with the Labor Alignment in 1984, it was estimated that nearly 13,000 housing units had been constructed for settlers in the West Bank and Gaza. This did not include considerable construction in the expanded environs of Jerusalem.[79]

On the other hand, Begin led Israel through the diplomatic thicket that in 1979 yielded a formal peace treaty with Egypt, under the terms of which the Sinai was restored to Cairo.[80] Yet Begin was acting consistently in seizing that opportunity to eliminate Egypt from the ranks of Israel's antagonists. His outlook had from the start been more flexible on the Sinai than on other occupied areas. For Begin and his followers, it was the West Bank and Gaza which demanded a firm commitment to retention.

However, neither Begin nor the leaders who succeeded him as prime minister in the early 1980s simply rejected the possibility of coming to some arrangement with Jordan and Egypt over the West Bank and Gaza. Yet Israel's clear determination to retain control over those areas seemed to leave little scope for a settlement. This was all the more true in view of the limitations on King Hussein's ability to speak for the Palestinians. Having acknowledged the PLO's right to represent the Palestinians, Hussein eventually came to hope for a formula that would allow him—in some sort of alignment with the PLO—to negotiate the future of the West Bank and Gaza. There was an air of unreality about the king's fruitless efforts throughout the 1980s to strike a bargain with PLO leaders—for Israel flatly refused to have any political contact with the PLO, whether or not Israel's right to exist was recognized by that organization.

None of the governments that sat in Jerusalem after 1967 was prepared to acknowledge the PLO as anything but a "terrorist organization." Although there was no dearth of evidence pointing to the PLO's use of violence, often against civilian targets, the official Israeli posture was not so much conditioned by this as by the PLO's central claim to uphold the Palestinians' national right to self-determination.[81] While Israel could officially acknowledge the necessity of solving the Palestinian refugee problem, and, eventually, accept the notion of granting closely limited communal responsibilities to the West Bank and Gaza Arabs, its governments rejected the concepts of a Palestinian "nation," Palestinian "national rights," or a Palestinian national right to "self determination."

The underlying reason for this was that the dominant view within Israel saw only Jewish national rights as applying to the lands claimed by the Palestinians. No Israeli government was willing to recognize the coexistence of Palestinian national rights; no Israeli government was prepared to surrender claimed Jewish rights to Palestinians in any portion of the disputed land. So long as this outlook prevailed, and so long as the PLO clung to the demand for national rights—however circumscribed and however limited the territory sought for their realization—there was no hope that Israel and the PLO would be parties to a settlement. On the other hand, given that the Hashemite monarchy's nineteen-year rule over the West Bank was founded on an accident of history, Israel's leaders felt it was not inconceivable that a bargain might ultimately be struck with Jordan in which their concept of Jewish rights there and in Gaza would prevail along with specially allocated Arab communal rights.

In the eyes of Israeli policymakers, the PLO barred the way to this alternative. Their solution was to launch the 1982 Israeli–PLO war in Lebanon. Victorious on the battlefield, and having grievously crippled the PLO's organizational structure, Israel's leaders hoped that Palestinian nationalism had been eliminated as a political force.

But if by the late 1980s Israel continued to look forward to a diplomatic accommodation with Jordan, it became progressively difficult to see how it could aspire to the same with Syria. The bitterness of Syrian–Israeli relations came second only to those between the PLO and Israel. Holding Damascus directly responsible for the events that led to the 1967 War, and highly conscious of the Golan Heights' strategic value, Israelis generally opposed returning the area to Syrian control. This view did not change in 1974, when a small part of the region was in fact returned to Syria. Nor did tacit understandings between Israel and Syria over spheres of influence in Lebanon in the mid–1970s lead to a thaw in relations between the two.[82] With the annexation of the Golan Heights in 1981, Israel's position seemed to be that if peace were ever to come with Syria, it would be based on Damascus' acceptance of irrevocable territorial loss.

During the two decades that followed the June War, the United States and Israel grew steadily closer. This is not to deny that their relationship was also marked by instances of friction. Controversies were sparked by occasional differences over a variety of issues, including political approaches to other significant actors in the Middle East, Israel's use of force in the area, and U.S. regional arms transfer policies. They did not, however, impede the progressive strengthening of U.S.–Israeli ties.

Even Israel's appetite for the occupied lands could not drive a wedge between Washington and Jerusalem, despite the consistency of U.S. declarations—as Assistant Secretary of State Richard Murphy would argue as late as 1988—that the key to a Middle East settlement remained "the exchange of territory for peace."[83]

Murphy's words only reiterated the same view expressed by U.S. spokesmen for over twenty years, a period during which Washington had never acted strongly to counter the challenge posed to its theory of Middle East peace by Israeli encroachments on the occupied territories. Indeed, the tone of U.S. reaction to steps binding the territories to Israel was established by Washington's reaction to the annexation of Jerusalem shortly after the June War. At that time, the White House and State Department issued a joint declaration:

The hasty administrative action . . . cannot be regarded as determining the future of the holy places or the status of Jerusalem in relation to them. The United States has never recognized such unilateral action by any state in the area. . . . [84]

However, having made this point, the United States proceeded to abstain twice at the United Nations on resolutions calling on Israel to rescind the measures affecting Jerusalem and to desist from further steps. On each occasion, the U.S. stand was explained on two grounds: that the resolutions in question "appeared to accept" Israel's actions as constituting annexation, a view the United States could not acknowledge; and that the Jerusalem problem (and by implication that of any other portion of the occupied lands) could not "realistically be solved apart from other related aspects of the Middle East situation."

In 1967, the latter argument signalled the Arab world that Washington was seriously determined to see an overall package settlement resolve the Arab–Israeli conflict. The former seemed to imply that U.S. policymakers confidently expected to put their narrow legalistic positions to effective use when it became necessary to roll back Israel's presence in the occupied territories.

By the 1980s, the United States had long since abandoned the goal of promoting a "package" settlement. Moreover, the deep roots that Israel had planted over the years in the West Bank, Gaza, and the Golan Heights raised serious doubts over Washington's ability, and will, to further "the exchange of territory for peace."

WASHINGTON EXPLORES TACTICS

The Johnson administration intially appeared to have little doubt that patience and determination would allow the United States to promote what it saw as an equitable tradeoff between territory and the specific principles of regional peace cited in the president's June 19 speech. During the nineteen months that lapsed between the end of the June War and Johnson's exit from the White House in January 1969, the administration's involvement with the Arab–Israeli conflict passed through three stages. The first, stretching from the termination of hostilities to the end of November, was devoted to searching for an internationally supported framework compatible with the objectives and requirements of Washington's pursuit of Middle East peace. The second lasted nearly a year and witnessed the administration's growing frustration and alarm over its failure to generate a productive diplomatic process between Israel and the Arab governments. The final phase came during the administration's last months in office and was used to establish grounds for a new departure in U.S. policy. The entire nineteen-month span marked a loss of original innocence as policymakers began to perceive more clearly the dimensions, difficulties and dangers attached to their postwar approach to the Middle East.

The process of debate and maneuver among the various actors in the Middle East drama began in mid-June at a U.N. General Assembly special emergency session that rapidly exposed the range of differences among key protagonists. The core issues at stake were the nature, timing, and extent of Israel's withdrawal from the occupied lands. Arab delegates demanded that the withdrawal be unconditional, immediate, and total. Israel insisted that the question could be approached only in the context of direct negotiations, and could be acted upon only as part of any peace settlement that might be concluded. In short, the timing would certainly not be immediate, the nature would certainly be conditional, and the extent—while unspecified—was hardly foreseen as total.

Having called for the emergency session, the Soviet Union initially extended full support to Arabs. However, while remaining committed to a total withdrawal, the Soviets soon dropped their demand that it should be immediate and unconditional. By July 19, Foreign Minister Andre Gromyko joined the U.S. ambassador to the United Nations, Arthur Goldberg, in calling for a complete Israeli withdrawal in exchange for Arab nonbelligerency and acceptance of Israel's right to exist. This early, and fleeting, sign of U.S.–USSR cooperation soon evaporated. The Soviets were unable at that time to overcome Arab opposition to the very notion of recognizing Israel. Israel opposed the Gromyko–Goldberg suggestion on grounds that a settlement could be arrived at only through direct negotiations with the Arab states.[85]

Since the U.S. posture at the General Assembly reflected the approach outlined by Johnson's speech on June 19, it both paralleled and differed from Israel's. The timing of any Israeli withdrawal was not to be immediate, but as part of a package comprising the elements indicated by the president's five principles. However, in keeping with Johnson's omission of any qualification limiting the process of arranging a settlement to a particular mode of negotiation, U.S. delegates were more flexible than their Israeli counterparts on the question of direct talks.

The deepest difference between the United States and Israel during the first weeks after the war lay in their respective assessments of the extent of withdrawal required for a final settlement. Goldberg's agreement with Gromyko was only one sign that Washington was then willing to speak out in favor of full withdrawal. Another indication came in the form of U.S. support for an unsuccessful Latin American resolution recommending withdrawal in the context of a peace settlement "from all territories occupied ... as a result of the recent conflict."[86] However, the suggestion that full withdrawal might be necessary was soon replaced by an open-ended stance supporting the idea that the extent of withdrawal must be determined by negotiation—and that later yielded to an overt stand in support of an unspecified degree of alteration of pre-war boundaries.

By late July, it was obvious that further efforts to break the deadlock in the General Assembly would be fruitless. With neither the Arabs nor Israel exhibiting flexibility, the emergency session referred the matter to the Security Council. Four months later, on November 22, that body adopted Resolution 242, a carefully crafted masterpiece of ambiguity that won approval precisely because of its ability to accommodate conflicting interpretations.

Resolution 242 called for "a just and lasting peace" based on two principles:

1. Withdrawal of Israeli armed forces from territories occupied in the recent conflict.

2. Termination of all claims ... of belligerency and respect for and acknowledgment of the sovereignty, territorial integrity, and political independence of every state in the area, and their right to live within secure and recognized boundaries. ...

It "further affirmed" the need for freedom of navigation through international waterways; a "just settlement of the refugee problem"; and guarantees of the territorial inviolability and independence of every state in the region through measures "including the establishment of demilitarized zones." Finally, the resolution asked that a special UN representative proceed to the Middle East to contact the disputing governments. His task was to "promote agreement and assist efforts to achieve a peaceful and accepted settlement" according to the resolution's "provisions and principles."[87]

The hallmark of these points was vagueness. The special represent-ative was given no real guidelines for promoting a settlement. It was unclear whether his role was to be limited to furthering direct contact between the Israeli and Arab governments, or whether he would be an indirect channel for communication, or, finally, whether he was expected to advance independent views and suggestions. Even were this proce-dural conundrum solved, Resolution 242 offered little direction for ef-forts to reconcile substantive differences between Arabs and Israelis. What constituted a "just" settlement of the refugee problem? Could guarantees of freedom of navigation, territorial inviolability, and political independence involve not only demilitarized zones but also border al-terations? If so, to what extent?

The significance of the resolution's two primary principles was equally elusive. The text called for an Israeli withdrawal "from territories" oc-cupied in the war. Did this mean from all or from part of those lands? The second principle upheld the need for terminating belligerency and acknowledging the sovereignty, territorial integrity and political inde-pendence of all states within "secure and recognized" borders. This raised a host of questions, chief among which were two. Did termination of the state of belligerency require a peace treaty jointly signed by the parties to the conflict or merely some form of declaration issued either collectively or individually? Were "secure" borders something other than previously acknowledged demarcation lines or not?

Finally, of course, the resolution made no reference to implementa-tion. It was unclear whether action on its several provisions should be taken simultaneously or sequentially, a problem that boiled down to whether withdrawal should be a prelude to or a consequence of accom-modation on other issues.

These ambiguities were not unrecognized when the Security Council approved the resolution. By then, however, it was clear that Arab–Israeli peace would not be produced simply and swiftly through the exchange of territory for political commitments. Under the circumstances, the resolution's significance was that it highlighted issues requiring resolu-tion were peace to come to the Middle East while making explicit an international consensus that lands taken by Israel should revert to Arab control as part of a settlement.

Washington was satisfied with this outcome, for the resolution upheld the five principles voiced earlier by Johnson. However, the same was not true of all parties directly involved in the recent conflict. Syria—until 1974—rejected the Security Council measure because of its call for termi-nating the state of belligerency in the Middle East and because to do other-wise appeared to imply recognition of Israel's legitimacy. Palestinian organizations took exception to the resolution's failure to refer to Palestinian political demands. Only Egypt and Jordan accepted the resolution with relative equanimity. Israel, although agreeing to receive a UN special representative, did not unequivocally accept Resolution 242 until 1970.

While the United States tried to preserve diplomatic flexibility by specifically avoiding any interpretation of the resolution's text, others eagerly went on record immediately. On the day the measure was adopted, Egyptian and Jordanian delegates insisted that the text justified their claim that the first step toward a settlement had to be Israel's full withdrawal from all lands occupied during the June War.

In contrast, Israel maintained that the resolution did not affect the policy it had followed since the end of the war. Speaking before the Security Council, Foreign Minister Abba Eban stated that Israel would continue to maintain the situation created by the cease-fire agreements until it obtained peace treaties "directly negotiated and contractually confirmed." Israel's interpretation of the UN special representative's role was also tightly limited. Jerusalem would accept his efforts to promote peace only to the extent that they aimed at bringing the parties together for direct negotiations.[88]

On November 23, Secretary General U Thant announced that Swedish ambassador Gunnar Jarring would serve as the Special UN Representative. A diplomat of long experience, Jarring took up the challenge with vigor. However, he was ultimately unable to overcome the deadlock between Arab demands for full withdrawal and Israel's insistence that substantive issues would be discussed only directly with Arab representatives. His mission terminated in early 1971.

That, however, lay in the future. For the moment, Washington saw Jarring's activities as a potentially useful instrument for breaking the diplomatic logjam. This hope was largely responsible for the administration's reaction to Levi Eshkol's trip to the United States in January 1968.

The Israeli leader's visit was a festive occasion, with crowds of admirers treating it as a victory celebration. In Texas, where Johnson received him at the LBJ Ranch, Eshkol's reception went "far beyond the requirements of normal protocol." Yet the effusive cordiality did not hide Eshkol's lack of success. He had come to convince the president of Israel's need for advanced weapons systems, particularly for F-4 Phantom warplanes. In support of his plea, Eshkol pointed to the Soviet Union's rapid rearming of Egypt and Syria. Though worrisome, and based on incontrovertible evidence, the prime minister's arguments were not deemed convincing in Washington, where in early 1968 the dominant feeling was that Israel's military superiority was not seriously threatened. Johnson promised only to keep Israel's defense requirements "under active and sympathetic review."[89]

The president could hardly have done less, for the administration was now committed to a course that left it no option but to ensure the nullification of Arab hopes to undo the consequences of their defeat through military means. With France having tilted politically toward the Arab world in the aftermath of the June War, the United States would clearly have to assume the major responsibility for sustaining Israel's military superiority. Still, Washington hoped to avoid a Middle East arms race that carried the potential of driving the Arab world into ever greater political and military reliance on the Soviet Union.

One possibility of averting this in early 1968 seemed to be an arms limitation agreement with the Soviet Union. Another was to encourage Israel to make maximum use of Jarring's efforts to explore chances for a settlement with the Arab states. Both of these considerations, together with the actual balance of forces in the Middle East, influenced Johnson's cautious reaction to Eshkol's request for advanced weaponry.

U.S. hopes of limiting arms shipments to the Middle East faded over the next several months. Moscow could not be shaken from its insistence that a Middle East settlement must precede an accord on arms transfers. By October, the U.S. abandoned efforts to alter the Soviet position. It was clear that Washington's desire to gain political mileage by preserving a balance of power in the Middle East favorable to Israel was equalled by Moscow's aim of capitalizing politically in the region by arming Egypt and Syria.

In the meantime, much attention focused on Israel's frustrated request for Phantom warplanes. Eshkol had departed from the United States publicly reaffirming that Israel would deal with the Arabs only through direct negotiations. It was widely believed that his failure to obtain the Phantoms left the United States with an option to exert "increased pressure on Israel to cooperate with U.N. efforts to achieve a peace settlement."[90]

The option began to be exercised openly in late February 1968, amid press reports of a letter from Secretary of State Dean Rusk to Foreign Minister Eban urging that Israel accept Resolution 242 unequivocally and embark on indirect negotiations with the Arab states through Ambassador Jarring. The Israelis were unmoved. On the day that Rusk's letter was reported in the *New York Times,* Eban reiterated his government's position before a meeting of the Labor World Zionist Movement in Jerusalem.[91] In March, Lyndon Johnson announced that he would not seek re-election. The decision did not prevent the Phantoms issue from becoming a part of election-year domestic politics.[92] In July, the House of Representatives unexpectedly attached an amendment to a pending foreign aid bill encouraging the president "to negotiate the sale of Phantom airplanes to Israel." Despite the administration's opposition, the Committee on Foreign Affairs approved the bill as amended.

In Israel, it became progressively apparent that the composite National Unity government would be split by any move to negotiate with the

Arabs through Jarring. Abba Eban touched off a domestic political storm in May by agreeing to Jarring's proposal to hold separate discussions with Arab and Israeli representatives at UN headquarters in New York. Even the relatively moderate *Jerusalem Post* charged the foreign minister with possibly blurring Israel's commitment to direct talks and "encouraging expectations on the part of friendly powers which by all odds will not stand the test of reality." Menachem Begin's Gahal faction threatened to withdraw from the governing coalition unless the policy on direct negotiations were officially reaffirmed. An official statement was duly issued asserting that "the only solution" to the Arab–Israeli problem was for the parties to embark on direct talks. The same theme was stressed days later in a peace proposal communicated to Jarring.[93]

By September, Israel was still fruitlessly awaiting positive action on its request for Phantoms.[94] At this point, President Johnson issued his first major Middle East policy statement since the "Five Principles" speech of June 1967. Significantly, he did not address the Phantoms issue, though he did note that the United States "had no intention of allowing the balance of forces in the area to become an incentive for war."[95]

The presidential message underscored the administration's two basic differences, one procedural, one substantive, with the direction taken by Israeli policymakers following the June War. It was, said Johnson, U.S. policy to support the Jarring Mission. Yet, he added, "the parties themselves . . . must make the major effort to begin seriously this much-needed peacekeeping process." Giving a somewhat more specific view of the requirements for constructing an overall settlement, Johnson argued that:

. . . the peacekeeping process will not begin until the leaders of the Middle East begin exchanging views on the hard issues through some agreed procedure . . . I urge them to put their views on the table . . .

Johnson's remarks clearly implied his disagreement with the claim that direct negotiations constituted the only possible procedure for exchanging views on "hard issues." Moreover, the president also indicated opposition to any significant expansion of Israel's borders. In this, he was acting in accord with arguments made by some of his advisors who called for steps to curb Israel's "growing appetite for territory."[96] Final boundaries between Israel and the Arab states, he said, "cannot and should not reflect the weight of conquest."

The underlying tensions between the United States and Israel surfaced again shortly afterward when Moshe Dayan publicly warned his countrymen against succumbing to U.S. preferences:

. . . we should get used to the idea that, as I believe, there are differences of view between us and the United States. The difficulties are about what kind of settlement there should be in the Middle East and the ways of solving the present dispute . . . to achieve a complete identity of views we should do what the USA wants. I hope we will not do this. We should not determine our policy according to the will of the USA.[97]

A few weeks later, amid mounting speculation that U.S. pressure would force Israel to present a plan for withdrawal from the occupied territories, Abba Eban spoke before the UN General Assembly. Although Eban did not suggest a concrete proposal for a peaceful settlement, his speech was delivered in moderate tones and appeared to signal a possible change in the Israeli stance on direct negotiations. Jerusalem, he said, was prepared to "exchange ideas or clarifications on certain matters of substance through Ambassador Jarring with any Arab government."[98]

However, while not specifying what "matters of substance" might be discussed through Jarring, his remarks strongly indicated that Israel had not altered its refusal to explore indirectly possible elements of a peace settlement:

The process of exploring peace terms should follow normal precedents. There is no case in history in which conflicts have been liquidated or a transition effected from a state of war to a state of peace on the basis of a refusal by one state to meet another for negotiations.

Eban's apparent concession on the possibility of communicating with the Arabs through Jarring was effectively cancelled by his renewed demand for direct negotiations to produce a "framework of peace." His comments were generally interpreted in Israel as marking no change in the government's position. The reference to Jarring's role as a mediary was taken to mean only that Jerusalem was not averse to intercourse that would lead to direct talks over substantive arrangements for peace. All doubts over this interpretation were removed a month later when Israel refused Jarring's request for an indication of its views on territorial arrangements that might be conveyed to the Arab states.[99]

In the meantime, official U.S. reaction to Eban's statement was subdued. State Department spokesmen labeled it "constructive" and said it moved away "to some extent from direct peace talks."[100] That restrained welcome seems not to have reflected any illusions over a change in Israeli policy so much as a desire not to appear totally disappointed at the failure of U.S. pressure.

And the pressure had failed. Twenty-four hours after Eban's UN speech, Johnson finally authorized the sale of the Phantoms requested by Levi Eshkol ten months earlier.[101] Domestic political considerations undoubtedly played a role in the decision. With only a month remaining before national elections, all presidential candidates, including the Democratic nominee, Vice President Hubert Humphrey, were supporting Israel's arms requests.[102] On the other hand, the president was not simply bowing to public pressure or the political requirements of the Democratic Party. The dynamic of the conflict in the Middle East was in its own right a major determinant of his final decision on the Phantoms.

The collapse in early October 1968 of U.S.–Soviet talks over limiting arms supplies to the Middle East indicated that no end was in sight to the rebuilding of Egyptian and Syrian forces.[103] If the more moderate aspect of the ambiguous stands taken by Egypt and Jordan after their defeat was to be cultivated and explored with a view to producing a Middle East settlement, Arab hopes of reversing the regional balance of power had to be thoroughly discredited. Under the circumstances, anything that appeared to weaken Israel's relative military advantage—or even any implication that Washington might weaken in its commitment to sustain Israel's position vis-à-vis the Arabs—worked against U.S. objectives.

So long as the United States saw a U.S.–Israeli partnership as the key to bringing the Arabs to a peaceful settlement, this posed an inevitable dilemma. For despite Israel's growing dependence on the United States, Washington had no effective form of pressuring Jerusalem into testing Arab hints of readiness to conclude peace in exchange for the lost lands.

Having discovered this harsh reality, the Johnson administration found itself locked into a diplomatic impasse as well as a Middle East arms race. It was a vicious cycle, one that might easily become a spiraling process of polarization and militarism as tentative Arab moderation yielded to militancy and Israeli hopes of negotiated peace were overwhelmed by expansionist ambitions and security calculations based exclusively on military might. Thus, Washington not only faced the threat of a continuing decline of its political influence in the Arab world, but also the spectre of further Middle East hostilities and the related danger of superpower confrontation. The gloomy fact facing U.S. policymakers was that in the absence of some Arab–Israeli bargaining process, the Phantoms decision seemed likely to enhance the very conditions that helped produce it.

In November 1968, the administration embarked on what State Department officials later described as a number of "initiatives."[104] Although U.S. officials denied that a specific blueprint for peace had been devised, it was soon apparent that Washington had approached Cairo, Jerusalem, and Moscow with a far-reaching proposal for an Egyptian–Israeli settlement. As explained to Egyptian officials, the United States favored a total Israeli withdrawal from the Sinai in return for peace between the two countries. The plan also called for free navigation through the Suez Canal and Strait of Tiran, a settlement of the refugee problem, and a signed peace treaty. In retrospect, the plan's most interesting feature was a suggestion for redeploying UN forces between

Israel and Egypt and at Sharm el-Sheikh. Secretary Rusk reportedly proposed that in contrast to the pre–1967 arrangement, UN forces should come under the direction of the Security Council. This placed the U.S. position far closer than it had previously been to those of France and the Soviet Union, both of which had for some time advocated a four-power guarantee as part of a Middle East settlement.[105]

There is little reason to suppose that U.S. policymakers were surprised when both Israel and Egypt rejected the November initiative. Israel had only recently repeated its refusal to consider peace terms not produced through direct negotiations. Egypt, on the other hand, could hardly have been expected under the prevailing circumstances to enter into a bilateral peacemaking process that left unspecified both the fate of the Palestinians and the nature of Israel's future relations with Jordan and Syria. Washington's November initiative seems to have been designed as the opening gambit in a new approach to the Arab–Israeli conflict. Having now lost hope of convincing or forcing Israel to embark on an indirect bargaining process, the United States turned to the possibility of escaping its dilemma through great power accommodation.

With Richard Nixon about to assume office, the Johnson administration could not hope to develop the new policy direction. However, it could leave the option to do so open to its successor. When the Soviets responded with a peace plan of their own in late December, the Johnson administration did not react for nearly two weeks. Then, although noting that a settlement could be reached only by the Arab states and Israel, the administration proposed the continuation of superpower talks on the Middle East conflict. It also requested so many clarifications of the Soviet proposal that this seemed ensured.[106]

The Johnson administration never abandoned the goal of an equitable peace based on the existing Middle East state system. However, by the end of 1968 it had fundamentally altered its tactical approach. No longer would Washington assume that persuasion or pressure would convert Israel into a compliant instrument for sounding out the prospects of, and possibly constructing a settlement based on, the U.S. vision of a peaceful Middle East. The door was now open for a far more direct U.S. role in Middle East peacemaking—a role to be directly shared with the Soviet Union. In a sense, it was a high price to pay. For just as U.S. policy had traditionally aimed at obviating or limiting Soviet influence in the region, Moscow's eagerness to accept the U.S. invitation was—at a minimum—motivated by the desire to establish "recognition of its legitimate interest and involvement in Middle East affairs."[107]

2

DIFFUSION OF AN
OBJECTIVE: 1969–1976

...somewhere along the line the question of what causes a Soviet
move becomes irrelevant; American policy must deal with its consequences, not with its causes.

Henry Kissinger

The Johnson administration failed to make substantial progress toward
resolving the Arab–Israeli quarrel. However, it left office with four significant accomplishments in the search for peace to its credit. First, the
administration had clearly established that Washington's goal was to see
the conflict terminated within the confines of the existing regional state
system through an exchange of territory and political concessions that
would not reflect "the weight of conquest." Second, it had recognized
that its chosen policy of keeping the regional power balance inclined in
Israel's favor might promote an open-ended arms race that could further
a U.S. decline, and a corresponding Soviet rise, in the Arab world. Third,
the administration had absorbed the uncomfortable lesson that in the
context of Superpower rivalry in the Middle East, the United States
lacked an effective means of pressuring Israel into even preliminary
indirect substantive negotiations with the Arabs. Finally, the administration had concluded that this dangerous dynamic might be reversed
by exploring possibilities for a Middle East settlement jointly with the
Soviet Union.

In the years that followed—the years of the Nixon and Ford presi-
dencies—the concept of peace developed during Johnson's tenure was
not formally abandoned. Nonetheless, it gradually lost its sharpness. By
the end of 1976 many Americans—as well as others—questioned whether

Washington retained the desire, or the ability, to further a definitive end to the drawn out Middle East conflict.

Henry Kissinger, whose influence on U.S. policy was critical during the period, was often seen as primarily responsible for this development. Some, in the harsh words of George Ball, faulted Kissinger for concentrating on immediate issues at the expense of purposeful goals: "[His] addiction to the tactical opportunity so often diverts him from his ultimate destination it is impossible to identify the stars from which he takes his bearings."[1]

Although both his diplomatic tactics and the broader concept of global politics he favored helped becloud the original purpose behind the post–1967 U.S. approach to the Middle East conflict, Kissinger's was but one of several influences on U.S. policymaking. Uncertainty over what if any role the Soviet Union should be allowed in the Middle East, and similar uncertainty over the extent to which the United States could, or should, press Israel into accepting any specific formula for a settlement, also undermined a consistent, purposeful pursuit of Washington's initial vision of peace. Then too, the direct repercussions of the Watergate scandal, and their indirect impact on the presidency of Gerald Ford, forced U.S. policy to be presided over during much of the period by a weak chief executive, a burden that added considerably to the government's difficulties in clinging to a consistent long-term approach.

External events over which the United States had little or no control also intervened to create circumstances that either detracted from the original "territory-for-peace" formula or seemed to threaten its viability in unfathomable ways. The PLO's development as the embodiment of Palestinian nationalism, the replacement of Gamal Abdel Nasser by Anwar Sadat, and the emergence of Arab "oil power" were phenomena that helped cause Washington to react to immediate issues in ways that often appeared to complicate the pursuit of its declared peace objective.

On balance, the years between 1969 and 1977, despite having opened with a major initiative designed to pursue a Middle East settlement along the lines outlined by the Johnson administration, constituted a period that was above all marked by reactive and tentative foreign policy steps.

NIXON CONFRONTS THE MIDDLE EAST

The outlook for Middle East peace did not seem auspicious in early 1969. Passions in the region had been kept at a boiling point by various incidents over the last months, and in January international outcries against a Christmas season Israeli commando raid on Beirut's airport were still reverberating. The attack, carried out without loss of life, had destroyed thirteen civilian airliners belonging to Lebanon's Middle East

Airlines. It had come in retaliation for an assault by PFLP guerrillas on an El Al plane at Athens airport.

The incident dramatically illustrated the spiral of action and reaction that kept Middle East tensions high. Although Israel did not accuse the Lebanese government of direct responsibility for the attack at Athens, the Beirut raid underscored Jerusalem's determination to hold "host" governments accountable for the activities of Palestinian groups. Justifying the reprisal by citing Lebanese press reports sympathetic to the Palestinians, Israeli spokesmen left no doubt that the most tenuous connection between Arab states and Palestinian guerrillas was sufficient to incur accountability.[2]

Such violent confrontations highlighted the lack of diplomatic momentum toward a settlement as well as Arab frustration over the lack of effective pressure on Israel. In Egypt, the first weeks of 1969 provided evidence of growing official despair over the diplomatic impasse. In early January, Nasser implied that Egypt had reached the limit of its diplomatic efforts:

We would not have accepted the 1967 Security Council resolution in spite of its shortcomings unless we believed that if there was a political means to erase the traces of aggression these means should be followed as long as possible.

I repeated, and I repeat now, that we do not call for war, but for peace. . . .

Our position is limited by two points: the first is that we will not give up any Arab land, and the second is that we will not sit down to negotiations of any kind with an enemy who is still occupying our land.[3]

Government spokesman Mohammed Hassan al-Zayyat emotionally elaborated the point when he told a press conference:

We want peace, we need it. It is not something to be ashamed of trying to get. But when we speak of peace, we are not speaking of surrender.[4]

At the same time, a series of newspaper articles published by Nasser's confidant, Mohammed Hassanein Heikal, in the authoritative Cairo daily *Al Ahram*, underscored the ambiguity that continued to surround Egyptian policy. In "Facts About the Middle East Crisis," Heikal distinguished between a "peaceful solution" and a "political solution" to the Arab–Israeli conflict. He concluded that the former, which implied direct negotiations capped by a formal peace treaty, was impossible. The choice was between a "political solution," by which he meant simply an Israeli rollback to 1967 boundaries, or war. Blaming Israel for the diplomatic stalemate, Heikal argued that only three avenues existed for shaking the Jewish state from its immobility: a sharp change in international conditions, increased political and psychological pressure by the Arab world, or "a sudden change in conditions now existing on the ceasefire lines." His analysis discarded the first two and supported the last as the only viable option. Several days later, Heikal returned to the same theme, the article's message being clearly indicated by its pessimistic title: "Diplomacy is No Solution."[5]

In March, Egyptian forces opened artillery barrages against Israeli positions on the east bank of the Suez Canal. A month later, Nasser announced that the 1967 cease-fire was no longer in effect, thus marking the beginning of what became known as "the War of Attrition." It was to last for sixteen months.

Only days after assuming office, Richard Nixon described the Middle East as a "powderkeg" capable of leading to a "confrontation between the nuclear powers." It was, he said, also an area in which the United States and the Soviet Union, "acting together," could serve the cause of peace. He promised "new initiatives and new leadership" toward this end.[6]

The new president prided himself on understanding international politics. Together with his National Security Adviser, Henry Kissinger, Nixon claimed to bring a new perspective on foreign relations to the White House. The Nixon–Kissinger view saw foreign policy as a field for the pursuit of national interests on the basis of rational calculation rather than ideological predisposition. Diplomacy, based on strength, was to be the key instrument for securing a world order that would not only be advantageous to the United States but also satisfy the legitimate interests of other powers in a rhythm reminiscent of the nineteenth century Concert of Europe. Military might was to be husbanded and developed, serving as the foundation of U.S. diplomatic strength, but to be employed judiciously and sparingly. American economic power and military technology would indirectly serve U.S. interests by enhancing the capacities of regional allies throughout the world.[7]

This global vision was predicated on achieving "detente" with the Soviet Union; that is, the replacement of strident, tension-filled competition by quiet diplomacy aimed at reaching mutual accommodation wherever possible. To the Nixon administration, detente did not imply an end to U.S.–Soviet competition, but its prosecution along more rational, and hence less dangerous, lines. Deep differences would still divide the Superpowers, but relations between them would largely be based on clearly understood rules.

The Nixon–Kissinger outlook gave great importance to "linkage"— the interrelated global nature of U.S. and Soviet interests—as an essential element permitting a process of reaching and sustaining detente. The argument was that U.S.–Soviet relations could be smoothed by the exchange of benefits in one area, or issue, for concessions in another.

This panoramic concept of global politics led naturally to the establishment of priorities for dealing with international issues according to their importance to the ultimate creation of a secure world order. In 1969, Kissinger and Nixon agreed that extricating the United States from Vietnam, pursuing an agreement with the Soviet Union on limiting strategic arms, strengthening the European alliance, and developing relations with the People's Republic of China were of primary importance to the United States.

It was not that the Middle East was deemed unimportant. The Nixon administration never lost sight of the region's strategic and economic value, and remained determined to bolster friendly regimes in the area while limiting the development of a Soviet presence. But the Arab–Israeli conflict was not accorded high stature in the pantheon of U.S. objectives during Nixon's first term.

The president was not unconcerned over the issue. Nor did he lack strongly held opinions, being not only apparently sincere in describing it as a "powderkeg," but also inclined to believe that U.S. policy had become excessively tilted in Israel's favor. Indeed, Nixon quickly came to believe that the danger inherent in the ongoing conflict would in the final analysis have to be eliminated by an imposed settlement. Yet he had several interrelated reasons for wanting to keep the issue at arms length.[8]

In part, Nixon's attitude reflected his eagerness to devote attention to issues he considered more pressing. This view was reinforced by the belief that little could be done, short of imposing a settlement on the Arabs and Israelis, to break the Middle East stalemate. It was also supported by Nixon's reluctance to embroil the White House in a taxing and time consuming controversy with the pro-Israel domestic lobby. Moreover, Nixon realized that any imposed solution would necessarily require a joint effort with the Soviet Union. During his years in office, the president would demonstrate an inability to settle in his own mind whether, or to what extent, the United States should cooperate with the Soviet Union in the Middle East.[9]

While Henry Kissinger concurred in assigning the Middle East problem a relatively low priority, he was never attracted to the idea of an imposed agreement. No did he share Nixon's ambivalence regarding a Soviet role in the Middle East. During his years as a Washington policymaker, Kissinger would unswervingly seek to reduce, and if possible eliminate, the Soviet presence in the Middle East.[10]

Although this occasionally led to differences between Kissinger and Nixon, it did not undermine the fundamental harmony of their respective perspectives on foreign policy. Sharing a basic distrust of the diplomatic bureaucracy, the two men nonetheless agreed that the Middle East should be delegated to the State Department. According to Kissinger, Nixon pointed out that while the messy Arab–Israeli problem might well prove intractable, the division of labor would "give State something to do while we handled Vietnam, SALT, Europe and China in the White House."[11]

Until Kissinger was given more direct responsibility for Middle East policy formulation in late 1971, the State Department spearheaded the U.S. approach to the Arab–Israeli issuse. The new secretary of state, William P. Rogers, was a lawyer who had served as attorney general in the Eisenhower administration. He had no experience in international politics and appears to have been chosen for his role because Nixon was looking "for a good negotiator, rather than a policymaker."[12] Yet, for the relatively short time that the Arab–Israeli problem fell within his domain, Rogers proved to be energetic and tenacious in trying to promote a settlement.

Under his direction, the Department adhered tightly to the territory-for-peace concept worked out by the previous administration. Israel's expansionist tendencies were considered contrary to U.S. interests, and the extended occupation of Arab lands was seen as threatening the long-term viability of moderate Arab regimes. State Department planners feared that prolongation of the stalemate in the Middle East would lead to a steady polarization in the region that could only enhance the Soviet's position in the Arab World. Equally disconcerting was the possibility that continuing Arab–Israeli tensions might erupt into major hostilities capable of plunging the superpowers into a confrontation. These considerations were at the core of the Department's conviction that movement toward a final settlement was urgently needed.

Rogers and his colleagues strongly welcomed the State Department's role in the "new initiatives" promised by Nixon. Actually an extension of the direction charted under Johnson at the end of 1968, the Nixon administration's policy initially seemed to be a dynamic and well integrated two-tiered effort to promote a Middle East settlement by coming to terms with the Soviet Union.

On one level, the bilateral U.S.–Soviet contacts developed under Johnson were pursued. On another, the United States accepted a long-standing French proposal for Four-Power (France, Britain, the USSR, and the United States) consultations on the Middle East. Both levels were theoretically united as means of facilitating the task of UN special representative Gunnar Jarring. In short, any guidelines for a settlement agreed upon at the bilateral level would be discussed, and presumably ratified, at the Four-Power talks. A consensus in that forum would then be passed on to Jarring for presentation to the Arab states and Israel.

Despite its aesthetically pleasing logic, the theory did not measure up to reality. It presumed that the two superpowers could agree on the essential elements of a settlement and, secondly, that they would then be able to promote acceptance of those elements by Israel and the Arab

states. The first assumption was eventually disproved as events showed
that neither the Nixon administration nor the Soviet government could
resist the temptation to strive for advantage in the Middle East. The
second assumption, of course, therefore went untested—although by the
end of Nixon's first term it would be clear that neither Washington nor
Moscow could ignore the capacities of Arabs and Israelis for independent
action.

A further assumption, one not directly related to the Nixon administration's chosen strategy toward the Middle East, but nonetheless a
necessary basis for any U.S. peacemaking effort, was overturned by
events. This was simply the belief that Washington could consistently
and purposefully adhere to a designated Middle East policy. More than
any other single factor, it was the emptiness of this premise that undermined the Nixon administration's hope of trying to end the Middle East
conflict.

Underlying the administration's vacillation were differences in the
assessments arrived at by Kissinger and the State Department regarding
the advisability of an active effort to promote a Middle East settlement.
Kissinger disagreed with both the State Department's view of the urgency
of ending the diplomatic stalemate and its belief that the optimum course
toward that end lay in seeking a coordinated approach with the Soviet
Union. In early 1969, Kissinger explained his reasoning to Joseph Sisco,
the newly appointed assistant secretary of state for the Middle East:

I thought delay was on the whole in our interest because it enabled us to demonstrate even to radical Arabs that we were indispensable to *any* progress and
that it could not be extorted from us by Soviet pressure. The State Department
wanted to fuel the process of negotiations by accepting at least some of the Soviet
ideas, to facilitate compromise. I wanted to frustrate the radicals—who were in
any event hostile to us—by demonstrating that in the Middle East friendship
with the United States was the precondition to diplomatic success. When I told
Sisco . . . that we did not *want* a quick success in the Four-Power consultations . . .
I was speaking a language that ran counter to all the convictions of his Department.[13]

Kissinger could not have been more correct. His outlook challenged
the State Department by holding that under the conditions obtaining in
the Middle East, time worked in favor of U.S. interests. This denied, or
at least deemed acceptable, the risks seen by the State Department as
inherent in protracted diplomatic inertia. Moreover, in contrast to the
State department's position, which foresaw the eventual necessity of pressuring Israel into greater flexibility, Kissinger's prescription required
that U.S. support for Israel be unwavering until political conditions
changed in the Middle East.

Kissinger points out that "the strategic disagreement was never really settled." To the extent that the Nixon administration never formally rejected one view in favor of the other, this is correct. In fact, however, the very ambivalence within the government's upper ranks rebounded to Kissinger's benefit. For by preventing the administration from giving full support to the State Department's energetic drive to lay the ground-work for a Middle East settlement, it inevitably undermined the De-partment's search for a settlement within the Two-Power/Four-Power framework.

As the final arbiter of U.S. foreign policy, Nixon was ultimately re-sponsible for the government's indecision. Fearing the Arab–Israeli con-flict's potentially explosive dynamics, Nixon no doubt wished to see the State Department's efforts yield fruit. Kissinger concluded that "deep down" Nixon "wanted to . . . impose a comprehensive settlement some-time during his term in office."[14] Yet the higher priority he granted other areas of foreign policy, his low confidence in professional diplo-matic bureaucracy, and his reluctance to challenge the pro-Israel do-mestic lobby combined with a deep suspicion of Soviet intentions to prevent him from strongly backing the State Department's initiative.

In the end, Nixon temporized. When, under the press of crisis in his second term, he did try to act decisively (and apparently unwisely) in favor of an imposed settlement, circumstances rendered him impotent.[15]

By then, the dangers in the diplomatic impasse warned of by the State Department seemed well on their way toward realization. Yet another Arab–Israeli war had erupted, the United States and the Soviets would shortly move close to a confrontation in the Middle East, and the PLO had so consolidated its position that the possibility of approaching the Arab–Israeli problem strictly within context of the regional state system would soon be radically reduced.

But if Kissinger's early analysis appeared badly shaken, it had not been destroyed. Egypt—even as it went to war in 1973—was visibly distancing itself from the Soviet Union. It was Kissinger's genius to seize the mo-ment, albeit somewhat belatedly, for launching his own, limited diplo-matic initiative and pursuing it with considerable immediate success.

WASHINGTON AS PEACEMAKER: 1969–1970

The State Department undertook the original initiative promised by Nixon amid a flurry of activity in March 1969, some six weeks after the new president's inauguration. Secretary Rogers informed the Senate Foreign Relations Committee that bilateral contacts on the Middle East had already been made with the Soviet Union, that these would continue, and that the United States would also utilize the Four-Power framework at the United Nations. Sketching out the U.S. position, Rogers called for a "contractual peace" between Israel and the Arab states and insisted on several requirements for any settlement, among which he included freedom of navigation and the necessity that any boundary change in the pre–1967 Middle East map to "be confined to those required for mutual security and not reflect the weight of conquest." Rogers offered no new ideas on the Palestinian refugee problem, limiting his comments to a reaffirmation that its elimination was also a necessary part of a total peace. The secretary rejected charges that by resorting to the Two-Power/Four-Power framework his department was undermining the Jarring Mission. "Regrettably," he noted, "in the twenty-two months since the war, Ambassador Jarring and the parties have not made any significant progress." He went on to argue forcefully that U.S. interests would be "ill-served" by the continued absence of a settlement.[16]

The first bilateral talks had been held nine days earlier in Washington between Assistant Secretary of State Joseph Sisco and the Soviet ambassador to Washington, Anatoly Dobrynin. The talks would continue, sometimes in Washington and sometimes in Moscow, into the fall. On April 3, the first Four-Power consultations were held. These talks went on regularly until the end of June, when they were suspended pending further progress at the bilateral level.

In addition to Great Power discussions, Washington explored prospects for a settlement through contacts with Israel and the Arab governments. King Hussein visited the United States in early April. He was quickly followed by Nasser's adviser on foreign affairs, Mahmoud Fawzi. Both men indicated their countries' eagerness for a settlement. Hussein publicly announced that he was authorized to confirm Egypt's willingness to uphold freedom of navigation through the Suez Canal in the context of a settlement. Fawzi privately added that Cairo "would not feel constrained by Syria's opposition...."[17]

On the other hand, Israel strongly opposed the U.S. initiative. Three days after Rogers spoke to the Foreign Relations Committee, the Israeli government publicly condemned the State Department's course:

Israel entirely opposes the plan to convene the representatives of states that lie outside the Middle East in order to prepare recommendations concerning the region. Israel is not and will not become the object of power politics, and will not accept any recommendations which are in conflict with her vital interests.[18]

The reference to Israel's vital interests was not as vague as it appeared at first glance, particularly since it came on the heels of Rogers' insistence that territorial adjustments should be governed by the requirements of "mutual security." In early March, the new Israeli national unity coalition created under Golda Meir's leadership after Levi Eshkol's death included in its policy program a promise that Israel's position in the occupied territories would be consolidated "in accordance with the vital needs of security and development."[19] At the same time, Mrs. Meir consistently condemned the United States for becoming involved in great power talks on the Middle East rather than simply insisting on direct negotiations between Israel and the Arab states.[20]

Israel's U.S. supporters embarked on a strenuous campaign to carry the message to the American public. Pro-Israel groups were rapidly and effectively mobilized. Before the end of April, 227 congressmen, including 48 senators, signed a declaration calling on the administration to "ensure direct negotiations . . . to secure a contractual peace settlement freely and sincerely signed by the parties themselves. . . ."[21]

Despite the obstacles, contacts between the United States and the USSR appeared to make some headway. During the following months, the Soviets probed to learn details of the U.S. stand on territory, while Washington sought explicit clarifications of Moscow's concept of security guarantees. By the end of summer, the USSR agreed that any settlement should be concluded as a "package," thus dropping its longstanding demand that withdrawal precede other elements of a negotiated peace. In what was seen as a major Arab concession, Egypt supported the Soviet position.[22] Soviet spokesmen further modified their position, claiming that Egypt concurred in this also, by agreeing that the parties to the conflict would negotiate on the basis of "Rhodes-type talks"—a reference to the indirect proximity negotiations Arabs claimed had been used to arrange the 1949 armistice agreements that ended Israel's War of Independence.

For its part, the United States developed more specific stands on various elements of a settlement, including, among others, such central features as the demilitarization of all areas evacuated by Israel; the determination of Gaza's final status through negotiations among Israel, Jordan, and Egypt; and the necessity of Arab parties to a settlement preventing Palestinian guerrilla attacks on Israel.[23]

However, while the U.S.–Soviet talks focused more closely on a possible Egyptian–Israeli settlement, Washington's position on the territorial dimension of an accord remained hidden. Although the State Department had convinced the administration as early as April to favor an Israeli pullback to the international frontier between Egypt and mandated Palestine, Kissinger prevailed upon Nixon to restrain U.S. negotiators from communicating this to their Soviet counterparts for nearly six months. Only slowly was the true U.S. position revealed. In July, the Soviets were informed that Washington considered an Israeli evacuation to the international frontier as "not necessarily excluded" from the terms of a final settlement. In September, the administration decided that the Soviets would be informed of the full U.S. stance if acceptable security measures could be devised for Sharm el-Sheikh and Gaza. Finally, in late October, the State Department convinced the president to allow the complete U.S. program for an Egyptian–Israeli settlement to be un-veiled.[24]

The procrastinating negotiating tactics followed by Washington dur-ing the spring, summer, and fall of 1969 may, as Kissinger argued, have induced greater flexibility on the part of Soviet negotiators. But they also entailed a cost, only part of which came in the form of irate Soviet charges that the United States was totally to blame for lack of progress toward a superpower agreement on the Middle East.[25] More important was the worsening situation in the Middle East—which seemed to render the area progressively less amenable to peaceful change.

The War of Attrition launched along the Suez Canal in March had steadily escalated. In July, the Israeli airforce initiated a major offensive and quickly established its supremacy. Before the end of the year, Israel reportedly downed over sixty Egyptian aircraft and destroyed up to twenty-four SAM 2 anti-aircraft missile batteries. By September, the first of the F–4 Phantoms promised by the Johnson administration arrived in Israel. Within months, they were put to effective use in "deep pen-etration" attacks on the Nile Valley.[26]

In the meantime, Palestinian guerrillas stepped up activities along the Jordanian and Lebanese borders. The theater of conflict widened no-ticeably following a PFLP decision in the summer of 1969 to mount a sustained terrorist campaign against Israeli targets outside the Middle East.

Pressed militarily by the Israelis, Nasser grew more truculent. In early October, Cairo denied having ever agreed to Rhodes-type negotiations with Israel.[27] Speaking at the UN in November, Nasser adopted a militant posture and stridently proclaimed Egypt's willingness to liberate all the occupied lands by war.

On the other hand, the Israeli government's opposition to Washing-ton's peacemaking venture was unaltered. Mrs. Meir arrived in the United States in September, making headlines by emphasizing her dif-ferences with the State Department:

Withdrawal is not the issue. The Arabs don't think it's the issue . . . the Arabs are in lack of a little more sand? That's the problem?[28]

In conversations with Nixon, the prime minister sought a favorable response to an Israeli request, first made in July, for an additional one hundred A–4 Skyhawk warplanes and twenty-five F–4 Phantoms. While Nixon deferred a decision, he did suggest the outlines of a new basis for an ongoing arms-supply relationship: "hardware" (arms) in exchange for "software" (greater Israeli political flexibility).

Political considerations had never been absent from U.S. decisions to help Israel acquire arms. However, the president's position soon virtually institutionalized the idea that weapons would be supplied to Israel not only on the basis of military requirements but also on the chance they might inject a greater spirit of compromise into Israeli policy. The approach was acted on within months. When Israel rejected its peace drive, the administration agreed to Jerusalem's requests for economic and military aid (though the latter did not then include action on the Skyhawks and Phantoms). With only minimal exaggeration, Kissinger concluded that a cycle had been established "in which every negotiating step of which Israel disapproved was coupled with a step-up of Israeli assistance programs without achieving a real meeting of minds with Israel."[29]

At the time of Meir's Washington visit, there seemed little possibility of purchasing Israeli flexibility with aid. National elections in Israel were scheduled for October. The prime minister returned home and undertook a series of actions that seemed to signal a hardening of her position. On October 13, it was announced that Israeli law would be extended to the occupied Golan Heights. Forty-eight hours later, Mrs. Meir again demanded that Egypt, Syria, and Jordan meet Israel for "unconditional negotiations." Some days later, she announced that seven additional settlements would be erected in the occupied lands, promising that further construction would "continue at the same pace."[30]

Israel's elections were held on October 28, 1969. While the Labor Alignment retained control of the Knesset, it no longer enjoyed an absolute majority. On the other hand, the Gahal party's representation increased by five seats. The elections were seen as reflecting "an ominous shift in Israeli public opinion toward the minority who favor outright annexation of the occupied territories." Observers tended to agree that the results left "little hope of greater flexibility in Israeli policy."[31]

Ironically, it was also on October 28 that the United States presented the Soviet Union with what the State Department hoped would become a jointly pursued plan for Middle East peace. Although Nixon had finally acquiesced in the Department's strategy, he also discretely disassociated himself from the domestic controversy that was bound to erupt. Kissinger recalls the incident:

Characteristically, he sought to hedge his bets by asking [Attorney General] John Mitchell and Leonard Garment—counselor to the President and adviser on Jewish affairs—to let Jewish community leaders know his doubts about State's diplomacy. Nixon implied strongly to them that he would see to it that nothing came of the very initiatives he was authorizing.[32]

On December 9, Secretary of State Rogers publicly revealed the content of a U.S. suggestion for an Egyptian–Israeli settlement. The proposal was quickly dubbed the "Rogers Plan." Nine days later, the United States presented the Four Powers (whose meetings had resumed on

December 2) with a parallel plan for a settlement between Israel and Jordan.

The proposed Egyptian–Israeli accord called for the two states to agree on a timetable for withdrawal from occupied territories that would "not exceed three months." Both countries were also charged with ending the state of war, refraining from acts of aggression, and "ensuring" that hostile actions by private organizations would not be carried out from their territory. Gaza's future was to be negotiated among Israel, Jordan, and Egypt under the auspices of Gunnar Jarring. Israel's withdrawal would be to the "frontier that existed between Egypt and Palestine at the time of the British Mandate," and secure and recognized final borders would be specified on maps. However, the withdrawal of Israeli forces from Egyptian territory would occur within the framework of demilitarized zones and "effective measures in the Sharm el-Sheikh area" to ensure Israel's access to the Gulf of Aqaba.

The plan required Egypt to allow Israel use of the Suez Canal, and specified that each state would recognize the other's "sovereignty, political independence, and right to live in peace within secure boundaries." The form such recognition should take was not specified.

The refugee problem was to be solved in accordance with arrangements that would first be agreed upon between Israel and Jordan. Finally, although the plan did not specifically discuss international guarantees, it called for the ratification of any final agreement by the Security Council. Upon that being done, the Four Powers were to "help" the two sides adhere to the settlement's provisions.[33]

The Jordan plan was similar to the first proposal, though it differed in some important areas. It also called for negotiations through Jarring and for agreement on a timetable for Israel's withdrawal, though no time limit was set. Neither did the proposal define the line to which withdrawal was to take place. It did, however, indicate that Israeli troops would pull back "from substantially all of Jordan's West Bank..."

Israel and Jordan were to "accept the obligations of a state of peace." This would commit Jordan to prevent "commando raids by Palestinian irregulars." Practical security arrangements for the West Bank, including the establishment of demilitarized zones, were to be negotiated. The plan also entailed Jordan's formal recognition of Israel's sovereignty, but as in the earlier proposal the form of recognition was not indicated.

A final accord between the two countries would be "endorsed" by the Security Council, while the Four Powers would "concert their future efforts" to help all parties abide by the settlement. Any agreement would be implemented "only with a simultaneous accord with the United Arab Republic."

Although the proposal did not specify the future boundary betwen Israel and Jordan, it indicated that the frontier should be on a line "approximating . . . the armistice demarcation . . . that existed before the 1967 war. . . . "Alterations would be allowed for security reasons and for "administrative and economic convenience." Gaza's future was left vague. Israel and Jordan were to conclude final arrangements for that area on the basis of the parallel settlement with Egypt. Jerusalem's final disposition remained unclear, although the proposal called for the city to be united, with Jordan and Israel sharing "civic and economic responsibilities."

Finally, the plan proposed solving the Arab refugee problem by giving refugees a choice between repatriation to Israel or resettlement, with compensation from Israel, in Arab countries. Israel and Jordan were to "agree upon a figure of refugees to be permitted repatriation annually." The first repatriated refugees should arrive in Israel "no more than three months after the conclusion of a negotiated settlement."[34]

Whatever hopes the State Department may have harbored for the success of its initiative soon drowned in an outpouring of opposition. Israel immediately denounced the proposed settlement with Egypt. The Israeli reaction intensified with the subsequent unveiling of the Jordan plan. Golda Meir branded the two-proposal package "appeasement" and expressed particular concern over the U.S. position on "peace, borders, refugees and Jerusalem." Although the prime minister must surely have been informed of Nixon's assurances to American Jewish leaders, she seized the opportunity to demonstrate resistance to anything hinting at U.S. pressure:

Israel won't accept this . . . nobody in the world can make us accept it. It would be treasonous for any Israeli government to accept it.[35]

Israel's U.S. supporters, including major Jewish organizations and prominent members of Congress, promptly joined the outcry. Typical was Senator Hubert Humphrey's charge that the administration was trying to sacrifice Israel's interests for the sake of an agreement with the Soviet Union.[36]

After delaying its response to the Rogers Plan for over a month, the Soviet Union rejected the proposal.[37] Nasser remained stonily silent. He would later imply that he had not deigned to respond since Israel was attacking Egyptian positions along the Suez Canal.[38] Apart from the State Department, only King Hussein supported the U.S. initiative. It was at this point, hoping to "quell Israeli fears," and no doubt also to dampen the blaze of domestic protest, that the administration decided to make an early, favorable response to standing Israeli requests for military and economic assistance.[39]

The "Rogers Plan," that is, both the interrelated Egyptian and Jordanian settlement proposals, still stands as the closest Washington has come to defining a comprehensive Middle East peace in structural terms that it could argue were simultaneously equitable and protective of U.S. interests. The development and collapse of the initiative have often been studied. Several explanations have been offered for this striking failure in U.S. diplomacy. At a level focusing strictly on the events of 1969, the most persuasive of these are three interlocking conclusions. The first is that the United States was unduly optimistic about the possibility of separating the Soviet Union from Egypt: "The United States was indeed willing to take its distance somewhat from Israel but this was not reciprocated by the Soviet Union."[40] A second conclusion is that the Rogers Plan was undermined by the low level of White House involvement in its development and promotion: "Perhaps a 'Nixon Plan' would have had better chances of success."[41] Finally, it has been suggested that the "bureaucracy" underestimated "Israel's will and ability to resist American pressure."[42]

While each of these elements undoubtedly figured in the Rogers Plan's demise, the interrelationships among them suggest more fundamental sources of difficulty in U.S. policy toward the Middle East. Thus, while it is true that Washington was ultimately disappointed by the lack of Soviet support for the Rogers Plan, it seems likely that Moscow had serious doubts about the United States' willingness or ability "to take its distance somewhat from Israel." For the Soviets were not only aware that the White House had removed itself to a marginal role in promoting the Rogers Plan, but also that the administration was divided over the wisdom of seeking a mutually acceptable arrangement with the Soviet Union over the Middle East.[43] To the degree that Moscow took this into account in its own policy formulation, the rejection of the Rogers Plan that capped its five week silence must be seen as a logical refusal to jeopardize its relations with Egypt by supporting a proposal from which Washington seemed likely to retreat. Moreover, while the State Department may have underrated the degree of Israeli resistance to the initiative, the other side of the coin was the Department's overestimation of Washington's readiness to confront Israeli ire. As aware as they were of Nixon's limited support for their strategy, Department planners could hardly have anticipated the president's willingness to undermine the U.S. initiative through informal channels.

In short, the pursuit of the Rogers Plan was afflicted by a malaise much deeper than simple optimism, White House non-involvement, or bureaucratic miscalculation. Washington's essential problem was a basic indecisiveness in the face of two key issues. The first was that of determining the extent to which the United States was willing to see the Soviet Union play a role in Middle East affairs as the price of Arab–Israeli peace. The second was the extent to which the U.S. government was prepared to exert pressure in an effort to force Israel's acceptance of an internationally approved framework for peace.

The demise of the Rogers Plan was not to be the last time that Washington's inability to settle on clear policies toward these issues would help undermine the U.S. search for peace in the Middle East.

PEACEMAKING AND NON-PEACEMAKING: 1970–1973

While the Rogers Plan was collapsing in late 1969, the War of Attrition raged on along the Suez Canal. In early January, Israel began using its new Phantoms with devastating effect on targets in the Egyptian heartland. This "deep penetration" strategy was designed not only to relieve pressure on Israeli troops along the Canal but also to undermine Nasser's domestic standing.

The Egyptian leader responded by making a secret trip to Moscow, where he successfully solicited urgent Soviet help.[44] At the end of January, Premier Kosygin sent messages to Washington, London, and Paris warning that unless Israel were restrained, the Soviet Union would "see to it that the Arab states have the means at their disposal" to offset Israeli military power. Nixon publicly retorted with an assurance that the U.S. would continue "to provide arms to friendly states as the need arises."[45]

Despite this gesture, the president was actually in a quandary created by the divided recommendations of his chief advisers. Notwithstanding mounting signs of growing Soviet involvement in Egypt, the State Department preferred to see the United States embark on a flexible effort to promote a Middle East settlement rather than a rigid approach designed to show that no amount of Soviet military aid could further Arab objectives. The Department, which in any case blamed Israel's escalation of the War of Attrition for having forced Egypt into greater reliance on the Soviet Union, therefore continued to oppose increasing U.S. arms supplies to Israel. This position received support from the Defense Department, where it was concluded that the balance of forces in the Middle East continued to favor Israel.[46]

Kissinger argued for just the opposite course. Although agreeing that Israel was not blameless for the deteriorating situation, his first preoccupation remained the Soviet's presence in the region: " . . . somewhere along the line the question of what causes a Soviet move becomes irrelevant; American policy must deal with its consequences, not with its causes."[47] In his view, the proper response to increased Soviet commitments in the Arab World could only be immediate and substantial increases in U.S. support for Israel.

Although Nixon was skeptical of the State Department's ability to make progress toward a diplomatic settlement, he allowed it to retain the lead in Middle East policy. However, the president proved inconsistent on the question of arms supplies. At the beginning of the year, he unexpectedly, and publicly, set a thirty-day limit for a decision on Israel's request for Phantom and Skyhawk airplanes. Yet he allowed the deadline to pass in silence. In March, swayed partly by recommendations of the departments of State and Defense and partly by discourteous treatment accorded to French President Georges Pompidou by American Jewish groups in Chicago, he chose to delay action on the Israeli request. By May, however, the president was undermining State Department hints that the delivery of arms already pledged to Israel depended on political developments. In July, Nixon finally authorized the shipment to Israel of sophisticated equipment to offset Egyptian antiaircraft defenses. He also promised to keep the arms pipeline open.[48]

In the meantime, the intervention of which Kosygin had warned in his January message to Western governments became a reality. By April, the first batteries of SAM 3 anti-aircraft missiles, together with Soviet crews, arrived in Egypt and were deployed around Cairo, Alexandria, and the Aswan Dam. As the missile build-up continued, Soviet-manned Mig–21s commenced regular combat patrols over the Nile Valley.

These measures quickly affected the War of Attrition. Israel sought to avoid a direct confrontation with the USSR by refraining from deep penetration raids. The scope of Israeli air activity threatened to become even more constricted as the SAM 3 network began extending toward the Suez Canal. By June, the creeping advance of SAM 3 emplacements led to the consolidation of the air defense system within twenty miles of the Canal. In July, Soviet-flown Migs began operating for the first time in the Canal Zone.[49]

By the end of July, a total of seven Israeli warplanes had been downed along the Sinai front. Goaded by the losses, the Israeli air force sprang a trap on a flight of Soviet-piloted Mig's over the Canal and shot down four. Shocked by the realization that events seemed to be getting out of hand, the Israelis and Soviets did not publicize the incident.

It was against this background that the State Department pressed its search for a political settlement. According to William Quandt, the Rogers Plan's failure had convinced the Department that less ambitious proposals probably stood a better chance of success.[50] Combined with the urgency of stemming the increasingly heated military confrontation along the Suez Canal, that conclusion helped shape the demarche that became known as the "Rogers Initiative." Although the initiative gave priority to bringing the parties to "stop shooting and start talking," it was not planned as a mere palliative. Focusing on procedural issues, and aimed at Israel, Egypt, and Jordan, its central purpose was to promote the comprehensive bargaining that had so far eluded the efforts of U.S. policymakers. The Rogers Initiative was therefore planned as a tactical change in approach rather than as a radical departure from the earlier Rogers Plan.[51]

Although the Two-Power/Four Power framework remained technically in use, the initiative was strictly a Washington product. In April, Joseph Sisco visited Cairo to assess Nasser's receptivity to a new U.S. effort. Shortly afterward, the Egyptian leader publicly encouraged U.S. diplomatic intervention. However, he also warned that opportunities for political solutions were fast running out.

Another indication that the timing might be favorable for a U.S. demarche came later that month, when Israel's prime minister responded to Nixon's assurances that military supplies would quietly continue flowing into Israel by formally announcing Jerusalem's acceptance of Security Council Resolution 242. At the same time, Mrs. Meir also agreed that talks with the Arabs could be conducted through a process along the lines of that used during the 1949 armistice negotiations at Rhodes.[52]

Despite these seemingly favorable signs, the ensuing U.S. initiative was severely flawed in several respects. Not the least of these, as it turned out, were the contradictory indications given by the Nixon administration of its intended arms supply policy. Nasser was left with the impression that restraint would be the order of the day. Israel had been simultaneously assured of continued military support. It was not duplicity but the ongoing failure of the White House and State Department to achieve a full meeting of minds that produced this ambivalence. Indeed, the administration's inconsistency on the question of arms supplies only reflected a deeper source of vacillation. Thus, when the U.S. initiative was publicly announced on June 25, the State Department presented it as an essential step toward final peace while Kissinger and Nixon issued statements—despite Secretary Rogers' outraged protests—indicating that the initiative's primary purpose was to counter the growth of Soviet influence in the Middle East.[53]

Cairo, Amman, and Jerusalem—together with the other Four-Power governments—officially received Washington's new proposal on June 19. On one level, the initiative was deceptively simple. The plan called for a ninety-day cease-fire during which UN mediator Jarring would facilitate indirect negotiations involving Egypt, Jordan, and Israel. Security Council Resolution 242 would provide the basis for progress toward a settlement: Egypt and Jordan would accept the principle of peace with Israel and that state's right to exist; Israel would accept the principle of withdrawal from territories occupied in 1967. On another level, although the U.S. proposal avoided the substantive positions taken in the Rogers Plan, the State Department obviously believed that pressures for a definitive political settlement would be maximized once all sides were engaged in a process of indirect bargaining. The department continued to hope that the eventual outcome would at least closely parallel the specific arrangements suggested by the Rogers Plan.[54] First reactions to the initiative were mixed. Israel and Egypt both denounced it. Despite bitter complaints over Washington's failure to formulate the proposal within the Two-Power/Four-Power framework, the Soviet Union found merit in the plan. Jordan's King Hussein remained carefully noncommittal.[55]

On July 22, following an extended visit to the Soviet Union, Nasser finally announced Egypt's acceptance of the Rogers Initiative. Jordan took a similar decision a week later. In the meantime, Israel slowly modified its original attitude upon receiving various U.S. assurances.

Eager to obtain Jerusalem's agreement, and to reassure Israel's domestic supporters that the administration was not abandoning the Jewish state, Nixon publicly pledged that Washington would prevent the regional balance of power from shifting against Israel.[56] In a message to Israel's prime minister, the president also made several far-reaching commitments, including promises that Washington would not pressure Israel to accept the Arabs' interpretation of Security Council Resolution 242; that the United States would not support a settlement of the Palestinian refugee problem that jeopardized Israel's security or Jewishness; that Israel would be expected to withdraw from occupied territories only once a satisfactory peace treaty were concluded; and that an ultimate withdrawal would not resurrect the 1967 borders.[57]

At the end of July, the Israeli cabinet voted to accept the U.S. proposal. Since this entailed accepting the principle of withdrawal from occupied territories, as well as dropping Israel's standing demand for unconditional face-to-face negotiations, the Gahal angrily withdrew from the government. The promises contained in Nixon's message to Mrs. Meir were instrumental in producing Israel's decision. Kissinger would later remark that it "was just as well" that no publicity attended the president's assurances against trying to pressure Israel into accepting the Arab view of Resolution 242. "The Arabs," he recalled, "had been given precisely the opposite impression when the ceasefire initiative was presented to them."[58]

On August 8, the cease-fire along the Suez Canal officially came into effect. Part of the U.S.-sponsored agreement provided for a military "standstill" within an area extending to fifty miles on either side of the Canal. However, the terms of the accord were so hastily arranged by the State Department that a separate U.S.–Israeli understanding defining violations of the "standstill" was not communicated to Egyptian authorities until thirty-six hours after the cease-fire began. The agreement also left verification of compliance to each side's "own national means." When the United States subsequently tried to assess the predictable torrent of charges and countercharges of violations that soon developed, its efforts were hampered by lack of firm knowledge of the on-ground situation at the cease-fire's outset and the confusion surrounding Egypt's understanding of its obligations during the agreement's first thirty-six hours.[59]

Shortly after the cease-fire took effect, Israel made the first of a series of claims that Egypt was violating the bargain by reinforcing its missile wall within the standstill zone. There followed fervent denials by Cairo, which in turn were soon joined by counter-claims that Israel was violating the agreement by enhancing fortifications along the Canal's East bank. Suspecting the Israelis of trying to torpedo the scheduled peace talks, the State Department initially waffled on the issue. Eventually, however, the Department publicly conceded that Egypt had significantly augmented its missile force. Israel was found to have also contravened the cease-fire in a variety of far less serious technical ways.

The controversy soon became public. Sensitive to what he saw as a direct Soviet challenge, Nixon ordered the secret delivery to Israel of sophisticated anti-missile weapons.

On September 6, Israel announced it would not participate in the projected peace talks until the situation along the Canal reverted to what it had been on August 7. When Egypt proved unwilling to consider that demand, the Rogers Initiative was effectively ended.

In retrospect, it is clear that all the involved parties saw the primary benefit of the Rogers Initiative as being in the cease-fire itself rather than in the peace negotiations that were supposed to follow. As the conflict along the Suez Canal escalated in the summer of 1970, none of the parties—Israel, Egypt, or the Soviet Union—wished to have it pass beyond control, yet all perceived the danger of that eventuality. The U.S. demarche provided each with an acceptable escape from the dangerous immediate dynamics of confrontation.[60] King Hussein followed Nasser's lead in welcoming the U.S. proposal not only because he had long hoped to find some means of settling his own dispute with Israel, but also in hope that his association with the Egyptian leader would strengthen the monarchy against the rising power of Palestinian guerrilla forces in Jordan.

Even the State Department, where hopes for the Rogers Initiative's long-range political impact were presumably strongest, succumbed to a sense of urgency. The rush to stop the shooting no doubt explains some of the glaring flaws that helped produce the cease-fire agreement's demise.

Having extricated themselves from the perilous spiral of hostility, none of the protagonists in the Middle East was eager to return to a high level of confrontation. Despite the Rogers Initiative's collapse, three years would elapse before serious fighting once again broke out along the Egyptian–Israeli front.

With one brief exception, the end of the Rogers Initiative led to a seven-year suspension of active U.S. efforts to promote definitive peace between Arabs and Israelis. The exception occurred in February 1971, when Washington encouraged Gunnar Jarring to undertake at least part of the mediating role he had hoped to play the previous summer. In effect, Jarring requested Israel and Egypt to agree on broad parameters of a settlement that his good offices might help define in detail. Israel was asked to state its willingness in principle to withdraw from the Sinai to the former international boundary between Egypt and mandated Palestine in return for acceptable security guarantees. Egypt was asked to accept in principle the notion of ending the state of belligerency with Israel. While Egypt agreed, though insisting on the re-establishment of 1967 boundaries, Israel refused to accept the principle of full withdrawal and reaffirmed its position that new borders would be defined only through direct negotiations. For all practical purposes, this ended Jarring's fruitless efforts as UN special representative.[61]

By then, much had happened in the Middle East. The U.S. search for a settlement in 1969–1970 had exacerbated divisions in the Arab world to the point of explosion. By the summer of 1970, rejectionist states, led by Syria and Iraq, were driven to fury as Nasser, and then Hussein, accepted the Rogers Initiative's call for indirect negotiations with Israel. Acrimonious charges flew back and forth across borders. The Soviet Union was also soon squabbling with Damascus and Baghdad over Moscow's defense of Egypt's decision. Not suprisingly, the Palestinian resistance movement stood out as the most adamant opponent of the U.S. peace drive. Repeated promises by Cairo and Amman that the Palestinian cause would not be sacrificed in any foreseeable settlement were dismissed as simply a cover for abandoning the struggle against Israel. In August, an exasperated Nasser closed Fateh's radio station in Cairo. King Hussein could not cope with the problem so easily.

Throughout the summer of 1970, armed clashes between Jordanian forces and Palestinian guerrillas provided a steady counterpoint to the international diplomacy surrounding the Rogers Initiative. Outside observers, as well as Hussein, worried over the King's loss of control and wondered if it was still recoverable. On August 28, the Palestine National Council met in Amman to denounce the U.S. plan and brand as "a traitor" anyone opposed to the campaign against Israel. At the same time, Fateh warned that if the Hashemite Monarchy sought "a showdown our revolution will be obliged to take action."[62]

On September 1, an attempt (the second that summer) was made on Hussein's life. Less than a week later, the PFLP perpetrated a spectacular series of highjackings that resulted in the guerillas holding three international airliners, along with their passengers and crews, on Jordanian soil. With this, Hussein ordered his army into action against Palestinian forces. Despite heavy resistance, the Hashemite troops soon proved their superiority.[63] At that point, Syria sent an armored column into northern Jordan. Fearing an all out invasion, Hussein quietly raised the possibility of U.S. intervention. After urgent consultations between the United States and Israel, it was decided that should it become necessary to save Hussein's throne, the Israelis would confront the Syrians while the United States guarded against Soviet involvement.

These drastic measures proved unnecessary. Israeli troop movements on the Golan Heights and the deployment of U.S. naval units in the Eastern Mediterranean inhibited Damascus from reinforcing its forces in Jordan or using its air force to support those already there. This allowed Hussein's limited air power to force a prompt Syrian withdrawal. At the same time, the Palestinian resistance in Jordan was broken. Most of the guerillas left the country, to wind up eventually in Lebanon. Those who remained in the Hashemite Kingdom were confined to the northern part of the country, from which the bulk of them were expelled within a year.

Although the Soviet Union had appeared to disapprove strongly of Syria's intervention in Jordan, Nixon and Kissinger saw the episode as part of an overall effort to radicalize the Middle East. Impressed by Israel's role in defusing the crisis, Washington became even more inclined to see the U.S.–Israeli relationship as "the key to combating Soviet influence in the Arab World and attaining stability."[64]

The pendulum of official opinion now began to swing decisively against the State Department's plea for urgency in the search for peace. Kissinger's strategy of fostering a stalemate was coming into its own. This was soon reflected in the administration's arms policy. In October 1970, Nixon approved a $90 million transfer of assorted arms to Israel. In January 1971 the administration approved $500 million in credits for Israeli arms purchases. By the end of its first term, the Nixon administration would extend some $1.5 billion in economic and military aid to Israel.[65]

The summer of 1970 saw the Middle East equation change further as a result of Gamal Abdel Nasser's death at the end of the Jordanian crisis. The new Egyptian president, Anwar Sadat, was not particularly well known in Washington. U.S. officials originally saw him as a figurehead who would in all probability soon be replaced. In his first private interview with the foreign press, President Sadat plaintively called for a resumption of U.S. peacemaking efforts. "And where is the American peace initiative that Rogers proposed," he asked; "we accepted it unconditionally."[66]

The next three years would show the futility of Sadat's repeated calls for a more active U.S. policy. Following the February 1971 failure of Jarring's efforts to rekindle Egyptian–Israeli negotiations—despite Washington's hopes that its generous arms supply measures would encourage Israel to make greater use of the UN mediator—the Nixon administration lapsed into an almost total diplomatic quiescence on the Middle East. The sole, and fruitless, exception was a State Department attempt in the spring and summer of 1971 to promote an "interim agreement" between Egypt and Israel providing for the reopening of the Suez Canal in return for a withdrawal of Israeli troops deeper into the Sinai. The plan was doomed by Washington's inability to bridge the gap between Egypt's insistence that any agreement be linked to further steps toward a final settlement and Israel's refusal to consider that option. Despite the energy expended by Secretary of State Rogers and Joseph Sisco, the administration was in any case only half-heartedly committed to exploring the approach.[67] Preoccupied by Vietnam, China, and particularly by the upcoming election year, Nixon asked Kissinger to play a more direct role in Middle East policymaking in order to ensure that no new departures would develop. The testing of Kissinger's thesis was now fully underway. With massive U.S. economic and military support continuing to flow into Israel, Kissinger could hope that political inertia would severely strain the Soviet position in the Middle East.

It was not long before the anticipated result began to develop. Having established an Egyptian air defense system ranking among the most modern in the world, Moscow found that "Egyptians tended to judge the Soviet effort more by what it had not, rather than by what it had, achieved." Unable to foment diplomatic progress, Sadat chaffed under Soviet hesitancy to provide adequate offensive weapons. In May 1972 a superpower summit meeting held in Moscow greatly increased Cairo's fears that the Soviet Union was consciously promoting a "no war, no peace" situation in the Middle East. The bland reference in the final U.S.–Soviet communique to the value of a Middle East peace based on Security Council Resolution 242 clashed sharply in Cairo's view with the emphasis given by the superpowers to establishing their relations firmly on the basis of detente.[68] Sadat became convinced that Moscow was seeking an accommodation with the United States at the expense of Arab and Egyptian interests. In July, he abruptly requested the departure of some fifteen thousand Soviet advisers.[69]

To the extent that this development signalled the end of the heyday of Soviet influence in Egypt, Kissinger's strategy was vindicated. However, opponents of his approach had all along argued against prolonging the Arab–Israeli stalemate not only on grounds that it provided scope for the growth of Soviet influence in the Arab world but also because it could provoke another Middle East war and heighten chances of a U.S.–USSR confrontation.

If Kissinger's analysis seemed partly borne out by Sadat's expulsion of Soviet advisers, that of his detractors was supported by later events. The diplomatic stalemate was ultimately broken by war, and the conflict appeared for a while to raise the danger of a superpower clash to uncomfortably high levels.

Although the last year of Nixon's first term was marked by the absence of both fighting along the Suez Canal and the acrimonious political manueverings typically generated by U.S. efforts to promote a settlement, other developments kept Arab–Israeli tensions high. Palestinian guerrillas, operating mainly from Lebanon, continued to attack targets in Israel, and Israeli forces mounted various assaults on targets in Lebanese territory. Palestinian terrorists also undertook a number of missions abroad, including a widely publicized attack on Israeli athletes at the 1972 Munich Olympics.

Meanwhile, Israeli policies in the occupied territories steadily fueled Arab resentment. Collective punishments against communities suspected of harboring guerrillas, land sequestrations under a variety of guises, the forcible exile of community leaders, and other measures were constant irritants.[70] More ominous in the long run, was the continuing construction of Israeli settlements in the occupied lands. By the end of 1972, at least forty-four settlements had been established.[71]

After his re-election in 1972, Nixon began thinking of a renewed diplomatic effort in the Middle East. The president believed that any initiative should come in the first year of his new term, since it would be inadvisable to attempt one in 1974 because of congressional elections, and "of course, not thereafter with '76 coming up." He was not inclined to let the matter be handled by the State Department. Yet Kissinger seemed leery of confronting Israel's U.S. supporters. In early 1973, Nixon noted in his diary:

... Henry has constantly put off moving on it each time, suggesting that the political problems were too difficult. This is a matter which I, of course, will have to judge. He agreed that the problem with the Israelis in Israel was not nearly as difficult as the Jewish community here, but I am determined to bite this bullet and do it now because we just can't let the thing ride and have a hundred million Arabs hating us and providing a fishing ground not only for radicals but, of course, for the Soviets.[72]

Despite his declared willingness to "bite the bullet" of domestic opposition, Nixon had no intention of going so far as pushing for an overall settlement. Although he blamed Israel for the diplomatic stagnation in the Middle East, the president carefully defined U.S. goals in light of what he thought Israel might accept:

... in some way we have got to get the Israelis off of their intransigent position. Needless to say, we can't move to the all-out Egyptian or Arab position either, but there is some place in between where we can move. The interim settlement is, of course, the only thing we can talk about, that's the only thing the Israelis will ever go for—and the Egyptians are just simply going to have to take a settlement of that sort—or the Arabs are—with the assurance that we will do the best we can to get a total settlement later.[73]

A few months later, with no new diplomatic effort having materialized in the interval, Nixon's view of the possible clashed strongly with a proposal made by Leonid Brezhnev for a private U.S.–USSR understanding to impose peace on the Middle East. The Soviet leader pressed the issue during a late night session while visiting the "California White House" at San Clemente in July. Warning that the absence of a settlement would lead to another Middle East war, Brezhnev advocated a superpower accord over the basic principles for final peace in the region. Only then could each power use its influence to bring about an Arab–Israeli agreement. The whole approach, he said, could be kept at the level of a secret oral understanding between Moscow and Washington. Among the principles he advanced were a complete Israeli withdrawal to 1967 lines; a declaration of nonbelligerency on the part of the Arab states; the establishment of final peace once a solution to the Palestinian problem was negotiated; freedom of navigation for all through the Suez Canal; and great power guarantees of a final settlement.[74]

Quite apart from the political constraints that prevented Nixon from entering into a secret oral agreement of such magnitude with the Soviet Union, it was obvious that Brezhnev's suggested "principles" were incompatible with key elements of Washington's position. Although the United States was technically committed to only insubstantial alterations in the 1967 borders, it was clearly opposed to any simple return to the pre–1967 map. Then too, while the U.S. was not insistent that an Arab–Israeli settlement be capped by a formal peace treaty, the administration would hardly find it possible to agree that the conversion of nonbelligerency, which would itself require Israel's full withdrawal, to "peace" be contingent upon a successful conclusion of negotiations over the Palestinian's future.

Despite his own tendency to view an imposed solution as the ultimate solution to the Arab–Israeli conflict, Nixon made no effort to discuss these points with Brezhnev. Instead, he rejected the Soviet leader's proposal out of hand.

Three months later, Nixon would reverse himself and seek to negotiate the basis of a joint U.S.–Soviet peacemaking effort. By that time, however, events unrelated to the Middle East severely hampered his freedom of choice.

STEP-BY-STEP-DIPLOMACY: 1973–1976

The 1973 October War marked a turning point in Washington's approach to the Arab–Israeli conflict. Henry Kissinger, having become

Secretary of State (while retaining his post as National Security Adviser) less than a month before fighting erupted on October 6, was soon the central figure of a remarkably energetic diplomatic campaign. Within twenty-three months, what quickly became known as the "peace process" altered the Middle East environment. During that period, Egypt and Israel concluded three agreements, one was reached between Syria and Israel, and the United States emerged in a relationship to Israel that has aptly been described as "a virtual alliance in all but name."[75]

Under Kissinger's guiding hand, the United States consciously refrained from pursuing a comprehensive resolution of the Arab–Israeli conflict. Justified by Kissinger as a necessary means of breaking psychological barriers to peace and building the protagonists' confidence in the possibility of an ultimate final settlement, the practice of "step-by-step" diplomacy was predicated on the premise that Washington's good offices would enable the parties to agree on relatively minor peripheral points without reference to the fundamental sources of conflict. Kissinger argued that such a process, if sustained, would engender a dynamic predisposition—or "momentum"—toward reconciliation that eventually would permit the resolution of core differences. In this context, then, the role of a third-party peacemaker was to facilitate consecutive agreements without becoming committed to the nature of any final settlement.[76]

Such, at least, was the theory. In practice it permitted the Nixon administration to claim overall peace as its final objective while assiduously avoiding the political costs—in terms of its relations with Israel and the pro-Israel lobby, the Arab states, and the Soviet Union—that would be incurred by delineating a specific framework for Middle East peace deemed compatible with U.S. interests. The strength of "step-by-step" was that under Kissinger's deft direction it managed to produce limited agreements. Its weakness lay in an inherent bias favoring the path of least resistance. While herculean efforts were capped by partial, though significant, agreements, the conflict's underlying central issues not only smoldered but became more complex.

In refocusing its attention on the Middle East after the October War, the Nixon administration labored under severe constraints. The Watergate scandal was cresting, with the president futilely struggling against the tide that would sweep him from office. The war itself, which cost Israel over 2,500 dead, shocked Israel's supporters and reinforced their determination to succor the Jewish state in its crisis. Finally, a hurtful oil embargo and reduction in crude output was aimed at the United States by Arab oil producers in retaliation for support extended to Israel during the war.[77]

On the other hand, a major opportunity to further U.S. interests began to appear even while the war was in progress. Virtually concurrently with the onset of hostilities, Egyptian president Anwar Sadat had sent the first of a series of communications to Kissinger indicating that Cairo's military goals were limited. Kissinger understood the message as inviting the United States to "participate in, if not to take charge of, the peace process."[78]

Sadat would soon establish the sincerity of his desire to extricate Egypt from the conflict with Israel. Personally distrustful of the Soviet Union, and disillusioned by what he saw as Moscow's inadequate support, Sadat set his sights on a partnership with the United States that would not only end the conflict but also be crucial to the revival and development of Egypt's stagnant economy.[79] In his eagerness to press on toward these goals, the Egyptian leader did much, in Kissinger's telling phrase, to make step-by-step "look good." Sadat quite consciously set out to make himself the point of least resistance in Kissinger's diplomatic efforts.

As a tactical approach, step-by-step developed in light of limitations and opportunities that impinged upon U.S. policymaking at a particular moment in time, and Kissinger proved a keen instrument for its employment. Yet, for all its emphasis on limited accords between Arabs and Israelis, the approach was not divorced from Kissinger's view of long-term U.S. objectives. Under his direction, step-by-step was consistently and successfully employed to keep the Soviet Union on the sidelines of Middle East diplomacy. It is, therefore, all the more ironic that while it was giving birth to step-by-step diplomacy, the October War also almost led Washington into exploring a partnership with the Soviet Union in Middle East peacemaking.

Neither Israel nor the United States was prepared when Egyptian troops suddenly stormed across the Suez Canal while Syrian forces simultaneously attacked Israeli positions on the Golan Heights. Unaware of the extent of Israel's losses in the war's opening phases, the Nixon administration assumed the Arabs would soon be crushed. The full dimensions of the situation began to emerge some days later when Israel urgently requested emergency arms supplies. Dropping its original call for a cease-fire based on a return to the lines of October 6, Washington now urged a simple cease-fire in place. At the same time, the administration permitted relatively small amounts of arms—far below what the Israelis were hoping for—to be flown to Israel. The Soviet Union, which was airlifting arms to Syria, joined the United States in calling for a cease-fire.[80]

However, the crisis refused to be contained so easily. On October 12, Israel announced its acceptance in principle of a cease-fire. Glorying in his forces' initial successes, Sadat demanded a prior Israeli agreement to "withdraw from occupied Arab territories."[81] These events triggered a massive flow of U.S. arms to Israel. Within days, the U.S. Air Force formed an "air bridge" to the Jewish state, delivering enormous amounts of war materiel over the next four weeks.[82]

The battle began to shift in Israel's favor even before the new arms could be hurled to the front. By October 16, Israeli units were crossing to the West bank of the Suez Canal. The movement eventually placed three Israeli armored divisions on the Canal's West bank and cut off the Egyptian Third Army in the Sinai. By then, Israel had also gone to the offensive on the Syrian front. Its own troops were in some areas only twenty miles from Damascus.[83]

On October 20, with the Arabs reeling under Israel's counter-offensive, Kissinger flew to Moscow to work out a joint stand on a cease-fire and subsequent peace process. He found the Soviets forthcoming, more interested in staving off further fighting than in lengthy bargaining. Agreement was soon reached. The superpowers jointly called for a cease-fire in place, for a peace based on Security Council Resolution 242, and for negotiations "under appropriate auspices" between the contending parties. They also agreed to serve as co-chairs of an overall peace conference.

This agreement was what Nixon and Kissinger had hoped for when the latter set out for Moscow. However, Kissinger was shocked by two messages he received from Washington just as his plane reached the Soviet capital. The first revealed that Nixon had independently informed Brezhnev that Kissinger enjoyed "full authority" to conclude an agreement, and, furthermore, that the secretary of state was bearing an oral message related to the president's conviction that final peace in the Middle East depended on strong and persuasive leadership by the U.S. and Soviet governments.

Kissinger records his horror upon learning the Kremlin could count on his "full authority." He worried that Nixon had effectively deprived him of the ability to stall should negotiations be difficult.

However, the secretary's discomfort over possible tactical problems dwindled to insignificance when he turned to the message informing him of what was to be communicated orally to Brezhnev. The president had decided that the argument made by Brezhnev during his stay in San Clemente was valid: the dangers of the Arab–Israeli conflict could only be eliminated by full peace, and it was time for the superpowers to force this outcome. Explaining his decision to Kissinger, Nixon argued that it was in Israel's interest to be pressured by the United States into accepting "a settlement which is reasonable and which we can ask the Soviets to press on the Arabs." The president ended by expressing determination to pursue his new policy "regardless of the domestic political consequences."

While relaying this to Brezhnev, Kissinger was to stress that Nixon could act in foreign policy matters without fear of congressional veto. Brezhnev was to be specifically informed that Nixon now accepted the essential validity of the arguments made by the Soviet leader in San Clemente. The president agreed that:

The Israelis and Arabs will never be able to approach this subject by themselves in a rational manner. That is why Nixon and Brezhnev, looking at the problem more dispassionately, must step in, determine the proper course of action to a just settlement, and then bring the necessary pressure on our respective friends for a settlement which will at last bring peace to this troubled area.

Kissinger was appalled:

American strategy so far had been to *separate* the cease-fire from a postwar political settlement and to reduce the Soviet role in the negotiations that would follow the ceasefire. What Nixon seemed to envisage now would involve us in an extensive negotiation whose results we would then have to impose on Israel as the last act of a war fought on the Arab side with Soviet weapons. Moscow would receive credit with the Arabs for having forced us into a course we had heretofore avoided.[84]

It is impossible to determine precisely what prompted Nixon's sudden attempt to reverse the basic thrust of policy developed under his administration. Given his inclination to think an imposed solution would eventually be necessary in the Middle East, it is possible he simply concluded that the opportunity for this had arrived. On the other hand, the timing of Nixon's initiative may have been influenced by immediate pressures. Arab oil producers had recently announced cutbacks in production, promising to sustain that policy pending an overall Middle East settlement. Then, on October 20, the Arabs reacted to the administration's request to Congress for $2.2 billion to pay for Israel's emergency arms supply by embargoing oil shipments to the United States. Finally, it is possible that Nixon's judgment may have been affected by a new twist to the Watergate affair—his quarrel with Special Prosecutor Archibald Cox—that degenerated on the day Kissinger arrived in Moscow into what became known as the "Saturday Night Massacre."

Whatever the sources of Nixon's change of heart, and whatever might be concluded in principle regarding the relative merits of pursuing comprehensive peace rather than limited agreements in the Middle East, there seems little doubt of the rashness of a decision taken so abruptly under such circumstances. With the ongoing fighting in the Middle East, a secretary of state suddenly informed of his orders while in Moscow would have faced enormous difficulties trying to negotiate the outlines of an adequate comprehensive Arab–Israeli agreement. Moreover, despite Nixon's brave pledges to presevere in his newly declared approach despite domestic political considerations, it is very doubtful that he could have done so. Within three days of the "Saturday Night Massacre," twenty-one resolutions for impeachment were under discussion in Congress.[85]

At any rate, Nixon's effort to redirect U.S. policy was stillborn. Kissinger simply ignored the order and proceeded to negotiate the joint cease-fire initiative in accordance with his original instructions. Never suspecting the secretary's curious position, Brezhnev apparently forgot to ask about Nixon's promised oral message.[86]

In the early hours of October 22, the Kissinger–Brezhnev understanding was adopted by the United Nations Security Council as Resolution 338. The measure called on all parties in the Middle East to observe a cease-fire within twelve hours, and to start implementing Resolution 242. With this obligatory bow to that earlier declaration, Resolution 338 introduced a new element into the Middle East equation:

...immediately and concurrently with the cease-fire, negotiations will start between the parties concerned under appropriate auspices aimed at establishing a just and endurable peace in the Middle East.[87]

Before leaving Moscow, Kissinger agreed with his hosts that the United States and the Soviet Union would serve as co-chairmen of the projected peace negotiations. Their responsibilities in this capacity were to be limited to "active participation" at the beginning of the peace talks "and thereafter in the course of negotiations when key issues of a settlement are dealt with."[88] Since this did not define "key issues," the extent to which the superpowers would be jointly involved in the negotiations remained unclear. Kissinger soon made it plain that he intended to minimize the Soviet role when the conference met in Geneva.

During a brief stop in Israel on his return to Washington, Kissinger found the Israelis opposed to a cease-fire now that the battle was running in their favor. However, Kissinger would not be put off. In the end, the Israelis seemed swayed by his insistence that Resolution 338 constituted a breakthrough by demanding direct negotiations to end the Middle East conflict. He left with assurances that Israel would accept the cease-fire.

The cease-fire duly went into effect on October 22. However, it broke down almost immediately.[89] Israel completed the encirclement of the Egyptian Third Army and over the next thirty-six hours struggled to press home its attack. Cairo loosed a volley of requests for U.S. and Soviet intervention to stop the Israeli advance. On October 23, yet another Security Council resolution failed to end the hostilities. Sadat's pleas culminated in a public request that both superpowers send troops to Egypt to impose a halt to the fighting.

From Washington's perspective, the problem now amounted to two intertwined crises. On the one hand, neither Nixon nor Kissinger wanted Israel to destroy the surrounded Third Army. Instead, they hoped to see the war end without a clearcut victor. On the other, the administration recognized that Sadat's urgent invitation raised a more immediate problem. It was inconceivable that U.S. troops confront Israelis on an Egyptian battlefield, and it was totally unacceptable to Washington for Soviet forces to do so. Realizing that Sadat's request would put the Soviet Union in an extremely embarrassing position that might virtually force Moscow to respond favorably, the administration countered signs of Kremlin interest in Egypt's proposal by promising to block any move in the Security Council to legitimize superpower intervention.

On the night of October 24, a letter from Brezhnev increased tensions. The message suggested joint action to produce a cease-fire in the Middle East. It also referred to possible unilateral Soviet action:

I will say it straight that if you find it impossible to act jointly with us in this matter, we should be faced with the necessity urgently to consider the question of taking appropriate steps unilaterally. We cannot allow arbitrariness on the part of Israel.... [90]

Amid reports that Soviet and East German troops might be poising for a leap to the Middle East, Washington rejected Brezhnev's suggestions. The point was emphasized by a series of obvious military moves, among which was an order placing U.S. forces—including the nuclear equipped Strategic Air Command—on enhanced alert.

At the same time, a message in Nixon's name was sent to Sadat, warning against the dangers of superpower confrontation and playing on the Egyptian leader's desire for U.S. political support:

I ask you to consider the consequences for your country if the two great nuclear powers were thus to confront each other on your soil. I ask you further to consider the impossibility for us undertaking the diplomatic initiative ... if the forces of one of the great nuclear powers were to be involved militarily on Egyptian soil.[91]

Cairo was impressed. Sadat requested the Security Council to send an "international force"—which by convention would not include great power units—to supervise the cease-fire. The Soviets abandoned the idea of intervention. Kissinger later described Washington's response to the possibility of direct Soviet involvement as "deliberate overreaction."[92] Events seemed to vindicate the tactic. Washington appeared virtually certain to inherit the field of Middle East diplomacy in the aftermath of the October War.

On October 25, a third Security Council cease-fire resolution was approved. The October War was over—almost. There remained the problem of Israel's determination to destroy the Third Army. Sadat continued complaining of a variety of Israeli military movements designed to force the Third Army's surrender. Washington now turned to the task of restraining Israel. While Kissinger berated the Israelis for intransigence, contingency plans were laid for a direct U.S. resupply of nonmilitary equipment essential for the Third Army's survival in its desert entrapment.

In the end, it was Sadat's willingness to countenance direct talks between Egyptian and Israeli commanders that defused the crisis. Pressured by Washington, and facing a beleagued but cohesive enemy force, the Israelis decided that limited face-to-face negotiations over the Third Army's future was sufficient gain. By the end of October 27, the war was finally over.

The issues facing U.S. policymakers at this point were dangerous and delicate. Washington had established its claim to preeminence as the outside actor that might decisively influence the political outcome of the recent hostilities. Yet the immediate political problem was to extricate the trapped Third Army. So long as this was not achieved, there remained the possibility that renewed fighting might immeasurably complicate, if not destroy, the chances for successful U.S. diplomacy. But solving the Third Army's predicament promised to be difficult. Egypt insisted that Israel withdraw to positions held at the time of the original cease-fire on October 22—that is, before the Third Army's encirclement. Israel maintained that any realignment of forces should amount to a return to prewar lines.

Having promised on various occasions during the war to search for a final solution to the Arab–Israeli conflict, Washington had to discover some means of generating activity dealing with immediate problems in the context of what could arguably be described as a process leading to accommodation on wider issues. The administration's awareness of the difficulties of doing this was sharpened by high level Israeli and Egyptian visitors at the end of the month. Golda Meir arrived in the United States still smarting over the U.S. pressure that had forced Israel to accept the cease-fire and deeply suspicious of Washington's intentions. Ismail Fahmy, about to be named Egypt's foreign minister, showed up almost simultaneously.

The Israeli prime minister focused on a multitude of specific issues, hoping to obtain maximum benefit from the Third Army's plight. Continued resupply of the Egyptian force, she said, depended on the return of wounded Israeli prisoners of war, the provision of a complete list of POWs in Egyptian hands, Red Cross visits to the POWs, the lifting of an undeclared Egyptian blockade of the Red Sea Bab el Mandab Straits, and continued Israeli control of access routes to the Third Army. Above all, she firmly opposed a return to the cease-fire lines of October 22. This list of detailed demands seemed to be mainly a means of avoiding long-term issues. Stunned by the number of Israeli casualties, facing a national election in December, and wary of the future course of U.S. policy, Israel's leaders adopted an exceedingly cautious approach to postwar bargaining: inch-by-inch.

In contrast, Ismail Fahmy arrived hoping to bargain leap-by-leap. His dual purpose was to prepare for a scheduled trip to Egypt by Kissinger and to promote a sweeping program of phased Israeli withdrawal that would culminate in an end of the state of belligerency between Egypt and Israel once the latter's forces pulled back to the international frontier.[93]

Kissinger suggested that these ideas were interesting and worthwhile, though perhaps overly ambitious. However, beneath this veneer of diplomatic restraint, the secretary of state was coming to believe that peacemaking efforts focused on Egypt and Israel might succeed. Fahmy had not only suggested an overall plan for phased peacemaking that did not necessarily imply Israel's return to 1967 territorial lines, but also—according to Kissinger—explicitly decoupled Egypt's diplomatic drive from the Palestinian question. "We have," said Fahmy in Kissinger's version, "no interest in putting Israel into the sea or invading Israel, irrespective of the Palestinian attitude." Fahmy disputes this account, claiming that no mention was made of the Palestinians during the conversation in question. In any event, whether by omission or commission on Fahmy's part, Kissinger concluded that the Palestinian issue was hardly central to Egyptian policy.[94]

In dealing with Egyptian and Israeli leaders, U.S. policymakers tried to cultivate the former's expectations and the latter's understanding. Fahmy received assurances that the United States would restrain Israel from further attacks on Egyptian forces and that Kissinger would pursue the Egyptian emissary's ideas with Anwar Sadat.[95] Golda Meir was told by both Nixon and Kissinger that the United States was committed to furthering its own relations with Egypt and advised that her government should become a partner in the endeavor without doubting Washington's commitment to Israel's security. Nixon argued as follows:

The problem you have to consider is whether the policy you have followed—being prepared with the Phantoms and Skyhawks—can succeed, lacking a settlement. The question is whether a policy of only being prepared for war—although even with a peace settlement you will have to be prepared—is sufficient.

This last war proves the overwhelming conclusion that a policy of digging in, telling us to give you the arms and you will do the fighting, can't be the end. Your policy has to be to move as you are moving toward talks.[96]

In early November, Kissinger departed on a world-circling journey to North Africa, the Middle East, and Asia. He met President Anwar Sadat for the first time during a brief stop in Egypt. The two men established the easy rapport that would characterize their relationship over the next years. Sadat quickly agreed to a six-point program suggested by Kissinger for dealing with the Third Army. The plan established conditions for the regular resupply of nonmilitary necessities to the Egyptian force. More importantly, it also sought to avoid the controversy over the October 22 cease-fire lines by proposing Egyptian–Israeli negotiations under UN auspices on the broader question of a full disengagement and separation of forces. The blossoming U.S.–Egyptian connection was highlighted when Kissinger and Sadat agreed that it was time to reestablish the diplomatic relations that had been broken in 1967.

Sending assistants to secure Israel's agreement to the six-point program, Kissinger went on to Amman and Riyadh. In each capital he endeavored to convince his interlocutors of Washington's determination to work for full peace. Already bouyed by the six-point agreement, and looking forward to promoting a general disengagement of Egyptian and Israeli forces, Kissinger's faith in incremental peacemaking was further boosted when Saudi Arabia's King Feisal encouraged him to bring Syria into the process. If limited agreements between Egypt and Israel could be repeated on the Syrian front, it seemed likely that the Arabs would cancel the oil boycott without awaiting a comprehensive peace settlement.[97]

By late November, Kissinger was planning for the Geneva Peace Conference envisaged by Resolution 338. However, he was determined that real diplomatic efforts would be left to bilateral Israeli–Arab working groups. The conference itself would be no more than a "symbolic act."[98] Its format was designed to facilitate the development of a major U.S. role while minimizing that of the Soviets.

The question of Palestinian participation proved less difficult than might have been expected. Although Kissinger had initially assured Sadat of Washington's readiness to seek some form of Palestinian presence, Israel's strong objections soon changed his mind. Egypt and Jordan agreed to attend on the basis of an invitation promising that "the question of other participants from the Middle East area will be discussed during the first stages of the conference." Syria decided to avoid the proceedings. This last development rather pleased Kissinger, who feared that the Israeli government—which had so far been unable to extract a list of prisoners of war from Damascus—might use Syria's presence as a pretext for resisting the considerable U.S. prodding that produced its own reluctant attendance at Geneva.[99]

The conference opened on December 21, and went as Kissinger hoped. Speeches were made by UN Secretary General Kurt Waldheim,

Soviet Foreign Minister Gromyko, the foreign ministers of Israel, Egypt, and Jordan, and Kissinger. The following day, it was decreed that Egyptian–Israeli talks should continue in subcommittee. The first—and only—session of the Geneva Peace Conference was over.

As empty as it seemed, the Geneva pantomime was not without significance. It marked the first time that Israel and Arab states openly shared a negotiating forum. It also underlined the complexities that any movement toward comprehensive peace would confront. Jordan, still anxious to regain control of the West Bank, attended under the cloud of an Arab summit meeting that in November had declared the PLO to be the sole legitimate voice of the Palestinian people. Finally, with neither the Palestinians nor Syrians in attendance, and Egypt's reliance on the United States becoming increasingly obvious, the Soviet Union's position on the margins of mainstream Middle East diplomacy was evident.

Washington did not delay seizing the opportunity that had developed. In keeping with the six-point program agreed to by Egypt and Israel, their military representatives had been meeting regularly at Kilometer 101 on the Cairo–Suez road to arrange the modalities of resupplying the Third Army and work out a general plan of disengagement. Pressures had built up on both sides. The Egyptian force was still languishing in the desert, and Israel was not only bearing the burden of maintaining troops to the west of the Canal but also experiencing the economically crippling impact of prolonged general mobilization. Although these conditions seemed to be propelling the parties toward a relatively rapid agreement, the talks suddenly bogged down when Israel's negotiator, General Aharon Yariv, backtracked from an earlier position. Whether or not, as some have claimed, Kissinger exerted pressure to abort promising negotiations in order to demonstrate his, and Washington's, adeptness at peacemaking, the Kilometer 101 talks were stymied.[100]

In early January (with the Labor Alignment having won Israel's elections, though losing seven seats to Menachem Begin's Likud), Kissinger travelled to the Middle East in order to assume a direct role in mediating the Egyptian–Israeli disengagement. His energetic jetting back and forth between Egypt and Israel gave birth to the term "shuttle diplomacy." Kissinger skillfully used his powers of persuasion, as well as the parties' own inclinations, to forge the first Egyptian–Israeli Disengagement Agreement, which was signed by military commanders at Kilometer 101 on January 18, 1974.

The agreement produced an Israeli withdrawal to a line some fifteen miles to the east of the Suez Canal, thus freeing the Third Army and returning all Israeli forces to the Sinai. Egypt retained its positions on the Canal's East bank but was required to reduce its forces and observe restrictions on armaments in the zone. A corresponding restricted zone was established on the Israeli side. The two forces were separated by a buffer area patrolled by an international UN contingent.

Beyond this, Egypt secretly committed itself to clear the Canal, permit passage of nonmilitary Israeli cargoes, and rebuild civilian population centers along the waterway. It was also understood that UN forces in the buffer area could be withdrawn only with the agreement of both Israel and Egypt. These points, set forth in a secret bilateral "memorandum of understanding" between the United States and Israel, were reinforced by Washington's promise to "make every effort to be fully responsive on a continuing and long-term basis to Israel's military equipment requirements."[101]

Encouraged by the success of the disengagement agreement, Kissinger began trying to arrange a similar accord on the Syrian front. He had met, and been intrigued by, Syrian President Hafez al-Assad in December 1973. However, Kissinger discovered that his new venture had to overcome deeper problems than those involved in arranging the Egyptian–Israeli disengagement. On one level, the issues were largely psychological—the legacy of years of hostility that had produced a particularly virulent hatred between Israel and Syria. Added to this was the smallness of the territory in which any disengagement would have to occur. Assad's fervent nationalism and pride as an Arab leader led to his rigid insistence that Syria would enter into a disengagement accord only if it regained, as had Egypt, at least some of the lands lost to Israel in 1967. Yet, it was virtually an article of faith in Jersualem that Israel would not withdraw from any portion of the strategic Golan Heights as part of a limited agreement. Not until the end of May, following a gruelling effort that reached its climax in a four-week marathon of shuttle diplomacy, was Kissinger able to finalize the Syrian–Israeli disengagement.

The agreement was patterned after its Egyptian counterpart. Again, both sides accepted limited force zones separated by a buffer and UN troops. Israel withdrew to a line that on the whole corresponded to its pre-October 6 positions. It did, however, return Quneitra, the shattered town that had been the capital of the Golan region before it fell to Israel in 1967. Both sides also agreed on U.S. surveillance flights as well as on the principle that UN forces could be withdrawn only by mutual consent. Assad offered private assurances that Palestinian guerrillas would not be allowed to attack Israel across the disengagement lines. As surety of the pledge, the United States publicly recognized Israel's right to retaliate if attacked by paramilitary forces. Israel also won Washington's promise to view sympathetically the possibility of establishing a long-term bilateral military relationship.

The Israel–Syria agreement was all the more notable because the process of arranging it showed the degree to which the U.S. peace process had gained active support in the Arab world. Saudi Arabia joined Egypt in encouraging Syrian flexibility in hope of seeing shuttle diplomacy succeed.

Although Kissinger made full use of these assets in dealing with Damascus, the Nixon administration was left to its own devices to overcome Israel's deep reluctance to yield territory on the Syrian front. Kissinger's imaginative persistence was combined with hints that U.S. aid policy would be formulated in light of Israeli responsiveness. To emphasize the message, the administration dramatically hesitated before waiving repayment of $1.5 billion of the $2.2 billion arms credits extended to Israel during the October War.[102]

The final outcome gave Nixon much reason to be pleased. The Syrian–Israeli agreement was a landmark event, involving as it did the most radical Arab state on Israel's borders. Then too, the determined U.S. campaign to promote the agreement was tangibly rewarded by the lifting of the Arab oil boycott.[103]

In June, the president embarked on a triumphal trip to the Middle East, where in contrast to the mounting condemnations over Watergate aimed at him in the United States, he was received with acclaim. Possibly a bit over-elated by the change, Nixon passed out assurances to Sadat, Assad, and Hussein that step-by-step diplomacy actually sought to push Israel back to its 1967 borders.[104] Whether this was simply ill advised bonhomie, or whether Nixon was articulating more fundamental hopes, his remarks reinforced what the Arabs wished to believe.

Nixon's Middle East tour was the highwater mark of the step-by-step approach. Thereafter, the pace of the administration's peacemaking efforts faltered. In one sense, the dissipation of step-by-step's apparent momentum resulted from weakened leadership in the United States and Israel. Golda Meir retired to private life just after the Syrian agreement was concluded. Her replacement as prime minister was Yitzhak Rabin, a former general, war hero, and ambassador to Washington, who was well known to U.S. policymakers but who lacked Mrs. Meir's commanding stature within Israel's fractious Labor Alignment. His two chief rivals for influence, Yigal Allon and Shimon Peres, sat in the the cabinet, serving respectively as ministers of foreign affairs and defense.

In the United States, Nixon's Watergate travail ended with his resignation on August 9. The new president, Gerald Ford, had stepped from congress into the vice-presidency only eight months earlier. Widely viewed as an honest, decent, and moderately capable individual, Ford seemed to have no outstanding leadership qualities and little knowledge of the Middle East. He retained Kissinger (whom Nixon recommended to the new president as "the only man who would be absolutely indispensable") as secretary of state.[105]

Apart from the impact of leadership changes, step-by-step began to suffer in the summer of 1974 from inherent limitations. It was, after all, essentially a reactive approach, a tactic for promoting limited agreements along the lines of least resistance. Now its scope was highly restricted. Another partial agreement between Syria and Israel seemed out of the question—at least for the moment—given the bruising effort required to arrange the first accord and the strategic significance of the Golan Heights. Kissinger had long held vague hopes of promoting a Jordanian–Israeli limited agreement, but on that front all issues were tightly linked to the central questions of Israel's final borders and the Palestinians' political future. This was hardly the stuff that fueled step-by-step. Although Hussein was so eager to reassert his claim to the West Bank that he was willing to accept a minimal initial Israeli withdrawal west of the Jordan River, Jerusalem was not prepared to entertain that possibility. After some hesitation, Kissinger decided against pursuing an interim agreement between the two.[106]

Of course, there was always the theoretical possibility of abandoning step-by-step, or at least enlarging it beyond recognition, by attempting to bring the Palestinians into the peace process. Nixon's Middle East trip had been capped by a joint declaration with Sadat describing the peace sought by the United States and Egypt as one "taking into due account the legitimate interest of all peoples in the Mideast, including the Palestinian people, and the right to existence of all states in the area."[107] But so long as Washington was unwilling to specify its view of Palestinian interests, references to the concept remained an empty bow to Arab sentiment rather than a statement of U.S. political goals. Seeing Palestinian political activism as an unwanted radicalizing force in the Middle East, and unwilling to challenge Israel's fundamental abhorrence of the concept of Palestinian national identity, Washington had no desire to deal with the central element of Arab–Israeli tensions. Indeed, after Hussein accepted the decree of an Arab summit conference at Rabat in late 1974 proclaiming the Palestinian Liberation Organization the sole legitimate representative of the Palestinian people, Washington's negative attitude toward Palestinian nationalism hardened.

Egypt therefore remained the natural focus for step-by-step diplomacy. Yet here—despite Sinai's wide spaces, Sadat's eagerness for another Israeli withdrawal, and the obvious benefits to Israel of cultivating Egypt's peaceful inclinations—thorny obstacles still existed. This was clear when Kissinger arrived in the Middle East in March 1975, once more hoping to return to Washington with an Egyptian–Israeli agreement in his briefcase. Preliminary contacts over the past several months, including an exploratory trip to the region in February, had shown that although the Egyptian and Israeli governments seemed interested in another accord, fundamental differences still divided them. Sadat argued that any new agreement should be of a strictly military nature and include an Israeli withdrawal from the strategic Mitla and Giddi passes in the Sinai and the oilfields around Abu Rudeis and Ras al-Sudr at the Gulf of Suez. Israel hoped to separate Egypt from other Arab states through a formal termination of belligerancy. Jerusalem was prepared to consider significant withdrawals in some areas, but resisted the possibility of returning either the Sinai passes or the oilfields.

Despite the apparent severity of this stand, Kissinger thought Israel's leaders might actually be a good bit more flexible. In late 1974, Prime Minister Rabin had publicly argued that Israel's international position had weakened in consequence of European and American dependency on Arab oil. He saw the situation as temporary, but possibly enduring for several years. Rabin recommended that Israel should therefore aim at gaining time, the implication being that it was in Israel's interest to avoid pressures for a final settlement. Step-by-step should be kept alive, in hope of promoting Egypt's estrangement from Syria and the Soviet Union. Significantly, Rabin did not insist on an explicit declaration of nonbelligerency as the price of the next agreement with Egypt.[108]

Another apparent indication that Israel's declared position concealed some readiness to compromise was given shortly afterward by Foreign Minister Yigal Allon, who offered Kissinger his "private" opinion that in return for full nonbelligerency Israel would hand over the oil fields and Sinai passes.[109]

Yet, when Kissinger went to the Middle East in March 1975 to secure another Egyptian–Israeli accord, he discovered that he had misinterpreted what had seemed to be Israeli political signals. Rather than growing from a hidden, purposeful flexibility, they turned out to reflect only the confusion and division prevailing within Israel's cabinet, in which— apart from their unceasing rivalry—Rabin, Allon, and Defense Minister Peres shared primarily a fear that the rightist Likud might cause the government's downfall at the first sign of weakness.

Arriving in Cairo on March 8, Kissinger was encouraged by his meeting with Sadat. The Egyptian president was ready to forgo linking a new agreement to subsequent diplomatic progress between Syria and Israel or within the Geneva Conference framework. He also acknowledged that some type of political concession (short of nonbelligerency) would be required to obtain another partial agreement. On the other hand, Sadat would not be moved from his demand for the Sinai passes and oilfields.

Kissinger's disappointments began the next day in Jerusalem. Israel refused to discuss territorial issues until Sadat's response to its central demands was clarified. These amounted to a call for a long-lasting agreement of nonbelligerency that would provide for practical steps toward peaceful relations without being tied to the vicissitudes of Israeli relations with other Arab states.

For the next two weeks, Kissinger engaged in another round of shuttle diplomacy. Sadat gave way, still rejecting formal "nonbelligerency" but accepting its "functional equivalent." He would, he said, accept provisions prohibiting resort to force and undertake de facto, though not formal, commitments to improve the general atmosphere between the two countries by limiting offensive propaganda and moderating Egypt's application of the Arab boycott of firms dealing with Israel. He was utterly inflexible on the issue of withdrawal, warning Kissinger that the Israelis should not think that he would permit them to remain in the Sinai passes or oilfields.

Eventually the Israelis also modified their stand—but only up to a point. In exchange for an Egyptian declaration upholding the non-use of force, Israel would consider pulling back halfway through the passes and permitting Egyptian access to the oilfields over Israeli-controlled roads.

A mortified Kissinger tried to convince the Israelis that Sadat would settle for nothing less than their complete abandonment of the passes and that the offer of functional nonbelligerency provided adequate assurances for Israeli security. He also argued that the Egyptian leader could not be expected to jeopardize his standing in the Arab world by formalizing the commitment. Neither Kissinger's eloquence nor a strongly worded letter from President Ford implying that Israeli intransigence could provoke a suspension of military and economic aid had any effect.[110]

Worried that step-by-step had now reached the end of the road, Kissinger anguished over the possibility that the entire edifice he had tried to construct in the Middle East was about to crumble. On March 22, just before returning to the United States, he unburdened himself to members of Israel's cabinet:

Step-by-step has been throttled, first for Jordan, then for Egypt. We're losing control. We'll now see the Arabs working on a united front. There will be more emphasis on the Palestinians, and there will be a linkage between moves in the Sinai and on Golan. The Soviets will step back onto the stage. The United States is losing control, and we'd all better adjust ourselves to that reality.[111]

It was no secret that Washington blamed Israel for having "throttled" step-by-step. Official U.S. displeasure took the form of ostentatiously delayed action on Israeli arms requests and a slowdown on the shipment of already committed supplies.

It was all part of a highly publicized "reassessment" of the Ford administration's Middle East policy. The reassessment identified two main options: to replace step-by-step with an effort to formulate, declare, and realize plans for a comprehensive settlement supportive of U.S. interests; or to try to reactivate step-by-step. A majority of academics and other unofficial experts whose opinions were solicited, as well as U.S. ambassadors to Egypt, Syria, Jordan, and Israel, were inclined to favor the first alternative.[112]

On the other hand, the pro-Israel lobby militated strongly against the "reassessment." Only a few congressmen, among whom was the chairman of the Foreign Relations Committee, Senator William Fulbright, urged the administration to risk the domestic consequences of pursuing a comprehensive Middle East peace. Edward Sheehan's description captures the situation:

In formulating the first option, Dr. Kissinger's advisors envisioned President Ford going to the American people, explaining lucidly and at length on television the issues of war and peace in the Middle East, pleading the necessity of Israeli withdrawal in exchange for the strongest guarantees. The President, too, was angry at Israel, and for a time toyed with this notion of appealing over the heads of the lobby and of Congress directly to the people. He hesitated. "How will it play in Peoria?" he asked. "You'll never know until you do it," J. William Fulbright urged him. "Do it first—then Peoria will follow."[113]

Domestic pressures came to a head in late May, with seventy-two senators signing a letter urging Ford to adhere to the established policy of extending large-scale economic and military aid to Israel. It was an unstable reminder that the president's overall need for congressional goodwill would be jeopardized by continued pressure on Israel:

Cooperation between Congress and the President is essential for America's effectiveness in the world. . . . We believe that the special relationship between our country and Israel does not prejudice improved relations with other nations in the region. We believe that a strong Israel constitutes a most reliable barrier to domination of the area by outside parties.

We believe that preserving the peace requires that Israel obtain a level of military and economic support adequate to deter a renewal of war by Israel's neighbors. Withholding military equipment from Israel would be dangerous, discouraging accommodation by Israel's neighbors and encouraging a resort to force. Within the next several weeks, the Congress expects to receive your foreign aid requests for fiscal year 1976. We trust that your recommendations will be responsive to Israel's urgent military and economic needs.[114]

The administration's reluctance to fall back on the Geneva forum in hope of pursuing a comprehensive peace and the strong tide of pro-Israel domestic sentiment soon killed further pretense that the touted "reassessment" might produce fundamental policy changes.

In June, Sadat and Ford met in Salzburg. Although failing to obtain a public declaration of U.S. support for an ultimate Israeli withdrawal to the international border, Sadat did receive private assurances to that effect. Apparently by now convinced of Washington's inability to pressure Israel into agreeing to his basic demands, Sadat also modified Egypt's minimal requirements for another partial accord. He suggested that the stalemate over the Sinai passes might be resolved by linking an Israeli withdrawal to the introduction of U.S. personnel manning early warning monitoring stations within the passes.

Some days later, Ford met Prime Minister Rabin in Washington. The president spoke of his willingness to recommend massive assistance in return for a partial accord with Egypt. The Israelis seemed more willing to negotiate. The rest of the summer was devoted primarily to U.S.–Israeli talks aimed at determining the price of Israeli flexibility over the passes and oilfields. By August 20, with the agreement all but achieved, Kissinger returned to the Middle East. The second Israeli–Egyptian partial agreement, "Sinai II," was initialed by both sides on September 1 and signed three days later. Israel surrendered the passes and oilfields but gained much: Egypt had for all practical purposes removed itself from the ranks of Arab confrontation states; the relationship between the United States and Israel was placed on a footing rarely achieved by the closest of formal allies.

Sinai II consisted of a Basic Agreement between Egypt and Israel, together with an Annex and Protocol; a U.S. "Proposal" (formally accepted by Egypt); a U.S.–Israeli "Memorandum of Agreement"; four "secret" agreements (three between the United States and Israel, one between the United States and Egypt); and a package of "secret understandings" involving all these parties.

Apart from committing Egypt to allow free passage of nonmilitary Israeli cargos through the Suez Canal (which in accordance with the first Sinai disengagement agreement had reopened in June), the Basic Agreement, Annex, and Protocol established the framework for Israel's withdrawal to a line curving east of the Sinai passes and the Abu Rudeis oilfield. These documents established that the conflict between the two states should "not be resolved by military force but by peaceful means," and committed them "not to resort to force or to the threat of force." They also established that while the Agreement was "not a final peace agreement," it would "remain in force until superseded by a new agreement."

As had the first Sinai agreement, Sinai II provided for limited force and armament zones and for an intervening buffer area in which an international UN force would be deployed. A significant innovation was based on the idea Sadat raised at Salzburg. Up to two hundred U.S. civilians would observe the operations of Israeli and Egyptian electronic surveillance stations (one each) in the passes, while at the same time independently monitoring the troop movements of both sides. The United States would also be responsible for aerial surveillance of the new disengagement lines.

The memorandum of "United States–Israeli Assurances" involved a sweeping set of undertakings committing the United States, "within the limits of its resources and congressional authorization and appropriation, on an on-going and long-term basis to Israel's military equipment and other defense requirements, to its energy requirements and to its economic needs."

Specific U.S. assurances included:

• A pledge to view Israel's arms requests "sympathetically, including its request for advanced and sophisticated weapons."

• A pledge to conclude a contingency plan "for a military supply operation to Israel in an emergency situation."

• A pledge to "take into account" when calculating annual financial assistance for Israel over the next five years the additional expense Israel would have to bear for importing oil after relinquishing Egypt's oil fields.

• A pledge to seek a congressional appropriation to help finance an oil reserve storage program for Israel.

• A pledge to guarantee for five years Israel's oil requirements should the need arise and should U.S. procurements meet its own normal needs.

In addition, Washington promised to "view with particular gravity" any threat to Israel "by a world power" and, should such a threat materialize, to consult promptly with Israel regarding what support, "diplomatic or otherwise," would be given.

Finally, three items in the Memorandum of Assurances collectively implied that whatever happened in the future, Egypt would be unable to revive its war option without confronting the U.S.–Israeli partnership:

• [Paragraph 6] The United States Government agrees with Israel that the next agreement with Egypt should be a final peace agreement.

• [Paragraph 12] It is the United States Government's position that Egyptian commitments under the Egypt–Israeli Agreement, its implementation, validity and duration are not conditional upon any act or developments between the Arab states and Israel. The United States government regards the Agreement as standing on its own.

• [Paragraph 15] In the event that the United Nations Emergency Force or any other United Nations organ is withdrawn without the prior agreement of both parties to the Egypt–Israel Agreement and the United States before this agreement is superceded by another agreement, it is the United States view that the Agreement shall remain binding in all its parts.[115]

The "Memorandum's" final paragraph confirmed that "the United States has informed the government of Israel that it has obtained the government of Egypt's agreement to the above."

One of the two "secret" agreements between the United States and Israel specified that Washington would consider Israel's requests for sophisticated weapons, including F–16 aircraft and Pershing ground-to-ground missiles with conventional warheads, "with a view to giving a positive response."[116]

The second U.S.–Israeli "secret" agreement ensured that the two states would coordinate their policies at the Geneva Peace Conference (if it ever reconvened). In this context, it also committed the United States not to "negotiate with or recognize" the PLO so long as that organization "does not recognize Israel's right to exist and does not accept Security Council Resolutions 242 and 338." This aspect of the Memorandum was later interpreted both in Jerusalem and Washington as precluding all direct contact between the United States and the PLO until the latter met the stipulated conditions.[117]

In a separate "Memorandum of Assurances" given to Egypt, the United States promised "a serious effort" to help promote further negotiations between Israel and Egypt and to "consult" with Egypt should Israel violate the Basic Agreement. More significantly, Washington reaffirmed its "desire to assist the economy of Egypt, subject to the approval of the United States Congress."

Given the import of paragraphs 6, 12, and 15 of the U.S.–Israeli Memorandum of Assurances, further secret undertakings deposited with the United States by Israel and Egypt were almost superfluous, though they probably bolstered each party's belief in the other's good faith. Egypt in effect promised that the Basic Agreement would remain in force for at least three years and that Cairo would flexibly apply the Arab economic boycott while reducing anti-Israeli propaganda. Israel committed itself to refrain from attacking Syria.[118]

Sinai II benefitted each of the states involved in its creation, though to different degrees. On balance, Israel gained most. Still occupying the bulk of the Sinai Peninsula, it simultaneously severed Egypt from the rest of its Arab antagonists and won significant economic, political, and military commitments from the United States. At a minimum, Rabin's goal of gaining time before having to come to grips with comprehensive peace had been achieved. As a senior Israeli official told *Time* Magazine, Israel "gave up a little for a lot."[119]

Sadat's Egypt also benefitted. Having re-opened the Suez Canal and encouraged the rebuilding of urban centers along its banks even prior to the Agreement, Sadat could point with pride to having regained Egypt's oilfields and pushed the Israelis into the desert beyond the passes. Domestic reconstruction and revival were the theme of the hour, and not only were the Israelis exiled to the vast reaches of Sinai but Egypt could also hope to enjoy American largesse. On the other hand, Sadat could not hide—however much he tried—the wedge that Sinai II drove between Egypt and much of the Arab World. Syria, Iraq, Libya, and the PLO roundly condemned the agreement. Jordan's King Hussein refrained from denouncing Sinai II, but explicitly withheld a wholehearted endorsement. Saudi Arabia, however, approved the agreement.[120]

The United States also gained from Sinai II, although incurring heavy costs in the process. Step-by-step achieved another victory. Precedents of Israeli withdrawal from occupied Arab lands were shown not to have been unique occurrences produced by the aftershocks of the October War. The major Arab confrontation state had not only shown its willingness to rely on U.S. peacemaking but also its willingness to continue doing so. It was virtually a formality when Egypt symbolically emphasized its rush into the U.S. orbit in 1976 by abrogating a treaty of friendship with the Soviet Union. Finally, Israel had been strengthened.

There was not much else that might be unequivocally claimed. How one evaluated the gains and costs of Sinai II depended on one's view of historical dynamics, of Israel's role in furthering U.S. interests, and of U.S. objectives in the area. Some, like Edward Sheehan, who saw the Palestinian issue as the central element of the Arab–Israeli conflict, clearly felt Washington had paid far too much for only minimal gain. Harvard professor Nadev Safran, who also saw peace in the Middle East as a vital U.S. interest, denied that the cost of Sinai II was "too excessive." He challenged critics to consider the price that might have been entailed by the agreement's absence.[121]

Despite different assessments, all agreed that the material cost to the United States of Sinai II was substantial. Fiscal year 1976 witnessed the outlay of $2.2 billion in economic and military assistance to Israel, while Egypt received $1 billion in U.S. foreign aid. By the time the Ford administration left office, total U.S. military and economic aid to Israel since Nixon's assumption of office amounted to $8.8 billion. Egypt had received some $2.3 billion.[122]

The political cost may have been less clear, but it too was substantial. Egypt's growing isolation in the Arab world not only tended to discredit step-by-step's claims to be moving toward comprehensive peace but also reinforced suspicions that U.S. policy had all along aimed at duping the Arabs into a process that would leave Syria, Jordan, and the Palestinians vulnerable to maximum Israeli demands. If taken literally (as it was), the U.S. commitment to refrain from recognizing or negotiating with the PLO would prevent Washington from exploring conditions under which Palestinians might play their two principal political cards: recognizing Israel and accepting Security Council Resolutions 242 and 338.

The question facing U.S. policymakers after Sinai II was "what next?"

Time, at least, had been purchased on the Egyptian front. Yet, while further progress there seemed for the moment out of the question, no new likely target for step-by-step appeared on the horizon. The passage of time might, in Rabin's view, benefit Israel but from Washington's perspective it began to appear that the U.S. approach had taken its last step into a blind alley.

By late 1975, with national elections scheduled for 1976, Washington began to slip into its traditional pre-election torpor on Arab–Israeli affairs. There were, however, some efforts by the administration to assure the Arabs that it had not abandoned the search for peace. The much publicized "Saunders Affair," in which Harold Saunders, one of Kissinger's top aides, raised before Congress the notion that the core of Arab–Israeli tensions was the Palestinian problem, flared and died away. Kissinger, later reported to have been behind Saunders' statement, minimized his subordinate's presentation. Arab attention was also drawn to the United Nations during 1976 as U.S. spokesmen suddenly offered rather specific condemnations of Israel's continuing construction of settlements in the occupied territories. This sort of verbal posturing may have been intriguing, but it did not obscure the central question. With step-by-step seeming to have no immediate target of opportunity, would the United States turn toward comprehensive peacemaking, and if so, would it have the will and capacity to succeed?

Jimmy Carter's election to the presidency in late 1976 meant that the answer would come under a new, politically unencumbered administration.

3

REVIVAL OF AN OBJECTIVE: JIMMY CARTER, 1977–1981

> I raised the question ... whether we should in fact be pushing so hard for an Egyptian–Israeli treaty if it is our intention to resolve also the West Bank issue. Once such a treaty is signed we will have less leverage.
>
> Zbigniew Brzezinski

Israel benefited greatly from its assocation with the United States during the Carter presidency. Total U.S. aid allocated to Jerusalem during the period soared to over $10.6 billion, some $360 million more than all U.S. aid extended to the Jewish state since 1948.[1] Yet Jimmy Carter was destined to leave office with the dubious distinction of being the U.S. president whose policies and intentions Israel had most distrusted since its birth.

Carter entered the White House determined to work for a comprehensive Middle East peace. Despite the admiration and protectiveness he felt for Israel—largely products of his Southern Baptist religious convictions—Carter revived the idea that the pursuit of peace should center on arranging the return of most of the occupied lands for Arab political concessions. Moreover, he recognized Palestinian political consciousness as a reality that demanded efforts to involve the Palestinians in the determination of their future.

Carter's approach inevitably placed him in conflict with dominant Israeli preferences. In the end, he saw his hopes for comprehensive peace wither. Although the 1979 Egyptian–Israeli peace was achieved with significant help from the United States, it caused both hope and concern in Washington: hope that it might provide a viable basis for building comprehensive peace; concern that it might not.

By then, however, Carter had lost much of the enthusiasm that marked his initial efforts as peacemaker. Bruised and disillusioned by the successive international and domestic political pitfalls he had encountered, and facing what promised to be a difficult—and proved to be a disastrous—election campaign, he turned his attention away from the Arab–Israeli problem. He could not, however, ignore the Middle East. Lebanon was caught in the throes of unending internal strife that threatened to provoke generalized regional conflict; the Soviet Union invaded Afghanistan; and the revolutionary regime that replaced the Shah in Iran directly challenged the United States.

These issues reinforced the administration's awareness of the Middle East's critical importance to the United States. Having presided over the historic Egyptian–Israeli peace without seeing it extended to other parts of the Arab world, Carter seems to have left office more than ever convinced that the continued absence of a comprehensive solution to the Palestine problem would exacerbate Washington's difficulties in coping with other problems in the Middle East.[2]

CARTER'S DRIVE TO GENEVA

Even before Carter's election, the divisions provoked by Sinai II in the Arab world were yielding to the creation of a broad constellation of Arab states that called for a resumption of the Geneva Peace Conference. With encouragement from Saudi Arabia, the rift between Egypt and Syria was healed in October 1976. Before the year ended, these three countries, with qualified support from Jordan, were urging that any renewed peace initiative deal with the central Palestinian question and entail some formula whereby the PLO might become involved in negotiations. Simultaneous efforts were made to enlist the PLO in the Arab demarche. These led in December to a rapprochement between Syria and the PLO, whose relations had been embittered by Damascus' mid–1976 intervention in the civil strife that had wracked Lebanon since the spring of 1975.

The outcome of Syrian, Egyptian, and Saudi efforts to reconcile the PLO and Jordan was even more dramatic. Formal meetings between PLO and Hashemite representatives were held in early 1977, and these in turn led to a friendly encounter between King Hussein and Yassir Arafat—their first such contact since the start of the 1970/71 civil war in Jordan. By early January 1977, President Sadat was speaking publicly, though not very precisely, of an "institutional link" between Jordan and any Palestinian state established as a result of a peace conference. The imprecision that characterized such official Arab visions of the Palestinians' future was linked on one level to the requirement, upheld at Rabat in 1974, that only the PLO could speak for the Palestinian people. Thus, a meeting between Sadat and Hussein in Mid-Janury produced a joint statement stressing the Palestinians' right "to set up their independent political entity" and Jordan's expectations of "very close relations" with that entity. Egyptian Foreign Minister Ismail Fahmy dexterously managed to straddle his government's support for the concept of a Jordan–PLO linkage and its determination to remain ambiguous on that point by noting that "the kind of link between Jordan and Palestine should be left to the two sides to decide, and we encourage such a link."[3]

More fundamentally, Arab inability to advance a comprehensive statement of aims regarding the Palestinians' political future was grounded in the PLO's own ambiguity. The 1968 Palestine National Charter identified the organization's aims in terms clearly calling for Israel's undoing. On the other hand, Yasir Arafat's leadership had moved the organization toward accepting an arrangement providing for a Palestinian state formed of the West Bank and Gaza Strip. Opposition to this trend came from "rejectionist" groups (primarily George Habash's PFLP) and was supported strongly in 1977 by Iraq and Libya. Caught between the demands of preserving internal cohesion and exploring possible political opportunities, the PLO wrapped itself in an intriguing, though noncommittal, nebulousness.

In early January 1977, Dr. Matti Peled, an Israeli peace activist, published a statement agreed to by an unnamed high-ranking PLO member. The statement called for the coexistence of Zionist and Palestinian states in Palestine. Dr. Peled said he was not free to divulge the name of the PLO member. His claim was immediately challenged by PLO Executive Committee member Farouk Kaddoumi. Yet, in early February, UN Secretary General Kurt Waldheim followed up a meeting held in Damascus with Yassir Arafat by praising the Palestinian leadership's "decision" to accept the creation of a Palestinian state alongside Israel.[4] In fact, no such clearcut "decision" had been taken.

The Palestinian movement's mixing of signals was evident at the Thirteenth Session of the Palestine National Council, held in Cairo from March 12 to 20. The meeting passed a stream of hardline resolutions, including a reaffirmation of the 1968 Charter, a rejection of any negotiations "at the Arab and international levels" based on Resolution 242 (which it charged "ignores the Palestinian people and their firm rights"), and a declaration rejecting "all types of American capitulationist settlement and all liquidationist projects." However, the PNC also countenanced more limited political goals by supporting the Palestinians' right to establish "an independent national state on their national soil" and authorizing the PLO to participate in international conferences dealing with the Arab–Zionist conflict.

Fending off opposition from "Rejectionist" delegates, who saw these last two items as establishing grounds for an accommodation based on a Palestinian mini-state sanctioned by the Geneva Peace Conference, the PNC unanimously elected a PLO Executive Committee that was overwhelmingly loyal to Yassir Arafat. The new executive body's independent authority was enhanced when the PNC did not reaffirm an earlier requirement that any decision to attend peace negotiations at Geneva would have to be ratified by a special PNC meeting.[5]

Watching the PNC from Jerusalem, Israeli Prime Minister Yitzhak Rabin opined that dialogue with the PLO should be limited "to the battlefield." Foreign Minister Yigal Allon suggested that the Palestinian organization was indeed divided into two camps: "extremist and more extremist."[6]

Other observers saw Palestinian waffling with kinder eyes. Arafat's hints of willingness to accept some form of association with Jordan, and the PNC's apparent acceptance in principle of an Arab state in part of Palestine, were taken as evidence of Palestinian readiness to explore conditions for coming to terms with the Jewish state. The PLO's refusal to issue a forthright statement of minimal conditions for a settlement was attributed to its narrow margin of maneuver, for in the final analysis the Palestinians' most potent claim to be taken seriously was the threat of undying struggle against Israel's existence. It was a position that Arafat and his colleagues could not lightly abandon, both because of their desire to maintain Palestinian unity and the prospect that acceptance of Israel's legitimacy might be the final trump card in negotiations leading to an Arab state in part of Palestine.

These considerations precluded PLO acceptance of the requirements established in 1975 for any meaningful dialogue with the United States: acceptance of Resolution 242, which made no mention of the Palestinians, and—even more importantly—acceptance of Israel's right to exist. The PLO seemed determined to wait for a firm political offer before unambiguously making one of its own. Jimmy Carter was quickly introduced to the uncertainties, and the perils, that this stand helped foster in the complex politics of the Middle East.

The Carter administration took office with a sense of urgency about the Middle East. The dominant feeling was that step-by-step had proved useful up to a point, but that U.S. policy had lapsed into dangerous inactivity during the past year. The new arbiters of U.S. foreign policy worried that the drift of events in the Middle East might, if not channelled into positive directions, undo the gains of step-by-step and possibly lead to another major Arab–Israeli war.

In planning for a prompt peace initiative, Carter and his chief advisers, Secretary of State Cyrus Vance and National Security Adviser Zbigniew Brzezinski, were also motivated by domestic political considerations. Repeating the calculation made by Richard Nixon when he contemplated the Middle East at the outset of his second term, they reasoned that the president would be strongest during his first year in office. Domestic pressures were expected to be much stronger in 1978, when congressional elections would be held. Even stronger pressures were anticipated as Carter drew closer to the end of his first term.[7] The renewed peacemaking effort therefore had to be launched immediately and aim at producing results by the end of 1977.

Carter, Brzezinski, and Vance began planning the administration's approach to the Middle East immediately after the inauguration. Their views harmonized, being largely influenced by conclusions reached earlier by a private think tank (the Brookings Institution) project on which Brzezinski had served.[8]

In striking contrast to previous administrations, the Carter team began by emphasizing the substance of overall peace rather than procedural questions. The essential points of the administration's concept of peace were the following:

1. Overall, comprehensive peace should be more than mere nonbelligerency. The Arabs should not only accept Israel's right to exist, but also the idea that peace must ultimately involve normal interstate relations, including commerce and peaceful interaction among private citizens.

2. Peace would require an Israeli withdrawal, approximately to its 1967 borders. Minor border modifications could be made in the interest of Israel's security.

3. Israel's security would have to be assured through various measures, possibly including the positioning of Israeli forces in Arab territory beyond Israel's political frontiers and the establishment of demilitarized zones.

4. The Palestinians would have to participate in the formulation of peace. Overall peace must include the creation of a Palestinian political entity, or "homeland," preferably in association with Jordan.

5. Final terms of peace should be negotiated among the parties under the framework of the Geneva Conference.

6. The Soviet Union's support for the peace drive should be enlisted.[9]

The administration's view of a settlement was not presented in comprehensive form as a proposal to be accepted or rejected by the parties in the Middle East. Still less was it advanced as an American decision that was to be imposed. Instead, its substance emerged in various comments made by the president and his advisers during Carter's first months in office.

Early deliberations in Washington led to key tactical decisions governing the new approach. The most important of these was that efforts would be made to bring the protagonists to agree as much as possible on substantive issues prior to reconvening the Geneva Conference. The Soviets would be kept informed but would not be involved directly until the process was well under way. Since Israel was expected to oppose the type of peace envisaged, it was essential that close contacts be maintained with the Arabs and that they be encouraged to perceive the projected conference as an "inducement" to be flexible in preliminary discussions of substantive issues. This logic—despite the administration's reluctance to admit it—required a readiness to exert strong pressure on Israel at some point. Brzezinski recalls:

I . . . told the President on more than one occasion that there would be no break-through to peace without U.S. persuasion of Israel. Israeli internal politics were so stalemated that no Israeli politician could take the responsibility for advocating a genuine compromise unless he could make also the added argument that otherwise U.S.–Israeli relations would suffer. Given the centrality of the U.S. pipeline to Israel's survival, most Israelis instinctively would shrink back from overt defiance of the United States, *provided* they were convinced the United States meant business.[10]

U.S. policy began to unfold in February, with Secretary Vance traveling to Israel, Egypt, Jordan, Saudi Arabia, and Syria. Vance was charged with assessing prevailing attitudes in the Middle East, though he was also to discuss substantive aspects of Washington's new departure with his hosts. Meeting with Rabin and his cabinet in Israel, Vance found the Israelis wary of a possible revival of the Geneva Conference and adamant that Israel would not attend were the PLO present in any guise.

Things went somewhat better in the Arab world, despite Vance's insistence that the PLO would not be welcome to participate in peace negotiations until it accepted Security Council Resolution 242 and Israel's right to exist. President Sadat publicly proposed resolving the problems of a Palestinian representation at Geneva and the final status of a Palestinian "entity" by establishing formal links between Jordan and the PLO before the convocation of a peace conference. On the other hand, Jordan's King Hussein—then engaged in the negotiations with PLO representatives that would lead to his meeting with Arafat the following month—was careful not to appear too enthusiastic over the Egyptian leader's suggestion. Hussein told Vance that formal ties with the PLO could be considered only after other Arab leaders rallied to Sadat's view. The Saudis, to Vance's great joy, expressed support for the peace initiative, and were hopeful that the Arabs would be flexible at Geneva. The tough Syrian, Hafez al-Assad, was cagey, voicing serious doubt that any progress toward a settlement was possible unless the United States was prepared to exert strong pressure on Israel. Still, it seemed clear that he too favored holding a peace conference and that Damascus might be willing to help solve the problem of Palestinian representation.[11]

While Vance had no contact with the PLO during his Middle East tour, the organization took advantage of his presence to let fly another hint of willingness to compromise. This time the vehicle was a statement by al-Fateh's Central Committee promising that the campaign of armed struggle would continue until Palestinian national rights were achieved and a Palestinian "democratic state" established. Palestinian spokesmen then immediately scrambled to point out that the usual qualifying terms "secular" and "in all of Palestine" had been omitted from the declaration. This, they implied, indicated the PLO's willingness to accept a state in part of Palestine. A somewhat more clear sign of PLO moderation came only days after Vance returned to the United States, when the organization reached agreement "in principle" with Jordan on strong, but unspecified, links between the Hashemite Kingdom and any Palestinian state established on the West Bank and Gaza.[12]

All in all, the administration saw reason for optimism in the results of Vance's trip. Key Arab states approved of Washington's initiative and, it could be hoped, would work to promote moderation within the Palestinian movement. Israel remained uneasy and suspicious of the new American approach, but its leaders had not been completely negative. Vance summarized his conclusions by noting that all parties seemed desirous of peace, though profound differences existed over the role of the Palestinians in the move toward a settlement.[13] The administration hoped these could be ironed out through talks between Carter and Middle East leaders that had been arranged by Vance. With the exception of his encounter with Assad, whom Carter would meet in Geneva, the president's high-level contacts on the Middle East were scheduled to be held in Washington.

Yitzhak Rabin called on Carter in early March 1977. The two men failed to establish a personal rapport. Carter found Rabin testy and rigid. When the president tried to break the thickening ice late one night by inviting his guest to look in on "First Daughter" Amy while she slept, Rabin replied with a simple "No, thank you."[14]

The mood reflected underlying political differences. Meeting privately with Rabin, Carter explained that the United States favored rapid negotiations and envisaged a peace based on minimal adjustments of the 1967 borders. What was more, Carter went on, "the Palestinians (including the PLO) would have to be somehow included in the discussion." Obviously upset by this, Rabin urged the president not to undermine Israel's bargaining position with the Arabs by voicing these views publicly. At a "working dinner" with congressional leaders and the president, House Speaker Tip O'Neill asked under what conditions Israel might accept PLO participation in peace talks. Rabin indicated that no such conditions existed. Speaking publicly for the record, the prime minister later rejected the notion that the PLO might attend Geneva as part of a Jordanian delegation.[15]

The next to arrive in Washington was Anwar Sadat. His encounter with the president was completely different from Rabin's. At their first meeting on April 4, Sadat and Carter seem to have developed an abiding mutual trust and confidence. Sadat confirmed his eagerness to see the Geneva Conference reconvene before the end of the year. While characterizing the Palestinian issue as "the core and crux" of the Middle East problem, he also promised to encourage modification of the PLO's formal opposition to Israel's existence. Although Sadat insisted that Egypt wanted peace, he initially balked when Carter urged that peace should involve normal diplomatic intercourse. However, at the end of his two day visit he pledged that "everything" would be "normalized" between Egypt and Israel in the context of a settlement. Carter was even more pleased when Sadat publicly conceded that "some minimal deviations from the 1967 borders" on the West Bank might be acceptable as part of overall peace. Finally, although Sadat was hoping for a substantial arms agreement with the United States, he did not insist on the issue.[16]

During the next six weeks, Carter met with King Hussein, Saudi Arabia's Prince Fahd, and Syria's Hafez al-Assad. Hussein and Fahd supported the administration's hopes for a peace conference, but each— particularly Fahd—stressed the Palestinian issue's centrality to prospects for diplomatic progress. Prince Fahd promised to work for PLO acceptance of Resolution 242.

The president's meeting with Hafez al-Assad was of a different order. During a long and cordial session, the Syrian leader forcefully listed Arab demands: full Israeli withdrawal from all lands occupied in 1967; the honoring of Palestinian refugees' right to return to their original homes or to receive compensation for their displacement; and the return of East Jerusalem to Arab control. This much said, however, he refused to be pinned down on the specifics of a settlement. He seemed to accept the idea that a Palestinian state might be created on the West Bank and Gaza Strip, or that an entity in confederation with Jordan might be established. He seemed favorably disposed toward Carter's initiative. As if to stress Syria's growing moderation, Assad promised to speak out publicly in support of the Carter administration's efforts to promote peace. He carefully pointed out to Carter that such a thing would have meant political suicide in Syria only a year earlier. Yet Assad remained evasive when the president requested his help in bringing the PLO to accept Resolution 242.[17]

As the meetings with Middle East leaders commenced, Carter began openly stressing the outlines of his administration's concept of peace. Ironically, the president's unfamiliarity with the code-word riddled intricacies of Middle East politics caused his first foray into public diplomacy to produce an impression that was exactly the opposite of what he sought to convey. Welcoming Prime Minister Rabin, Carter expressed support for Israel's demand for "defensible" borders. Since Israel's established preference for that term over the phrase "secure and recognized borders" had given it an expansionist connotation, Carter committed a notable blunder. Two days later, he clarified his views by calling for "sovereign and recognized" borders based on substantial Israeli withdrawal and possible security arrangements extending beyond Israel's frontiers.[18]

Carter's largest verbal bombshell came on March 16. Speaking in Clinton, Massachusetts, he set forth various principles for Middle East peace, among which were included Palestinian acceptance of Israel's legitimacy and the need for a Palestinian "homeland." This time, it appeared the president had chosen his words with care. It was widely noted that the term "homeland" was associated with the Balfour Declaration, the 1917 milestone in the Zionists' march to Jewish statehood. Arab reaction was positive, while Israeli spokesmen were predictably dismayed. Carter preferred to allow the ambiguous term to stand on its own. He issued strict instructions forbidding any official "elaborations or clarifications."[19] Several months would pass before the administration finally clarified its position on the possibility of a Palestinian state.

In the meantime, the "homeland" issue provided grist for much Middle East commentary. While Israel's U.S. supporters castigated Carter for having brought up the concept, others urged the president to specify just what he meant by "homeland" in order to bolster moderate Arab forces. In late April, British Foreign Secretary David Owen extended support to the "homeland" concept. In May, following a visit to Moscow by Yasir Arafat, the Carter administration did not deny unconfirmed reports that the Soviet Union had conveyed Arafat's willingness to accept Israel's right to exist in exchange for Israeli endorsement of a Palestinian "homeland." The reports appeared to take on further substance when Carter called on Israel to accept a Palestinian "homeland" in return for PLO acceptance of its legitimate existence. Some days later, the PLO indicated its agreement in principle to the creation of a Palestinian state embracing the West Bank and Gaza Strip and called on Carter to define the location of his envisaged Palestinian "homeland."[20]

Whatever possibilities the administration may have thought existed for pursuing an Israeli–Palestinian accord suddenly seemed undermined by events in Israel. Since the beginning of the year, political activity there had focused on elections scheduled for May 17. In early April, Yitzhak Rabin resigned under a cloud of financial impropriety. Defense Minister Shimon Peres functioned as prime minister during the weeks leading to the elections. To the surprise of almost everyone, Menachem Begin's Likud bloc emerged victorious, ending the string of Labor-dominated coalitions that ruled Israel since its establishment.

Begin's rise to power raised serious questions in Washington. The Likud's insistence that the West Bank (Judea and Samaria) and Gaza were inalienable parts of Israel were well known, as was Menachem Begin's personal history as a terrorist leader under the Mandate and as an ideologically rigid political figure after Israel's creation. The new Israeli government could be expected to take strongly negative positions on the main issues raised by the Carter administration's peace initiative: the idea of a Palestinian "homeland" and the possibility of PLO representation at Geneva. Indeed, the Likud's campaign platform had not only promised that "between the sea and the Jordan River sovereignty will be exclusively Israeli," but also taken an inflexible view of the PLO:

The PLO is not a national liberation movement but an organization of assassins which is a political instrument and an arm in the service of Arab states and which serves the ambitions of Soviet imperialism. A Likud government will seek to bring about its disappearance.[21]

Washington could do little but wait. However, with Begin scheduled to visit in July, the administration started publicly emphasizing the main ideas behind its peace drive. In mid-June, Vice President Mondale delivered a strong speech reiterating the argument that peace required both an Israeli withdrawal approximately to the 1967 borders and the establishment of a Palestinian "entity." He added, however, that Israel should pull back only under conditions of "real peace" and, even then, enjoy special security lines until the permanence of any negotiated settlement was assured. Mondale also said that a Palestinian entity would preferably be linked to Jordan. In making these points the vice president presented them as general policy directions rather than ironclad positions. The United States, he said, had no intention of imposing its view. White House sources described Mondale's speech as an effort to outline the administration's approach to peacemaking while calming the growing ire of Israel's U.S. supporters.[22]

Mondale's assignment to these twin tasks was not accidental. The vice president's political career had established his reputation as a staunch friend of Israel. There was some hope in administration circles that Mondale's presentation of U.S. policy might help enlist the support of American pro-Zionists against Begin's expected onslaught on the developing U.S. peace initiative.[23]

The hope was unwarranted. No sooner had Mondale spoken than New York Senator Jacob Javits delivered a well publicized discourse on Capitol Hill attacking the administration for trying to wring political concessions from Israel. Various prominent senators quickly supported Javits' view.[24]

Javits' attack was only one shot in an ongoing volley of pro-Israeli criticism of the administration's Middle East policy.[25] By early June, Carter was feeling the pressure. In the administration's inner councils he pondered the advisability of a "public showdown" with domestic opponents of his peace campaign. Secretary of State Vance favored a firm stand. Brzezinski sounded out Speaker of the House Tip O'Neill:

I spoke with Tip O'Neill and asked him for his assessment of the situation. He told me point-blank that if the choice came down between the President and the pro-Israel lobby, the country would clearly choose the President—but only if the choice was clearly posed.

Brzezinski also recalls the outcome: " . . . such a choice was never presented directly. The President felt it would be too divisive."[26]

Instead, the administration devoted itself in the weeks preceding Begin's arrival to reaffirming its concept of Mideast peace while simultaneously reinforcing its credentials as a staunch supporter of Israel. Mondale's speech was one step in this direction. Various meetings between Carter and Jewish leaders were another. Then too, despite ostentatious official denials in Washington, an announcement in late June that the administration was willing to approve massive arms deliveries to Israel was taken as another sign of official eagerness to assuage domestic pro-Israeli sentiment. The same was true of Carter's almost simultaneous avowal that Israel's survival was a "pre-eminent priority" of U.S. policy.[27]

The results were just the opposite of what the administration hoped. Instead of gaining support, Carter created an image of vulnerability. In early July, Sol Linowitz, then serving as an unofficial link between the administration and American Jewish groups, spoke with Vance:

The word is out in the Jewish community that if they press hard enough the President will yield. This is apparently the effect of the meeting [Carter] had a couple of days ago with the Jewish leaders.[28]

On July 19, Begin arrived in Washington for a two-day stay. Despite the uneasy state of U.S.–Israeli relations, Carter was impressed by the prime minister's personality. Carter outlined his concept of an Arab–Israeli peace, including "secure borders" and "a Palestinian entity." Begin seemed amenable to all points, save the notion of a Palestinian entity. Carter also raised the question of Jewish settlements in occupied Arab lands, reminding Begin that the established U.S. position held them to be in violation of international law.[29]

The two leaders parted amicably. Carter had presented his views, heard the prime minister's objections, and avoided a public confrontation. Instead, he acceded to Begin's request to refrain from speaking publicly of either Israel's withdrawal to borders approximating those of 1967 or a Palestinian "homeland." In turn, Carter urged Begin to exercise restraint in the creation of settlements in occupied areas. Begin made no commitments. The issue was soon to become a sore point in U.S.–Israeli relations. Days after returning to Israel, the prime minister approved the establishment of three new settlements on the occupied West Bank.

Secretary of State Vance returned to the Middle East at the end of July. This time he carried a set of principles which he hoped would be approved by Arabs and Israelis, and of which the Soviet Union would be informed in the context of a proposal to reconvene the Geneva Conference. The major elements of the package Vance carried comprised the following points:

1. Comprehensive peace should be embodied in peace treaties.
2. Peace negotiations should be based on U.N. Security Council Resolutions 242 and 338.
3. Peace should entail normal inter-state relations.
4. There should be a phased Israeli withdrawal to secure and recognized borders, coupled with mutually agreed security arrangements.
5. "A nonmilitarized Palestinian entity with self-determination" should be created.[30]

Vance also took along various proposals for Palestinian representation at the Geneva Conference. Of these, the administration favored the idea of a unified Arab delegation in which Palestinians would participate.[31]

The trip produced no startling results. Having already refused to deal with the PLO, even should that organization accept Resolution 242, Begin's government was as opposed to Palestinian representation at Geneva as it was to the concept of a Palestinian entity. The Arabs, by now growing increasingly doubtful of the implications of Washington's concept of an "entity," were cautious and noncommital. Vance came to the obvious conclusion that wide gaps still separated the parties to the conflict, though he seemed to place the lion's share of the blame on Israel.[32]

Still, the demonstration of U.S. determination to proceed to Geneva seemed to have some productive impact. Syria, at long last, joined Egypt and Jordan in informing Vance that the Arabs were willing to sign peace treaties with Israel as part of a Middle East settlement. Near the end of August, Assad—much to Carter's relief—also moved closer to the U.S. preference for a joint Arab delegation by suggesting that Arab representation at Geneva might be accomplished under the auspices of the Arab League. By the end of September, Syria and Jordan explicitly came out in support of a joint Arab delegation to the peace conference.[33]

However, the problem of Palestinian representation was still unresolved. Whether or not a joint Arab delegation attended the conference's opening session, the unanswered question was what role, if any, would be assigned to the PLO in actual negotiations.

Because of its 1975 commitment to Israel, Washington felt unable to explore possible conditions for PLO participation through direct contact with the organization's spokesmen. The upshot was a veritable ballet of public diplomacy, with U.S. and PLO leaders exchanging messages through the world press. A flurry of declarations and statements produced by both sides during September and August brought no agreement but did clarify the basic gulf between the administration and the PLO. Each seemed anxious to inaugurate direct contact, yet neither could see the way past its minimal requirements for doing so. For Carter, the sine qua non of dialogue (and of the PLO's participation in the Geneva Conference) remained PLO acceptance of Resolution 242 and Israel's right to exist. Apart from this, however, the administration was willing to be flexible—the PLO was invited to "accept" the UN resolution with reservations regarding its implications for Palestinian rights. Yet, given Israel's refusal to meet the PLO under any circumstances, Washington could not definitely promise that Palestinian cooperation would be rewarded by a seat at Geneva. Instead, U.S. spokesmen referred to Washington's readiness to "work with" the PLO and to support its bid to attend the peace conference.[34]

Arafat and his colleagues were intrigued, but they were also wary. Having already accepted in principle the prospect of a Palestinian state comprising the West Bank and Gaza, with some unclear relationship to Jordan, the PLO would accept Resolution 242 only at the price of gaining support for its political claims. Various ideas were advanced by PLO leaders. They suggested that the organization might accept the UN resolution were it amended to acknowledge Palestinian national rights, or, failing that, accept a new Security Council measure that reaffirmed Resolution 242 while supporting Palestinian national rights. In effect, PLO leaders indicated a willingness to accept the substance of Resolution 242 if the United States would balance its commitment to Israel's existence by upholding the goal of a Palestinian state on the West Bank and Gaza.

Throughout this ultimately sterile exchange, Israel remained opposed to PLO involvement in the peace process.[35] However, the Israeli government did agree that individual Palestinians might participate in the Geneva proceedings as part of a unified Arab delegation. Various indications that Israel would accept Palestinians on a Jordanian delegation led Washington to hope a workable arrangement might be within reach.[36]

By late September 1977, Arab governments believed the United States was committed to a Geneva format that would involve a unified Arab delegation "possibly including not well-known members of the PLO." The plan called for the Arab delegation to negotiate with Israel through national subcommittees after an opening plenary session. The West Bank, Gaza, the Palestinian question, and the refugee issue would be dealt with in talks among "Israel, Jordan, Egypt, the Palestinians and perhaps others."[37]

THE GENEVA BUBBLE BURSTS

The problem of Palestinian representation at the Geneva Conference had not been settled when Egyptian Foreign Minister Ismail Fahmy arrived in Washington on September 21. Fahmy and his assistants dealt with a high level U.S. team that included Carter, Mondale, Vance, Brzezinski, and several advisers.

Fahmy entered the discussions convinced that the United States was embarking on a pivotal stage in its pursuit of peace in the Middle East:

My discussions with Yasser Arafat had made it clear that a major obstacle to the PLO's acceptance of [UN Resolution 242] was the clause referring to "the right of every state to live in peace." Arafat rightly feared that if the PLO accepted that clause it would in practice unilaterally recognize the state of Israel and its right to live in peace, but would receive no guarantee for or recognition of the right of the Palestinians to live in peace within an independent national entity. It was imperative that the Palestinians be given a guarantee that the United States recognized the Palestinians' right to statehood.[38]

The foreign minister put forward various options. He first suggested that the U.S. acquiesce in a new Security Council resolution that would support Palestinian national rights while upholding Resolution 242. Carter was firm: "I want to be very clear that, if your proposal is to amend 242, the United States will veto it."[39]

Trying another approach, Fahmy proposed that Carter extend an indirect commitment to the PLO by assuring Egypt that "a national homeland for the Palestinians would be established in the West Bank and Gaza." "I cannot give you the assurance," replied the president. The foreign minister then suggested that Washington might push for mutual recognition by Israel and the PLO:

Mr. President, you want us to put pressure on the PLO to accept Resolution 242. We, in turn, believe that it is fair and equitable to ask you to bear pressure on Israel to recognize the PLO.

Carter did not see this as an option. Apparently believing that U.S.–PLO contacts would be productive, and seemingly convinced that time remained for cultivating relations between the two, he urged Fahmy to work toward that end. Fahmy recalls that in trying to explain some of the constraints binding the White House, the president argued that Arabs exaggerated his ability to sway Israel:

It is important that you do not forget that my influence on Israel is proportionally related to the scope of support which I get from American public opinion, Congress and the Jewish circles in this country. I want to be abundantly clear that in the absence of such triangular support my ability to influence Israel is minimal.[40]

A week after this encounter, Carter tried once more to elicit a PLO concession that would help finalize plans for the Geneva Conference. Although the Israeli government remained opposed to the inclusion of PLO members on a unified delegation at Geneva, Carter's remarks were the clearest public indication of the strength of his desire to involve the PLO in the peace process:

If the PLO should go ahead and say "we endorse UN Resolution 242, we don't think it adequately addresses the Palestinian issue because it only refers to refugees and we think we have a further interest than that," that would suit us O.K. We would then begin to meet and work with the PLO.[41]

Actually, Carter's overture had been made privately some weeks earlier when, with Saudi Foreign Minister Prince Fahd serving as intermediary, Cyrus Vance offered the PLO leadership a U.S.-drafted statement that Washington was prepared to acknowledge as constituting the required acceptance of Resolution 242:

The PLO accepts United Nations Security Council Resolution 242 with the reservation that the resolution does not make adequate reference to the question of the Palestinians since it fails to make any reference to a homeland for the Palestinian people. It is recognized that the language of Resolution 242 relates to the right of all states in the Middle East to live in peace.

Vance's offer failed to win the votes required for acceptance by the PLO Executive Committee. Prince Fahd attributed the outcome to the heavy opposition of extremist elements within the PLO as well as to a generalized reluctance within the organization to accept Israel's right to exist without guarantees that minimal Palestinian political demands would be met.[42]

By resurrecting the offer publicly, Carter clearly seems to have been trying to bolster the position of PLO moderates. Moreover, he carefully tied his move to coincide with a startling new twist in his search for Mideast peace.

On October 1, 1977, two days after Carter's appeal to the PLO, the United States and the Soviet Union issued a joint statement on the Middle East. The PLO immediately endorsed it, a stand that reflected the generally positive reaction the statement evoked in the Arab world.[43] On the other hand, Israeli opposition was immediate and unyielding, and U.S. domestic reaction was massively negative.

Since the United States and the Soviet Union were technically still co-chairing the suspended Geneva Conference, the joint statement was intended as a basis for reconvening that forum. It had taken shape during the previous months over the course of several meetings between Secretary of State Vance and Foreign Minister Gromyko. The dramatic reversal of Kissinger's policy of excluding the Soviets from peacemaking efforts stemmed from the Carter administration's belief that compre-hensive peace could not be attained without Moscow's active support.

Superficially, the U.S.–Soviet declaration was largely a reiteration of the administration's well-known position in favor of a settlement based on Israel's withdrawal from "territories occupied...in 1967" and the establishment of "normal peaceful relations" between Israel and her neighbors.[44] However, as an expression of U.S. policy it contained—in addition to the radical change it implied in Washington's view of the Soviet factor in Middle East peacemaking—some potentially significant innovations. For example, the text made no mention of Security Council Resolution 242. Moreover, the joint statement argued that a settlement should ensure "the legitimate rights of the Palestinian people." This was not only a new aspect to Washington's approach, but it also ran counter to Israel's view that Palestinians had no collective rights.

The U.S.–Soviet statement would almost certainly have drawn heavy fire from Israel at any point during Carter's presidency. However, the declaration's timing could scarcely have been better calculated to increase the chances of an emotionally bitter reception in Jerusalem. Only two weeks earlier, the Carter administration had apparently pressured re-luctant Israeli policymakers to abort a planned massive assault on PLO forces in Lebanon.[45]

Israeli officialdom, pro-Israeli American groups, and U.S. proponents of a hardline policy toward the Soviet Union shared an immediate—and deep—hostility toward the October 1977 declaration. Concern for Israel led many of the administration's critics to focus on the possibility that Washington was edging toward acceptance of a Palestinian state as part of a Middle East settlement. Others objected to the new policy direction because they saw it as needlessly offering political gains to the Soviet Union.

Within three days, the White House received some nine thousand telegrams of protest from Jews around the country. One hundred fifty members of the House of Representatives signed a letter expressing "grave concern" over the U.S.–Soviet statement. A typical charge was made by New York City mayoral candidate Edward Koch, who accused State Department arabists of selling Israel "down the river." Numerous public figures charged the administration with preparing to impose a settlement on Israel while allowing the Soviet Union back into the main-stream of Middle East diplomacy.[46]

The outpouring of opposition propelled the administration into im-mediate efforts to mollify its critics. Speaking before the United Nations on October 4, Carter rejected the possibility of an imposed Middle East peace and stressed the relevance of Resolution 242 to the peace process. While repeating his support of Palestinian "rights," he carefully included a novel stress on the notion that such "rights" would have to be defined through negotiations. Rabbi Alexander Schindler, chairman of the Con-ference of Presidents of Major American Jewish Organizations, was re-portedly pleased by the president's presentation.[47]

That same evening, President Carter and Israeli Foreign Minister Moshe Dayan held a crucial meeting in a New York hotel. Present also were Israeli Ambassador Simcha Dinitz, Vance, and Brzezinski. It was a tense encounter. As the price of going to Geneva, the Israelis demanded guarantees that the United States would neither pursue the idea of a Palestinian state nor seek to pressure Israel into a settlement not to its liking. Carter tried to salvage what he could of the U.S. initiative. Both parties threatened the ultimate sanction of appealing against the other to U.S. public opinion. Citing passages from his private journal, Brze-zinski recalls the confrontation:

A long negotiating session during the day with Dayan which extended into late at night, interrupted by dinner which the President had to attend.... Dayan in effect blackmailed the President by saying that unless he had assurances that we would oppose an independent West Bank and that we would give [Israel] eco-nomic and military aid, he would have to indicate our unwillingness in his public comments here in the United States. The President clearly indicated that this was impossible but at the same time tried to get Dayan to approve an approach to Geneva which would permit the Israelis to attend. Both men were aware of the psychological value of threatening a confrontation. At one instance, Dayan said, "We need to have some agreed formula, but I can go to Israel and to the American Jews. I have to say that there is an agreement and not a confrontation." To which the President replied, "We might have a confrontation unless you are willing to cooperate. But a confrontation would be very damaging to Israel and to the support of the American public for Israel."[48]

Despite his reference to possible confrontation, Carter did not want an open clash. The outcome of the talk with Dayan was a joint statement and a "working paper." Brzezinski appraised the results:

In the end, we got a compromise statement which pledges the Israelis to go [to Geneva], but I wonder whether Dinitz and Dayan did not emerge from the meeting with an excessively self-assured view of the degree to which the President is susceptible to pressure. In some instances and on some issues [Carter] was quite tough; but he didn't go far enough, in my judgment, to indicate that if challenged he would go to the country and there would be an all-out confrontation.[49]

Released in the early hours of October 5, the U.S.–Israeli statement reaffirmed the importance of Resolutions 242 and 338 as the agreed basis for negotiations at Geneva. It also stated that "acceptance of the joint U.S.–USSR statement of October 1, 1977, by the parties is not a prerequisite for the reconvening and conduct of the Geneva Conference."[50] Even more upsetting to Arab opinion was the U.S.–Israeli "working paper" establishing a framework for the projected Geneva Conference. The document envisaged a unified Arab delegation that would include Palestinian Arabs but which, after the conference's opening session, would be split into national groups for separate substantive negotiations with Israel. The West Bank and Gaza "issues" would be "discussed" in a working group formed of Israel, Jordan, Egypt, and the Palestinian Arabs.

Arab disillusionment deepened when it became known that the first draft suggested by the United States differed markedly from the final U.S.–Israeli "working paper." Washington's original version included clauses calling for the participation of low-level PLO members and indicating that the question of a Palestinian "entity" should be part of the Geneva Conference agenda. In addition, the earlier draft had proposed that the plenary meeting involving the unified Arab delegation remain in session throughout the conference. It had also stated that the question of the West Bank and Gaza would be "negotiated," rather than merely "discussed."[51]

In essence, the position now taken by the Carter administration suggested that Geneva would simply provide a cover for separate direct negotiations between Israel, on the one hand, and Egypt, Syria, Jordan, and possibly Lebanon on the other. PLO participation was clearly out of the question, and it was exceedingly doubtful that a Palestinian "entity" would even be "discussed," much less "negotiated." Syria, the PLO, and Jordan were dismayed by the U.S.–Israeli stand. Among Arab leaders, only Sadat still claimed passionate interest in the Geneva Conference and even he futilely urged the working paper's amendment to permit PLO participation.

The man most anxious to save the meeting at Geneva was Jimmy Carter. In the turmoil caused by the U.S.–Soviet declaration, the U.S.–Israeli statement, and the "working paper," he worried that "the whole process was breaking down."[52] As a last resort, he appealed to Anwar Sadat for a strong public endorsement and statesmanlike gesture to help revive momentum toward Geneva.

Sadat's answer arrived in early November. He suggested resolving the

Middle East problem by convening a meeting in East Jerusalem of the leaders of China, Egypt, France, Britain, Israel, Jordan, the PLO, Syria, the United States, and the USSR. Carter, Mondale, Vance, and Brzezinski wondered whether the Egyptian president was "losing his sense of reality."[53]

In retrospect it seems doubtful that Sadat's balance was impaired. More likely, his bizarre proposal was simply a means of responding to his "friend Jimmy" with a message that manifested good intentions but could hardly lead to practical results. For Sadat was in the process of deciding—or perhaps had already decided—that Geneva was no longer worth pursuing. On November 9, he announced his willingness to meet with Begin in Jerusalem. Astonishing the world by his quick acceptance of the forthcoming invitation, Sadat appeared before the Knesset and delivered an eloquent plea for peace while admonishing his listeners that a settlement required the return of all occupied lands, including East Jerusalem, and acceptance of the Palestinians' right to statehood.[54]

It is impossible to determine precisely what impelled the Egyptian leader to undertake the historic journey. Interviewed shortly after his trip, Sadat pointed to the procedural nitpicking over Geneva as the root of his decision. His autobiography makes much the same claim, but the account is imbued with hints of lofty inspiration belying the notion that the action was taken in a pique of procedural impatience. It is, of course, possible that both impatience and highmindedness drove him. But it may also be that mundane, pragmatic political calculations were centrally important.[55]

Without telling Carter, or Foreign Minister Ismail Fahmy, Sadat had sent an emissary to a secret rendezvous in Morocco with Israeli Foreign Minister Moshe Dayan in mid-September. It is uncertain just what transpired. Some have suggested that the initial contact with Dayan paved the way for Sadat's trip to Jerusalem on the basis of confidential Israeli pledges to return the Sinai to Egyptian control in exchange for a separate peace. Ismail Fahmy later considered this explanation but found no evidence to support it. He concluded that Sadat acted impulsively in undertaking his journey without really contemplating its repercussions.[56]

In any case, Sadat had good reason to grow increasingly concerned about the options available to him once Carter's Geneva scheme began to unravel. Sinai II had undermined Egypt's war option, and probably completely destroyed that alternative under Sadat's leadership. The Egyptian president was locked into an agreement that could be superseded only by a peace treaty with Israel—unless he was willing to demolish the budding special relationship between his country and the United States. And that was hardly a choice to be contemplated. Cairo's growing ties to Washington had produced some $2.5 billion in U.S. aid since 1975, as well as the beginning of an arms supply relationship, and it promised to be steadily more fruitful in the future. On the other hand, Sadat's bridges to the Soviet Union seemed burned beyond repair.[57]

With the U.S. approach to the Geneva Conference having alienated Arab opinion, Sadat's alternatives were limited. He could futilely stand by Carter's Geneva plan—without altering Egypt's predicament while almost certainly suffering the unforeseeable, but surely uncomfortable, consequences of a renewed estrangement between the Arab world and the United States—or he could take radical action that might benefit his country by fundamentally altering the diplomatic environment. To the extent that such considerations motivated him, Sadat had very strong reasons to believe that once Cairo embarked on direct negotiations with Israel, Egypt could fully count on Washington to support its territorial claim to all of Sinai up to the international border.[58] In choosing the latter course, Sadat did not simply turn his back on Israel's other Arab antagonists, including the Palestinians. In the months ahead, he would strive for a firm linkage between progress toward Egyptian–Israeli peace and the demands of these other Arab actors. Yet, it would also be clear that Sadat accorded priority to removing all traces of Israel's presence from Egyptian soil.

The decision to go to Jerusalem was costly. Algeria, South Yemen, Libya, Syria, Iraq, and the PLO were outraged. Saudi Arabia and the Gulf States were visibly shocked and displeased. Foreign Minister Fahmy resigned, and when Sadat tried to replace him with Mahmoud Riad, then serving as Minister of State for Foreign Affairs, he too resigned. Yet the majority of the Egyptians, and, more importantly, the army, stuck by the president.

Upon returning from Jerusalem, Sadat proceeded as though nothing unusual had happened. He invited the prospective Geneva Conference participants to gather for a preparatory session in Cairo. The only ones to arrive were the United States and Israel, whose representatives met the Egyptians on December 14 for the essentially empty exercise.

At almost the same time, Menachem Begin arrived in Washington with a peace plan he was preparing to submit to the Egyptians. The proposal's central features focused on the Sinai, the West Bank, and Gaza. Egyptian sovereignty over most of the Sinai was recognized, though Begin's plan demanded that Israeli settlements in the area be preserved. The West Bank and Gaza were considered areas over which Israel would refrain from pressing, while not abandoning, its claim to sovereignty for at least five years. In the interval, the areas' Arab inhabitants would be granted "administrative autonomy" while Israel would remain responsible for overall security. Israeli citizens would retain rights of settlement.[59]

Left at loose ends by the recent twist of Middle East events, the Carter administration tried to put the best face possible on these suggestions, knowing full well they would be unacceptable to Egypt or any other Arab actor. Brzezinski believed that Begin's "administrative autonomy" would probably be seen by Arabs as no more than a formula for creating a Palestinian "Basutoland." Yet Begin advanced the suggestion as an interim arrangement, and that implied the necessity of further developments at some point. Brzezinski bowed to necessity, recommending that the administration abandon the wrecked search for comprehensive peace and return to step-by-step.[60]

The administration had little alternative. Carter's stalled drive to Geneva could not be restarted. Begin's proposal was received warmly, if with reservations. Somewhat to its own surprise and discomfort, the Carter administration found itself committed to promoting a separate Egyptian–Israeli peace.

The new direction made the Palestinian issue of less immediate concern. Carter, who had previously expressed reservations about the ultimate creation of a Palestinian state only as a matter of personal "preference," now reiterated that position in a context (the debate between Sadat and Begin over just that issue) that gave his words virtually the force of a policy statement. Yet, while the broader elements of the Arab–Israel conflict were pushed to the perimeter of American attention, the administration remained uneasy. Its fear was that a separate peace between Egypt and Israel not linked to Israel's relations with its other neighbors would result in an unstable situation that could ultimately redound to Soviet benefit.[61]

TOWARD AN EGYPTIAN–ISRAELI PEACE

Menachem Begin responded with fixed purpose to the overture symbolized by Sadat's Jerusalem trip: he wanted a separate peace with Egypt that would leave Israel in control of all areas it had occupied since 1967, except for the Sinai Peninsula. Even there, although Begin realized from the beginning that Israel's presence in the Sinai would have to be greatly reduced to achieve a settlement with Cairo, he hoped to extract maximum concessions.

Contrasting with this was the position taken by Anwar Sadat before the Knesset: Israel should withdraw from all Arab territories occupied in 1967, including East Jerusalem, and the Palestinians' right to statehood should be upheld.

Having failed to resurrect the old territory-for-peace formula as the guiding principle of an effort to promote a definitive end to the Arab–Israeli conflict, the Carter administration gave up Geneva as a lost cause to support the thrust toward an Egyptian–Israeli accommodation. At the request of both parties, it was not long before the United States assumed a central role in the new peacemaking venture. However, a major concern of the Carter administration was that an Israeli–Egyptian rapprochement neither be, nor be perceived as, simply a self-contained separate peace. There was, therefore, a marked convergence of preferences from the outset between Washington and Cairo, and it was obvious that Sadat counted heavily on U.S. pressure on Israel benefitting the Arabs.

Sadia Touval succinctly describes the essential nature of the trilateral negotiations that in fits and starts characterized the sixteen-month interval between Sadat's Jerusalem journey and the signing of the Egyptian–Israeli peace treaty in March 1979:

The agenda for the negotiations...crystallized around three main issues. One was the bilateral Egyptian–Israel issue—the time schedules of Israel's withdrawal from Sinai, security and arms limitations arrangements, the future of the Israeli settlements in the Sinai, and the pace of the normalization of Egyptian–Israeli relations. The second was the Palestinian question and the future of the West Bank and Gaza. The third was the form and degree of the link between the first two issues. Would the settlement of bilateral issues in a peace treaty stand on its own, be conditional upon the settlement of the Palestinian problem, or would it perhaps be linked to the Palestinian problem only in a vague and imprecise manner?[62]

From the outset, Anwar Sadat failed to appreciate the depth of the Carter administration's reluctance to be exposed to charges of pressuring Jerusalem into a peace agreement. Still smarting from the unproductive 1977 confrontation with Israel and its American supporters, the administration had no heart for being accused once more of trying to impose a pro-Arab settlement. Part of its concern over this was manifested by a firm decision to refrain from using U.S. aid as a lever to generate Israeli flexibility in the peace negotiations with Egypt.[63]

While this helped the administration avoid public conflicts with Israel that approched the dimensions of its losing struggle in the fall of 1977, U.S.–Israeli relations never became really harmonious during the remainder of Carter's tenure. Three issues produced serious frictions between Jerusalem and Washington after plans for the Geneva Conference collapsed. Two were longstanding problems arising from Israel's policies toward Jewish settlements in occupied Arab lands and toward Lebanon. The third, which became a major point of controversy in the spring of 1978, was the transfer of U.S. arms to Saudi Arabia and Egypt.

Although the United States had generally refused to support UN condemnations of Israel's construction of Jewish settlements in the occupied territories—and, indeed, made use of its veto to prevent the Security Council from formally acting on the issue until 1979—Washington's official position was that the settlements violated international law. In March 1976, ambassador to the United Nations William Scranton offered this description of the U.S. position:

... my Government believes that international law sets the appropriate standards [for judging Israeli settlements in occupied areas]. An occupier must maintain the occupied areas as intact as possible.... The Fourth Geneva Convention speaks directly to the issue of population transfer in Article 49: "The occupying power shall not ... transfer parts of its civilian population into the territory it occupies."

Clearly then substantial resettlement of the Israeli civilian population in occupied territories, including East Jerusalem, is illegal under the Convention and cannot be considered to have prejudged the outcome of future negotiations between the parties on the location of the borders of states of the Middle East.[64]

In late 1976, the United States adhered to a Security Council "consensus statement" strongly deploring all Israeli steps to alter the occupied territories' demographic composition or geographic nature. The statement particularly denounced the establishment of settlements, declaring the practice to have "no legal validity" and to constitute "an obstacle to peace."

With Menachem Begin promising an accelerated settlement program, the issue was thrust to the forefront of international discussion. Israel's new minister of agriculture, Ariel Sharon, was recognized as a staunch supporter of the extremist Gush Emunim movement. He was soon voicing long-range plans for populating a security arc stretching through the Jordan Valley to the tip of the Sinai Peninsula, with up to two million settlers.[65]

Disturbing though Sharon's enthusiasm may have been to many, he seemed to be revelling in grandiose dreams rather than immediate threats. Yet, if millions of Jewish colonists were at most a distant possibility, Begin's government took prompt, effective, and sustained action to bind the occupied lands closer to Israel by substantially increasing the numbers of settlements and settlers.

By early 1978, Israel had constructed sixty-two settlements in the occupied areas. The corresponding figure at the end of 1976 had been twenty-nine.[66] Demographic changes strikingly reflected Likud policy. Excluding Jerusalem's expanded environs, the Jewish population of the West Bank was only 3,176 by the end of 1976. Under Begin, this figure rose in 1978 to over 7,000 thousand; in 1979, to 10,000; and by the end of 1983 to 27,500.[67]

The rapid rate of expansion was largely the result of the Likud's development of semi-urban and suburban bedroom-commuter settlements, rather than the rural-agricultural settlements associated with Zionist tradition. Attracted by a modern suburban lifestyle, government subsidized loans, and publicly financed infrastructural amenities—particularly an expanded and modern highway system—thousands of middle class, white collar workers opted to reside in the West Bank while retaining professional and social ties to Israel's urban centers.[68]

The settlements issue soured U.S.–Israeli relations throughout Carter's term of office. From his first meeting with Begin, Carter fruitlessly pleaded for Israel to moderate the campaign to settle the occupied areas. By the end of 1977, the frustrated and embittered president fumed over the situation and privately expressed unwillingness "to maintain a policy in which in effect we are financing their conquests and they simply defy us in an intransigent fashion and generally make a mockery of our advice and our preferences." Secretary of State Vance, an experienced international lawyer who was personally convinced of the illegality of Israel's actions, urged that Washington retaliate for further settlement construction by rescinding its commitment not to negotiate with the PLO.[69]

Despite irate private outbursts, Carter took no substantial action against Israel. The greatest manifestation of the administration's displeasure came in 1979, when a U.S. abstention finally permitted the Security Council's fourteen other members to pass a resolution demanding a halt to Israel's settlement program.[70] The inescapable conclusion appears to be that Carter, having felt the full brunt of Israel's influence on domestic politics in the fall of 1977, and still hoping to achieve some major step toward Middle East peace, was convinced that a major confrontation over the settlements issue had best be avoided.

U.S.–Israeli relations were also adversely affected by Israel's policy toward Lebanon, where Palestinian guerrillas had secured a solid foothold along Israel's northern border. Fearing that major hostilities in Lebanon would derail hopes for a negotiated peace, the Carter administration was annoyed by what it perceived as the Begin government's excessive inclination to intervene in that country. Carter and Begin had already clashed in September 1977 over an Israeli incursion into South Lebanon. In March 1978, goaded by a terrorist raid that left over thirty dead, Israel launched a major invasion that took its forces up to the Litani River. Although Washington expressed understanding of Jerusalem's security concerns, it pressed for a prompt Israeli withdrawal. The United States joined in a Security Council resolution calling for an Israeli pullback and the deployment in south Lebanon of a UN peacekeeping force. Relations between the United States and Israel were strained until Israeli troops withdrew in mid-June, after having installed a rebel Lebanese Army major, Saad Haddad, as head of a friendly surrogate security force in south Lebanon.[71]

However, the issue that overshadowed other differences between the United States and Israel during much of 1978 was the administration's ultimately successful effort to link the sale of warplanes to Israel, Egypt, and Saudi Arabia in a "package deal." Announced in mid-February, the proposed sale involved sixty F–15 aircraft for Saudi Arabia, fifteen F–15's and seventy-five F–16's for Israel, and fifty F–5E airplanes for Egypt. Anxious to cultivate the support of moderate Arab regimes, and mindful of U.S. dependency on Saudi oil, the administration let it be known that negative congressional reaction to any part of the proposed sale would result in a presidential veto of the entire package. The strategy was designed to circumvent the predictable opposition of Israel's supporters to the transfer of advanced weapons to Arab countries. It soon embroiled the administration in a protracted and convoluted struggle that was, with great difficulty, narrowly won in May 1978.[72]

Although controversies over Jewish settlements, Lebanon, and the aircraft package were prominent features of U.S.–Israeli relations during the winter and spring of 1977/78, they did not prevent Washington from rapidly, albeit ineffectually, becoming involved in the effort to produce an accord between Israel and Egypt. On Christmas Day, 1977, Menachem Begin and Sadat met on the banks of the Suez Canal at the city of Ismailia. The two leaders did not get on well, and the encounter was decidedly chilly. Begin presented his proposals for an Israeli withdrawal to the international border and "administrative autonomy" for the Arabs of the West Bank and Gaza. The plan also called for Israel's retention of settlements and civilian-controlled airfields in the Sinai.

Apprised earlier of the Begin plan by the United States, Sadat had already informed Israeli Defense Minister Ezer Weizman that it was unacceptable. He repeated this to Begin, insisting that no Israeli presence could remain in Sinai. He suggested that agreement be reached on a brief statement of principles calling for peace based on Israel's full withdrawal from territories occupied in 1967, Security Council Resolution 242, and a just settlement of the Palestinian problem founded on the right to self-determination. The talks ended with Begin's refusal to join in such a declaration.

However, the two leaders agreed to establish two joint committees. A "political" committee was to meet in Jerusalem and continue searching for a mutually acceptable set of principles. At the same time, a "military" committee would sit in Cairo to discuss security arrangements between the two countries.

The differences were simply too great for such easy resolution. The political committee ceased functioning almost immediately after its first session on January 17, 1978; as Sadat, convinced of Israel's intransigence, ordered the Egyptian delegation to suspend its work.

In the meantime, having become a de facto participant in the Egyptian–Israeli negotiations by virtue of Begin's effort to gain its approval of his peace plan, Washington became progressively more involved. In early January, Carter saw Sadat briefly in Egypt and announced a position that later became known as the "Aswan Formula." The "formula" tried to bridge the gap between the Egyptian and Israeli positions on the Palestinian question by affirming that peace required resolving the Palestinian problem "in all its aspects" as well as recognition of "the legitimate rights of the Palestinian people." Its key point, however, was that a settlement must "enable the Palestinians to participate in the determination of their own future."[73]

In effect, this placed the United States on record against the application of the principle of self-determination to the Palestinians. As Seth Tillman puts it:

The Palestinian people were by this means put on notice that although they might "participate" in deciding their own future, Israel and perhaps others would participate as well, guaranteeing that there would be no independent Palestinian state. The Wilsonian postulate was thus amended so as to retain most of its language while being divested of most of its meaning.[74]

The Aswan formula would underlie Washington's approach to the Palestinian factor in its subsequent efforts to promote peace between Egypt and Israel.

No progress was made over the next several months toward reconciling the Egyptian and Israeli positions on the West Bank and Gaza and the possible retention of a minimal Israeli presence in Sinai. By late March 1978, both Sadat and Begin had journeyed to Washington, the former to be encouraged in his commitment to the peace process, the latter to be scolded for denying Resolution 242's applicability to the West Bank and Gaza and for his generally rigid approach to Egypt.[75]

Carter was convinced that Sadat would never agree to an Israeli presence in the Sinai. Yet the president felt strongly that the Egyptian leader would not insist on a Palestinian state and that he could be brought to accept an interim arrangement for the West Bank and Gaza based on the withdrawal of Israeli forces to security enclaves and the granting of self-rule to the local populace. On this basis, he forcefully confronted the Israeli delegation in Washington:

In the meeting with Begin and Dayan I described the presumptions that Sadat and I had worked out for a possible peace settlement, namely: no complete withdrawal by Israel from the West Bank; no independent Palestinian nation; self-rule in the West Bank–Gaza Strip; withdrawal of Israeli forces to negotiated security outposts; some modification of the western boundaries of the West Bank; devolution of power to the local authorities from both Israel and Jordan; no claim of sovereignty (by either nation) for a five-year period; at the end of the five-year period the Palestinian Arabs who live in the occupied zones will have the right to vote on either an affiliation with Israel or Jordan or continuation of the so-called "interim government"...; the ceasing of new or expanded settlements during the time of active negotiation.... I then read to Begin and his group my understanding of their position: not willing to withdraw politically or militarily from any part of the West Bank; not willing to stop the construction of new settlements or the expansion of existing settlements; not willing to withdraw the Israeli settlers from the Sinai, or even leave them there under UN or Egyptian protection; not willing to acknowledge that UN Resolution 242 applies to the West Bank–Gaza area; not willing to grant the Palestinian Arabs real authority, or a voice in the determination of their own future.... Although Begin said this was a negative way to express their position, he did not deny the accuracy of any of it.[76]

A later meeting with Begin in May was equally unproductive. Yet Carter's growing frustration did not lead him to consider challenging the Israeli government by threatening or taking restrictive action on economic and military aid. Instead, the president was tempted to end U.S. involvement in the stalled Israeli–Egyptian talks and publicly place the blame on Israel. The president's short flirtation with this possible course apparently stemmed from weariness with what he was beginning to see as as thankless task that was eroding his standing within the Democratic party.[77]

Tempting though the option may have been, its exercise would have been very costly. Throughout the spring and early summer, high administration officials, including Cyrus Vance and Walter Mondale, invested much effort traveling to the Middle East to seek an end to the Israeli–Egyptian deadlock while simultaneously reassuring moderate Arab regimes that Washington's endeavors constituted steps toward an eventual comprehensive peace. To have simply dropped out of Middle East diplomacy would not only have underscored Washington's reluctance to pressure Israel, and possibly increased chances for renewed conflict in the area, but also exposed the administration to criticism from every side of the domestic spectrum for having permitted U.S. policy in the Middle East to fall into tatters. At the same time, such an ignominious end to the administration's Middle East peacemaking could have been expected to provide opportunities for a resurgence of Soviet influence in the region.

In late July 1978, Carter decided on a daring gamble. He would meet Anwar Sadat and Menachem Begin in the secluded presidential retreat at Camp David for open-ended discussions aimed at breaking the deadlock. It was, of course, a step carrying great risk for his personal prestige. Yet, by dramatizing the urgent necessity of smashing the diplomatic logjam that threatened the hopes for peace raised months earlier by Sadat's journey to Jerusalem, Carter created heavy indirect pressures on the leaders of Egypt and Israel, each of whom for reasons of his own still hoped an accommodation might be possible:

Mediation at the summit carried the usual advantages and disadvantages of summit diplomacy. Carter, who convened the conference, and by virtue of his role as mediator, took the greatest political risk. But the prestige of Sadat and Begin were also at stake. By its very conspicuousness, and because the prestige of all three leaders had become committed, failure would have been dramatic. It would have hurt all three politically; worse, it would have increased tensions in the Middle East...the circumstances of the conference itself created strong pressures on Egypt and on Israel to make concessions, and greatly intensified the American motivation to secure success....[78]

None of this diminished the validity of the insightful admonition Brzezinski delivered to Carter on the summit's eve:

Sadat cannot afford a failure and knows it; both Sadat and Begin think you cannot afford a failure; but Begin probably believes that a failure at Camp David will hurt you and Sadat, but not him. He may even want to see Sadat discredited, and you weakened, thus leaving him with the tolerable status quo, instead of pressures to change his lifelong beliefs concerning "Judea and Samaria."

Sadat will define success in terms of substance, and in particular on Israel's commitment to the principle of withdrawal on all fronts. Begin will define success largely in terms of procedural arrangements and will be very resistant to pressures for substantive concessions.[79]

The outcome of twelve grueling days of negotiations at Camp David—during which Carter deservedly gained fame as a tireless and energetic master of mediation—verified most of Brzezinski's analysis.[80] Sadat was able to claim success in substantive terms—having won Israel's agreement to the principle of total withdrawal from the Sinai, including the settlements and airfields. Begin could claim success very largely because the procedures agreed upon for the ultimate disposition of the West Bank and Gaza Strip seemed to ensure continuing Israeli control of those areas.

The proceedings at Camp David produced two accords that were signed on September 17, 1978: "The Framework for the Conclusion of a Peace Treaty Between Egypt and Israel" and "The Framework of Peace in the Middle East." As their titles indicated, the accords did not constitute a settlement, but rather agreements in principle on substantive and procedural elements of agreements yet to come. Various letters exchanged among the participants established their respective positions on significant matters that remained unresolved.

The framework for Egyptian–Israeli peace stipulated the two countries' goal of concluding negotiations for a full peace treaty within three months. The treaty itself was to be completely implemented not later than three years after coming into effect. Within three to nine months of its signing, there would be an interim withdrawal of Israeli forces in Sinai. This was to be followed by the establishment of "complete, normal relations" between Egypt and Israel, including full recognition, diplomatic, economic, and cultural relations, the termination of economic boycotts, and the evacuation of Israeli forces and civilians from all Egyptian territory. The framework committed Egypt to allow Israeli ships passage through the Suez Canal, the Gulf of Suez, and the Strait of Tiran. It also established broad outlines for military arrangements in areas leading to the international frontier, including the positioning of UN forces. Details were to be worked out in negotiations leading to the peace treaty. In an exchange of prearranged letters with Jimmy Carter, Begin promised to submit to the Knesset a measure authorizing the removal of Israel's Sinai settlements provided all other outstanding issues between Israel and Egypt were satisfactorily settled. A letter from Sadat placed Egypt on record as not being bound by the framework unless the Knesset reacted favorably.[81]

The framework for Middle East peace was more complex. It too affirmed the goal of reaching a negotiated Egyptian–Israeli peace treaty within three months. However, its most significant elements focused on the related questions of the Palestinian people and the future of the West Bank and Gaza.

Expressing the parties' commitment to reaching "a just, comprehensive, and durable settlement . . . through the conclusion of peace treaties based on Security Council Resolutions 242 and 338 in all their parts," the Framework for Peace in the Middle East called for Egypt, Israel, Jordan, "and representatives of the Palestinian people" to resolve the Palestinian problem "in all its aspects." It proposed that negotiations among the parties proceed in three stages. The first step would aim at defining the substance of "full autonomy," a condition that was to apply to the inhabitants of the West Bank and Gaza Strip during a "transitional period" of at most five years' duration. Second and third stage negotiations would deal respectively with the post-transitional phase, the final status of the West Bank and Gaza, and the formulation of peace treaties between Israel and Jordan.

As pat as this sounded, it could not conceal the existence of potentially overwhelming complications, not the least of which were that Jordan had taken no part in the framework's formulation and that the Arab world still recognized the PLO as the sole legitimate representative of the Palestinian people. Apart from these considerations, the framework in effect gave Israel a veto over arrangements for the West Bank and Gaza. Defining the "full autonomy" to be exercised by a "self-governing authority" was left to negotiations among the parties, who would have to agree on the transitional regime's powers and responsibilities. Then too, while the self-governing authority in the West Bank and Gaza was to be "freely elected," elections would proceed under the auspices of

Israel's military government of occupation. No provision was made for independent supervision of the proceedings.

Moreover, according to the framework for Middle East peace, once the transitional "self-governing authority" was established, unspecified numbers of Israeli forces would be redeployed into unspecified numbers of "security locations." At the same time, unspecified "arrangements for assuring internal and external security and public order" in the West Bank and Gaza would come into effect. All these issues were to be settled by agreement among the parties prior to the creation of the "self-governing authority."

By tying required steps in the West Bank and Gaza to Israeli agreement, the framework for peace in the Middle East did much to legitimize the possibility that de facto Israeli control would continue indefinitely. Any fair reading of the document must uphold the conclusion arrived at by the Palestinian scholar Fayez Sayegh: " . . . the Camp David Framework . . . in fact fully protects Israel against any changes of which it does not freely approve."[82]

The same principle held true when the framework turned from purely political issues to the question of refugees. It stated that during the transitional period "representatives of Egypt, Israel, Jordan, and the self-governing authority will constitute a continuing committee to decide *by agreement* on the modalities of admission of persons displaced from the West Bank and Gaza in 1967. . . ."As for those Palestinians who became refugees prior to 1967, Egypt, Israel, and "other interested parties" were to work toward an agreement.[83]

Neither of the Camp David frameworks mentioned Jerusalem. As an issue that defied efforts to reconcile the Egyptian and Israeli positions even through the vaguest and most general formulas, Jerusalem was dealt with in letters exchanged among Begin, Carter, and Sadat. Sadat insisted that East Jerusalem was a part of the West Bank and must be restored to Arab sovereignty, although the city should be undivided and governed by a municipal council composed of an equal number of Arabs and Israelis. Begin's letter simply affirmed that the entire city was an integral and undivided part of Israel and the capital of the state. At Menachem Begin's vehement insistence, Carter's letter indicated Washington's position by only referring to—but not repeating the substance of—statements made in 1967 and 1969 by U.S. ambassadors to the United Nations. The U.S. stand that Begin preferred not to see renewed in print was in any case well known: Washington did not accept the validity of efforts to change Jerusalem's status unilaterally, East Jerusalem was considered to be occupied territory, and the city's final status should be determined through negotiations.[84]

However, after the high drama of the summit meeting, flaws in the outcome seemed less important than the existence of an agreement. An understandable sense of euphoria prevailed when the accords were signed on September 17, 1978. Carter could justifiably claim a great deal of responsibility for the success. The United States had also given tangible proof of its importance to the peace process, breaking a major deadlock over Israel's two airbases in the Sinai by undertaking to replace them with comparable facilities in the Negev Desert. As never before, Washington could claim to be the key to Middle East peace. The president noted with undisguised satisfaction:

> ... the document calls for the completion of the peace treaty negotiations within three months. And I have noticed the challenge extended by [Begin and Sadat] to each other. They will complete [peace negotiations] within three months—I might say this document encompasses almost all of the issues between the two countries and resolves those issues. A few lines remain to be drawn on maps and the question of settlements is to be resolved. Other than that, most of the major issues are resolved already.... [85]

Carter was soon to be disillusioned. Whatever hope he had that the Camp David frameworks would be the seed of an eventual comprehensive peace in the Middle East depended largely on his belief in Israeli good will. Yet, almost before the proverbial ink dried on the Accords, he was confronted with what appeared to be duplicity on Begin's part.

By September 17, Carter believed he possessed the Israeli prime minister's clearcut promise to freeze the construction of Jewish settlements in the occupied areas pending the outcome of negotiations for the establishment of Palestinian self-rule. Having, in fact, rejected an earlier letter from Begin on grounds that its commitment along those lines was inadequately expressed, Carter was told by the Israelis that a version more to his liking would be prepared. However, when the new letter arrived, the day *after* the Camp David accords were signed:

> ... it ... contained an altogether different version of what had been agreed: the Israelis limited the settlements freeze only to the time provided for negotiating the Egyptian–Israeli peace treaty—namely, three months—and not for the duration of the negotiations aimed at the establishment of Palestinian self-rule.... [86]

While the Israelis denied the U.S. version, Carter and his top aides appear to have remained convinced that Begin had simply gone back on his commitment. Begin used the days immediately following the Camp David summit to publicize his determination to continue establishing settlements in the occupied areas as well as his insistence that the Accords did not contain anything to prevent Israel from retaining a presence in those regions even after the proposed five-year transitional period expired.[87] These were only the first links in a chain of post-Camp

David statements that would culminate in 1981 with the prime minister's well known public vow:

I, Menachem, son of Ze'ev and Hana Begin, do solemnly swear that as long as I serve the nation as Prime Minister, we will not leave any part of Judea, Samaria, the Gaza Strip, or the Golan Heights[88]

THE EGYPTIAN–ISRAELI PEACE

Negotiations toward an Egyptian–Israeli peace treaty started in October, with Washington serving as the venue in order to facilitate U.S. mediation. The talks quickly proved far more difficult than anticipated. The three month deadline for completing the talks passed with no agreement in sight. Not until late March was the peace treaty finally signed.

The basic issue dividing Israel and Egypt was predictable from the outset. Egypt entered the post-Camp David talks hoping to forge tight links between a peace with Israel and progress toward an overall settlement of the Arab–Israeli conflict. Jerusalem was committed to separating its new ties to Egypt from the nature of Israeli or Egyptian relations with other Arab actors.

Although both countries agreed that full peace between them should be based on Israel's total withdrawal from Egyptian land, their distinct orientations to the broad implications of a settlement crystallized into specific areas of contention. Focusing on the self-governing authority that was to be negotiated for the West Bank and Gaza after the treaty with Israel was concluded, Cairo sought a firm deadline for the elections to establish that body. Israel strongly opposed this. Egypt wanted an exchange of ambassadors to occur only after the autonomous Palestinian regime came into being. Israel wanted the exchange to occur before its full withdrawal from the Sinai. Egypt wanted the treaty's text to specify that peace with Israel was a step toward comprehensive peace. In view of Egypt's many mutual defense pacts with other Arab states, Israel not only opposed this, but also insisted that the treaty explicitly establish its own legal priority over Egypt's other international obligations. Then too, Egypt hoped to gain a special role in Gaza, including the right to station liaison officers there during the negotiations for Palestinian autonomy, and, moreover, pressed for the self-governing authority to be established first in Gaza and then in the West Bank. These demands were also opposed by Israel, which for its part—and in the face of stubborn Egyptian opposition—persistently demanded special rights to purchase Egyptian oil.

In approaching the Egyptian–Israeli peace negotiations, the Carter administration was above all anxious that the momentum toward peace generated by Camp David not be lost. In the end, this redounded to

Israel's benefit. For although Carter and his top assistants wished to see the Egyptian–Israeli peace linked to a process culminating in a comprehensive Middle East settlement, they wanted even more to see the ongoing negotiations end successfully. Thus, while the administration clearly sympathized with Sadat's efforts to tie the negotiations to broader questions, Israel's resistance led the United States to promote a series of compromises that in effect made the outcome a separate Egyptian–Israeli peace.

By late October 1978, the Washington talks had bogged down. Direct intervention by Carter produced some forward movement. The Israeli delegation, still refusing to accept mention of comprehensive peace in the body of the proposed treaty, agreed to language in the document's preamble indicating both states' commitment to the goal of an overall settlement. In return, Egyptian representatives accepted a treaty clause establishing the agreement's priority over their country's other international obligations. However, this apparent progress proved ephemeral. Dissatisfied with several points agreed to by the Egyptian team, particularly the wording of the obligations clause, Sadat sought to reopen the negotiations. On the other hand, the Begin cabinet approved in principle of the work done in Washington but wished to water down the preamble's reference to comprehensive peace.

Israel and Egypt also remained at odds over the relationship between the treaty and autonomy for the West Bank and Gaza. Having agreed that the question could not be handled within the treaty's provisions, Sadat wanted a joint letter, to be signed by himself and Begin, that would establish a timetable for arranging Palestinian autonomy and link the Egyptian–Israeli exchange of ambassadors to progress on that issue.

The tensions created by these problems were suddenly increased when Begin announced plans to expand existing West Bank settlements. When negotiations resumed in Washington under this cloud, both sides appeared to have hardened their positions. While the Egyptians continued to push for a clear connection between the treaty and Palestinian autonomy, the Israelis now denied—in contradiction to the Camp David Accords—that the inhabitants of the West Bank and Gaza were to have the right to participate by vote in deciding the regions' final status.[89]

Despite these ominous signs, U.S. spokesmen continued to proclaim the emerging Egyptian–Israeli settlement as a viable step toward comprehensive peace. In October, the administration replied to a series of questions forwarded by King Hussein, who had not yet responded to Camp David's invitation to join the peace process. The King sought to commit the United States to a posture that would favor the Arabs in any negotiations that might develop with Israel. His queries covered such issues as the U.S. stand on Israeli settlements, Palestinian self-determination, the status of Jerusalem, the withdrawal of Israeli forces from occupied territories, the return of Palestinian refugees, and the ultimate political disposition of the occupied areas.

Hussein's effort to pin Washington to unequivocal positions failed. The replies, basically reflecting well known U.S. stands, were generally ambiguous. For example, in answer to Hussein's request for clarification of the U.S. position on the withdrawal of Israeli forces from the West Bank–Gaza area after the establishment of a self-governing authority, Washington replied that the United States "did not oppose the stationing of limited numbers of Israeli security personnel in specifically designated areas if agreed to by the parties." Referring to the role of West Bank and Gaza Arabs in determining the areas' final status, Washington said its policy "did not preclude" the possibility that upon the conclusion of an agreement among the involved states the inhabitants might elect representatives "to whom that agreement will be submitted for a vote." When Hussein asked for the U.S. view of the territories' final status after the five-year transitional period proposed at Camp David, he was told that "would be a matter for discussion" during the peace process.[90]

It was hardly surprising that these answers did not satisfy Hussein, who now decided against becoming involved in the peace process. Nor were the Israelis pleased, seeing the administration's ambiguity as preserving a U.S. option to exert eventual pressure toward an unwelcome resolution of the questions posed by the Jordanian monarch.[91]

Little had changed by November. Israel was willing to accept the proposed treaty, but not a side letter suggested by Washington as a means of committing both sides to start negotiating the autonomy issue within a month of the treaty's conclusion and to accept the end of 1979 as a non-binding "target date" for the election of a Palestinian self-governing authority. Nor was the Egyptian government, which wanted a firm deadline rather than a "target date," satisfied by the U.S. formulation. Cairo also still insisted that modifications were needed in the draft treaty's clause establishing the agreement's priority over Egypt's other international obligations.

Hoping to break the deadlock, Carter sent Vance to the Middle East. The secretary of state arrived in Cairo on December 10. To allay Egyptian concerns without reopening negotiations on the body of the treaty, he proposed appending "interpretative notes" to the document. One part of the proposed appendix would have offered Washington's legal opinion that the Egyptian–Israeli peace treaty would not prevent Cairo from coming to the aid of an ally who was attacked. Another would have provided at least a broad link in principle between the Egyptian–Israeli peace and a wider regional settlement by describing the treaty as having been concluded "in the context of a comprehensive peace settlement in accordance with the provisions . . . agreed at Camp David." Finally, Vance again suggested a side letter fixing the end of 1979 as a target date for electing the Palestinian self-governing authority.[92]

Sadat was satisfied. He was, of course, pleased by Vance's suggested interpretative notes. However, he was also growing increasingly concerned over events in Iran, which threatened to bring down the Shah's regime and send disturbing political ripples throughout the Middle East. To the dismay of his cabinet, the Egyptian president agreed to accept the draft treaty and the U.S. interpretative positions. Although Egypt still hoped to win a special status in Gaza as well as to delay exchanging ambassadors with Israel until the self-governing authority's establishment, Vance was encouraged. However, on arriving in Jerusalem he found the Israelis outraged over the proposed U.S. interpretations. Israel refused to proceed on the basis outlined by Vance. Upon returning empty handed to the United States, the secretary of state publicly blamed the Israelis for preventing the treaty from having been concluded.[93]

The outcome jarred the administration. Washington was at least as concerned as Sadat over the deteriorating Iranian situation. The unforeseeable implications of the turmoil in that country lent renewed urgency to the administration's desire to finalize Egyptian–Israeli peace. At the same time, Carter and his advisers were becoming convinced that Begin was seeking to frustrate their peacemaking efforts in order to undermine the president's chances for re-election.[94] Despite the setback suffered by Vance, the administration saw no option but to try again.

After unproductive talks in Brussels among Vance, Egyptian Prime Minister Mustafa Khalil, and Israeli Foreign Minister Moshe Dayan, the administration resorted to another session at Camp David. This time it was convened by Vance and attended by Dayan and Khalil. The futile encounter began on December 23 and lasted two days. In the aftermath of this sterile exercise, Carter invited Begin to Washington. The two leaders held talks between March 2 and 4, 1979, in sessions that were often stormy and riddled by bad feelings. However, at the price of conceding several points, Carter managed to reach agreement with the prime minister on key issues. Among these was an agreement to modify the U.S. interpretation of the treaty's obligation clause. In order to downplay the interpretation's U.S. origin, it would be appended to the treaty as an "agreed minute" instead of as an interpretative note. More importantly, a sentence would be added cancelling the interpretation that had swayed Sadat. By such diplomatic sleight of hand was the treaty's clear priority over Egypt's other international obligations restored— while permitting Cairo, if it wished, to point selectively to phrases that, out of context, appeared to indicate otherwise.[95]

Carter also agreed to modifications in the joint Begin–Sadat letter referring to Palestinian autonomy. At Begin's behest, the word "goal" was substituted for the phrase "target date." Much more significantly, however, the non-binding "goal" in question would only refer to the hope of concluding negotiations over the timing and modalities of establishing the self-governing authority, rather than to elections to create that body.[96]

Finally, although Begin would not be swayed from Israel's consistent demand for special rights to Egyptian oil, Carter offered guarantees that Israel's energy requirements would be met.

Aware that these concessions virtually eliminated any substantial connection between the projected peace with Egypt and Palestinian autonomy or Israel's overall relations with the Arab world, Begin promised to recommend positive action by his government.

Carter decided to follow up his efforts by going to the Middle East to supervise the final stages of the negotiating process. The president was motivated both by the belief that his involvement would probably be necessary to finalize the peace and the attraction of receiving personal credit for a diplomatic breakthrough.[97] At the time, Carter's image as a leader was certainly in need of a boost. It was not only the tensions with Israel during the frustrating months of negotiations over the Egyptian–Israeli peace treaty that harmed his political standing at home. The fall of the Shah and the return to Iran of his nemesis, the virulently anti-American Ayatollah Khomeini, strongly enhanced Carter's need for a Middle East success.

Just before leaving Washington, the president sent Brzezinski to Cairo. The national security advisor was to point out to Sadat that not only the Iranian revolution but also Carter's domestic difficulties lent urgency to the need for successfully concluding the Egyptian–Israeli negotiations. He was also to stress Carter's commitment to continue pursuing a comprehensive Arab–Israeli peace.

Brzezinski carried out his instructions to the letter:

I met with Sadat...on March 6....I analyzed the security problems of the region, emphasized our determination to enhance Egyptian–American cooperation, reaffirmed the President's commitment to a wider peace in the Middle East, indicated that in our view success in moving toward such a peace was essential to the President's political fortunes, and suggested that Begin's inclination was to stall and perhaps even contribute to the President's political defeat.[98]

Sadat was moved, apparently to a great degree by the thought of helping Carter out of a politically threatening domestic situation. The result was his virtually complete agreement to the new developments in the U.S. position. "In effect," writes Brzezinski, "Sadat gave Carter carte blanche for his subsequent negotiations with the Israelis."[99]

After first stopping in Egypt, Carter arrived in Israel on March 10. The final negotiations were difficult. Although most issues were now settled, the Israelis resisted Egypt's standing demand for special arrangements in Gaza, while retaining their own for special access to Egyptian oil. Differences also still existed over the timing of exchanging ambassadors.

However, the last major obstacle was removed when Israel agreed to drop its claims on Egyptian oil in return for a fifteen-year U.S. oil guarantee. Morever, in exchange for Egypt's abandoning its position on Gaza and agreeing to earlier action on the question of ambassadors, Begin "hinted he might be willing to take some unilateral steps on the West Bank, symbolic of his commitment to autonomy."[100]

With this rather meager offer, Carter returned to Cairo to seek Sadat's final agreement. It was quickly obtained.

The treaty was signed in Washington, amid great ceremony, on March 26, 1979. Together with the treaty, various annexes, interpretative notes, letters, memoranda, and maps elaborately documented the terms of the new relationship between Egypt and Israel. The essence of the relationship rested on Israel's withdrawal in stages to the international border that separated the Palestine mandate from Egypt in return for Egyptian political commitments.

An interim withdrawal, to occur within nine months after the treaty went into effect, would be followed by the normalization of relations— including an exchange of ambassadors—between Egypt and Israel. Israel was guaranteed free passage through the Suez Canal and the Strait of Tiran, the latter acknowledged by Egypt to be an international waterway. Egypt would regain full sovereignty over areas evacuated by Israel, but would observe specified force limitations—as would Israel in an area along its southern border. Israel was committed to withdraw completely behind the international border within three years of the treaty's ratification.

The priority of the obligations incurred under the treaty was established in article VI, which committed the parties, inter alia, to fulfill the terms of peace "without regard to action or inaction of any other party and independently of any other instrument . . . ," not to enter into any agreement "in conflict with the treaty," and to recognize that in case of a conflict of treaty obligations "the obligations under this Treaty will be binding and implemented." The import of an appended "agreed minute" left these commitments unmodified.[101]

The treaty's preamble described the document as "an important step in the search for comprehensive peace in the area and for the attainment of the settlement of the Arab–Israeli conflict in all its aspects." The appended joint Sadat–Begin letter stated that negotiations aimed at defining the modalities for establishing a Palestinian self-governing authority and determining its powers and responsibilities would commence within a month of the treaty's ratification.[102] The parties set for themselves "the goal of completing the negotiations within one year...."

Having been a "full partner" with Egypt and Israel in negotiating the peace, Washington was also a full partner in the peace. Through identical letters sent by Carter to Sadat and Begin, the United States committed itself to conduct aerial monitoring of the limited force zones, to secure the deployment of UN forces in the Sinai or, failing that, to take steps toward establishing and maintaining an acceptable alternative multinational force, and to act in effect as guardian of the peace by consulting with the parties and taking "such other action as it may deem appropriate" should there be a violation or threatened violation of the treaty.[103]

Additional U.S. involvement came in the form of the fifteen-year guarantee that Israel's oil needs would be met. Washington also signed a bilateral Memorandum of Agreement with Israel that, although heavily circumscribed by qualifications, not only seemed to commit the United States to support Israel should the treaty be violated by Egypt but also—quite apart from any possible violation—reaffirmed Washington's sympathetic view of Israel's "military and economic assistance requirements."[104]

The U.S.–Israeli "Memorandum of Agreement" surprised and embarrassed the Egyptians. Prime Minister Mustafa Khalil learned of it just twenty hours before the treaty was signed. Writing to Vance, he criticized the Memorandum for presuming "that Egypt's compliance with its obligations is in doubt," and accused the United States of having abandoned its role as "full partner" in the peace by assuming "the role of the arbiter in determining that there has been a violation or threat of violation of the Treaty."[105] In a subsequent letter to Vance, Khalil raised a host of arguments against the Memorandum.[106] There was, however, little he could do but inform the secretary of state that Egypt would "not recognize the Memorandum and considers it null and void...."

The United States also assumed a heavy financial burden. A document prepared by the U.S. General Accounting Office described the U.S. financial contribution through 1981 in these terms:

The Special International Security Assistance Act of 1979...authorized $4.8 billion supplemental security assistance in support of the peace treaty. For fiscal year 1981, an additional $200 million was authorized in the Arms Export Control Act for financing additional redeployment costs. Israel received $800 million in grant in aid for air-base construction in the Negev Desert and $2.5 billion in foreign military sale credits for financing the relocation of its forces. Egypt's package consisted of $300 million in economic aid and $1.5 billion in foreign military sales credits to modernize its armed forces.[107]

Long after celebrations over the treaty's signing subsided, the Carter administration continued to insist that the peace treaty was not an isolated development but rather part of a move toward a comprehensive settlement. But mounting evidence indicated the opposite. The Arab states and the PLO were soon in an uproar over Egypt's defection. Cairo's ostracization from the Arab World, already begun in the wake of Sadat's Jerusalem trip, was rapidly and thoroughly completed. Arab capitals were virtually unanimous in condemning the peace treaty, breaking diplomatic ties with Egypt and suspending the country's membership in the Arab League. Although Saudi Arabia had been reluctant to act strongly against Egypt's go-it-alone policy, it too was galvanized by the peace treaty into joining the general boycott.[108]

In the wake of the peace treaty, Carter distanced himself from the Arab–Israeli issue. The problem had consumed an inordinate amount of his time and had on the whole been a frustrating experience. With an eye on the approaching 1980 elections, he also decided—despite the protests of Cyrus Vance—to reduce State Department involvement with the Arab–Israeli issue. He needed, he said, to appoint a special Middle East Negotiator who would be a "political shield" while serving as pointman for U.S. involvement in negotiations over Palestinian autonomy.[109] Robert Strauss took the position in the spring of 1979 and stayed on until October, when he was replaced by Sol Linowitz. Both men had close connections with the American Jewish community and in Carter's mind would be effective buffers against domestic political pressures.

It is doubtful that Carter expected much from their efforts to promote a successful outcome to the "autonomy talks." Without the administration's determined and active backing, neither Strauss nor Linowitz had much chance of bridging the gap between Cairo and Jerusalem. The desultory negotiations, marked by Egypt's efforts to lay the basis for meaningful Palestinian self-determination and Israel's efforts to prevent just that outcome, dragged on long after Carter's defeat at the polls. The talks were finally terminated by Egypt in the aftermath of Israel's 1982 invasion of Lebanon.

Jimmy Carter stands out as the president who in the years after 1967 was most actively committed to promoting a comprehensive Arab–Israeli peace based on the return of occupied territories in exchange for political concessions. He was also distinguished by his obvious conviction that any viable comprehensive settlement must somehow satisfy Palestinian nationalism. It was, of course, this issue that ultimately entangled the president's policy in enormous logical and practical difficulties, for while Carter's references to the need of a "homeland" seemed to raise the possibility that Palestinians might obtain self-determination in part of Palestine by reducing their territorial claims, he eventually lapsed into a logically untenable commitment to limited self-determination.

Some years after leaving office, Carter would conclude his reflections on the Middle East by arguing that peace remained contingent on Arab recognition of Israel's reality and Israeli acknowledgment of "Palestinian claims to civic equality and their right to express themselves freely in a portion of their territorial homeland."[110] Whether by design or accident, the phrasing is uncomfortably reminiscent of the document that gave birth to the Palestine problem. For seven decades, Palestinians have castigated the carefully calculated omission of "political rights" in the 1917 Balfour Declaration's caveat that British support of Zionism should do nothing to prejudice the "civil and religious rights" of Palestine's inhabitants.

Ex-president Carter's assertion that peace demands that "Palestinian human rights, including the right of self-determination, must be ac-knowledged," only underscores the point.[111] Recognition of the distinction between the communal and individual spheres of human activity requires that self-determination be defined as a "political," not a "human," right. Simply put, it has always been logically impossible to uphold and simultaneously qualify the applicability of the political principle of self-determination to the Palestinian people.

Soon after Camp David, Brzezinski and Carter found themselves agreeing that Israel's objectives were to have "essentially a separate peace, then U.S. payments, and finally a free hand in the West Bank."[112] Brzezinski brought up what can be seen in retrospect as the most significant problem in the administration's entire involvement with the Arab–Israeli conflict:

I raised the question...whether we should in fact be pushing so hard for an Egyptian–Israeli treaty if it is our intention to resolve also the West Bank issue. Once such a treaty is signed we will have less leverage.[113]

The president's response is not recorded. However, two (not mutually exclusive) answers suggest themselves. One is that after having become committed so publicly to Middle East peacemaking, Carter could not bring himself to reject a significant achievement—even though it might set back, or utterly undermine, possibilities for the comprehensive peace he originally envisaged. Another is that the president clung to the belief that in time the hopes with which he entered Camp David might yet be realized.

By the latter half of the 1980s, that belief perhaps found its strongest support in realms indicated by the title of Carter's memoir, *Keeping Faith*.

LEBANON

The problem of Lebanon festered throughout Carter's presidency. Rooted partly in Lebanon's own socio-political makeup, yet also an outgrowth of the Palestine problem, the issue could not be dealt with in isolation from the Arab–Israeli conflict. Washington's policy toward Lebanon was therefore intimately connected to its approach to Middle East peacemaking.

Lebanon's uneasy political system had rested since 1943 on an unwritten power-sharing agreement reached by leaders of the country's major religious groupings. This "National Pact" committed the various sects to put aside particularistic aims and to work in tandem, if not in unison, for the welfare of the country's heterogeneous society. Maronite Christians abandoned traditional hopes for special status under French protection, while Moslem communities retreated from their own desire for incorporation into a wider Arab political entity. A key feature of the arrangement was the confessional system, in which political power was allocated among religious communities according to a fixed formula. The result was a decidedly oligarchical polity within which each sect's established elites generally benefited sufficiently to justify the necessity of continual accommodation.

The arrangement functioned for three decades. It did not, however, function smoothly. Lebanon was a polity in which communal loyalties so outweighed national identity that central authority survived mainly through a judicious combination of promises and payoffs to competing groups. But if the Beirut government had no option other than working under tight strictures imposed by the domestic environment, it also constantly walked a tightrope in foreign affairs. Notwithstanding the spirit of the seminal National Pact, Lebanese politics were thoroughly penetrated by competing international ideologies and movements.[114] Crisis and crisis management were normal features of political life.

With a politically marginalized Palestinian community that by the mid-1970s totalled some 350,000, it was unavoidable that Lebanon would be affected by the post–1967 heightening of Palestinian activism. On the one hand, Palestinian guerrilla and terrorist activities soon called forth Israeli retaliation that underscored the Lebanese government's inability to protect citizens or property. On the other, the intensification of the Palestinians' struggle encouraged Pan-Arabist and leftist trends while simultaneously alienating conservative Lebanese nationalist (mainly Maronite) currents. When added to the considerable strains already accumulated under Lebanon's modernizing oligarchy—the erosion of traditional values, the rise of a non-traditional urbanized middle class, increasing demands for expanded political and economic participation by the growing and neglected Shi'a community—these pressures proved disastrous.

Despite efforts by Lebanon's established elites to preserve the status quo, the traditionally effective politics of compromise steadily yielded to a process of polarization fueled by sectarian fanaticism, ideological differences, and personal rivalries. In the spring of 1975, these tensions erupted in an orgy of violence that has not yet ended.

The civil war's outbreak, coming as it did months before the successful conclusion of Henry Kissinger's pursuit of the Sinai II Agreement, gave rise to much speculation that a hidden U.S. hand had helped kindle the blaze. After some fifteen months of fighting—with both the PLO and Syria by then fully drawn into the fray—the late Malcolm Kerr explained the logic of these suspicions to a Senate subcommittee:

Was this Dr. Kissinger's toy . . . [perhaps] the objective of American policy had already been achieved with the simultaneous neutralization of Egypt, Syria and the Palestinian Liberation Organization. Instead of fighting Israel, they are now fighting each other, and the PLO is struggling for its very existence.[115]

Kerr did not subscribe to this interpretation, though he labeled it "perhaps mistaken but certainly plausible." A decade later, the proverbial benefit of hindsight offers no help in conclusively establishing the covert role—if any—of the United States or other actors in initiating or pro-longing the Lebanese conflict.

Nonetheless, available evidence lends credence to William Quandt's conclusion that Washington reacted to the civil war's onset with "no game in mind other than to prevent a full-blown Arab–Israeli war."[116] This does not, however, necessarily imply that U.S. policymakers remained unreceptive to the possible advantages—precisely those suggested by Malcolm Kerr—to be found in a situation not of their own making. There appears to be substantial truth in Walid Khalidi's understated contention that "it would be disingenuous to assume that the U.S. was altogether displeased with the course of events in Lebanon."[117]

Still, there was good reason for the Ford administration's initial alarm. Kissinger's post–1973 step-by-step stalking of peace seemed to have proved its worth by achieving the Sinai I disengagement and winning Anwar Sadat's eager participation. No less important was the apparent progress made toward reconciling the United States and Syria. By mid–1974, President Hafez al-Assad seemed to have fallen in with the pace of step-by-step, accepting disengagement on the Golan Heights and the interposition of UN forces between Israeli and Syrian troops. Then too, U.S.–Syrian relations took a qualitative leap forward that same year when Damascus opted to resume normal diplomatic ties after an estrangement of seven years.

These gains were jeopardized by the Lebanese conflagration. As the situation deteriorated after April 1975, Washington at first sought to contain the crisis and achieve the restoration (with possible minor mod-ifications) of the status quo ante.

This initial U.S. stance entailed strong opposition to outside intervention in Lebanon. However, as the conflict in that country became obviously more uncontrollable, and as U.S. policymakers modified their original perceptions of Syria's reaction to the crisis, Washington's policy underwent significant changes. The result was that between the Ford administration's early approach and the Carter administration's ultimate position, U.S. policy toward Lebanon fell into three broad stages.

The first can roughly be dated from the beginning of the civil war to the spring of 1976. During that period Washington favored palliative action to restore pre–1975 conditions. U.S. pronouncements upholding the ideal of peace in Lebanon, as well as the country's territorial integrity and sovereignty, were frequent. Hard upon these followed calls (aimed largely at Syrian ears) for outside parties to refrain from intervening.[118]

The second stage in the U.S. approach developed as events threatened to bring victory to radical forces in Lebanon, a contingency that found Washington and Damascus sharing profound misgivings. Syria perceived the breakdown of Lebanese civil society as a threat to its military and political position against Israel. Thus, although Washington was slow to acknowledge it openly, the Syrian regime had from the start of the crisis tailored its actions to three clear goals: preventing a "rightist" ascendancy that would eclipse the Palestinian resistance in Lebanon, and therefore undermine the entire Arab bargaining position against Israel; preventing a "radical" ascendancy beyond its control that might spark a war with Israel at a time, and under circumstances, not of Syrian choosing; and, finally, preventing a deterioration into simple chaos that might permit Syria to be outflanked by Israel in the event of war.[119]

By the late spring of 1976, the course of the civil war exacerbated Syrian fears. The "National Movement," a leftist alliance of Sunni, Druze, and Shi'a forces supported by substantial numbers of Lebanese Greek Orthodox Christians, was cooperating closely with the PLO and pressing hard against the rightist "Lebanese Front," the largely Maronite nationalist block spearheaded by the Phalangist militia.

Under the circumstances, Washington and Damascus found common cause. Although Syria's initially sub rosa intervention in late 1975 had aimed at forestalling the defeat of radical forces, Damascus now switched sides.[120]

Recognizing the convergence of interests, the Ford administration began to rely openly on Syria's potentially stabilizing role. By April 1976 the facade of U.S. opposition to Syrian involvement had all but crumbled. Ford, although still condemning the possibility of "regular" foreign forces entering Lebanon, tacitly approved the use of thinly disguised Syrian surrogates. It was not long before the president publicly expounded the theme that U.S. diplomats must have been repeating for some time to governments throughout the Middle East: "We hope the Israelis will stay out and that Syria will help. . . ."[121]

U.S. approval was preordained when the first of some 30,000 regular Syrian troops crossed the frontier to prevent the Lebanese Front's defeat in June. Washington also had been instrumental in arranging a tacit Syrian–Israeli understanding, the so-called "Red Line Agreement," that permitted Syria's intervention. In effect, the accord acknowledged Lebanon's division into zones of influence, sanctioning Syria's presence in approximately two-thirds of the country while granting Israel a green light to dominate events in the remaining southern portion.

While President Ford and Kissinger viewed Syria's incursion as an expedient shield against radical enemies of step-by-step diplomacy, Jimmy Carter's new administration welcomed it as a necessary support for a comprehensive peace conference in Geneva. Shortly after taking office in early 1977, Carter was heaping praise on Syria's "self-sacrificing role in Lebanon."[122] The ensuing relative heyday in U.S.–Syrian relations saw major steps taken toward symbolically important cultural and air traffic agreements with Damascus. At the same time, the Carter administration established policy guidelines that led to State Department approval of the sale to Syria of four L–100 aircraft, the civilian version of the C–130 military transport.[123]

Such efforts to pave the way for Syrian participation in the projected Geneva Conference were outdated by the end of 1977. The administration's rapid turnabout in the face of Israeli and domestic opposition to the U.S.–Soviet declaration of principles on the Middle East was followed within weeks by Sadat's trip to Jerusalem. Geneva became irrelevant, and Washington was soon concentrating on an Egyptian–Israeli settlement.

These events ushered in the third stage in U.S. policy toward Lebanon, a phase that lingered on without substantial modification until the Reagan administration was forced to react to Israel's 1982 invasion of the country.

The collapse of Carter's drive for comprehensive peace altered Washington's appraisal of the value of Syria's presence in Lebanon. No longer was Damascus' stabilizing presence seen as a welcome restraint against radical forces or as a generalized asset that would redound naturally to Lebanon's benefit once Geneva disposed of the Arab–Israeli conflict. Instead, Syrian involvement gained more importance as a distraction and burden, reducing the effectiveness of opposition to the Egyptian–Israeli peace process. In short, while Syria served U.S. interests by preventing an all-out renewal of war in Lebanon, it seemed equally beneficial from Washington's perspective to have Assad bogged down in Lebanon.[124]

Once the Carter administration refocused its peacemaking efforts on Egypt and Israel, the tacit Syrian–Israeli understanding in Lebanon was inevitably undermined. Damascus was hardly prepared to stand by tranquilly and watch Egypt remove itself from the ranks of Israel's enemies. Israel, seeing no diplomatic avenue to resolve its problems with Syria, was not prepared to allow Syria to consolidate its position in Lebanon.

Yet neither side was eager for a prompt showdown. Israeli policy-makers were loath to provoke an open war that might bury chances for a separate peace with Egypt. Syria, already becoming regionally isolated in its Lebanese venture, was unwilling to face Israel's superior firepower alone. Nonetheless, the two states' jockeying for position in Lebanon intensified in the late 1970s. It is in this context that Israel's 1978 incursion into south Lebanon, and its installation there of Major Haddad as the area's warlord-in-chief, must be understood.

Wedded to the goal of an Egyptian–Israeli settlement, the Carter administration reacted ambivalently to the Israeli invasion. Although Washington prominently insisted on a prompt withdrawal, publicly upheld Lebanon's right to sovereign existence, and introduced the Security Council resolution that placed UN troops along the country's southern border, it feared that antagonizing Israel would complicate negotiations toward peace with Egypt.

U.S. ambivalence was partly manifested by Washington's patient acceptance of Israel's three-month stay in Lebanon and Jerusalem's undisguised sponsorship of Major Haddad. It was even more strikingly apparent in the administration's handling of Israel's misuse of U.S.-supplied weapons during and after the invasion.

The Carter administration had no doubt that Israel had violated restrictions limiting the use of U.S.-supplied arms to defensive purposes and prohibiting their unauthorized transfer to third parties. Yet, in response to public charges to this effect, it merely advised congress that violations might have occurred. It then avoided making the final determination that, if based on its own information, would have by law required the suspension of further arms shipments to the Jewish state.[125] Moreover, although the United States quietly pressured Israel into recovering a small amount of arms from Major Haddad early in the summer of 1978, it generally turned a blind eye to Jerusalem's arms arrangements with Lebanese factions. While the extent of Israeli arms transfers is still not publicly known, it was no doubt substantial. By mid–1980 unconfirmed reports in the *New York Times* placed total Israeli aid to Christian militia forces at somewhat over $1 billion.[126]

Washington's tolerance of Israel's deepening involvement in Lebanon was mirrored by its continued support of Syria's presence. Amid the tensions provoked by the Syrian–Israeli competition, the administration continued to reassure Damascus of its commitment to the already obsolete vision of tranquil spheres of influence implied by the "Red Line Agreement." These assurances took tangible form in the continuation of U.S. financial aid to Syria, justified in terms of Damascus' contribution to Lebanon's "uneasy stability."

The pursuit of a policy that perpetuated controlled instability in Lebanon was automatically reflected in the nature of Washington's commitment to the resurrection of centralized authority in the country. By 1980, after five years of civil war, Lebanon had received some $115 million in U.S. economic aid. However, approximately $55 million was emergency disaster relief, which did nothing to meet the immense need for infrastructural reconstruction. Other aid came in the form of a three-year $100 million credit announced in 1977 as a move toward recreating the Lebanese Army. Yet, even in this important area Washington seemed to lack determination. Despite the Lebanese Army's ability to replace Syrian troops in some sectors of Beirut in early 1980—the Army's first credible showing in nearly five years—the administration soon recommended a cut of over $8 million in the previous year's military aid level.[127] Critics were quick to charge that the reduction would be seen as signalling a weakening of support for the Lebanese government's efforts to reassert itself.[128] By the same token, a tiny, but vocal, group of pro-Lebanese congressmen were appalled by the administration's 1980 request for only $7 million in economic assistance, a sum amounting to only $2 per capita in terms of Lebanon's population, while simultaneous requests for Jordan, Egypt, and Israel yielded respective per capita breakdowns of $16, $20 and $200.[129]

By 1980, it was all too clear that Washington's oft-expressed support of Lebanese sovereignty and territorial integrity referred to long-term hopes rather than firm objectives. There was nothing necessarily startling in this. It was, indeed, only the sad, but necessary, conclusion to be drawn from the realization that Lebanon's future would be largely determined by the search for Arab–Israeli peace.

Still, it was one thing to promote "uneasy stability" in Lebanon pending a comprehensive Arab–Israeli settlement and quite another to apply the same formula in the context of step-by-step peacemaking. The former approach sought to drive to the root of the Arab–Israeli problem, and therefore held out the possibility of a new regional and local political configuration that would facilitate reconciliation among warring factions in Lebanon. The latter at best promised Lebanon open-ended suffering until step-by-step eventually, if ever, confronted the irreducible conflict between Israeli aspirations and Palestinian nationalism.

Forced away from the search for comprehensive peace and back into the mold of incremental peacemaking, the Carter administration managed to contain the Lebanese situation until the Egyptian–Israeli settlement was achieved. The Reagan administration was left with the problem of how next to deal with it.

4

ABANDONMENT OF AN OBJECTIVE: RONALD REAGAN, 1981–1988

This is America's moment in the Middle East.

Alexander Haig

Ronald Reagan's election to the presidency in November 1980 came packaged as a resounding victory. Allowing Carter to carry only six states, Reagan won 489 Electoral College votes to the incumbent's 49. By the time it was over, Reagan outdistanced Carter in the popular vote by a margin of over eight million votes. Carter conceded even before the polls closed on the West Coast.

On entering the White House, Reagan gave priority to reviving the U.S. economy. He did not, however, neglect international affairs. Arguing that Soviet expansionism posed an increasing threat in the global arena, the new president promised to contest and defeat the Soviet Union for international influence.

The formula made for exciting rhetoric. But to many who had closely followed Reagan's campaign statements in the months before the election, his approach to international affairs failed to delineate clear policy guidelines for dealing with myriad specific issues. Some saw this as particularly true in regard to the Middle East. *New York Times* columnist Anthony Lewis put it this way:

A large unknown in the foreign policy outlook of President-elect Reagan is his view of the Middle East. Except for a few campaign simplicities, he has said little about how he would approach the Arab–Israeli conflict or handle . . . the area.[1]

Lewis was wrong. Candidate Reagan had made known his foreign policy outlook on the Middle East. Those who thought otherwise did so only because they refused to take seriously what they heard. In a sense, their doubts were understandable. Reagan's campaign pronouncements, while strongly pro-Israel, gave little indication that he had considered the two key problems then besetting the U.S. search for Middle East peace: how to bring the Camp David process to a successful end by breaking the deadlock over the autonomy talks, and—secondly—how to broaden the Egyptian–Israeli peace by bringing in other Arab actors.

On the other hand, Reagan had expressed clear and firm positions during his campaign. By the spring of 1980, the essence of his views on the Middle East were open to examination: the Soviet Union was the principal factor to be considered in devising a U.S. approach to the region; Israel's role in the United States' anti-Soviet stance was of major importance; Palestinian radicals should look for no succor from the United States; Israel, as a major ally in broader U.S. geostrategic objectives, should not feel that Washington might inhibit its local ambitions.

"An undivided city of Jerusalem means sovereignty for Israel over that city," Reagan declared approvingly. "I believe in [Israel's] right of settlement in the West Bank," he added. On the PLO, the candidate saw no reason "to negotiate with a terrorist group." And if the PLO accepted Security Council Resolution 242, and therefore acknowledged Israel's right to exist? "I'd still," said Reagan, "want to know whether they represent the Palestinian people they claim to represent."[2]

The underpinnings of Reagan's dismissal of outstanding points of contention between Israel and the Arab World were open to examination:

Israel is the only stable democracy we can rely on in a spot where Armageddon could come. The greatest responsibility the United States has is to preserve peace—and we need an ally in that area. We must prevent the Soviet Union from penetrating the Mideast. The Nixon administration successfully moved them out; if Israel were not there, the U.S. would have to be there.[3]

The theme was developed and sharpened throughout the campaign. By September, Reagan was accusing Carter of a unique and regrettable folly. "Until this administration," he argued, "no administration had ever deluded itself that Israel was not of permanent strategic interest to the United States." Flying in the face of accuracy, he went on to say that the solution to the problem of Palestinian refugees "could be assimilation in Jordan, designated by the UN as the Arab-Palestinian state."[4]

Notwithstanding the excesses of campaign rhetoric and the limited knowledge a candidate might be expected to bring to bear on an issue so complex as the Palestinian problem, Reagan's comments accurately indicated the approach his administration would adopt toward the Middle East. Critics such as Anthony Lewis failed to appreciate the extent to which both aspects of Reagan's public stance—his strong support for Israel and his small concern with the peace process—reflected the new president's views. By 1986 a former staff member of the pro-Israel lobby, the American Israel Public Affairs Committee (AIPAC), would recall the significance of Reagan's first six years as president by noting:

a . . . powerful force—the personal views of Mr. Reagan. Even his harshest critics in the liberal Jewish community acknowledge he is the most viscerally pro-Israel president since the founding of the state.[5]

SEARCHING FOR "STRATEGIC CONSENSUS"

To Ronald Reagan and his new secretary of state, Alexander Haig, the Arab–Israeli conflict was not the primary issue that demanded attention in the Middle East. In their eyes, the principal focus of U.S. policy should be the threat of Soviet penetration of the economically and strategically vital oil-rich Persian Gulf. There were understandable grounds for their preoccupation with the Middle East hinterland. Iran was embroiled in a post-revolutionary upheaval that was to become immeasurably complicated by the war launched by Iraq in September 1980 in an effort to seize the oil-producing province of Khuzistan. At the end of 1979, the Soviet Union invaded Afghanistan and became involved in a slogging war against fiercely resisting tribesmen. Pro-Western Arab regimes on the Gulf's Western shore feared the turbulence would cross their frontiers.

From Washington's vantage point, protecting the Persian Gulf entailed several requirements: the priorities of U.S. interests in the Middle East must be made plainly evident; Arab regimes in the Gulf must be convinced of Washington's active commitment to their security; available U.S. resources, both its own and those of proxies, should be visibly marshalled in support of U.S. resolve; the firmness of U.S. opposition to "radicalism" throughout the area should not be doubted.[6]

These considerations produced the two chief features of the policy pursued by the administration toward the Middle East during its first year in office. One was a determined effort to create a viable and visible anti-Soviet bloc in the Middle East. The other was an equally emphatic determination not to allow what were seen as secondary issues to interfere with efforts to promote the desired anti-communist grouping.

Relegated to "secondary" importance, the Arab–Israeli conflict was assumed by the new administration to be irrelevant to its primary aim of securing the Middle East against Soviet incursions. Events would show this to be a serious miscalculation. The mistake eventually led to the fading of grandiose geopolitical hopes. More importantly, it permitted on-the-ground events in the Middle East to go their own relatively unrestricted way while Washington fixed its gaze on overarching strategic scenarios.

The administration's failure was not so much a lapse in logic as a lapse of perspective. In itself, the vision of countering a perceived Soviet menace by mustering a Middle East anti-communist bloc was coherent. The problem was that when taken "in itself," the concept led to a futile effort to impose abstract Cold War premises on the dynamics of Arab–Israeli relations. Thus, while the administration would spend ineffective months attempting to translate its logic into effective policy, ramifications of the Palestinian–Israeli struggle soon enough had Washington reacting as best it could to unexpected developments.

When it took office in January 1981, the Reagan team did not hide its lack of interest in the slogging Egyptian–Israeli autonomy talks. The negotiations had dragged on, broken by sporadic suspensions, since 1979 with no sign of progress. Now, nearly a full year after the good-faith time limit set by the Egyptian–Israeli peace treaty, Cairo continued to insist that a formula be devised to grant full autonomy to the West Bank and Gaza—a concept that Egypt saw as requiring the devolution of political power on the Arab inhabitants of those areas, including East Jerusalem.

Menachem Begin's government clung to its original position: Israel would not yet claim sovereignty over the territories, but neither would it permit them to be severed from the Jewish state. Under all conditions, Jews must continue to enjoy an absolute right to settle the territories. Palestinian Arabs might establish some form of "administrative," but not "executive," council. Jerusalem must remain undivided under Israeli sovereignty.[7]

It was clear that under the best of circumstances, there was no easy way to break the stalemate. However, with Israel gearing up for national elections in June 1981, immediate chances of inducing flexibility in the negotiations were even further reduced. Still, within the State Department bureaucracy, pressures built up for the administration to establish a basis for future action on the autonomy question. By early March, however, the *New York Times* carried what amounted to an obituary of these hopes:

The Near East Bureau of the State Department is said to have sought and failed to receive from Mr. Haig a public commitment to Palestinian rights. So far, he has shown little interest in that question. . . . [8]

Later that month, the secretary of state outlined the administration's Middle East strategy to the Senate Foreign Relations Committee. Washington, he said, would concentrate on forging a "strategic consensus" to counter the Soviet Union in an area stretching from Egypt to Pakistan, including Turkey, Israel, and Saudi Arabia. Haig did not call for a formal alliance, but rather for a tacit arrangement—a "consensus."

As imprecise as this was, its implications were sufficiently clear to create almost immediate difficulties. For what the Reagan administration had in mind not only entailed increased reliance on Israel as a surrogate military instrument in the Middle East, but also on building up the military capacities of the Arab component of the projected anti-Soviet defensive arrangement. The issue rapidly boiled down to the specific question of U.S. arms sales to Saudi Arabia.

Shortly after speaking to the Foreign Relations Committee, Haig journied to Egypt, Israel, Jordan, and Saudi Arabia. At each stop he developed the theme that Soviet expansionist designs and subversive machinations constituted a common threat binding these countries to the United States. He stressed that "the United States was once again a reliable friend and ally."[9]

Haig appeared to disregard all evidence that his message failed to strike a universally responsive chord. Foreign Minister Prince Saud, while acknowledging that the United States and Saudi Arabia shared "an overall direction and perception," argued that his country saw Israel, rather than the Soviet Union, as the "main cause" of instability in the Middle East. King Hussein made much the same point. Reporters in the secretary of state's entourage noted that "despite statements to the contrary by King Hussein and Prince Saud," Haig unhesitatingly claimed that "with regard to regional concerns we had a unanimity of view with every leader." Those who accompanied him agreed that no Arab leader with whom Haig met, except Anwar Sadat, seemed enthusiastic over Washington's push for a "strategic consensus."[10]

But Haig was not one to doubt his own assessments. Years later, he offered this version of his Middle East visit:

In every capital, I was given the same urgent message: dangerous forces had been set loose in the region, and only a credible new assertion of American influence, coupled with the influence of moderate Arab regimes, could oppose them. There was, in a real rather than a theoretical sense, a strategic consensus in the region. This had nothing to do with American phrase making or with an American tendency to turn the Middle East into a theater for East–West confrontation. Three great fears ran through the region: fear of terrorism . . . fear of Islamic fundamentalism . . . fear of the Soviet Union. In reality, this was one consolidated fear: that terrorism and fundamentalism would so destabilize the region that the Soviets would either subvert the Islamic movement . . . or seize control of Iran and possibly the whole Gulf.[11]

Haig clung to this strategic vision throughout his tenure as secretary of state. The perspective was so inflexibly held that it seemed to diminish his ability to take into account the significance of regional political dy-

namics. He was not unaware of the view that the Arab–Israeli conflict
was a central concern that in one way or another affected the considerations given by Middle East policymakers to most major regional issues.
Yet Haig saw this as harmfully misguided:

The tendency to focus on the Palestinian issue [had] distracted the West from
consideration of the fact that many Middle East conflicts, and especially those
around the Gulf, had little to do with Israel and could not be solved by Israeli
concessions.[12]

Few would have claimed that Israeli concessions could resolve all Middle East conflicts. The real question was the extent to which the United
States could count on isolating its approach to the area from ramifications
of the Arab–Israeli conflict. Notwithstanding Haig's insistence to the
contrary, indications that broad strategic policy could not be immunized
against the impact of Arab–Israeli tensions continued to pile up.

A sizeable portion of this ominously growing mountain of evidence
took shape during his Haig's April visit to Israel. Somehow, it failed to
alert him that something less than "a unanimity of view" existed between
himself and Middle Eastern leaders.

Haig found Menachem Begin's government girding for the June elections and struggling with a host of difficult issues, including spiraling
economic inflation. He also noted that the autonomy question posed a
problem for the government. Yet his lack of concern over the issue is
amply evident in his recollection that:

The prime minister was preoccupied also with the complicated issue of granting
some form of local autonomy to Palestinian settlements [*sic*] on the West Bank
of the Jordan River, as provided in the Camp David accords. . . .[13]

On the other hand, the secretary carefully heeded his hosts' agreement
that "Soviet influence and the instability . . . it breeds were mortal enemies
of Israel's national safety." Yet, the Israelis strongly challenged the
administration's desire to encourage a regional anti-Soviet alignment.
Only Israel, and not the Arabs, they argued, would "fight the Soviets."

Begin and his colleagues particularly opposed the administration's
plans to sell sophisticated military hardware to Saudi Arabia. Unim-
pressed by Haig's argument that upgrading the military capabilities of
"moderate" Arab states was a logical step, the Israelis solidly supported
Defense Minister Yitzhak Shamir's caustic observation that "Saudi Arabia
is no moderate nation where Israel is concerned."[14]

The proposed arms transfer included equipment to enhance the utility
of the F–15 fighter planes purchased earlier by the Saudis. The entire
package, ultimately worth $8.5 billion, was composed of fuel tanks,

Sidewinder air-to-air heat-seeking missiles, six KC–135 aerial refueling tankers, five ultramodern E–3A radar surveillance aircraft (known as Airborne Warning and Control Systems, or AWACS), and a complex of twenty-two electronic ground stations to provide support for the AWACS and F–15s. Although Jerusalem opposed any significant enhancement of Arab military power, it was especially alarmed by the prospect of Saudi Arabia acquiring AWACS. These, argued the Israelis, would not only boost Saudi military power (and therefore potentially that of other Arab states as well), but also reduce Israel's defensive capacity.[15]

The "AWACS controversy" consumed much of Washington's time and energy over the next six months. At the end of October 1981, the arms package was finally rescued from congressional defeat by a Senate vote of 52–48. It was an exceedingly narrow victory. The House of Representatives had already rejected the proposal by the overwhelming margin of 301–111. Negative action by the Senate would have meant total defeat.

The victory was politically costly. Despite compensation to Israel in the form of an additional squadron of F–15s to offset the Saudi deal, and $200 million of military assistance funds to be used largely for purchases from Israel's own defense industry, Jerusalem remained opposed to the Saudi deal.[16] Reagan had found it necessary to intervene personally in order to overcome pro-Israeli sentiment on Capitol Hill. The heated controversy eventually propelled the president into declaring that it was "not the business of other nations to make American foreign policy."[17]

At the same time, Saudi Arabia's government had been angered and visibly humiliated by the proceedings. The Saudis were particularly embarrassed by a widely publicized letter sent by Reagan to Senate Minority Leader Howard Baker on October 28. "We have," wrote the president, "reached agreement with the Saudi government on a number of specific arrangements that go well beyond . . . all the standard terms. . . ." The conditions to which Reagan referred included restrictions on the use and maintenance of the AWACS, which in effect would limit Saudi employment of the system for well over a decade.[18]

With Israel discomfitted, Saudi Arabia chagrined and resentful, pro-Israeli domestic sentiment dismayed, and the narrowness of the administration's victory having attracted as much attention as the outcome, the "AWACS controversy" underscored the difficulties of creating a viable anti-Soviet front in the Middle East.[19]

The six-month AWACS battle gave Washington no respite from Arab–Israeli tensions. On the contrary, while the administration tried to erect a consensual anti-Soviet barrier across the Middle East, events seemed determined to emphasize the far-reaching implications of Arab–Israeli hostility. The immediate daily fare of the decades-old Palestine problem—violence—soon forced Washington to turn at least some of its attention away from visions of a strategic umbrella. The eruptions came in Lebanon, involving Syria, Israel, the PLO, and local Lebanese factions, and in Iraq, where Baghdad was suddenly converted into a target on the basis of Israeli fears that a future nuclear threat might be sprouting.

The first of the multiple crises came in early April, as Haig set out to promote the doctrine of strategic consensus. Serious clashes broke out in the Lebanese city of Zahle. A predominantly Greek Orthodox community of some 200,000 inhabitants, Zahle's location in the Bekaa Valley astride the Beirut–Damascus highway made it strategically important to the balance of power within Lebanon.

The problem began as Maronite Phalangist forces, already holding a bastion in Zahle, sought to expand and consolidate their grip on the city by building a road to the Maronite stronghold of Mount Lebanon.

On April 2, Syrian troops encircled Zahle and shelled Phalangist positions. The struggle intensified in the following weeks, playing itself out in the city and surrounding hills. Tensions simultaneously multiplied throughout the country. Fighting flared in Beirut as well as in south Lebanon, where Palestinian and Israeli forces fell into a series of encounters.

The siege of Zahle finally ended on June 30, with an agreement mediated by an Arab League committee requiring the Phalange to withdraw. In the meantime, however, the initial Syrian–Phalange confrontation had metamorphisized into a far more threatening situation. The escalation began in late April, when the Israeli air force intervened on behalf of the hard-pressed Maronites and shot down two Syrian helicopters. Damascus immediately moved batteries of SAM–6 surface-to-air anti-aircraft missiles into the Bekaa Valley and into Syrian territory adjacent to the Lebanese border.

With this, the "Syrian missile crisis" was born. Israel demanded the missiles' immediate removal. Damascus insisted the missiles would not be redeployed. The prospect of a major confrontation, perhaps even of war, between the two states appeared to grow.

Former Undersecretary of State Philip Habib was urgently recalled from retirement and sent to the Middle East as a special presidential emissary. Reagan also personally urged Prime Minister Begin to allow time for a diplomatic resolution before resorting to force. Near the end of July, Habib's efforts met with success. By then, however, the "missile crisis" had merged into other interlocking crises that inflamed passions throughout the region.[20]

The first major development complicating Habib's mission had nothing to do with Lebanon, but much to do with the overall nature of the Arab–Israeli conflict—particularly the legacy of past traumas and the fear of long-range intentions that so often fueled the parties' actions. In early June, Israeli warplanes suddenly streaked in a low-flying arc across

Jordan and Saudi Arabia to bomb and destroy a nearly completed French-built nuclear reactor on the outskirts of Baghdad. Israel justified the attack by charging that the installation was part of a scheme to produce nuclear weapons for use against the Jewish state. Baghdad hotly denied the accusation, and the French government and the International Atomic Energy Agency (IAEA) dismissed the contention that Iraq was close to acquiring a nuclear military capability.

Official U.S. reaction was ambivalent. Aware that Israel had set a new and disturbing precedent by carrying out history's first successful attack on a nuclear installation, and worried over the affair's implications for Habib's mission and the deteriorating situation in Lebanon, some of Reagan's top advisers urged "strong, even punitive" measures against Israel. Others shared the secretary of state's opinion that "the suspicion that Iraq intended to produce nuclear weapons was hardly unrealistic."[21]

Haig's view was not unreasonable. Amid a general consensus that Israel had possessed a nuclear capability since the late 1960s, there was logic in the conclusion that some of its Arab antagonists would not balk at seeking nuclear arms of their own. Nor could Israeli fears of the consequences of an Arab nuclear capacity be discounted as unwarranted paranoia. For no one could say with any degree of certainty what might result from efforts to achieve a nuclear balance of terror in the Middle East.

If, in these terms, Israel's strike on the Baghdad reactor was understandable (whether actually motivated by fear of Iraq's potential as it then stood or intended as a signal that Jerusalem would take extreme measures against any Arab nuclear potential, however remote), it also provided much food for thought. To some, it might have reinforced the urgency of working for a resolution of the Arab–Israeli struggle before time and technology injected beyond recall a new, threatening, and perhaps exceedingly unstable element into the Middle East political equation.

But this was not Haig's inclination. Although he was understanding of the reasons behind Jerusalem's decision, he advanced neither Baghdad's possible intentions nor the broader issue of nuclear rivalry in the Middle East as basic considerations for determining a U.S. response to Israel's attack. Instead, solidly bound to his initial global strategic vision, he could not go beyond arguing that "while some action must be taken to show American disapproval, our strategic interests would not be served by policies that humiliated and weakened Israel."[22]

Washington officially decried the attack, and acknowledged that U.S.-supplied equipment had been used in its execution. The U.S. delegation at the United Nations supported a Security Council resolution condemning the Israeli strike. The secretary of state also formally notified congress that a substantial violation of Israel's commitment to utilize U.S.-supplied weapons only for defensive purposes might have occurred. Finally, Reagan suspended a scheduled delivery of four F–16 fighter planes to Israel.

On the other hand, these steps were openly diluted. While official spokesmen were denouncing Israel's action, the president announced that it was "very difficult" for him "to envision Israel as being a threat to its neighbors." At the United Nations, Ambassador Jeanne Kirkpatrick stressed that Washington would support a condemnatory resolution only if it did not imply sanctions against Israel. The United States (together with Israel) also voted against an IAEA resolution, adopted by a margin of 29–2, censuring the attack on Iraq's reactor. Then too, although the administration had notified congress of a possible violation of the terms under which Israel received U.S. arms, it never offered a final judgment on the matter.[23]

The furor over the Baghdad raid was soon overshadowed by other manifestations of the Arab–Israeli conflict. Under the impetus of the Zahle and missile crises, clashes involving the PLO, Israel, and the Israeli-sponsored forces of Major Haddad in south Lebanon multiplied during the early summer of 1981. By June, a buildup of Palestinian guerrillas in the area was well underway, and Israeli planes were frequently attacking Palestinian supply routes and bases.

The situation deteriorated drastically on July 17, as Israeli warplanes dive-bombed a residential section in the heart of Beirut. The target was a PLO complex, but according to the Lebanese government three hundred civilians were killed and over eight hundred wounded in the attack. Israel disputed the claim, arguing that the raid occasioned only about one hundred deaths. In any case, the sobering demonstration of Israeli firepower against an Arab capital produced an international outcry. The Reagan administration decided to delay another scheduled delivery of F–16s to Israel. Haig described the decision as not taken in response to "any specific action" but rather stemming from the president's belief that Middle East tensions made it "highly inappropriate" to send additional arms into the area.[24]

Days after the Beirut air raid, Israel indicated its willingness to have Philip Habib negotiate what amounted to a cease-fire along the Lebanese border. Although Habib was not authorized to communicate directly with the PLO, negotiations with that body were conducted through a chain of intermediaries. With discreet help from Saudi Arabia, the emissary managed to arrange a cease-fire that went into effect on July 24. Three weeks later, the Reagan administration approved the delivery of the blocked warplanes to Israel.

With the PLO refraining from attacking targets across the border, and

Israel suspending aerial warfare in Lebanon, the Syrian missile crisis was also defused. Damascus' missiles would remain in place until they were destroyed when the cease-fire collapsed ten months later.

The end of the four month Lebanese crisis gave Washington some relief from immediate Middle East pressures. However, it did not produce any sign that the administration was ready to accord higher priority to searching for a resolution of the Arab–Israeli conflict. In August, the man who was soon to become Saudi Arabia's king, Prince Fahd, unveiled a peace proposal that seemed to imply acceptance of Israel's right to exist.

The Fahd Plan called for Israel's withdrawal from all occupied territories, and the removal of all Israeli settlements from the area. It envisaged the establishment of a Palestinian state, with Arab Jerusalem as its capital, and the establishment of guarantees for freedom of worship of all religions at Jerusalem's holy places. Acceptance of Israel's right to exist was implied by the plan's provision for a settlement based on the right of "all countries of the region to live in peace," guaranteed by the United Nations.[25]

At the time, Washington saw nothing in the plan that merited exploration as a possible avenue for diplomatic progress. That same month, Anwar Sadat arrived in the United States urging the U.S. government to become more active in trying to broaden the Egyptian–Israeli peace. He was treated cordially, but his main proposal—inclusion of the PLO in the peace process—was flatly rejected.[26]

These events reflected the administration's continuing concern with "strategic consensus." Still deeply embroiled in the AWACS battle, U.S. policymakers were too preoccupied with the idea of a geopolitically secure Middle East to pay much heed to the Arab–Israeli question.

The point was emphasized when Menachem Begin visited the United States in early September. Talks between President Reagan and the Israeli leaders reportedly concentrated so much on possibilities for strategic cooperation that neither the strike against Iraq's nuclear reactor nor the bombing of Beirut was ever discussed.[27] By the time Begin departed, agreement had been reached that lower level negotiations would work out specific areas of the U.S.–Israeli military cooperation. Despite the publicity accorded to this development, many observers, noting that Israel had long been considered an informal U.S. ally, saw the move toward more formal ties primarily as a play to reduce congressional opposition to the Saudi arms deal. Haig reinforced this interpretation by stressing the proposed strategic agreement's symbolic nature.[28]

Arab reaction was nonetheless predictably adverse. At the end of November 1981, Israeli and American negotiators produced a memorandum of understanding committing the two countries to a variety of coordinated activities designed to counter "the threat to peace and security of the region caused by the Soviet Union or Soviet-controlled forces from outside the region. . . . "Although the explicit mention of the Soviet Union was intended to indicate that military cooperation did not extend to the Palestine conflict, Arab bitterness was not assuaged.[29]

In the meantime, apparently hoping to cast Saudi Arabia in a favorable light just prior to the crucial senate vote on the Saudi arms deal, as well as to mitigate growing Arab ire over the new twist in U.S.–Israeli relations, Washington somewhat modified its earlier coolness toward the Fahd peace plan. Having originally dismissed the proposal as no more than a reformulation of established Saudi positions, the administration had already informed Fahd that the plan could not be regarded as a practical suggestion for peace. However, in late October U.S. spokesmen suddenly directed moderate praise at the Saudi overture as a step toward peacemaking.[30]

During the Reagan administration's first year in office, this low-keyed gesture would be the high water mark of official indications that the United States remained interested in broadening the Egyptian–Israeli peace.

It came too late to help Anwar Sadat claim that in going to Jerusalem and Camp David he had furthered Egyptian as well as wider Arab interests. Sadat was assassinated in early October 1981 by Islamic fundamentalists, who considered him a traitor to the Arab cause. Although the Arab world did not mourn his passing, his successor—Vice President Hosni Mubarak—vowed to maintain the fallen leader's commitment to peace.

The Fahd Plan fared no better in the Middle East than it had in the United States. Israel saw the proposal as a device to achieve the Jewish state's destruction. Although Yassir Arafat expressed an interest in the Saudi suggestion, dissident Palestinian factions, together with hardline Arab regimes such as Syria, Libya, and Iraq, strongly opposed the implication that the Arab world would recognize Israel.[31]

An Arab summit meeting at which the plan was to be discussed in late November collapsed when 13 of 21 Arab League members failed to attend. It was not long before the Saudis themselves began waffling, finally denying in early 1982 that Saudi Arabia was prepared to recognize Israel under any circumstances.

The Fahd Plan's demise came in the midst of an international furor sparked by Israeli legislation that effectively annexed the Golan Heights.[32] The move was followed within three weeks by the announcement of plans to settle an additional twenty thousand Israelis in the Golan area. These measures not only led to riots among the region's fifteen thousand Druze inhabitants, but also to a wave of international protests and new strains in U.S.–Israeli relations. On December 7, the United States supported a Security Council resolution declaring Israel's action "illegal" and "null and void." The resolution further called on Israel to rescind the decision, and committed the Council to consider "appropriate measures" should Jerusalem fail to comply by January 5, 1982. When the Security Council met again in January, however, the United States vetoed a call for the application of sanctions against Israel.

Washington unilaterally showed displeasure over the Golan Heights annexation by suspending ongoing talks over further strategic cooperation and placing in abeyance a projected purchase of Israeli-made military equipment. These steps had been strongly encouraged by Secretary of Defense Casper Weinberger, who argued that unless some "real cost" were imposed on the Israelis, the United States "would never be able to stop any of their actions." The U.S. ambassador to Israel, Samuel Lewis, informed Begin that the revival of strategic collaboration depended on progress in the autonomy talks as well as Israeli restraint in Lebanon.[33]

Begin accepted the challenge, accusing the United States of treating Israel as a "vassal state" and pledging that the Golan decision would not be reversed. Israel, he said, understood that by suspending discussions on strategic matters, Washington had "cancelled" the November memorandum of understanding.[34] Although U.S. spokesmen later disputed this interpretation, nobody seemed disposed to deny that the brief period of formal military cooperation with Israel was temporarily over.

After a year in office the Reagan administration's record in the Middle East was not enviable. Its major unblemished accomplishment had been to smooth the way toward the consummation of the Egyptian–Israeli peace treaty, under the terms of which Israel was to evacuate its last outposts in the Sinai by the end of April 1982. In this area, U.S. diplomacy successfully arranged for an international force, known as the Multinational Force and Observers (MFO), to monitor the peace once the area reverted to Caro's control. Washington was scheduled to provide nearly half of the 2600 MFO troops. The first unit of the force, comprising 670 Americans, was to be deployed in mid-March, 1982.[35]

Apart from this, however, the administration had accomplished little on behalf of its declared view of U.S. interests in the Middle East. Although formally committed to broadening the Arab–Israeli peace process, nothing of significance had been attempted in that realm. The Palestinian autonomy talks remained comatose and were of obviously low interest to Washington. The Fahd Plan had come and gone, with only mild expressions of U.S. interest that were in themselves of questionable sincerity. While the administration won the AWACS battle, the victory raised serious questions regarding the degree to which Arabs could rely on the United States as an ally. An overlapping U.S.–Arab–Israeli "strategic consensus" remained as far from realization as had been true a year earlier.

Finally, the year ended with the bitter aftertaste of the quarrel with

Israel over the Golan Heights. The demands put by Ambassador Lewis to Menachem Begin as conditions for reviving the strategic understanding indicated more than irritation over Israel's independent course of action. At bottom, the Lewis–Begin confrontation seemed to reflect the administration's dawning realization that most major political questions in the Middle East could not be isolated from the impact of the Arab–Israeli conflict.

Although this appeared to signal a budding change in Washington's perception of the Middle East, it left unresolved the problem of establishing a policy. During the following months, the administration would give signs of considering the need to devise a clear approach to the Arab–Israeli conflict. However, it would also consider, and ultimately follow, a strategy suggested, and then acted upon, by Israel.

"AMERICA'S MOMENT IN THE MIDDLE EAST": LEBANON

In June 1981, Israel's electorate returned the Likud to power. The event was a significant departure in the country's politics. While Begin's 1977 victory over the dominant Labor alignment had been widely interpreted as the result of a protest vote, the Likud now stood as a major political force in its own right. In the words of one Israeli analyst, the 1981 election indicated "no less a positive choice *for* the Likud than a negative vote *against* the Alignment."[36]

The significance of this went beyond establishing the transformation of Israel's domestic politics from an essentially single dominant party system to a dual party-bloc system. A decisive number of Israelis now supported the Likud's expansionist aims as well as the tactics through which these were sought. The latter, by 1981, included not only the highly visible drive to settle the occupied territories launched after 1977, as well as Begin's outspoken claims to sovereignty over the areas and his often abrasive diplomacy, but also an increasingly evident shift in the Israeli government's perception of military force as an instrument of national policy.

Faced by the Arab world's rejection after 1948, Israel's leaders long saw little possibility of forcing a change in Arab mentality at gunpoint. Time, the argument went, was the key element; for with repeated demonstrations of the Jewish state's viability and impregnability the Arabs must eventually reconcile themselves to its existence. As developed under successive Labor governments, Israel's military doctrine emphasized defense of the status quo by limited demonstrations of military superiority and a readiness for large-scale pre-emptive action. As is true of so much in Israel, the doctrine was neither universally held nor adhered to strictly. As demonstrated by Labor governments after 1967, the doctrine was

taken to mean that changes in Israel's borders effected by arms in a pre-
emptive war could constitute a new situation to serve as the object of
defense. Nonetheless, Yoram Peri's assessment of the dominant Labor
view of the military's role in national policy is essentially correct:

[The] concept had always accepted the assumption that Israel cannot enforce
her will upon the Arab World by military means, owing to her inferior geostrategic and geopolitical positions. Israel's objective was the preservation of the
status quo.... This was in essence a negatively-oriented defensive, preventive
concept, although it was designed to lead to the ultimate achievement of a positive
objective—Arab acceptance of Israel's existence.
This defensive character influenced the various dimensions of Israel's security
concept . . . since Israel cannot resolve the Jewish–Arab conflict in war, however
great her victory may be, we must avoid any war which is not essential. A war
which cannot be prevented must be brief and inexpensive.[37]

The perception changed fundamentally under Menachem Begin's
stewardship. In part a natural consequence of Begin's militant Revisionist
Zionist ideology, the trend was accelerated by Egypt's elimination from
the ranks of Arab belligerents, by the resignation from the cabinet in
the spring of 1980 of Ezer Weizman, who as minister of defense since
1977 had been the government's most prominent advocate of flexibility
on political and territorial questions, and by the rising influence of Israel's hawkish chief of staff, General Raphael Eitan, and his erstwhile
colleague, ex-general, and (since 1977) minister of agriculture, Ariel
Sharon. Thus, the Likud's program of expanding and consolidating
Israel's presence in the occupied territories was increasingly complemented in the late 1970s by Israel's growing military involvement in
south Lebanon and its open support of Lebanese Christian militias to
the north.

These three key elements of Likud policy were accompanied by a basic
change in Israeli military doctrine. No longer was it assumed that Arab
attitudes could not be altered by force. On the contrary, the dominant
belief in the upper echelons of the government came to be that a purely
"military solution" to the Arab–Israeli conflict was within grasp:

. . . the primary objective was not one of thwarting Arab intentions to harm Israel
and preservation of the status quo until the Arabs accept and recognize the State
of Israel, but rather a fundamental modification of the status quo and the en-
forcement of an Israeli solution upon the Arabs either by peaceable means or
through creating a new political order in the Middle East which will significantly
and radically weaken Arab ability.[38]

Put another way, the militancy of Israel's leadership was fueled by the
belief that the threat or use of military power could alter the regional

status quo in order to realize the dream of a secure, and expanded, state. The immediate geopolitical target of Israeli power was clear. Lebanon would be invaded in order to smash the PLO and establish a friendly, if not dependent, regime. Syria could either resist, and also be crushed, or nurse its own bitter hostility in isolation while watching its sway over Lebanon evaporate. In either case, with the Palestinian movement eliminated, the core of Arab–Israeli hostility would be removed. Jordan, claimed by some of Israel's leaders to be already a Palestinian state, would perforce become the sole realistic focus for Palestinian political aspirations.[39]

It was a dangerous calculation. However, the new Begin government that assumed power in mid–1981 found Ariel Sharon serving as minister of defense and Rafael Eitan still in the chief of staff's chair. The threesome, which in less than a year would launch the Israeli–PLO war in Lebanon, was eager for the test.[40]

Begin chose not to act in Lebanon until the final step toward peace with Egypt was accomplished. In the interval, Jerusalem was preoccupied by the evacuation of settlements in the areas that would revert to Egyptian control in the spring. To encourage voluntary compliance by some five-thousand Jewish settlers in the Sinai, the government allocated approximately $270 million as compensation—a sum that averaged about $200,000 per settler-family. Still, a minority of settlers, supported by members of Gush Emunim and Rabbi Meir Kahane's Jewish Defense League, gathered in the Israeli-built north Sinai town of Yamit promising to resist all efforts to expel them. However, Israeli Army units finally managed to remove them with no loss of life or injuries.[41]

On April 25, 1982, Egypt regained control of virtually all the Sinai Peninsula up to the 1967 international border. A strip of coastal land, Taba, on the Gulf of Aqaba adjacent to Eilat, was temporarily placed under the MFO's administration pending final agreement with Israel on the precise location of the international frontier.

A month later, Secretary of State Haig delivered a major address before the Chicago Foreign Policy Association. Proclaiming the arrival of "America's moment in the Middle East" Haig reflected the administration's belated awareness of the need to consider the impact of local Middle East issues on Washington's pursuit of its own goals in the region. Warning that the United States "must shape events in the Middle East if we are to continue hoping for a more peaceful international order," Haig promised a broad new approach. He did not specify particulars, but pledged that Washington would revitalize the Palestinian autonomy talks, promote an end to the Iran–Iraq war, and reduce tension along the Lebanese–Israeli border.[42]

Despite the promise of his words at Chicago, Haig was fully aware that the administration still had not settled on any concrete plans for pursuing these objectives.[43] He was, in short, expressing only the hope of a new departure, not a commitment.

On June 6, Israel unleashed a massive invasion of Lebanon. Any plans for U.S. initiatives in the Middle East evaporated. Washington was soon reacting to events.

Jerusalem initially described the invasion, dubbed "Operation Peace for Galilee," as a limited action to clear Palestinian guerrillas from a 40-kilometer strip in south Lebanon. The pretext was a chain of events that began with the wounding of Israel's ambassador in London by non-PLO Arab gunmen on June 3. In response to the attack, Israeli planes bombed PLO positions in south Lebanon. This, in turn, produced a PLO reaction in the form of rocket attacks on Israeli targets across the border. Claiming a breakdown of the cease-fire engineered by Habib nearly a year earlier, Jerusalem sprang the invasion, its spokesmen stressing that Syrian troops would not be engaged unless they forced the issue first.

These official Israeli pronouncements were inaccurate. Israeli forces did not pause at the proclaimed 40-kilometer goal. One of the three invading columns was directed through central Lebanon, making a clash with the Syrians inevitable. By June 7, Israeli troops were initiating action against Syrian units. Over the next two days, major encounters between the Israeli and Syrian air forces took place. Israel not only destroyed Syria's anti-aircraft missile batteries in the Bekaa Valley but also reportedly shot down sixty Syrian warplanes.

By June 9, the Israeli Army was on the outskirts of Beirut. Along the way, the advancing forces, accompanied by an estimated twelve hundred tanks and supported by heavy air and naval bombardments, swept through the towns of Tyre, Sidon, and Damour, eliminated the Palestinian stronghold at Beaufort Castle, and gained control of major inland population centers. By the 14th, with close to 90,000 Israeli troops in Lebanon, Beirut was cut off by land and sea.

Trapped inside West Beirut were some 6,000 Palestinian fighters, a virtually equal number of Syrian troops, and a sizeable portion of the city's 500,000 civilian inhabitants. The siege lasted ten weeks. Leery of the casualties its own forces might suffer in a frontal assault, the Israeli military command relied on artillery, air, and naval bombardment to inflict maximum damage on the city's defenders—a tactic that wreaked havoc on the civilian population as well.

The campaign was marked from the outset by heavy civilian casualties, not only in Beirut but throughout the area swept by the invading forces. Although the actual numbers of dead and wounded remain in dispute, it seems likely that between June 5 and the end of the Israeli–PLO war, over 12,000 noncombatants were killed.[44] Although Israel claimed that this figure was highly exaggerated, the toll was undoubtedly high.

It was, of course, not the nearly fatal wounding in London of Israeli Ambassador Shlomo Argov that caused Lebanon's painful summer. The invasion was an outgrowth of the Begin government's belief that Israel had the capacity to alter decisively the political context of the Middle East by force. Little effort was made to hide this after the first flurry of flimsy rationalizations offered during the attack's opening stages.

In addition to its primary objectives of facilitating the creation of a friendly government in Lebanon, rendering the Syrian position there untenable, and—above all—destroying the PLO, Israel retained a subsidiary hope of securing the deployment of U.S. troops as part of a peacekeeping force in southern Lebanon. When combined with the U.S. contribution to the MFO in the Sinai, such a force would have done much to encase Israel within a U.S. military tripwire defense.

These ambitions were all referred to, though not all with equal precision, in an Israeli cabinet statement on June 13. The cabinet's least precise reference was to Israeli objectives vis-à-vis the PLO, for the statement indicated only Jerusalem's determination to secure the withdrawal of that organization from Lebanon.[45]

Other Israeli spokesmen were more explicit. In Washington, Israeli General Aharon Yariv acknowledged that his government's declared goal of securing a "buffer zone" in Lebanon had been "perhaps misleading." The invasion's real purpose, he said, was to "demolish the infrastructure of the PLO," and "to do our best to see it was not reestablished."[46]

Yariv spoke truthfully. The invasion of Lebanon was not undertaken for limited purposes—it sought neither to chastise the PLO, nor simply to remove its forces from Israel's borders. The goal was to eradicate the PLO once and for all, to give both its political and military dimensions a blow from which they could not recover. In short, the Begin government hoped to kill and bury the organizational manifestation of Palestinian national consciousness, and by doing so to destroy, or at least render impotent, the consciousness itself.

The rationale behind this was also not long hidden. It was summarized best in then Foreign Minister Yitzhak Shamir's observation that "the defense of the West Bank starts in Beirut."[47] The comment went to the heart of Israel's decision to launch the war in Lebanon. For it was not simply the PLO's organizational structure—nor, certainly, its limited military capacity—that Israel's leaders perceived as a threat. The greatest menace in their eyes was that the PLO embodied Palestinian nationalism, the primal force that voiced an irreducible claim to Palestinian self-determination in the occupied areas Begin had sworn never to abandon.

To Israel's leaders, the PLO's destruction was therefore a crucial step toward the absorption of the occupied territories. The hope was that smashing the Palestinian national movement would demoralize the inhabitants of the occupied territories and lead to their acceptance of some form of administrative "autonomy" compatible with the Israeli government's maximalist territorial ambitions.[48]

The plan had been discussed at the upper levels of the Israeli government for at least a year. Despite opposition from high ranking intelligence officers who insisted that an attempt to restructure and control Lebanon would be inordinately costly and almost certainly doomed to failure, the government's eagerness for the venture grew, spearheaded by Ariel Sharon's single-minded determination.[49]

Jerusalem's hawkish confidence was reinforced by the attitude of Bashir Gemayel, the leader of the Maronite-dominated Lebanese Forces, who not only had long urged Israel to rid Lebanon of the PLO and promised his troops' cooperation in the effort but also wanted very much to be the country's president. The invasion's timing had been linked to the necessity of ensuring Gemayal's victory when Lebanon's parliament elected a new president in August 1982.[50]

U.S. policymakers were not ignorant of Israel's plans. As early as September 1981, Sharon discussed the possibility of an invasion with U.S. officials. In October, Prime Minister Begin told Haig that Israel might enter Lebanon in order to rearrange the situation there more to its own liking. By the end of the year, Sharon had outlined to Philip Habib and Ambassador Lewis the rationale and plans behind the anticipated invasion "in some hypothetical detail."[51] In early 1982, the director of Israeli military intelligence, General Yehoshua Saguy, informed Haig of plans for a large-scale advance to Beirut aimed at destroying the PLO infrastructure. On the eve of the invasion, in late May, Sharon shocked a group of State Department officials in Washington by sketching out a military campaign "that would rewrite the political map of Beirut in favor of the Christian Phalange."[52]

Many lower level U.S. officials were outspokenly opposed to the Israeli plan. Years later, Ambassador Lewis recalled that he and Habib "were rather dumbfounded by the audacity and the political concept this seemed to involve." Habib responded "very vehemently" to Sharon's overture: "He made it extraordinarily clear to Sharon that this was an unthinkable proposition as far as the United States was concerned." Haig records that Sharon's exposition in late May "shocked a roomful of State Department bureaucrats."[53]

However, Israel's leaders were understandably far more impressed by the reactions they elicited from the secretary of state and the president. Upon first hearing of Israel's plans for Lebanon, Haig established a formula from which he and Reagan never departed. The United States would not support a major assault on Lebanon unless it came "in response to an internationally recognized provocation and [was] proportionate to that provocation."[54] Over time, the patient repetition of this caveat came to seem progressively more like tacit approval. In early January 1982, Reagan sent a message to Begin urging Israel to exercise "restraint" vis-à-vis Lebanon. According to Haig, Begin then sought "to redefine the conditions under which the United States would consider an Israeli attack justified." Haig repeated the well-worn formula: any action would have to be strictly proportionate to an "internationally recognized provocation."

Begin agreed, then changed his mind, and in one of his exercises in creative nuance, told Reagan that there would be no major Israeli action "unless [Israel was] attacked in clear provocation."[55]

Creative nuance did not elicit creative firmness. Over the next several months the administration's sole response to the rising signs of Israel's readiness to invade Lebanon was the level reiteration of Haig's formula. When Sharon "shocked" State Department bureaucrats in May, the Israelis studied Haig's reaction closely:

Sharon and his delegation took careful note of Haig's presentation of the American position. Haig issued no threat against Israel's forthcoming military action. He confined his comments to the issue of the cease-fire. He emphasized that it would take an unquestionable breach of the cease-fire by the PLO to warrant an Israeli riposte. Without such a breach, he said, an Israeli attack would be neither understood nor accepted in the international arena.[56]

According to Israeli military correspondent Ze'ev Schiff, Israel's ambassador to Washington saw Haig a few days later. The ambassador, having presumably heard yet another recitation of Haig's formula, reported "that he had discussed in a positive atmosphere Israel's need to seize a security zone in southern Lebanon."[57]

It appears impossible to doubt Schiff's conclusion:

Whether wittingly or unwittingly, Washington gave Jerusalem the green light to invade Lebanon, and Israel interpreted the lack of a strong American position as support for all its objectives.[58]

Washington, at least at the vital levels of the president and secretary of state, seemed willing on the eve of the invasion to countenance a heavy Israeli strike against the PLO. However, the administration as a whole seems to have failed to understand that Israel's leaders were driven by uncompromising nationalistic ambitions to seek the organization's annihilation. During the summer of 1982, the difference in outlook, not a minor one, was mirrored most clearly in the administration's embarrassed concern over the sustained ferocity of Israel's attack. The high numbers of civilian casualties, Israel's indiscriminate use of U.S.-supplied cluster-bombs (an anti-personnel weapon of such devastating power that Israel was pledged to utilize it only in defense against attacking regular military forces), the shelling and bombing of West Beirut, and the prolonged suffering of the area's civilian inhabitants—all led to strains between Jerusalem and Washington.

Yet none of this caused Washington to reverse its basic support of Israel's invasion. Paradoxically, the fundamental reason for this appears to lie in the lesson gleaned by the administration from its first eighteen months in office. Having finally recognized the futility of ignoring the Arab–Israeli conflict, U.S. policymakers acknowledged the need for a new approach. And here they encountered an intellectual vacuum. When Haig spoke in Chicago, the administration still had little, if any, idea of what its promised initiative on the Palestine issue might be.

The answer was provided by Israel's invasion of Lebanon. The rapidity with which Israel smashed the Syrians and bottled up the PLO in Beirut provided Haig with a "strategic plan," an approach fit for what he saw as "a great opportunity."

Syria and the PLO . . . had been defeated. The Syrians and the Soviets were at each other's throats in the aftermath of Syria's humiliating defeat at the hands of the Israelis. . . .
The moment had come to move all foreign forces—Syrian, Palestinian, and Israeli—out of Lebanon. . . . The elements [of U.S. policy] were clearly defined: withdrawal of all foreign troops, reestablishment of effective government in Lebanon, a safe northern border for Israel.[59]

Haig saw the key to success as a U.S. effort to "use the shock of the Israeli attack to force the PLO out of Beirut."[60] Haig's vision foresaw that once this were accomplished there would be fresh horizons for U.S. efforts to resolve the Palestine problem:

[A] settlement in Lebanon would have significant consequences . . . Syria and the PLO, the heart of Arab opposition to Camp David, had been defeated. With the PLO's "military option" gone, Israel's arguments against granting a wider measure of autonomy to the Arabs of the West Bank and Gaza would be negated . . . [creating] a fresh opportunity to complete the Camp David peace process. . . .[61]

Whether Haig really thought that the Begin government had launched the war in Lebanon as a prelude to surrendering, or reducing, its claims on the occupied territories is a moot question. It seems likely that he was relatively unconcerned with the future of the West Bank and Gaza so long as the political effectiveness of those who used the Palestine issue to complicate U.S. policy in the Middle East was undermined.

Haig's "strategic plan" for the Middle East jelled almost totally with Israel's vision of a restructured regional environment. With the elimination of PLO and Syrian influence in Lebanon, a settlement in that country could hardly result in anything other than a government dominated by the Lebanese forces. Washington was undoubtedly aware of, and concurred with, Israel's plans to see Bashir Gemayel installed as Lebanon's president.

However, there remained the disparity between the U.S. and Israeli views of the PLO's fate. The difference was largely one of degree, although nonetheless significant. While Haig was certainly prepared to see the PLO rendered impotent as a political actor, he thought in terms of its organizational effectiveness. Moreover, it must be presumed that Haig, and the administration as a whole, saw a need to balance the effort required to destroy the PLO against broader concerns of international opinion and the administration's desire to cultivate moderate Arab regimes. The siege of Beirut would show that Begin, Sharon, and their colleagues thought in terms of the PLO's elimination, and were not particularly concerned that the political cost of seeking that end would be too high. Seeing the battle as crucial to the essence of the Jewish state, Israel's leaders set no great store by world opinion, and even less by that of moderate Arab regimes.

It was not long before Haig experienced at firsthand the import of this basic difference. In late June, with the Palestinians securely trapped in the Lebanese capital, Israel's ambassador to Washington passed on a message from Ariel Sharon: "If Israel could "do more" in West Beirut, it "could bring the PLO to its knees." The secretary of state reacted sharply:

I expressed my disapproval; it was not our idea to bring the PLO to its knees under the guns of Israeli soldiers, but to rid Lebanon of the PLO under circumstances that would enhance the prestige and influence of the Lebanese government.[62]

This was the last element of Haig's "strategic plan" for the United States. Washington would support Israel's use of force to rearrange conditions in Lebanon, expel the PLO from that country, and chastise the Syrians. It would not, however, provide the Israelis with a carte blanche to eradicate the PLO at all costs. The melody and counterpoint of U.S. policy toward the invasion of Lebanon would combine encouragement and restraint. Syria would be humbled, Lebanese politics would be recreated, and the PLO would be neutralized, though in somewhat less drastic a fashion than that preferred by Sharon.

Haig lost his job shortly after replying to Sharon's "PLO-to-its-knees" message. The full story of Reagan's decision to dispense with Haig's services remains murky. It was, however, reported that the president was displeased by Haig's handling of the Falklands-Malvinas crisis as well as by what appeared to have been the encouragement he gave to Israel during the Lebanon invasion's planning stages.

The irony was that by the time he left office, Haig had convinced the administration, or at least the president, of the wisdom of his "strategic plan." Thus, although (much to Haig's annoyance) the new secretary of state, George Shultz, spoke at his confirmation hearing on July 13 of the need to recognize "the legitimate needs and problems of the Palestinian people," U.S. policy throughout the long siege of Beirut adhered closely to the course charted by Haig.[63]

Even before Haig left Washington it was evident that Reagan had adopted the suggested approach. Although the United States voted for a Security Council resolution on June 6 calling upon Israel to withdraw from Lebanon "forthwith and unconditionally," an official statement issued twenty-four hours later implied that an Israeli pullback should be conditional upon the elimination of Palestinian attacks from south Lebanon.[64] When Israel ignored the resolution and pushed on to Beirut, the Council considered a draft resolution threatening sanctions. Reagan first wanted the U.S. delegation to support the measure but was persuaded by Haig to order it vetoed.

On June 21, Prime Minister Begin visited the White House. Reagan and his guest met in the Oval Office as Israeli naval and artillery fire continued to fall on West Beirut. Reagan was worried that the Israelis would escalate the attacks, and perhaps even enter the city to eliminate the PLO. He outlined the U.S. position developed by Haig, who recalls the president's demeanor as "firm and stern."[65]

Yet Begin was publicly received with warm friendliness. Although Reagan expressed some reservations over Israel's intervention in Lebanon, he stuck to the view that U.S.–Israeli objectives were essentially harmonious:

It's clear that we and Israel both seek an end to the violence [in Lebanon] and a sovereign independent Lebanon under the authority of a strong central government.... We agree that Israel must not be subjected to violence from the north.[66]

In the meantime, the administration had also been trying to arrange for the withdrawal from Beirut of the trapped Palestinian forces. Philip Habib, still serving as diplomatic point-man in the Middle East, led the search for a formula to evacuate PLO fighters—although once again he was precluded from direct contact with the Palestinian leadership. As the weeks of negotiations dragged on, the administration continued its purposeful two-pronged policy, relying on Israel's military pressure to force the PLO into evacuating while manifesting visible, though hardly harsh, signs of displeasure over what it considered excessive Israeli force.

Amid sporadic and ever-collapsing truces, the siege of West Beirut continued through July and August. Although Yassir Arafat had agreed in late June to a PLO withdrawal, an operational plan acceptable to all parties remained elusive. The PLO leader alternated between swaggering among the defenders (and newsmen), more or less daring the Israelis to come and get him, and hinting that his organization was ready to come to terms on the basis of a Palestinian state comprising the West Bank and Gaza. In late July, he gave U.S. congressman Paul McCloskey a signed note stating his acceptance of all UN resolutions "concerning the Palestine questions."[67] Though the ploy won Arafat and the PLO some favorable publicity, it had no impact. The PLO was simply in no position to bargain for such high stakes.

The Arab world vociferously condemned Israel, but proved strikingly unable to do much else. Libya's Colonel Qaddafi advised Beirut's defenders to die gloriously in the rubble. Damascus would no doubt have liked to pounce upon the Israelis, but its lack of military capacity had already been painfully demonstrated. Iraq, bogged down in its own war and separated from the fighting in Beirut by the rival Syrian regime, was in no position to enter the fray. Egypt expressed outrage over the invasion but was clearly unwilling to undo the diplomatic gains of years by renouncing the peace treaty. At the end of summer, Cairo angrily recalled its ambassador to Israel. Jordan could not hope to face the Israelis militarily, even had it (which it did not) wished to do so. Saudi Arabia and the Gulf states were unwilling to exert indirect pressure on Israel by imposing an oil boycott on the United States.

The basic issue was that no Arab state saw the option of taking action, whether military or economic, to help the PLO as commensurate with the costs that would be incurred. At the same time, it is likely that most Arab regimes were not overly sorry to see the PLO take a beating. Conservative regimes had no liking for the organization's radical tendencies; radical regimes had no love for its efforts to retain an independent, flexible identity.

While the war highlighted cracks in Arab ranks that had in any case never been hidden by reams of rhetoric about common interests, it also exposed strains within Israel. For the first time in Israel's history, domestic opposition to a government's wartime policies became common. In late June, thirty soldiers on leave from the fighting in Lebanon picketed Begin's residence to protest the possibility of an assault on West Beirut. In July, a group of over 120 reservists, including officers, publicly accused the government of having embarked on an "unjustified" and "aggressive" war. A popular colonel, Eli Giva, resigned the command of an armored brigade on grounds that his conscience would not allow him to serve while the prospect loomed of being ordered to take his men into Muslim West Beirut. Earlier in July, an anti-war rally reportedly drew 80,000 people.

It was not only at home that the Begin government came under heavy criticism. While visiting the United States in June, the Israeli prime minister was strongly challenged in official quarters other than the White House. A meeting with the Senate Foreign Relations Committee was described by Senator Paul Tsongas as unique: "In my eight years in Washington, I've never seen such an angry session with a foreign head of state."[68] Much of the ire directed at Begin stemmed directly from the growing volume of reports of civilian casualties. Not surprisingly, particular attention focused on Israel's use of cluster-bombs.

Not all senatorial anger was directed at the immediate effects of Israel's war in Lebanon. Senator Charles Percy seized the occasion to urge a change in Israel's settlements policy, arguing that a moratorium should be placed on the construction of new settlements in order to facilitate progress in the autonomy talks with Egypt. Begin would not be moved. Jews, he responded, had a right to live in the West Bank.[69]

On July 19, Reagan suspended the shipment of further cluster bombs to Israel and advised congress that a breach of Israel's obligation regarding the use of U.S.-supplied weapons "may have occurred." In late July and early August, stepped-up Israeli ground advances and air attacks against Beirut prompted another presidential rebuke. Writing to Begin on August 4, Reagan termed Israel's assaults on beleaguered West Beirut "disproportionate" and warned that serious doubts were being created as to whether Israel's use of U.S. arms was strictly for purposes of "legitimate self-defense." The message reportedly also listed a variety of possible economic, military, and diplomatic sanctions that might be considered by Washington should Israel not show greater restraint. A similar message the following day warned that U.S.–Israeli relations would be jeopardized by continued "unnecessary bloodshed."[70]

In the meantime, public discussion had broken out in the United States over the possibility of U.S. troops being sent to Lebanon as part of an arrangement to end the crisis. In early July, the White House announced its conditional readiness to take such a step. However, it was unclear just what role might be assigned to U.S. forces.

Two options soon emerged. One, closely paralleling the view expressed by Israel's government soon after the invasion started, called for the employment of U.S. troops on a long-term basis to help separate Israeli forces from local combatants. The alternative was to utilize U.S. forces only for the limited purpose of facilitating a PLO evacuation from Beirut.[71] Considerable congressional opposition developed to the possibility of an extended military involvement. By the end of July, it was evident that were U.S. forces sent to Lebanon, it would probably be on the basis of the second option.

On August 6, the PLO agreed to an evacuation plan forwarded by Philip Habib through intermediaries. However, despite Reagan's August 4 message to Begin, the Israelis seemed to redouble their efforts to wreak as much destruction as possible before Habib's evacuation plan could be implemented. In a highly publicized message to Reagan that some took as casting doubt on the prime minister's grasp of reality, Begin had earlier replied to a presidential birthday greeting by noting:

I feel as a prime minister empowered to instruct a valiant army facing Berlin, where amongst innocent civilians, Hitler and his henchmen hid in a bunker deep beneath the surface.

Now he seemed determined to unleash ever greater violence on the city housing his Palestinian enemies. On August 5, *The Times* correspondent described "the most savage bombardment" yet carried out against Beirut:

...the Israelis fired artillery rounds into houses and apartment blocks at the rate of one every ten seconds, smashing dozens of homes and killing or wounding their occupants. To describe the shelling as indiscriminate would be something of an understatement.[72]

Referring to another bombardment at about the same time, the U.S. ambassador in Beirut sent a confidential report to Washington describing ninety "unbelievable minutes."

Simply put, tonight's saturation shelling was as intense as anything we have seen. There was no "pinpoint accuracy" against targets in "open spaces." It was not a response to Palestinian fire. This was a blitz against West Beirut....

At best this will be interpreted as another example of U.S.–Israeli collusion in the war in Lebanon.[73]

Perhaps no other battle in history has received more sustained first-hand journalistic coverage. Reporters flocked into the city, both the Christian and Israeli-dominated eastern sector and the Muslim-Palestinian western area. Most of those covering the latter were appalled by the carnage resulting from Israel's late-July/early-August attacks. Horror stories of civilian deaths, hospital emergency rooms sporting stacks of severed limbs alongside piles of human entrails, and the diabolical effects of phosphorus bombs on innocent civilians sprouted in the world press.

The reporters were aware, and did not hide their awareness, that the PLO was partly responsible for Beirut's suffering. The organization had

turned West Beirut into a bastion, and then, while accepting the principle
of withdrawal, tenaciously negotiated for the best deal it could get.

Still, the heavy Israeli attacks raised journalistic passions. *New York
Times* correspondent Thomas Friedman risked his life to get a wide view
of the Israeli shelling and bombing on August 4, then filed a story
terming the attack "indiscriminate." When his editors deleted the word,
Friedman telexed an incensed protest that made its own way into print
not long afterward:

... I don't just throw words like indiscriminate around. I knew I was using a
strong word. . . .

It was clear ... that what took place yesterday was "indiscriminate" bombing
and shelling. My God, your own reporter's hotel was hit thirty feet from his
room and there are no Palestinian positions in the Commodore. . . .

It is perfectly obvious that you deleted the point out of a fundamental lack
of courage. You knew I was correct and that the word was backed up by what
I had reported. But you did not have the courage—guts—to print it in *The New
York Times.*[74]

But if the *New York Times* hesitated to describe Israel's attacks as "indiscriminate," other news organs did not. Even before the August 4
assault, NBC's nationally renowned television commentator, John Chancellor, raised deep doubts about the nature of Israeli policy. Delivered
against the backdrop of Beirut rubble, Chancellor's remarks were broad-
cast nationally in the United States on August 2:

The Israel we saw here yesterday is not the Israel we have seen in the past. The
stench of terror was all across the city. Nothing like it has ever happened in this
part of the world. I kept thinking of Madrid during the Spanish civil war. What
in the world is going on? Israel's security problem on its border is fifty miles to
the south. What is the Israeli army doing here in Beirut? The answer is that we
are now dealing with an imperial Israel which is solving its own problems in
someone else's city—world opinion be damned.

The bruised sensibilities of on-the-spot observers did not predominate
in Washington's orderly hallways. Reagan reacted to the August 4 bombing with harsh words, and even openly wondered whether Israel was
employing U.S.-supplied arms for "legitimate self-defense." Yet, virtually at the same time, Vice President George Bush and Secretary of
State George Shultz reportedly assured a group of American Jewish
leaders that the administration would take no sanctions against Israel,
that it was determined to see the PLO leave Lebanon, and that Israel
remained a key U.S. strategic ally.[75] When Israel's attacks continued in
the wake of the PLO's acceptance of the Habib Plan, and even after the

Israeli cabinet agreed "in principle" to the proposal on August 10, the administration was still slow to react.

Then, on August 12, the Israeli air force followed up several hours of continuous shelling by unleashing the heaviest bombing of the war on West Beirut. The bombing, which lasted for eleven hours, was supplemented by further Israeli advances on the ground. Incomplete casualty figures released the same day by the Lebanese government reported at least 128 dead and 400 wounded. Lebanese intermediaries angrily withdrew from the effort to arrange the PLO's evacuation from Beirut.[76] Reagan was reportedly outraged and telephoned Begin personally to express his ire. At an urgent meeting of the Israeli cabinet, Defense Minister Sharon was roundly criticized for having ordered the August 12 assault without consulting his colleagues. The air raid delayed finalization of Habib's plan for the removal of PLO and Syrian troops from Beirut. Finally, on August 19, Israel's government formally approved the scheme.

With the Israeli army now occupying most of Beirut, the first stages of the evacuation were underway when Lebanon's new president was chosen by sixty-two members of the national parliament. To nobody's surprise, Bashir Gemayel ran—unopposed—for the post and was elected by a margin of 57–0. Five deputies abstained. A majority of Muslim deputies did not attend the proceedings. Israel welcomed the predictable outcome. Washington also reacted favorably.

The first Palestinian and Syrian troops had begun leaving the city two days earlier. The movement continued over the next several days. By the time it was over, some fourteen thousand individuals, including PLO and Syrian troops as well as several hundred civilians, departed by land and sea. Over half of the evacuees went to Syria. The PLO leadership, together with approximately one thousand guerrillas, were eventually to reach Tunisia, where the organization established new headquarters. Smaller PLO units were destined for relocation throughout the Arab world, including Algeria, Jordan, the Sudan, North Yemen, South Yemen, and Iraq.

The PLO did not take the finale as a defeat. While their leaders claimed "victory" for having withstood Israel's onslaught, rank and file fighters—deprived now of heavy weapons but retaining personal arms—displayed a morale that was almost jubilant. Popular Arab sentiment, anxious to find some peg on which a mantle of pride might be hung to cloak at least partly the humiliation of the Arab world's recently displayed impotence, promptly took up the theme. Well beyond the Middle East, many observers concluded that the siege of Beirut had indeed ended with a Palestinian "political victory."

On the level of image and symbolism, there was some truth in this. The ten-week spectacle of numerically stronger Israeli forces hammering away with some of the most modern military equipment in the world at a basically defenseless city, but kept at the gates by a few thousand relatively lightly armed irregulars, generated much sympathy for the Palestinian underdogs. Widely publicized scenes of mayhem and suffering caused many of Israel's friends to feel that Jerusalem had carried things too far. Moreover, the PLO's stubborn defiance helped cast the Palestinians in a new light in Western press reports. The defenders of West Beirut were not simply cowardly terrorists bent on obliterating innocent victims. They were, at least, also proud fighters prepared to wage hopeless combat against overwhelming odds. Amid the horror, the summer's events underscored the Palestinians' commitment to their national cause.

Yet the value of this sort of "victory" was hardly as important as Beirut's Palestinian survivors wished to believe. Image and symbolism alone do not define actual or potential political influence. Perhaps the triumphant proclamations of Yassir Arafat and his followers on the eve of their departure from Beirut were merely the Palestinian version of a stiff upper lip. Or perhaps the plain joy of having survived caused PLO leaders to forget a premise they had clung to since the organization's founding: that political success depended on the ability to have recourse to force. This had been a basic feature of the PLO's calculations when it clung to the goal of undoing Israel, and it had still been accepted as valid when the organization manifested its later tendency to settle for a Palestinian state on the West Bank and Gaza. In each case, whether it was to be relied on for direct confrontation with Israel or employed indirectly to threaten open-ended regional instability unless Palestinian demands were satisfied, a credible force option remained vital to the PLO's chances of realizing its objectives.

Having lost what by its standards were enormous amounts of materiel, suffered the deaths of an estimated one thousand guerrillas and the loss of some six thousand others captured by the Israelis, seen its organizational infrastructure in Lebanon smashed, and, above all, its remaining fighters scattered to the far corners of the Arab world, the PLO was grieviously weakened as a relevant political actor.[77] Whatever face Arafat and his colleagues tried to put on it, the reality was that the Palestinians' ability to determine their national fate was now more questionable than at any time since 1948. The lesson would be driven home in a particularly vicious form only days after the evacuation from Beirut.

Yassir Arafat left Beirut by sea on August 30, going first to Greece and then on to Syria. On September 11, 800 U.S. marines sent earlier to help supervise the PLO's withdrawal and maintain public order left Lebanon. It has frequently been charged that the United States, which under the Habib Plan had pledged to "do its utmost" to ensure that

Israeli guarantees regarding the security of noncombatants would be observed, was precipitate in withdrawing the marines.[78]

The issue remains controversial. Given Washington's lack of a clear program for dealing with the problem of Palestinian homelessness—and its policy of supporting Israel's intervention in Lebanon—the Reagan administration had few alternatives in disposing of the marines. Apart from assigning them to protect Palestinian civilians for an indefinite period or trusting Israel to provide security, there seemed little else to be done.

Under these circumstances, and having already committed itself to a temporary intervention in Lebanon, the administration chose to count on Israel. To the extent that Washington shared blame for the ensuing tragedy, its real culpability lay not so much in the immediate decision to withdraw the marines as in its overall failure to recognize, and act on, the need for a clearly defined objective vis-à-vis the Palestine problem.

Three days after the U.S. withdrawal, Bashir Gemayel was assassinated. No group claimed responsibility for the president-elect's murder, but no group involved in Lebanon's tangled politics escaped being named by Beirut's energetic rumor mill. The Palestinians, it was said, did it for revenge; or, again, it was the Syrians; or, on the other hand, it was the Israelis who found the new president less pliable than anticipated; or, others alleged, it was Gemayel's own rivals within the Lebanese Forces. In the end, however, the balance of evidence appeared to lead to Damascus.[79]

Gemayel's death was immediately followed by an Israeli takeover of West Beirut, a move that violated the terms of the cease-fire arranged by Habib. The Palestinian refugee camps of Sabra and Shatila came under Israeli control. Israel justified the occupation of West Beirut by citing the need to ensure order in the aftermath of Gemayel's assassination.

On Thursday evening, September 16, with the United States having supported a Security Council resolution condemning Israel for entering West Beirut, Israeli authorities allowed units of the Lebanese Phalange to enter the refugee camps. It was later claimed that the Phalangists had been authorized only to search out guerrillas suspected of hiding in the area. However, over the next thirty-six hours, while the Israeli army stood on the camps' boundaries, there ensued a massacre of unarmed men, women, and children. The death toll has not been definitively established. Israeli intelligence later put the figure at 700–800; Arab sources placed it as high as 2000.[80]

In Israel, a large segment of public opinion reacted sharply, quickly, and with horror to the suspicion of official collusion. On September 25, an estimated 350,000 Israelis demonstrated against the possibility that their government saw tactics bordering on the genocidal as the only means of coping with Palestinian nationalism. Forced by the tide of outrage, Menachem Begin reluctantly permitted a blue ribbon panel of inquiry chaired by Israeli Supreme Court Justice Yitzhak Kahan to investigate the Sabra and Shatila massacre.

The Kahan Commission eventually concluded that Defense Minister Sharon should be held indirectly responsible for the tragedy. Under this shadow, Sharon was dismissed from his position—though not from the cabinet. He became a minister without portfolio.[81]

Time Magazine assigned Sharon a far more direct responsibility, alleging that he had encouraged the Phalangists to take revenge for Gemayel's murder. Sharon charged libel and sued the periodical for $50 million in a New York federal court. Both sides claimed victory after the final verdict was handed down in 1985. *Time*, the court ruled, failed to prove its charge. Sharon, it said, had failed to establish that the magazine acted maliciously in publishing the story. *Time* unrepentently stuck by the essentials of its account. Sharon received no compensation.[82]

The United States was widely held to share the onus attached to Sabra and Shatila. Obviously embarrassed, and hoping to mitigate some of the criticism, the Reagan administration ordered the marines, this time 1200 of them, once again into Beirut. They were there, said Reagan initially, for the limited purpose of helping the Lebanese government provide security for Beirut.

Sabra and Shatila also froze the PLO's winning smile in place. The erstwhile "political victory" was revealed in all its emptiness for what it was: the temporary glow of words and pictures of little, if any, consequence. The victims of Beirut's most recent killing grounds were the families and friends of many of those who had shouldered a Kalishnikov and marched off with the triumphant assurance of having focused world attention on their cause. The memory would haunt them. Numbers of them would inevitably blame the leader who had rejected Qaddafi's free advice to die among the rubble and instead chosen a negotiated withdrawal. The organizational wreckage of the PLO begun by the Israeli invasion of Lebanon seemed likely to be fully accomplished in the wake of the Beirut massacre.

WASHINGTON'S TWO-TRACK APPROACH

As Beirut's bloody summer ground to its end, the Reagan administration decided that the final elements for restructuring the Middle East along more congenial lines were falling into place. With Syria cowed and the PLO badly mauled, Washington looked forward to a regional environment that would isolate and eventually totally frustrate radical Arab forces.

By the time Yassir Arafat's fighters evacuated Beirut, this broad ambitious vision had been refined into a two-track political approach. On one level, the United States would do its utmost to encourage Jordan's assumption of the role assigned to it under the Camp David Accords. That, of course, would require King Hussein to join Israel in determining the nature of Palestinian autonomy in the West Bank and Gaza Strip. On a second level, U.S. policy would promote the consolidation of the newly installed Gemayel regime in Lebanon and that country's incorporation in a U.S.-sponsored regional peace.

In the administration's view, Israel's military prowess now made it possible to achieve success on both fronts without the need for compromise with either the PLO or Syria. Washington would remain opposed to any form of Palestinian statehood in the expectation that the Arabs of the West Bank and Gaza would soon see no realistic alternative to life under Israeli occupation other than acceptance of whatever role in their affairs might be devised for Jordan. By the same token, the extension of the peace process to Jordan and Lebanon could proceed without regard for Syrian sensibilities. In both cases, the predictable cries of outrage by the PLO and Damascus would be inconsequential.

As had consistently been true of its plans for the Middle East, the administration's new strategy proved to be a costly miscalculation. Events would show that Damascus, which despite its recent defeat still had some 30,000 troops in Lebanon and retained substantial influence among approximately 7,000 Palestinian guerrillas in Syrian-controlled territory, could affect both the politics of Arab–Israeli peacemaking and the nature of things in Lebanon. Nor was the PLO as inconsequential as Washington hoped. No moderate Arab leader, including King Hussein, proved willing to ignore the organization's claim to represent the Palestinian people. On the other hand, the administration also mistakenly assumed that Israel would readily follow the U.S. lead in peacemaking.

By the end of Reagan's first term, these miscalculations would be all too apparent. In the meantime, however, the policies to which they led helped propel the United States into an ill conceived intervention in Lebanon.

The administration unveiled what was billed as a "fresh start" in its approach to the Middle East on September 1. Delivering a nationally televised address, President Reagan espoused a dynamically upbeat outlook. Yassir Arafat and the last Palestinian guerrillas had abandoned Beirut forty-eight hours earlier. A week before that, Bashir Gemayel had been elevated under Israeli guns to Lebanon's presidency.[83] Sabra and Shatila were still some days away.

Arguing that the new situation now offered the possibility of building a "stable and revived Lebanon essential . . . for peace in the region," Reagan indicated the two-track policy his administration intended to pursue:

But the opportunities for peace in the Middle East do not begin and end in Lebanon. As we help Lebanon rebuild, we must also move to resolve the root causes of conflict between Arabs and Israelis.[84]

Driving home the import of his newly acquired awareness of the Palestine issue's centrality to regional peace, Reagan projected a novel personal concern for the Palestinians' fate:

The departure of the Palestinians from Beirut dramatizes more than ever the homelessness of the Palestinian people. Palestinians feel strongly that their cause is more than a question of refugees.
    I agree.

In addition to the human dilemma, the president saw two political lessons arising from the recent conflict in Lebanon:

First, the military losses of the PLO have not diminished the yearning of the Palestinian people for a just solution to their claims; and second, while Israel's military successes . . . have demonstrated that its armed forces are second to none in the region they alone cannot bring just and lasting peace to Israel and her neighbors.

The essential issue, he argued, was that of reconciling Israel's "legitimate security concerns" with the Palestinians' "legitimate rights." The solution, said Reagan, could be discovered only through negotiations based on the Camp David accords. However, in what seemed to be the most significant part of his remarks, he added that although the United States had long refrained from "public comment on key issues," it was now evident that "some clearer sense of America's position . . . is necessary to encourage wider support for the peace process."

Having promised a more active approach to substantive issues, Reagan's remarks did not materially depart from what had long been Washington's established preferences. He did, however, sharpen the United States' standing opposition to both a Palestinian state and Israel's permanent retention of the occupied territories.

. . . as we look forward to the future of the West Bank and Gaza, it is clear to me that peace cannot be achieved by the formation of an independent Palestinian state in those territories. Nor is it achievable on the basis of Israeli sovereignty or permanent control over the West Bank and Gaza . . .

The "Jordanian Option" was placed squarely at the center of U.S. policy toward the Palestinian question:

... it is the firm view of the United States that self-government by the Palestinians of the West Bank and Gaza in association with Jordan offers the best chance for durable, just, and lasting peace.

Although reaffirming the principle that an Arab–Israeli settlement should result from "an exchange of territory for peace," the president stressed that Washington had no fixed position regarding the amount of land to be returned to Arab control. Final U.S. policy on that issue would be "heavily affected" by "the extent of true peace and normalization and the security arrangements offered in return." On Jerusalem, Reagan limited his comments to the standard official formula: the city should remain undivided and its final status ultimately decided through negotiations.

But all this referred to Reagan's view of a final settlement. His immediate concern, rooted solidly in the Camp David accords, was to promote a transitional arrangement that would prove "to the Palestinians that they can run their own affairs, and that such autonomy would not threaten Israel's security."

Clearly hoping to encourage Jordanian participation in revived autonomy talks, Reagan pledged that Washington would become far more active in working for a transitional arrangement for the West Bank and Gaza. The United States would support reasonable compromises and put forward "detailed proposals" of its own when this seemed likely to facilitate agreement.

To encourage the receptivity of the key protagonists, Reagan's message simultaneously sought to reassure Israel of U.S. support and play upon Arab fears that the future would be even more grim than the present.

... make no mistake, the United States will oppose any proposal—from any party and at any point in time—that threatens the security of Israel. America's commitment to the security of Israel is ironclad. And I might add, so is mine.

While this carrot was intended to foster Israeli cooperation in the search for Palestinian autonomy, the Arabs were urged on with a thinly veiled stick:

The United States will not support the use [by Israel] of any additional [occupied] land for the purpose of [establishing] settlements *during the transitional period.*[85]

In contrast, the president's admonition to Israel that "the immediate adoption of a settlement freeze" would do much to create Arab confidence in the autonomy talks was delivered in the context of friendly advice rather than as a firm principle of U.S. policy.

The message was unmistakable. Until the establishment of a "transitional period," the United States would continue to support, or at least not oppose, Israel's policy of settling the occupied areas. If the Arabs were unwilling to see Israel steadily increase its hold on the occupied lands, they would best rush to accommodate the U.S. desire for an autonomy agreement. Washington must have fully expected that Arab governments, as well as Palestinians, would believe that only a bad deal could result from any negotiations undertaken in the immediate aftermath of the war in Lebanon. Reagan's point was that delay would only result in a worse one.

Just over a week later, Secretary of State George Shultz reinforced the president's remarks. In a statement delivered before the House Foreign Affairs Committee, Shultz stressed that the administration's objectives vis-à-vis Lebanon and the Arab–Israeli problem were essentially distinct and therefore susceptible to pursuit through independently erected policies. In Lebanon, the United States would help rebuild the country and revive the central government's authority. Conceding that chances of achieving this would "be helped by progress in the overall search for a Middle East peace," Shultz nonetheless maintained that Lebanon's problems were "distinct and must be addressed whenever possible separately from our Middle East peace initiative. . . ."[86]

In planning its pursuit of Middle East peace, said Shultz, the administration had now reached two "paramount conclusions":

(1) It is time to address, forcefully and directly, the underlying Palestinian issues, and (2) genuine success depends upon broadening participation in the negotiations to include, as envisaged in the Camp David accords, Egypt, Israel, Jordan, and the representatives of the Palestinian people.

Promising "renewed dynamism" in the search for peace, Shultz accorded priority to arranging the five-year period of autonomous self-government for the occupied territories. He argued, as had Reagan, that final peace, though requiring "peace for territory" could be arrived at only once "Israel and her neighbors, Jordan, Egypt and the Palestinians engaged in fair, direct and successful negotiations. . . ."

Shultz repeated many other points made by Reagan. He noted that the ultimate U.S. position on the extent of Israel's withdrawal from the territories would be "significantly influenced by the extent and nature of the peace and security arrangements . . . offered in return," that Jerusalem should remain undivided and its final status resolved through negotiations, and that Washington would seek "some form of association" with Jordan for the West Bank and Gaza. Yet, by elaborating on other aspects of the U.S. position on a final settlement he also more clearly indicated key strictures that Washington hoped to see imposed on the Palestinians' eventual political status:

In the Middle East context, the term "self-determination" has been identified exclusively with the formation of a Palestinian state. We will not support this definition of self-determination.

Even more alarming to Arabs trying to assess the full implications of Washington's "fresh start" were Shultz's statements regarding the future of Israeli settlements in the occupied territories. Not only did the Secretary of State dispose of the precedent set by Anwar Sadat's demand for the removal of all settlements from the Sinai as part of the price for peace with Israel, he also retreated from the standing U.S. position that the settlements contravened international law.

The status of Israeli settlements must be determined in the course of the final status negotiations. We will not support their continuation as extraterritorial outposts, but neither will we support efforts to deny Jews the opportunity to live in the West Bank and Gaza under the duly constituted governmental authority there, as Arabs live in Israel.

Having said this, it was almost superfluous for Shultz to add that in suggesting a "freeze" on Israeli settlements the administration's concern was "not with their legality or illegality, but with their effect on the peace process."

Shultz ended his remarks before the House committee with a plea for sustained congressional support in pursuing a goal that "could hardly be accomplished in a few short weeks." The administration, he promised, would persevere in searching for a long-term, just solution. In words that would soon seem empty as well as unintentionally ironic, he offered an apparently ironclad commitment:

I pledge to you that we will be exercising the creativity, the persistence, and the dogged determination to succeed which marked the successful effort in Beirut.

It was evident that the new U.S. initiative was predicated on the exclusion of both the PLO and Syria from the envisaged peace process. By clinging firmly to the provisions of the Camp David accords, Washington in effect upheld the veto that had been granted to Israel over who might represent the inhabitants of the West Bank and Gaza in any negotiations. At the same time, the intention to exclude Syria from the peace process was amply indicated by Reagan and Shultz. Although the president had explicitly stressed the inadmissibility of "Israeli sovereignty over the West Bank and Gaza," he was loudly silent on the Golan Heights. Indeed, neither Reagan nor Shultz made any mention of Syria in launching the "fresh start." A close examination of the comments made by both men shows that only their brief references to the applicability of Security Council Resolution 242 "to all fronts" might be interpreted as a possible allusion to the necessity of an eventual Israeli withdrawal from Syrian territory.

While Arab reaction to the U.S. peace initiative was mixed, Israel's was prompt, clear, and overwhelmingly negative. The Israeli cabinet accused Reagan of deviating seriously from the Camp David framework. Prime Minister Begin went before the Knesset and was supported in his rejection of the Reagan Plan by a vote of 50–36. Israel also rejected Reagan's suggested settlement freeze, on grounds that "such settlement is an inalienable right and an integral part of our national security." The point was emphasized four days after Reagan's speech when the Israeli government allocated $18.5 million for the construction of three new Jewish settlements and approved plans for the creation of seven more. At the same time, Begin fired off an angry letter to Washington warning that Reagan's proposal would lead to a PLO-dominated state and the expansion of Soviet influence in the Middle East.[87]

Washington received the rebuff philosophically. The State Department announced it was neither surprised nor disappointed by Israel's reaction and that it still hoped Jerusalem might reconsider its position should the general principles embodied in the president's plan win Arab acceptance. A statement was issued strongly condemning the decision to build new settlements.

That was virtually the end of overt U.S. efforts to promote Israel's acceptance of the new peace initiative. Thereafter, the striking thing about the "Reagan Initiative" was its rather ghostlike character—a supposed presence that was, with increasing infrequency, sometimes referred to, but which somehow never materialized. By the latter half of the 1980s, even the more faithful of true believers were tired of waiting for the specter's incarnation. Menachem Begin seemed to have described the initiative correctly from the start by labelling it "a lifeless stillborn."[88]

But while Reagan's "fresh start" initiative only increased the Begin government's tenacious grip on existing policies, it provoked much political activity in the Arab world. The president's comments had not, of course, fully satisfied any Arab actor, and they fully infuriated some. Even the most moderate Arab voices continued to insist on the return of East Jerusalem to Arab control, on Israel's full withdrawal from the occupied territories, and on the Palestinians' right to self-determination.

Yet in the months—and then years—that lay in the future, the Reagan Plan became the lodestone that guided attempts by the chief Arab moderate parties—Jordan, the mainstream PLO under Yassir Arafat, Egypt, Morocco and Saudi Arabia—to construct a clear position that might generate a sympathetic U.S. reception.

Efforts along these lines promptly ran into obstacles. Damascus refused to countenance a peace process that ignored its interests. Opposition also came from radical rejectionists, to whom the idea of any possible settlement with Israel remained anathema. Although the latter, principally comprising Palestinian splinter groups and the radically nationalist Libyan regime, did not share Damascus' apparent pragmatic readiness to settle the conflict with Israel under certain circumstances, the continuation of Syria's exclusion from the U.S. search for peace undermined the distinction.

The tortuous political maneuvering and bloodshed that continued to mark inter-Arab politics after 1982 was, therefore, largely the consequence of three interrelated phenomena: the efforts of moderate Arab actors to devise a program for a settlement with Israel that would win U.S. support and lead to the return to Arab control of the West Bank and Gaza; the failure of Arab moderates to ascertain whether any program they might realistically support in the Arab world would enlist Washington's commitment to their minimal territorial claims; and, finally, the fundamental division between Arabs prepared to seek a political settlement and the rejectionists.

In the aftermath of the Lebanon war, the cutting issue was whether or not moderate Arabs could formulate, support and successfully promote a plan to settle the conflict with Israel on the basis of a Palestinian West Bank entity linked in some form to Jordan. Encouraged particularly by Egypt and Saudi Arabia, Jordan and the PLO began to explore the extent to which Palestinian nationalism might bow to Washington's preference for the "Jordanian option."

Although portents of this development were only obliquely indicated by immediate Arab reaction to the Reagan Plan, Washington's initiative was cautiously welcomed by important Arab voices. Egypt and Jordan quickly issued statements greeting the apparent revival of U.S. interest in peacemaking as "positive." PLO "foreign minister" Farouk Kaddoumi described the president's comments as "not altogether bad."[89]

On September 6, 1982, an Arab summit conference met in Morocco, convened by Morocco's King Hassan for the purpose of formulating an agreed-upon peace plan. Except for Libya, all members of the Arab League, including Syria, attended. The PLO was represented by Yassir Arafat. Egypt, its League membership suspended after Cairo signed the peace treaty with Israel, was, of course, absent.

The proceedings at Fez were carefully handled to avoid producing a single criticism of the Reagan Initiative. Instead, the summit resulted in the unanimous approval of an Arab peace proposal. The Fez Plan called for a total Israeli withdrawal from the West Bank and Gaza, and the establishment there of a Palestinian state whose capital would be East Jerusalem. Reaffirming the PLO's status as the Palestinian people's sole legitimate representative, the plan called for the occupied territories to be placed under UN rule during a short transitional period leading to Palestinian statehood. It upheld the principle of freedom of worship for all religions at holy places, and implied Arab willingness to accept Israel's legitimacy by proposing that a settlement include a Security Council guarantee of "peace among all states of the region."[90]

There was no doubt that unanimity had been achieved at the price of ambiguity. The suggestion of a Security Council guarantee was as much an effort to dilute the U.S. role in any peace process that might develop as a way to avoid the earlier Fahd Plan's call for the recognition of the right to exist of all states in the area—an approach that to the hardline Arab position seemed too strong an indication of Israel's acceptance by the Arab world.

Israeli spokesmen correctly described the Fez Plan as a restatement of known Arab views. Still, the leaders gathered at Fez saw the plan as an opening bargaining position. Over the next few weeks, there was much talk in the Arab world about the possibility of bridging the gaps between the Fez and Reagan proposals.

In late October, an Arab League delegation, headed by Morocco's King Hassan, and including representatives of Algeria, Jordan, Saudi Arabia, and Tunisia, arrived in Washington to discuss the matter directly with Reagan. The president was cordial, but his Arab visitors failed to generate interest in the Fez Plan as a basis for serious negotiations. They departed with King Hassan insisting that a settlement required Israel's full withdrawal from occupied lands but noting that the delegation's effort showed "that we ourselves want to live in peace with Israel."[91]

The gesture had in any case probably been futile from the start. Reagan had made it plain in his September address that Washington wanted to pursue peace via the autonomy talks, and that meant that the United States was above all interested in Jordan's entry into the Camp David process. Twenty-four hours before the Arab delegation reached Washington, the State Department let it be known that what it sought from the Arab League was authorization for Jordanian participation in the Palestinian autonomy negotiations—in other words, an abandonment of the League's position upholding the PLO as the Palestinians' sole legitimate representative.[92]

At the same time, the United States was endeavoring to convince King Hussein to ignore all constraints and seize the opportunity to be Israel's negotiating partner. Much as he wished to see a Jordanian presence returned to the West Bank, Hussein would not cooperate. Two face-to-face sessions with President Reagan in late December produced nothing more than the King's refusal to join the autonomy talks without PLO and Arab League support.

By then, Sabra and Shatila's gory shadow had been cast over the Middle East. The massacres altered neither the objectives nor strategies of any of the main protagonists in the Middle East drama. The dynamics of the Arab–Israeli conflict remained unchanged. However, the slaughter of unarmed Palestinian refugees graphically highlighted the Palestinians' plight. It also lent renewed urgency to the expectations of those in the Arab world who hoped to see Washington turn its efforts to the promotion of a settlement that would uphold the minimal claims of Palestinian nationalism.

Chief among these was Yassir Arafat, who had realized from the start of Israel's invasion of Lebanon that what had been placed in most jeopardy was the credibility of his willingness to explore avenues for a settlement. As early as June 6, Arafat's spokesmen had scoffed at Jerusalem's initial claims that the invasion sought only to sweep Palestinian guerrillas from a strip along Lebanon's southern border. Israel's real intent, they said, was "to crush the PLO." Aiming their remarks at world opinion, and particularly at the United States, they warned that should Israel succeed, "the hardest of hard liners would dominate Palestinian politics."[93] It was not a threat but a cry for help in avoiding an outcome that the established PLO leadership dreaded as tantamount to placing the Palestinian cause in the grip of extremist tendencies that were doomed to failure.

It was largely to buttress the credibility of their moderate vision among their own following that Arafat and his cohorts steadily insisted during the dark days of their entrapment in West Beirut that the PLO was chalking up a "political victory." It was for the same reason that PLO leaders urgently searched for political gains once the evacuation from Beirut was effected.

Farouk Kaddoumi's guardedly positive reaction to the Reagan Plan was as much designed to explore openings to Washington as to reassure the Palestinian rank and file that the PLO leadership still saw a chance for progress through negotiations. Days later, Arafat successfully arranged something of a political coup by having himself received in a private audience by Pope John Paul II. From the PLO's perspective, the meeting was a significant political event signalling that Palestinian moderates enjoyed important moral support at the international level. Again, that message seemed aimed primarily at the Palestinians themselves.

Israel's government was visibly infuriated by the PLO's political ploys. It had galled Begin and his colleagues to see the world press publicizing, and sometimes apparently sympathizing with, Arafat's claims of political victory from the wreckage of Beirut. It was even more irritating that the PLO managed to seem receptive to the Reagan initiative while Begin felt compelled to denounce the scheme in the strongest possible terms. Arafat's reception at the Vatican was the last straw. On the eve of the papal audience, Jerusalem issued a scathing denunciation:

The same Church which did not say a word about the massacre of the Jews for six years in Europe and did not say much about the killing of Christians in

Lebanon for seven years is ready to meet the man who perpetrated the crime in Lebanon and is bent on the destruction of Israel, which is the completion of the work done by the Nazis in Germany.[94]

The Vatican immediately branded the Begin government's statement as "an outrage against the truth." Arafat must have been well pleased. By embroiling itself in an intemperate conflict with the Roman Catholic Church, Israel only reinforced the impression that PLO leaders had strong friends in high places.

Then, the day after Arafat met the Pope, came the massacres at Sabra and Shatila.

Aware that his willingness to settle for a Palestinian West Bank–Gaza mini-state had long since led to divisions within the national movement, Arafat could not have failed to understand that the passions unleashed by Sabra and Shatila would make it more difficult than ever to convince his followers of the need for political flexibility. Yet he saw no viable option but to persevere in the search for a political opening that would sustain the viability of moderate Palestinian hopes. Given the context created by Israel's invasion of Lebanon and Reagan's announced initiative, Arafat's direction was virtually predetermined. He focused on Jordan, on the possibility that an arrangement might be reached with King Hussein which would, while not sacrificing the minimal claims of Palestinian nationalism, still be acceptable to the United States.

It was a direction sure to increase the strains on Arafat's position as Palestinian leader. Although PLO–Jordanian relations had thawed considerably in the wake of Egypt's move toward a separate peace with Israel after 1977, memories of the 1970 civil war in Jordan made many Palestinians see little difference between Hussein and Begin as enemies. Moreover, Damascus was bound to react violently against any effort to create a moderate Arab peace drive that downplayed Syrian interests.

Contacts between the PLO and Amman were stepped up throughout September and October. Rumors of a secret agreement between Arafat and Hussein were soon widespread. However, the first concrete sign of a rapprochement came in early October with the freeing of some seven hundred Palestinians who had been held in Jordanian jails since 1970.[95]

Arafat and Hussein met in Amman several days later. The PLO leader emerged from three days of talks giving the impression that he and the king shared a basic interest in a Palestinian–Jordanian federation. Indicating that he understood this solution to be in keeping with the Reagan Plan, Arafat mildly praised that proposal for containing "some positive elements." However, he also strongly criticized the U.S. initiative for failing to endorse the creation of a Palestinian state and for not acknowledging the PLO's right to represent the Palestinian people.[96]

Amid mounting speculation that Arafat had in fact agreed to abandon the national cause in return for the procedural figleaf of an empty juridical moment of Palestinian "statehood" that would be immediately followed by the creation of a federation of Gaza, the West Bank, and Jordan, PLO spokesman Mahmoud Labadi offered the following explanation:

Our basic aim . . . is to secure an Israeli withdrawal [from the West Bank and Gaza], get Israel to recognize our right of self-determination, set up a Palestinian state on the returned territory, and then talk of a federation or association.[97]

Given Washington's opposition to Palestinian statehood, and Hussein's ambition to recover as much as possible of his authority over the West Bank, this statement seemed to describe an almost certainly fruitless negotiating position. It did nothing to dispel the suspicion that Arafat was discarding the struggle for statehood in order to save a Hashemite-dominated remnant of Palestinian political existence through the good offices of King Hussein and Washington.

Nonetheless, no agreement was reached between Arafat and Hussein in the fall of 1982. However, another meeting between the two men at the end of November ensured that further efforts would be made to reach an understanding.

Meanwhile, tensions mounted within the Palestinian movement. Following the first meeting of Arafat and Hussein, Syria had strongly castigated the PLO chairman for acting without a mandate from the organization's executive committee. Amid some confusion as to the accuracy of the report, Damascus announced that five PLO groups joined it in denouncing the idea of federation.[98] By early 1983, the internal Palestinian controversy showed no signs of abating. It was becoming increasingly doubtful that Arafat could find some formula to paper over the differences.

In January, leaders of the same five Palestinian groups earlier alleged to have denounced Arafat's policies—the PFLP, the DFLP, the PFLP-GC, Saiqa and the Palestinian Popular Struggle Front—met in Tripoli under the auspices of Muammar Qaddafi. This time, there was no doubt of their position. They issued a hardline communiqué condemning and rejecting the Reagan Plan. Arafat rushed to repair the damage and was at least partly successful. Within days he apparently succeeded in convincing the leaders of the PFLP and DFLP, George Habash and Nayef Hawatma, of the vital need to preserve Palestinian unity.[99]

Still, it was impossible to hide internal frictions when the Palestine National Council (PNC) met for the first time since the evacuation from Beirut. The meeting, which opened in Algiers in mid-February, was marked by stormy sessions at which Arafat was sometimes forced to shout down his adversaries. While Arafat emerged still clearly in charge of the PLO, the outcome was a series of compromises between the hard-line and moderate positions.

While the PNC did not rule out PLO participation in U.S.-sponsored Arab–Israeli talks, it refrained from approving efforts to establish a joint Jordanian–Palestinian negotiating team. At the same time, although rejecting "all schemes which harm the PLO's right as the Palestinian people's sole representative," the PNC accepted the principle of a confederation with Jordan after the establishment of a Palestinian state.[100] Arafat and his colleagues sought to reassure the conclave that they had no intention of diluting the PLO's political role. Speaking for Fateh, Saleh Khalaf referred to a possible confederation with Jordan and proclaimed that "if any confederal base is established, it must be on the basis of an independent Palestinian state. . . . Any confederation without a Palestinian state means Reagan and means annexation with Jordan."[101]

The stand taken by the PNC on the question of a political settlement also reflected an uneasy compromise between the mainstream PLO leadership and Syrian- and Libyan-backed radical groups. The Fez Plan was described as the "minimum" program "for Arab political action," though it was to be "complemented" by military action. The Council's position on the Reagan Plan was phrased in these words:

The Reagan Plan in its procedure and contents does not respond to the Palestinian people's inalienable national rights. The Reagan Plan negates the Palestinian rights of repatriation, self-determination, and the establishment of an independent Palestinian state. It also ignores the PLO as the Palestinians' legitimate representative and contradicts international legitimacy. The PNC declares its refusal to consider the plan as a sound basis for a just and permanent settlement to the Palestinian question and the Arab–Zionist conflict.[102]

On the basis of this statement, PLO spokesmen insisted that "the PNC is not rejecting [the Reagan] Plan." Helena Cobban points out that by linking their statement to a refusal to "consider" the plan, PLO leaders felt able to uphold this interpretation. Arafat and his colleagues, she notes, believed that "they had won enough room to continue, in the months which followed, their exploration of the value of the U.S. initiative." Similar significance could be attached to the carefully-phrased declaration's precise affirmation that the Reagan Plan was not viewed as a "sound" basis for settling the Arab–Israeli conflict. This seemed to indicate that the PNC did not reject the plan as a basis for discussion toward that end.

The PNC's delicate balancing act was also evident in its pronouncements on terrorism and Egypt's relations with Israel. The former was denounced, though with special emphasis on what was described as "systematic and official American and Israeli terrorism against the Palestinian people, the PLO, the Lebanese people, the Arab nation, and all other liberation movements in the world." Egypt's relations with Israel were also denounced, and solidarity was expressed with Egyptian sentiment favoring abrogation of the Camp David accords. This last step only further embarrassed Arafat's effort to project a moderate Palestinian image. It also plunged the PLO into a bitter public controversy with the Egyptian government.[103]

Despite the shaky foundation of Palestinian unity erected at the Algiers meeting, Arafat was committed to the ongoing talks with Jordan. By spring, significant progress appeared to have been made toward an understanding between the PLO and the Hashemite kingdom. Agreement in principle was reached on the ultimate goal of a confederation between Jordan and the West Bank–Gaza area. Although the proposed arrangement seemed to aim at allowing Palestinians to claim parity with Jordan under a confederal umbrella, and therefore ran counter to the U.S. preference for Jordanian predominance, Washington did not openly attack Hussein's efforts to reach an understanding with the PLO. Apart from infrequent statements supporting in principle Hussein's efforts to form a Jordanian–Palestinian negotiating team, the United States remained aloof from the diplomatic maneuvering between Jordan and the PLO.

Movement toward an agreement on the principle of confederation did not prevent Amman and the PLO from being divided over key procedural issues as they looked forward to possible negotiations over the occupied territories. Having already obtained Soviet support for a "confederation on the basis of voluntarity between the independent Palestinian state after its creation and Jordan," Arafat sought to diminish the U.S. role and preserve as much as possible of the PLO's position as sole representative of the Palestinian people. To this end, he insisted that negotiations should proceed under guidelines established at the Fez Summit; that is, under auspices of the Security Council. Hussein hoped for a repetition of the purely U.S.-sponsored process that had brought peace to Egypt. He urged that Jordan and the Palestinians agree to negotiate with the United States and Israel on the basis of Security Council Resolutions 242 and 338, using the Reagan Plan as a point of departure.[104]

At this point, with Israel unmoved from its original condemnation of the Reagan Plan, the central issue for the PLO was the degree to which modification of its nationalist stand could be counted on to elicit U.S. support against Israel. Even Arafat's closest advisors took a dim view of the prospects. Farouk Kaddoumi and PLO military chief Khalil Wazir reportedly argued that any alteration of Palestinian aims would be a useless concession since Washington could not be expected to influence Israeli policy. It was also argued that unilateral concessions would simply enhance Damascus' chances of undermining the PLO by exerting leverage on Palestinian forces in Syrian-controlled parts of Lebanon.[105]

On the other hand, Hussein argued that only by entering into an arrangement with Jordan would the PLO stand a chance of ending the expansion of Israel's presence in the occupied territories. He was confident, and claimed to base himself on U.S. assurances, that Washington would respond to a Jordanian–Palestinian agreement by seriously endeavoring to halt Israeli settlement activities.

Arafat arrived in Amman in early April 1983 for what was heralded as a crucial encounter with Hussein. Two days of talks apparently left things much as they had been. When a final agreement proved elusive, Arafat—still speaking optimistically of an impending accord—flew to Kuwait to confront PLO colleagues.

But if Hussein or Arafat were hoping for some sign from Washington that might bolster arguments in favor of a Jordanian–PLO agreement, they were sorely disappointed. On April 8, State Department spokesman John Hughes issued a statement that was widely noted in the Middle East:

If Jordan announces its willingness to enter such negotiations [with Israel] we are determined to do our best to assure that the results of those negotiations are not prejudiced from the outset by the activities of any party which reduces the prospects of a negotiated peace.[106]

Asked whether the construction of Israeli settlements could be considered that sort of prejudicial action, Hughes replied in the affirmative. However, he then promptly added that his statements should not be interpreted as "a threat to cut off aid or take any other action against Israel."

The reply could only have added to Arafat's difficulties in seeking authorization for diplomatic flexibility in his talks with Hussein. Despite Arafat's apparent optimism upon leaving Amman for the meeting with other Palestinian leaders in Kuwait, the PLO refused to conclude the deal with Jordan. Hussein was obviously embittered by what he saw as PLO backtracking. An official statement issued in Amman declared with undisguised pique that Jordan would now:

leave it to the PLO and the Palestinian people to choose the ways and means for the salvation of themselves and their land, and for the realization of their declared aims in the manner they see fit.[107]

It was a heavy blow to Arafat and his strongest supporters. They remained mired, now even more deeply, in their dilemma. They had hoped that a confederal solution would advance their cause by wrapping the essence of Palestinian statehood in ambiguous trappings. However, ambiguity had swayed neither the United States nor Jordan. Moreover, it was clear that many within the Palestinian national movement saw Arafat as having come dangerously close to surrendering the goal of statehood without provoking any sign of interest on Washington's part. The waning credibility of Arafat's political approach redounded to the benefit of those who argued that the Palestinians' only hope lay in extremist militancy.

Yet Arafat continued searching for a viable middle ground between abandonment of Palestinian national aims and what he perceived as self-destructive militancy. Following the Amman statement, he immediately dispatched two representatives to reopen the dialogue with Hussein. Convinced that no other option existed, he clung to the goal of a Jordanian–Palestinian partnership throughout the turbulent period that lay ahead. Twenty-two months would pass before it seemed that his efforts might succeed.

In the meantime, strife mushroomed within Palestinian ranks. Dissidents challenged Arafat's authority, accusing him of having betrayed the cause. In May 1983, open rebellion broke out among PLO forces in Lebanon. The trouble soon spread to Fateh members. Supported by Syria, and led by a former Arafat associate, Abu Musa, the mutiny pitted pro- and anti-Arafat forces in a series of battles that erupted sporadically throughout the summer and into the fall. By November, Arafat had joined beleaguered loyalists in the port city of Tripoli. Over the next six weeks, Arafat's PLO troops, together with anti-Syrian Sunni Lebanese forces, were besieged by Palestinian dissidents and elements of the Syrian Army.[108]

By mid-December, as Israeli gunboats rounded out the spectacle of Middle East political paradox by shelling Tripoli's defenders from the sea while Syrian surrogate forces closed in by land, the United Nations completed preparations to evacuate the Palestinian leader and some four thousand of his followers. The pro-Arafat fighters eventually boarded PLO-chartered Greek ships flying the UN flag en route to ultimate destinations as far afield as Yemen, Algeria, Tunisia, and the Sudan.

The event was fraught with irony. Expelled from Beirut fifteen months earlier by Israelis who labeled him an inflexible fanatic, Arafat now underwent similar treatment at the hands of Arabs accusing him of an unseemly readiness to compromise. That Syria, Palestinian militants, and Israelis found themselves in a curious alliance against Arafat's forces underscored their common antipathy to the notion of a negotiated settlement. For above all, Arafat had managed to attract the wrath of each of them by seeking to explore possible diplomatic avenues opened by the Reagan Initiative. A final irony was that the Palestinian leader's efforts to attract U.S. attention at last paid off—in a very limited way, and under circumstances he had hardly anticipated. Apparently galvanized by the international outcry raised by a world that still remembered the bloodletting at Beirut, Washington pressured Israel into withdrawing the gunboats that had been preventing the UN fleet from evacuating the trapped Palestinians.

As it watched the blossoming of intra-Palestinian tensions after 1982, the Begin government never wavered in its view that Arafat, and the position he symbolized, posed the greatest threat to Israel's desire to absorb the occupied territories. Extremists who focused with single-minded dedication on armed struggle and maximalist demands faced Israel's overwhelming superiority of military power. Begin and his colleagues had no doubt that challenge could be met.

On the other hand, Palestinian moderates had proved tenacious and politically adept. They had to be met in the slippery realm of diplomacy, where conditions are subject to so many influences that little can be taken as given and complacency can be disastrous. It was there that Israel's grip on the occupied territories might begin to be loosened.

In mid–1983, Israel's then-foreign minister, and future prime minister, Yitzhak Shamir, accurately attributed the split between Palestinian moderates and militants to the PLO's "demoralization and disappointment in the wake of the tremendous [1982] defeat . . . in Lebanon." He did not see the main danger this might pose for Israel as lying in the possibility that the schism would lead the PLO into extremist positions:

I am not afraid of the radicalization of the entire organization. Practically speaking, it may be that Arafat's tactics are sometimes more dangerous to us.[109]

COLLAPSE OF AN APPROACH

Menachem Begin's characterization of the Reagan Plan as "stillborn" could not have been more apt. The "initiative" produced virtually nothing, apart from the fanfare of its announcement. On the other hand, the second level of the administration's proclaimed new two-track approach—Lebanon—was the focus of much attention in Washington after September 1982. The administration seemed not to have intended this development. Reagan and Shultz had taken care to stress that *both* the Palestinian issue and Lebanon would be dealt with. Shultz, although arguing that the two issues were largely distinct, had nonetheless postulated a politically important connection between them. The rebuilding of Lebanon, he said, could "only be helped by progress in the overall search for a Middle East peace."

However, when caught between Israel's total rejection of the Reagan Plan and its own conviction that any concession to Palestinian nationalism would further radicalism in the Middle East, the administration chose to abandon its initiative. Washington found that Lebanon had become not just a major object of its Middle East policy but the very heart of its approach to the region.

The shift was never explicitly acknowledged by U.S. policymakers. Officially, the two-track policy remained in force. Yet, as the Reagan Initiative languished from neglect while U.S. intervention in Lebanon steadily grew, Washington struggled to provide rationalizations. By late 1982, Lebanon was being officially termed the "key" to Middle East peace as well as a "vital interest" of the United States.[110] The connection drawn by Shultz between the Palestine issue and Lebanon was suddenly reversed. Unnamed "high ranking officials" were now telling the press:

You can't solve the Palestinian question without solving the Lebanese problem. And you can't have peace without solving the Palestinian problem.[111]

Cast in these terms, with Palestine placed safely beyond immediate concern, the U.S. goal seemed virtually indistinguishable from Israel's grand design for reordering the Middle East. By November, a former U.S. chief of naval operations described the impact of Israel's concept in terms that recalled Alexander Haig's early enthusiasm:

Within the Administration . . . there has been a recognition, right from the start [of Israel's invasion of Lebanon] that Israel's strategic objectives in the war closely paralleled American interests. There is now a dawning realization that the outcome of the sweeping victory opens the possibility of additional gains beyond Lebanon. Indeed, while the political situation is static to deteriorating in much of the rest of the world, Lebanon is emerging as the one place where we can see a decisive gain for the West and a clear setback to the interests of the Soviet Union and its radical allies.[112]

To be sure, differences existed between Israeli ambitions and the objective that came to be adopted by the Reagan administration. Washington looked to the conclusion of peace between Israel and the Lebanese government in the expectation that Jordan would then find it easier to strike a deal with the Jewish state. In Israel, the matter was more complex. Although not adopting Ariel Sharon's view that Jordan itself should become a Palestinian state at Hussein's expense, the Begin government remained committed to the retention of the occupied territories.[113]

In essence, Jerusalem was far more concerned that the outcome of the Lebanon war enhanced Israel's military security than that it serve as a political prelude to negotiations over the occupied territories. Israel's immediate strategic objective was to ensure the neutralization of Palestinian and Syrian power in Lebanon. The problem was that with its military victory in hand, the Begin government found itself uncertain as to how to achieve this.

Begin had originally banked on the long-term benefits of installing Bashir Gemayel as the friendly head of a Phalangist-dominated central Lebanese government. That hope, an outgrowth of years of Israeli support of the Phalangists' struggle in Lebanon, was strengthened by the Gemayel clan's steady encouragement of Israel's 1982 invasion. However as the battle for Beirut ended, serious doubts were cast on the wisdom of this course.

On August 30, 1982, the Lebanese president-elect arrived in the northern Israeli town of Nahariya to meet with Menachem Begin. Although strongly pressed by the prime minister to conclude a full peace treaty by the end of the year, Gemayel was evasive. He was suddenly protective of Lebanon's sovereignty and clearly worried that rushing into an Israeli embrace might spark intolerable opposition from the Arab world and Lebanon's fractious non-Maronite factions. According to Ze'ev Schiff, his answer was framed as follows:

We are with you on a long haul on a genuine peace, not an artificial one.... I cannot decide on such matters alone. There is a government and political institutions in Lebanon, and they must be involved. We will continue to move in this direction, as I have said again and again. But the hasty signing of a treaty is not justified, either from a political or security standpoint.[114]

Gemayel's coyness fueled existing doubts within Israeli policymaking circles over the strategy pursued by Begin and Sharon. At the upper levels of Israel's intelligence community there was particularly strong resistance to the idea that Jerusalem could promote the emergence of a central Lebanese regime strong enough, or reliable enough, to guarantee the security of Israel's northern border. It would be far better, went the counter-argument, to rely on more direct involvement within a limited security zone in South Lebanon and on efforts to strike bargains with Lebanon's Shi'a and Druze communities, which in exchange for Israeli support for autonomy from the central Lebanese government might become strong allies against the resurgence of a Palestinian presence south of Beirut. In the months following Bashir Gemayel's interview with Menachem Begin, Israeli officials unsuccessfully explored these options with Shi'a and Druze leaders.

As the single largest community in Lebanon, and because it was concentrated in the country's southern portion, the Shi'a were an especially attractive potential ally. Moreover, by 1982 the Palestinians' presence in Shi'a territory had left a legacy of tension between the two groups that Israel could hope to capitalize upon. In the wake of its invasion of Lebanon, Israel would spend not only months, but years, engaging in secret efforts to forge a partnership with Nabih Berri, the leader of Amal, the Shi'a political organization.[115]

Bashir Gemayel's death heightened the uncertainty that led Israel to entertain a possible strategy based on ties with other Lebanese factions while it was ostensibly committed to furthering Phalangist predominance in Lebanon. Although Amin Gemayel, who succeeded his brother to Lebanon's presidency on September 21, 1982, pledged to be an even better friend than Bashir, the Israelis had little faith in his sincerity or leadership qualities.

Thus, while the Begin government negotiated throughout the rest of 1982 and into the spring for a peace treaty as the price of withdrawing its troops from Lebanon, it progressively redefined its goal as the maintenance of an Israeli presence in South Lebanon.

On the other hand, Washington became steadily more committed to promoting a viable Lebanese central government. On September 29, the first of 1200 marines ordered to Lebanon in the aftermath of Sabra and Shatila returned to Beirut and took up positions near the airport. They were there, together with French and Italian contingents that had already arrived, to help maintain security in the Lebanese capital.[116]

Yet, as George Ball points out, the marines' new mission was "indeterminant." Although it was announced that the marines would remain in Lebanon "until all foreign forces were withdrawn," imprecision surrounded their objective. A day before the marines returned to Lebanon, Assistant Secretary of State for Near Eastern and South Asian Affairs Nicholas Veliotis informed the House Foreign Affairs Committee that the withdrawal of Syrian and Israeli troops from Lebanon was not a "criterion" but an "expectation." U.S. troops, he predicted, would be home by the end of 1982 as an "outer limit."[117]

In the meantime, Washington had already expressed enthusiasm for the new presidency of Amin Gemayel. As early as September 16, Philip Habib's chief aide, Morris Draper, informed Gemayel that he would enjoy full U.S. support as his late brother's replacement.[118]

Amin counted heavily on this support, believing that his government could only avoid becoming an Israeli client by forging strong links to the United States. He also hoped that avenue would permit his fledgling government to avoid the disruptive domestic consequences of rushing into close ties with Israel.[119] In October, the new Lebanese leader met Reagan in Washington. "You are president not only of the United States but of Lebanon as well, and I will not depart from your advice," he reportedly gushed.[120] Still later, once negotiations between Israel and Lebanon opened near the end of the year, the Gemayel regime countered Israeli insistence that U.S. representatives sit in only as observers by urging Washington to be a full participant.

Gemayel's attitude encouraged the Reagan administration's belief that the fragility of the Beirut government's hold on power could be overcome so that Lebanon might become the focus of a peace process similar to that which had culminated in the Egyptian–Israeli treaty. Jerusalem, however, was in no mood to consider an extended process. Its approach was dictated not only by a distrust of Amin Gemayel's true intentions, as well as by skepticism over his ability to rule, but also by the growing conviction that Israel would do better to keep the security of South Lebanon under its own control. The Israeli outlook was not softened when Gemayal appeared at the United Nations in mid-October to call for the removal of all foreign forces from his country and singled out the withdrawal of Israeli forces from Lebanon as "the fundamental objective" of relevant Security Council resolutions.[121]

Tactical differences in the U.S. and Israeli approaches to Lebanon emerged quickly. Washington did not support Israel's demands for an immediate formal peace treaty and normalization of relations. Nor was it fully in accord with Jerusalem's insistence on special arrangements in south Lebanon that would place Israeli military observers in the area. Moreover, although the United States and Israel agreed in principle that all foreign troops should leave Lebanon, they disagreed on questions of procedure and timing. Israel envisaged a preliminary evacuation of remaining PLO troops that would be followed by a simultaneous withdrawal of its own and Syrian forces. Washington was prepared to countenance a mutually phased withdrawal of all foreign troops.

These disparities were not overcome by December 28, when Israeli and Lebanese officials met at the negotiating table. Much of the delay in convening the talks—at which Morris Draper represented the United States—had stemmed from the difficulty of finding a venue acceptable to all parties. Israel unsuccessfully demanded that negotiations be held alternately in Beirut and Jerusalem, a proposition rejected by Lebanon on grounds of its refusal to recognize Jerusalem as the Jewish state's capital.

There was an air of unreality surrounding the negotiations. U.S. policymakers had known since early October of Damascus' declared willingness to participate in a general withdrawal of forces that restored full Lebanese sovereignty. Yet neither the United States nor Israel had the slightest intention of trying to involve the Assad regime in discussions toward that objective. The prevailing feeling in Washington was captured by Reagan's reported comment to Foreign Minister Yitzhak Shamir: "let's leave the Syrians on the outside looking in." Washington chose to believe that the good offices of friendly Arab regimes would convince Syria to accept the role assigned to it by the tripartite talks in Lebanon.[122]

As the negotiations dragged on, and it became increasingly obvious that the Begin government would not easily be moved from its original demands, Washington began to complain openly of Israeli intransigence. When little progress was achieved by late March 1983, the White House suspended the delivery of seventy-five F–16 airplanes contracted by Israel a year earlier.

In the meantime, the U.S. and Israeli governments faced mounting doubts at home over the necessity of maintaining forces in Lebanon. The Israelis suffered a continuing trickle of casualties in the country. With troops still as far north as Beirut and no negotiated settlement in sight, Jerusalem was under rising domestic pressure to find a way to conclude the intervention.

On the other hand, the initial welcome that greeted the international force's arrival in Beirut faded by early 1983. In February and March, an Iranian-backed Shi'a organization, Al Jihad Al-Islamia, claimed responsibility for a series of attacks on French, Italian, and U.S. troops. At the same time, various serious confrontations occurred between Israeli forces and U.S. marines. In mid-March, the Defense Department published a letter sent to Secretary of Defense Casper Weinberger by the Commandant of the Marine Corps charging Israel with harrassing U.S. military forces for political purposes.[123] The spectacle of U.S. Marines facing unfriendly Arabs as well as Israelis in Beirut led to questions about the rationale behind their presence in Lebanon. The issue was raised to dramatic proportions on April 18, when a suicide driver detonated a truck-bomb at the entrance of the massive U.S. embassy in Beirut. Some sixty individuals, including seventeen Americans, died in the blast. The embassy was destroyed.[124]

Secretary of State Shultz arrived in the Middle East later that month to deal personally with the Lebanon negotiations. During nine arduous days, he travelled between Jerusalem and Gemayel's presidential palace in Baabda, with side trips to Riyadh and Damascus. His approach to mediation was multifaceted. To the Lebanese, he stressed the dilemma they confronted: to accept an accord that only barely disguised the granting of special status to Israel in the south, or, on the other hand, to refuse the accord and perpetuate the country's de facto division between Syria and Israel. He approached the Israelis by pointing to Gemayel's domestic difficulties and Washington's growing impatience with the prolonged negotiations. He also emphasized Israel's own dilemma: to salvage an agreement that met most of its political and security concerns, or to sustain an open-ended occupation of nearly half of Lebanon.

His efforts were successful. Once the outlines of the Israeli–Lebanese agreement were firm, the Saudis were urged to speak to Damascus in support of a Syrian withdrawal. Shultz simply informed Assad of the agreement's main features.[125]

The pact was signed by Israeli and Lebanese representatives (not, at Lebanon's insistence, by the countries' respective heads of state) on May 17, 1983. It was not a formal peace treaty, but it formally terminated the state of war that had existed between Lebanon and Israel since 1948. The two sides committed themselves to begin negotiations promptly toward a full normalization of relations.

Israel did not win the right to station military personnel inside Lebanon, although arrangements for the security of approximately the southern third of the country would be undertaken jointly. Among the projected security measures were mixed Israeli–Lebanese military patrols. Secret agreements concluded between the United States and Israel guaranteed that Jerusalem's obligation to withdraw was contingent upon a Syrian withdrawal and, further, that Washington acknowledged Israel's right to retaliate for guerrilla attacks launched from Lebanese soil.[126]

It seemed—to Washington at least—to be a great moment; Reagan pronounced the May 17 agreement "an important threshold on the path to peace."[127] Actually, the accord opened the door to stormy winds of chaos that would soon blow away the last vestiges of the administration's Lebanon policy.

Neither the Israelis nor the Lebanese were satisfied by their new relationship. The agreement fell short of giving Israel either a full peace treaty or the degree of control over south Lebanon desired by the Begin government. There is evidence that Begin sanctioned the pact in order to avoid further friction with the United States while remaining confident that the agreement would be effectively nullified by Syria's refusal to accept it as an adequate basis for a troop withdrawal. He seemed to have this in mind when noting that if the agreement did not work, "we are free to do as we wish."[128]

Instead of reducing intercommunal tensions in Lebanon, the pact caused a crisis. Druze and Muslim leaders, joined by the anti-Phalangist Maronite followers of former president Suleiman Franjiyeh, fumed over what they saw as a Phalangist bid for hegemony. Walid Jumblatt, the leader of the Druze community, voiced the common theme:

Secretary of State George Shultz came to the area to achieve any agreement.... We should have stuck to the United Nations resolutions [calling for an Israeli withdrawal].... Instead we have given Israel more than it expected, which means that certain internal parties, namely the Phalange, wanted more for their own ends.[129]

Damascus condemned the agreement, charging that it not only violated Lebanon's sovereignty but also—by giving Israel undue advantages in the country—constituted a threat to Syria. With strong Syrian encouragement, the Phalangists' Lebanese rivals began preparing for a concerted move against the Gemayel regime.

At the end of July 1983, a loosely-knit "National Salvation Front" announced it would force the Lebanese government to abrogate the May

17 agreement and acquiesce in a new formula for power-sharing in the country. It was a potentially formidable group whose chief spokesmen were Walid Jumblatt, Suleiman Franjiyeh, and Rashid Karami, the last a Sunni notable with considerable experience as a prime minister, acceptable to both pan-Arabist and moderate Lebanese nationalist currents. The front also won support form Lebanon's Shi'a community.

While these developments were brewing, the Begin government was coming under increasing domestic criticism over the steadily mounting toll of casualties among Israeli forces in Lebanon. By June, as the number of Israelis killed since the PLO's evacuation from Beirut nine months earlier rose to over 180, Jerusalem announced plans for a partial pullback to a new line along the Awali River, approximately sixty miles from Beirut. The cabinet approved the proposal a month later. The movement was scheduled to begin in September.

It was no secret that the coming withdrawal would lead to fighting in the Chouf Mountains. The area was traditionally a Druze stronghold, but it had been penetrated during the occupation, with Israel's approval, by Phalangist forces, which the Druze were anxious to expel.

The anticipated fighting began on schedule, with Druze forces immediately gaining the upper hand. The conflict spread as Lebanese Army units came to the aid of the Phalange militia. Amid reports from Phalangist and Lebanese government sources of active Syrian–Palestinian involvement in the hostilities and Druze denials of the claim, the battle for the Chouf reached ferocious proportions. Each side accused the other of slaughtering unarmed civilians.

U.S. marines guarding Beirut's international airport soon came under fire, initially as a result of misdirected artillery rounds. This passive involvement quickly progressed to more active levels. In mid-September, Reagan authorized U.S. forces to call on naval and air support. Within days, American warships were firing in support of the Lebanese army, and U.S. planes were flying cover for Lebanese air strikes against Syrian-backed Druze and Shi'a forces.

A cease-fire was declared at the end of September. Gemayel agreed to meet his enemies for "national reconciliation talks." With the cease-fire regularly punctuated by breakdowns, preliminary discussions among the various Lebanese factions took up most of October. The participants eventually decided to begin formal negotiations in Geneva in late October.

In the meantime, there occurred an event that, although having no notable impact on the immediate political situation, marked the end of an era. Menachem Begin retired from political life. Foreign Minister Yitzhak Shamir was elected to replace Begin as the Herut Party's leader. He formally became Israel's new prime minister in early October.

Begin cited personal problems that prevented him from functioning adequately. It was widely reported that he suffered from depression brought on by the death of his wife a year earlier and exacerbated by the complications arising from the invasion of Lebanon.

Menachem Begin would be remembered for many things by many people. Tragedy had filled his life from the days that his immediate family was caught up in Hitler's genocidal campaign. But he had also savored success—as leader of the anti-British Jewish terrorist Irgun prior to Israel's independence; as an opposition leader who moved from being virtually ostracized by Israel's dominant Labor Party leadership prior to 1967 to prime minister of his country a few years later. As a leader, he left no doubt that he *was* a leader. Whatever other memories might be held of his political career, that of his inflexible commitment to Israel's cause as he saw it would be among them. It would remain the task of biographers and historians to attempt a final evaluation of the significance of that commitment for Israel and for the Arab world.

Begin left the stage just as the declared objective of his policy toward Lebanon was about to be frustrated. The Lebanese "national reconciliation" talks in Geneva, which had been attended by U.S. and Syrian observers, ended by producing agreement in principle on Lebanon's identity as "an Arab country," the advisability of "freezing" the May 17 pact with Israel, and the need for constitutional reform.[130]

However, agreements in principle arrived at in Geneva did little to stem the rising violence in Lebanon. On October 23, 1983, another Iranian-supported militant Islamic group, Hizb al-Allah, sent a suicide driver in a bomb-laden truck crashing into a U.S. marine barracks. A similar attack was carried out against French troops. Over 260 U.S. marines and 50 French soldiers died. A few days later, yet another attack caused much loss of life at the Israeli military headquarters in the south Lebanon city of Tyre.

With the cost of war brought home so suddenly and viciously, the American congress and press began urgently questioning Washington's Lebanon policy. Arguing that Lebanon remained vital to U.S. interests, the Reagan administration maintained that the United States could not capitulate to terrorism and that a precipitous withdrawal from Lebanon would only enhance the positions of Syria, the radicals, and, through them, the Soviet Union, in the Middle East. Still, Reagan seemed to be delicately trying to establish an exit for the marines when he commented that should there be a "collapse" in Lebanon, U.S. forces would have no mission.[131]

What was quickly collapsing was the administration's early hope of using Lebanon as the foundation of an overall political rearrangement in the Middle East. Throughout November, fighting swept the country. Israeli planes retaliated for the attack in Tyre by bombing a suspected terrorist headquarters. The French re-bombed the same target. Yassir

Arafat, by then carrying on his own battle against Syrian-backed Palestinian enemies and Israeli gunboats, was trapped on the coast at Tripoli. The Druze, under Damascus' benign gaze, renewed their fight with Lebanese government forces and the Phalange. Beirut's international airport became a favorite target for Druze gunners. Lebanon's Shi'a militia, Amal, was fighting the Lebanese Army in West Beirut. Israeli forces, now dug in behind the Awali River line, were out of the thick of the fighting but still exposed to guerrilla attacks.

By December 1983, U.S. warships were again shelling Druze, Shi'a, and Syrian positions. A major attack by some two dozen U.S. warplanes was made on Syrian forces. The Syrians shot down two aircraft, killing one pilot and capturing another.

At the beginning of 1984, there was no denying Washington's own dilemma. The choice was between committing more men and firepower to try to impose the Gemayel regime's supremacy or extricating the troops from Lebanon with as much grace as possible. The first option was unpalatable for two major reasons. On the one hand, the Gemayel government's fundamental weakness had been shown up in such stark terms by recent events that the Reagan administration could not avoid recognizing the false optimism of its own early hopes for the revival of central authority in Lebanon. On the other hand, 1984 was an election year in the United States, and a major new military venture in Lebanon promised to become a focal point of criticism against the administration's handling of foreign affairs.

In early February 1984, as though venting Washington's frustration in a last roar of cannon fire, the battleship *New Jersey* used its well-advertised sixteen-inch guns to devastate a thirty-square mile area near Beirut. A week later, Gemayel agreed to a Saudi peace proposal calling for the abrogation of the May 17 pact with Israel. Twenty-four hours later, the already pending evacuation (officially termed "redeployment") of U.S. marines began. The international incursion sparked by Israel's 1982 invasion was at an end. The Israelis, who were not to withdraw their forces from Lebanon until June 1985—and even then to retain a strong presence in the country by virtue of their support of the South Lebanese Army—remained. So too did the Syrians and Palestinians. The Gemayel government was left to fend for itself.

The marine's evacuation ended Lebanon's growing role in U.S. domestic politics, but not that of the Middle East. Shortly before the U.S. withdrawal, Jesse Jackson's search for the Democratic Party's presidential nomination led him to Damascus, where he obtained the release of the captured U.S. pilot. Some observers felt that if Jackson hoped to enhance his political standing by acting in the Middle East, he had already been outmanuevered by the administration. In November 1983, Washington had suddenly concluded a new Strategic Cooperation Agreement with

Israel. The Arab world reacted with shock. For while the United States still claimed to be committed to the Reagan Plan and the withdrawal of Israeli troops from Lebanon, the accord appeared to reward Israeli recalcitrance on both fronts. George Ball indicates the range of considerations that seem to have influenced the move:

The simplest explanation ... may be the most plausible: the decision ... and the timing of that decision were the reactions of officials rattled, befuddled, frustrated, feeling intense domestic pressure, facing an election, and at a loss to know what else to do.[132]

In any case, it was obvious that the two-tiered policy declared by the United States in September 1982 had come to grief. The Reagan Initiative now seemed consigned to history, while the hope of expanding the Egyptian–Israeli peace through Lebanon was no more than the memory of a shattered ambition. Far from having been neutralized, the very forces the administration sought to render insignificant emerged stronger. The Assad regime not only claimed credit for having staved off the threats it perceived in each of Washington's twin tracks, but was also receiving unprecedented Soviet aid to build its military capacity to hitherto unreached heights.[133] And the most uncompromising Palestinian forces were still celebrating Arafat's expulsion from Tripoli.

After cutting its losses in Lebanon, the Reagan administration appeared unperturbed by the disarray into which U.S. Middle East policy had fallen. The strategic agreement with Israel was followed in 1984 by a series of steps reinforcing the impression that Washington had abandoned even minimal interest in serving as a mediator between Israel and the Arab world. In the spring of 1984, friendly Arab states were antagonized by the administration's denial of Jordanian and Kuwaiti requests to purchase hand-held defensive anti-aircraft "Stinger" missiles. Saudi Arabia was permitted to buy only a third of its original order for the same weapon. Charges that the United States had fully aligned itself with Israel appeared to take on new credibility.[134]

The heightened sensitivity to Israeli concerns that characterized much of U.S. policy in 1984 was clearly fueled by election-year politics. While the administration openly bowed to pro-Israel pressures in handling Arab arms requests, both houses of congress did the same by competing to promote larger appropriations for Israel than were suggested by the White House. Meanwhile, most potential presidential contenders eagerly sought to garner pro-Israel support.[135]

However, conditions in the Middle East also contributed mightily to what almost amounted to a moratorium on the search for peace throughout 1984. Jordan and the mainstream PLO still failed to agree on a common position with which to approach the United States on the basis of the Reagan Initiative. Israel not only remained unmovingly hostile to the Initiative, but was also soon preoccupied by its own upcoming elections. In the summer, these would produce an uneasy Labor–Likud coalition government.

Despite repeated frustrations, moderate Arabs preferred to hope that Washington's lack of interest in Middle East peace was transitory. Although in the spring of 1984, King Hussein issued a harsh pronouncement to the effect that the United States had disqualified itself as a disinterested peacemaker, he had no wish to believe his own analysis. The same was true of Saudi and Kuwaiti leaders, who in their initial outrage at being denied U.S. arms threatened to turn elsewhere, including the Soviet Union, for weapons.[136]

The truth was that the Jordanians, Saudis, and Kuwaitis could not afford to conclude that the United States had turned its back on a negotiated peace in order to rely solely on Israel as an anti-Soviet (and anti-radical) regional bulwark.

Hussein saw Jordan's stability, and his rule, menaced by an open-ended prolongation of the Palestine conflict. Saudi Arabia, Kuwait, and other Gulf regimes feared that the absence of an Arab–Israeli settlement would generate the spread of hostile radical forces in the Arab world. Each recognized the United States as the key to a settlement based on the territory-for-peace formula. None, in any case, could seriously contemplate a close, long-term association with the Soviet Union. The moderate Arab camp was solidly joined in these considerations by Egypt, which was for the foreseeable future inextricably committed to the extension of the U.S.-sponsored peace process, and by Yassir Arafat, whose relations with radical militants were now in tatters.

Paradoxically, then, 1984 was marked by moderate Arab leaders' bitter recriminations against the United States as well as by redoubled efforts among the same group to attract U.S. interest in a compromise settlement of the Palestine question. While Arafat travelled about the Arab world trying to muster support, Egyptian President Hosni Mubarak devoted increasing attention to fostering an agreement between the PLO and Jordan.

Despite the pro-Israel hyperbole generated by the ongoing U.S. political campaigns, a prominent Arab view was that the Reagan administration only awaited a second mandate before putting the full power of the United States behind an energetic drive based on the framework announced by the president in 1982. Supporting evidence for this optimistic outlook was found in the administration's opposition to a bill introduced by New York Senator Patrick Moynihan calling for the U.S. embassy in Israel to be moved from Tel-Aviv to Jerusalem. The outcome of Israel's election, which produced a coalition government headed by Labor Party leader Shimon Peres, reinforced hopes that U.S. peacemaking might be more productive under a second Reagan presidency.

Arab efforts to pave the way for capitalizing on these expectations seemed to bear some fruit in November 1984, when the Palestine National Council (PNC) met in Amman. Egypt had been particularly active in helping to arrange the meeting, the first PNC assembly to be held on Jordanian soil. In the face of fulminating tirades from Syria and its dissident-Palestinian allies, the PNC reiterated its support in principle for a PLO–Hashemite agreement on a confederal arrangement between Jordan and the West Bank and Gaza, which would, in turn, serve as the foundation of a negotiated peace.[137]

Arab moderates were jubilant. The impasse between Jordan and the PLO that had blocked a firm moderate position since 1982 now seemed likely to be overcome in final negotiations between the two sides over details that might be relatively easily arranged. The foundations for meaningful negotiations with the United States and Israel seemed at last to be under construction. The opening for an energetic thrust by Washington to cap its eighteen year search for Mideast peace appeared to have been created.

There was no doubt that differences still divided Jordan and the PLO. This was true even after King Hussein and Yassir Arafat reached what appeared to be another major milestone three months later. In February 1985 the two leaders announced agreement on a joint peace initiative. Although full details of the accord were not revealed, the two sides proposed resolving the Arab–Israeli dispute on the basis of an international conference that would lead to the creation of a Palestinian state in confederation with Jordan.[138] What could not be hidden was Arafat's continuing commitment to the goal of Palestinian statehood. Hussein, on the other hand, hoped to win Palestinian acceptance of something less under a confederal umbrella.

This essential distinction undermined the apparent harmony that prevailed when the two leaders met in February. The PLO conceived of an international conference as a forum with binding powers, an arrangement that would offset the U.S. role in devising a peace formula. Jordan, far more ready to see the United States as a mediator, was also more willing to view a conference as only a framework for substantial negotiations with Israel and the United States. Moreover, while the PLO's willingness to accept Security Council resolutions 242 and 338 was ultimately contingent on reciprocal recognition, by the United States, if not by Israel, of the Palestinian people's right to self-determination, Jordan urged the resolution's acceptance as a key step toward inaugurating formal negotiations.

The divisive effects of these different outlooks would become apparent during the course of 1985. However, in the early part of that year, they were overshadowed by optimism in the moderate Arab camp. With Reagan back in the White House for a second term, and the Jordanian–

PLO agreement in hand, a renewed campaign was undertaken to rekindle active U.S. interest in Middle East peacemaking.

THE FINAL REAGAN YEARS

Most of Ronald Reagan's second term was destined to be characterized by the continuing absence of any U.S. interest in reactivating the stalled search for Mideast peace. Only in its final year of office did the administration show evidence of feeling compelled by events to project itself once more as an active peacemaker. In the meantime, the initiative remained with local actors in the Middle East. Pro-Western Arab regimes and the PLO first tried, and failed, to form an effective united front that would generate momentum toward a political settlement. However when that failed, they too lapsed into an unfruitful torpor. It was ultimately the Palestinians living under Israeli occupation who finally rekindled signs of broader interest in resolving their plight.

By early 1985, Jordan and the PLO had settled on a strategy they hoped would eventually win U.S. support for a negotiated peace based on Israel's withdrawal from the occupied territories. As a first step, the new approach called for the opening of a dialogue between a Jordanian–Palestinian delegation and the United States. Washington would be offered an opportunity to circumvent its own ban on direct contact with the PLO by limiting Palestinian delegates to individuals not officially associated with, but approved by, the PLO.

If the projected talks satisfied all parties, the second stage of the Arab initiative would entail formal PLO acceptance of UN Resolutions 242 and 338. With Washington and the PLO then able to engage in direct relations, it would be possible to negotiate toward a Middle East peace utilizing bilateral U.S.–PLO contacts as well as an international conference.

That, at least, was the theory as Hussein explained it a year after he and Arafat agreed on their joint peace initiative.[139] The problem, of course, lay in the link between the first and second stages of the Arab approach. Washington might agree to meet a Jordanian–Palestinian delegation, but the United States showed no indication of abandoning its opposition to any form of Palestinian statehood. On the other hand, the PLO's insistence that acceptance of the Security Council's resolutions must be reciprocated by recognition of the Palestinian people's right to self-determination remained unshaken.

In trying to promote a Jordanian–Palestinian–U.S. meeting, Hussein did not specify just what outcome he sought. However, he could only have counted on one of two eventualities: either Washington would modify its stand on Palestinian statehood, or the PLO would surrender the final vestiges of its nationalistic goal.

The Reagan administration greeted the Arab demarche cordially, but without enthusiasm. Hussein was dutifully praised for his active interest in peacemaking, although Washington rejected the notion of an international conference. Meeting with Reagan and other top level officials in May, the king tried to generate a more active response by delivering a statement to which Yassir Arafat had earlier agreed:

. . . on the basis of the Jordanian agreement with the PLO signed on 11 February [1985], as a result of the talks which I recently held with the PLO, and in view of our sincere desire to achieve peace, we are determined to negotiate to achieve a peaceful settlement within the framework of an international conference on the basis of the related UN resolutions, including Security Council Resolution 242 and 338.[140]

The underlying differences between Jordan and the PLO prevented Hussein from publicly straying beyond carefully worded ambiguity in describing the final settlement envisaged by the moderate Arab camp. Arguing that peace negotiations should be conducted "under the auspices" of the five permanent Security Council members, Hussein called for a solution "which would ensure the Palestinian people their right to self-determination within the context of a Jordanian–Palestinian confederation." He evaded questions on the structural features of such an arrangement. At almost the same time, however, Jordanian Foreign Minister Taher al Masri was giving assurances in Washington that a confederal solution "means that there will be no independent Palestinian state."[141]

The vagueness of the confederation proposal undermined Arab hopes of generating an immediate revival of the Reagan Initiative. It quickly became obvious that the U.S. preferred to stand on its refusal to countenance Palestinian self-determination in the expectation that Hussein would soon part with the PLO in order to move alone toward an accommodation with Israel over the occupied territories.

On the other hand, Hussein's call for a Jordanian–Palestinian–U.S. dialogue offered the Reagan administration an opportunity to become industriously involved in procedural—as opposed to substantive—considerations related to peacemaking opportunities. By April, despite Israeli objections, Washington agreed in principle to meet with a Jordanian–Palestinian delegation, provided no leading members of the PLO or other resistance organizations were included. Although the issue was not dealt with in a sustained way at the highest levels of government, U.S. diplomats, under the leadership of Assistant Secretary of State for Southwest Asia Richard Murphy, devoted considerable time over the next few months to establishing criteria for identifying acceptable non-PLO Palestinians who could serve as de facto PLO representatives.

Much public attention was given to this academic quest. However, while official Washington spokesmen in one breath touted the task as an essential part of the peace process, in the next breath they consistently reiterated the administration's known positions on substantive questions. This strange position prompted some skeptical observers to urge U.S. policymakers to heed the likelihood that the substance of what might be said to the Palestinians—if and when a dialogue was held—might be more important to the "peace process" than the meeting itself.[142]

At any rate, after winning U.S. agreement to accept four non-PLO Palestinians on the planned joint delegation, Hussein returned to Jordan for further consultations with PLO leaders. By July, the PLO Executive Committee and the Fateh Central Committee had settled on several candidates for positions on the joint delegation. The list was relayed to Washington through King Hussein, giving the United States the final say in the selection process.

At this point, the world press unexpectedly learned the identities of the nominated Palestinians.[143] The projected meeting between U.S. representatives and PLO surrogates became a focal point of public interest. Although the State Department initially proclaimed that Israel would not be allowed to determine whether the U.S. would meet with a joint Jordanian–Palestinian team in preparation for eventual peace talks, the administration was soon backtracking. Hussein was first told that the United States found only two of the prospective Palestinian delegates acceptable. In the first week of September, the king was informed that Washington no longer found it possible to meet the joint delegation.[144]

Having abandoned a path that it had touted for most of the year as a potential path to Middle East peace, Washington was momentarily left at loose ends. In October, U.S. officials began trying to create a new approach by falling back on Hussein's plan for an international conference.

Another visit by the king provided the setting for Washington's first tentative expressions of interest in an international conference. Hussein placed on record the basic difference between the emerging U.S. concept of a conference and his own:

The United States submitted a proposal concerning the international conference, which, after careful examination, seemed to suggest a conference in name only. We, on the other hand, insisted that the conference should have clear powers.[145]

Another major divergence was over the PLO's role in an international conference. Hussein argued that prior PLO acceptance of Security Council Resolutions 242 and 338 should suffice to guarantee the organization's participation. The U.S. initially maintained that it could not commit itself to accept PLO participation, even under such circumstances.[146] During the remainder of the year, a possible international conference continued to be a main subject of discussion between the U.S. and Jordan. In November, under prodding from both Jordan and Egypt, Yassir Arafat issued a statement that was intended to disassociate the mainstream PLO from international terrorism. The "Cairo Declaration," as it came to be called, condemned "all [violent] operations outside [Palestine] and all forms of terrorism." Although promising immediate efforts to deter violations of this position, the declaration reaffirmed "the right of the Palestinian people to resist the occupation in the occupied territories. . . ."[147] As interpreted by senior PLO spokesmen, this did not rule out violent actions in the occupied territories or Israel.

In early January 1986, Hussein met Assistant Secretary of State Richard Murphy in London. The king urged Washington to agree that PLO acceptance of Security Council Resolutions 242 and 338 would win the organization a seat at an international peace conference. He also repeated his view that a conference should have decisive powers.

On January 21, Hussein received a reply in which Washington slightly modified its position. The United States still viewed an international conference as essentially ceremonial, with substantive movement toward peace depending on direct talks between the parties in conflict. Nor would it approve of a conclave with decisive powers. However, Washington now agreed that the negotiating parties might submit any disagreements between them to the conference.[148] Hussein also received a reply on the question of PLO participation. The message from Washington stated:

When it is clearly on the public record that the PLO has accepted Resolution 242 and 338, is prepared to negotiate peace with Israel, and has renounced terrorism, the United States accepts the fact that an invitation will be issued to the PLO to attend an international conference.[149]

It was a small enough concession. Not only did the American message by implication establish that the United States did not consider the Cairo Declaration to be a renunciation of terrorism, it also presented the PLO with an additional requirement to be met before the organization could be invited to a peace conference: getting "clearly on the public record" that it was "prepared to negotiate peace with Israel."

PLO leaders could not but look upon this with deep suspicion. In contrast to the Carter administration's relative flexibility on the issue, the Reagan administration had developed a rigid insistence that only "unconditional" PLO acceptance of Resolutions 242 and 338 would be acceptable.[150] Were the same stringent spectacles used to judge forthcoming expressions of the PLO's readiness "to negotiate peace with Israel," the organization might never sit at a peace conference, for it was hardly conceivable that the PLO would proclaim an unqualified readiness for peace with the Jewish state.

By this time, however, Hussein was under growing pressure. His peace initiative seemed to be going nowhere. He was also awaiting an imminent decision from Washington on a request to purchase nearly $2 billion of sophisticated arms. During the final days of January, the king tried to convince Arafat to issue a clear declaration accepting Security Council Resolutions 242 and 338.[151]

Arafat would not be swayed. Insisting that the U.S. position was unacceptable, he urged Hussein to seek an additional U.S. commitment to support the Palestinians' right to "self-determination."

When Hussein complied, he was rebuffed. The United States, he was informed, would adhere to its original position. Upon relaying this to PLO leaders, Hussein was asked to approach the Americans once more with the same request. Again he did so, only to receive the same reply. At the same time, Washington suggested that Jordan proceed independently of the PLO in its efforts to arrange a settlement with Israel.

Hussein rejected the overture. Still, although having almost simultaneously received word that congressional opposition made it impossible for the Reagan administration to conclude the pending arms deal, he continued to encourage the PLO to accept the UN resolutions.

At this point, Hussein received some token support for his dealings with the PLO. The Reagan administration, apparently hoping to mitigate the King's disappointment over the arms deal, embellished its earlier declaration regarding possible PLO participation in a peace conference with a statement supporting the "legitimate rights of the Palestinian people."

There was nothing at all new in this formulation. It had long appeared in U.S. policy statements, including that embodying the Reagan Initiative. This did not escape the notice of PLO leaders.

Pointing this out, Arafat handed the King three differently worded texts of a "conditional acceptance of 242" which the PLO was prepared to issue simultaneously with a U.S. government "pledge to affirm the right of self-determination of the Palestinian people." Here too, there was little that was new. The drafts explicitly stated the PLO's readiness to participate in an international conference for the purpose of negotiating a settlement ensuring the Palestinians' right of self-determination "within the context of a Jordanian–Palestinian confederation." They also indicated the PLO's view that negotiations would be based on "United Nations and Security Council resolutions relevant to the Palestinian question, including Resolutions 242 and 338." Finally, each draft "reaffirmed" the PLO's "denunciation and rejection of terrorism, which it had confirmed in the Cairo Declaration."[152]

There were subtle differences in the texts. The most significant of

these related to the PLO's stand on the nature of an international conference. The first draft referred to the organization's willingness to attend a conference "with effective powers." The absence of the qualifying
phrase in the other drafts implied some flexibility.

However, even the most favorable interpretation of the proposed declarations left no doubt that each would be unacceptable to the Reagan
administration. By linking acceptance of Resolutions 242 and 338 to all
Security Council and General Assembly resolutions relevant to the Palestine question, the PLO invited a negative U.S. reaction. There was no
denying a later state department critique of the PLO drafts:

The phrase "all pertinent UN resolutions" encompasses a very mixed bag of
documents, some objectionable to the U.S. and to Israel. The PLO may cite its
preferred resolutions but not in such a way as to place them on a par with 242
and 338 or to dilute its acceptance of these resolutions.[153]

If PLO leaders hoped to exert political pressure by offering Washington a choice between abandoning its opposition to Palestinian self-
determination or standing nakedly before the bar of world opinion as
the sole obstacle to clear-cut PLO recognition of Resolutions 242 and
338, they badly overplayed their hand. For, by so hedging their proposed
acceptance of the Security Council resolutions, Arafat and his colleagues
were in effect not only asking the United States to reverse its stand on
Palestinian statehood but also to modify one of its central conditions for
dealing directly with the PLO.

The U.S.–Palestinian impasse remained firmly entrenched. Seeing no
immediate prospects for proceeding with the joint peace initiative, Hussein once again broke with the PLO. Without discussing the significance
of the full range of conditions included in Washington's note of January
21, he charged that Arafat had violated an earlier understanding by
refusing to accept Resolution 242 after the United States had agreed to
PLO participation in an international conference. Jordan, announced
the king on February 19, was no longer "able to cooperate politically
with the PLO leadership until such time as their word becomes their
bond. . . . "

The PLO was not slow to defend its approach. In a statement issued
from its headquarters in Tunis, the PLO Executive Committee offered
its own version of the failed year-long Arab peace drive:

[A] meeting was supposed to take place between a Jordanian–Palestinian joint
delegation and [Assistant Secretary of State Richard] Murphy. Agreement was
reached with the Jordanian government to draft an integrated program that
included U.S. recognition of the PLO and the Palestinian people's legitimate
national rights, including their right to self-determination, as well as other political guarantees for the PLO, in order to convene the international conference

in return for the PLO's acceptance of international resolutions, including 242 and 338. However, as is known to everyone, the joint delegation's meeting with Murphy did not take place because the United States retreated from its promises to Jordan. How can our organization alone be asked to recognize Resolutions 242 and 338 while the United States refuses to recognize in return the Palestinian people's right to self-determination and refuses to provide all the political guarantees for the PLO which formed the crux of the talks with Jordan regarding the arrangement of the joint delegation's meeting with the U.S. envoy? Moreover, how can the PLO be held responsible for the retreat while the PLO has never accepted Resolution 242 without its being linked to all the other UN resolutions and to the right to self-determination. . . .

There is no doubt that the responsibility for the failure rests with the U.S. retreat, and that it is U.S. credibility that has always been doubtful.[154]

Nonetheless, the PLO statement indirectly appeared to lend some substance to the King's contention that he had been misled about the extent of the organization's flexibility:

The PLO has fulfilled its promise to its people and its Arab nation. It has never retreated from struggle. . . . Therefore, the real criterion for its credibility is its firm commitment to its people's rights and its struggle for the sake of these rights.

In the wake of the collapsed cooperation with the PLO, the Jordanian government embarked on an undeclared challenge to the PLO's role as the sole representative of the Palestinian Arabs. Days after the Hussein–Arafat talks ended, the lower house of Jordan's parliament issued a declaration supporting the king's position and asserting that the parliament spoke for West Bank Palestinians. While Hussein affirmed his readiness to "respect" a decision by Palestinians to retain the PLO as their only representative organization, he added that Jordan would welcome another "apparatus."

The Palestinians must now make a decision. . . . Are they happy with creeping annexation of their land by Israel and their possible expulsion from Palestine? If they're unhappy, what do they want us to do about it?[155]

Jordanian–PLO relations deteriorated further in the following months. Reports soon surfaced that a former PLO intelligence chief was responding to Hussein's call for a change in Palestinian leadership by organizing an anti-Arafat movement in Jordan. In July, Amman closed all Fateh offices in the country and expelled one of Arafat's leading lieutenants.[156]

U.S. reaction to the breakdown of cooperation between the PLO and Jordan was instantaneous. "The PLO has now failed the King's test and history moves on," said a State Department spokesman. To no one's surprise, his remarks were an early signal that Washington supported Hussein's efforts to bypass the PLO by appealing directly to Palestinians in occupied territories:

[A]ll parties will now have to find another basis to move towards the undiminished imperative of a negotiated peace, including the resolution of the Palestinians' problem.[157]

Equally unsurprising was Israel's reaction to the PLO–Jordan split. Having never modified its opposition to PLO participation in the peace process, nor its insistence on direct negotiations with Jordan as the way to resolve the future of the West Bank, Jerusalem welcomed the new development.[158]

During the rest of 1986, Israel and the United States sought to enhance Hussein's prestige among Palestinians in the occupied territories. In August, Hussein announced a $1.3 billion five-year development plan for the West Bank and Gaza.[159] The money was to be largely raised from international donors. In November, a branch of the Cairo–Amman Bank was established in Nablus. It was the first Arab bank permitted by the Israelis to open in the occupied territories since 1967. The step was reportedly taken on the basis of a secret agreement between the central banks of Israel and Jordan permitting joint supervision of the new facility.[160] With the PLO now on the diplomatic sidelines, it appeared that Palestinians were to be shown the tangible benefits that Hussein's leadership could bring. In the summer, Israeli Prime Minister Shimon Peres took another step that seemed at least partly intended to bolster the king's image by supporting the concept of an international conference that would serve as an "umbrella" for direct peace negotiations.

Few expected any of these moves to revive the peace process in the near future. For one thing, Peres was scheduled to hand over the prime ministry to his coalition partner, Likud leader Yitzhak Shamir, in the fall. When the change occurred in October, Shamir—as expected—retained his strong opposition to any form of international peace conference. On the other hand, although welcoming plans to bolster their flagging economy, the majority of Arabs in the occupied territories remained loyal to the PLO. Their position was made plain through a variety of means, including opinion polls and mass demonstrations. Finally, King Hussein, although no less eager than before to reassert his authority over the West Bank, showed no signs of willingness to enter into negotiations with Israel without substantial support from the Arab world.[161]

At the same time, the Reagan administration was clearly not enthusiastic about exploring possible avenues to peace. The occasional desultory gestures that had marked U.S. involvement with the Palestine problem since the marines withdrew from Lebanon in February 1984 tapered off into virtually complete inertia. Washington increasingly devoted what attention it could grant to the Middle East to other issues. Chief among these were the international wave of terrorism initiated by anti-PLO Arab factions in 1985 and the war between Iran and Iraq. By the winter of 1986, and through much of 1987, the drawn out scandal caused by clandestine U.S. arms sales to Iran (and the transfer of substantial portions of the proceeds to CIA-supported Nicaraguan rebel forces) not only crippled the administration domestically but also further eroded its credibility among moderate Arab states.

Following a visit to Washington by Israeli Prime Minister Yitzhak Shamir in early 1987, an anonymous State Department official graphically described the degree to which U.S. interest in a Middle East settlement had waned. Against the backdrop of nearly three years of neglect by the United States, Shamir's adamant opposition to both an international conference and further terrritorial concessions by Israel, and U.S. national elections scheduled for late 1988, the unnamed functionary pronounced the peace process to be "comatose, but not dead."[162] To some, there appeared to be growing grounds for wondering whether that was not an unduly optimistic diagnosis.

Such misgivings were not allayed during the remainder of the year. Yet, neither in the United States nor the Middle East did any generalized feeling of disquiet over the lack of efforts to move toward an Arab–Israeli settlement appear until the end of 1987. The new sense of urgency developed as a result of sustained rioting, which spontaneously broke out in December among the populations of the Gaza and the West Bank.

With worldwide attention focused on the months-long spectacle of Israeli troops suppressing Palestinian civilians, Washington launched the new peace initiative referred to in the next chapter. However, by the spring of 1988 evidence indicated that the U.S. proposals offered little if anything that had not been heard before.

It remained to be seen whether the comatose U.S. search for peace was at last to be revived or simply giving a final twitch before settling into the enduring stillness of rigor mortis.

5

CONCLUSION: PRELUDE TO REQUIEM?

An appraisal of U.S. efforts to promote an end to the Arab–Israeli conflict yields mixed results. Two decades have seen much change in the Middle East, some for the better—and some that raise the question of whether the accrued benefits will endure.

In terms of the Arab–Israeli conflict itself, the clearest U.S. achievement to date is the peace between Israel and Egypt. Whatever the future offers, this will remain a political milestone in the history of the Middle East, as well as in the history of American diplomacy. Sinai II and Camp David also rightfully take their places in the annals of imaginative and productive diplomatic efforts.

In terms of broader U.S. interests, the seminal roles of Henry Kissinger and Jimmy Carter in bringing Sinai II into existence and then nurturing it into the 1979 Egyptian–Israeli peace treaty not only drastically reduced the disturbing impact of Arab–Israeli tensions on U.S. policymakers, but did so while simultaneously excluding the Soviet Union from the mainstream of contemporary Middle East political currents. With Moscow marginalized, and local Arab opponents of Egypt's turnabout unable to do more than vent frustration in bombastic rhetoric and annoying, but essentially inconsequential, occasional slashes of violence and terrorism, Washington seemed to have secured its niche as the Middle East's dominant outside power.

On the other hand, Sinai II, Camp David, and the U.S.-sponsored Egyptian–Israeli peace were not pristine diplomatic coups. The proverbial fly in the ointment was present from the outset in the form of a question: "What next?"

To the extent that consideration was given to the problem of extending the Egyptian–Israeli peace process to other realms, the difficulty was embryonically inherent in Sinai II. Under Kissinger, however, with a step-by-step philosophy dictating the avoidance of core issues, the question was bypassed. After the 1979 Jerusalem–Cairo treaty, step-by-step reached the end of the road, at least on the Egyptian–Israel axis. "What next" assumed compelling proportions in the U.S. search for Mideast peace.

The first major effort to find an answer came under the Reagan administration—between 1982 and 1984, in Lebanon. The significance of the U.S. marines' eventual withdrawal from that country was not hidden by public relations jargon of "redeployment." If local Middle Eastern parties opposed to the direction of U.S. peacemaking efforts were not strong enough to block the arrangement between Egypt and Israel, they were at least capable of preventing the imposition of a regional Pax Americana not to their liking.

Burned in Lebanon, Washington eschewed further major initiatives, contenting itself with probing possibilities for an agreement between King Hussein and Israel. After mid–1987, much public attention was given to the possibility of an international peace conference to settle the Arab–Israeli quarrel once and for all.

Despite the fanfare, there were serious doubts that such a conference could be held, or, if it were, that grounds for productive negotiations existed. Some of these sprang from immediate considerations: the onset of active campaigning in the United States for the 1988 presidential elections, which, if tradition was a guide, was sure to preclude forceful U.S. diplomacy in the Middle East; deep divisions in Israel pitting Labor against the Likud over the wisdom of participating in an international conclave; and the thorny question of whether, and if so how, Palestinians might be represented in such a gathering.

Other doubts arose from more fundamental issues. As Israel's most outspoken champion of an international peace conference, Labor leader Shimon Peres' public comments indicated that he envisaged no more than an internationally sanctioned umbrella for direct talks with Jordan aimed, it appeared, at establishing a sort of Israeli–Hashemite condominium over the remaining occupied territories. It remained highly problematical whether Hussein could be induced to accede to such a deal. Then too, Washington—in support of Israel's basic tenet—remained unshaken in its stand that full Palestinian self-determination was not to be a viable option under any negotiating format.

Under these conditions, the end of the Reagan administration's second term approached without instilling grounds for optimism. "What next" seemed to take on not only compelling but possibly ominous proportions as a long-term question. With the Middle East balanced between the conflicting objectives of major actors, what seemed to be in play was not only the extension of the Egyptian–Israeli peace but also, ultimately, the preservation of what had so far been achieved by peacemaking.

THE U.S. APPROACH: 1967–1988

In 1967, the United States set its sights on a final resolution of the Arab–Israeli conflict. The extent of Israel's victory in the Six Day War, and above all the expanse of Arab territory that fell under Israeli control at the end of hostilities, were taken to offer the key to a just and lasting regional peace. Territory-for-peace was the straightforward formula that Washington felt would secure an enduring reconciliation between Israel and the Arab world. Although U.S. policymakers refrained from defining the full extent of the territory that should be returned by Israel, William Rogers' stand in favor of only minimal border changes was heralded much earlier by President Johnson's warning that true peace could not reflect "the weight of conquest."

Today, the territory-for-peace approach seems farther from realization than at any time in the past. By 1987 there were a total of 130 Jewish settlements in the West Bank alone. Sixty thousand Israelis live within the confines of these settler-towns. These figures do not include the settler-neighborhoods constructed in the expanded environs of East (Arab) Jerusalem, nor the more than 85,000 Israelis who populate them. Moreover, Israel's energetic settlement policies in areas other than the West Bank have had a telling effect. At least fifteen settlements, peopled by nearly 1500 settlers, dot the tiny Gaza strip while some thirty-eight settlements and over seven thousand Jewish residents are to be found in the Golan Heights.[1]

The political significance of this is not revealed by simply considering the settler population's numerical inferiority in comparison to the 1.5 million Palestinians living in the occupied areas. The settlers represent the vanguard of overtly expansionist sentiment that mushroomed in post–1967 Israel and which has exerted growing influence over Israel's policies. The turmoil and cost generated by the Begin government's 1981 eviction of a relative handful of Jewish settlers from the Sinai—an area never accorded the importance of the West Bank and Gaza in expansionist ideology—give but a pale notion of the problems that would probably attend a similar attempt in the remaining occupied lands.

Then too, any assessment of Israeli encroachments in the territories must go beyond enumerating settlements and settlers. In addition to these—and the extensive infrastructure of transportation, electrical, and water systems linking them to Israel—what must be counted is the enormous amount of land that has been removed during the occupation from Palestinian control. Israel's government has made wide use of a variety of measures to wrest land from the local populace. Meron Benvenisti estimates that by mid–1985, expropriations and land-use restrictions had placed 52 percent of the West Bank under Israel's effective control. Don Peretz argues that "up to 70 percent of the land in the

West Bank could be available for exclusively Jewish use." Ann Lesch calculates that by 1985, 30 percent of the Gaza Strip was covered by Israeli settlements and their access roads.[2]

In brief, the past twenty years not only witnessed the growth of expansionist ideology and political power within the Israeli body politic but also the forging of substantial ties between Israel and significant amounts of the territorial currency Washington originally hoped to see bartered for a lasting settlement in the Middle East. Neither process has been hidden. Both were visible virtually within days of the end of the 1967 war; both blossomed in the intervening years. Equally noticeable has been the high cost of Israel's settlement program. Although conclusive and precise figures are difficult to come by, it appears that between 1967 and 1983 Israel's capital investments in civilian projects in the West Bank alone totalled $1.5 billion.[3]

Inevitably there arises the question of what factors influenced the U.S. search for Mideast peace in ways that permitted this state of affairs to develop.

It is, of course, true that U.S. policy did not unfold in a vacuum. Arabs, Israelis, and others pursued their own interests as they saw them. Yet, while far too many participants have affected events for any one party to be assigned sole responsibility for developments since 1967, the history of Washington's involvement with the Arab–Israeli conflict reveals several major features in the formulation and execution of U.S. policy that helped shape the current state of the issue.

In an overall sense, it is clear that Washington failed to settle on a consistent concept delineating the purpose and nature of the peace it hoped to promote in the Middle East. This is evident in the different views the United States took of the roles to be played by the Soviet Union, Israel, and the Palestinians.

In 1967, the Johnson administration decided to press for a definitive settlement because of its conviction that U.S. aims in the Middle East would no longer be served by approaching the Arab–Israeli conflict on the basis of the territorial integrity formula. The objective of seeking a resolution was therefore limited to the essential goal of eliminating a problem that could no longer be controlled and that had already proved its capacity to disrupt the pursuit of U.S. interests in the Arab world. From an American perspective, what was sought was an equitable arrangement under which Arab governments would accept Israel as a permanent reality in exchange for what would amount to a virtual restoration of the territorial status quo ante.

This vision saw the Palestinian factor only as a humanitarian refugee issue, which required attention to reduce or eliminate its irritating impact on the regional political climate. It was predicated on continuing close ties between the United States and Israel, though not at the expense of alienating the Arab world. By the same token, while the Soviet Union was not to be permitted to enhance its influence in the region by aiding Arabs to recover their losses without coming to terms with Israel, the Johnson administration did not reject possible Soviet participation in an overall settlement. Indeed, once the administration concluded that Israel's refusal to explore peace terms indirectly could further a continuing decline of U.S. influence in the region, it began examining prospects for a joint peacemaking initiative with the Soviet Union.

During the early Nixon years, Secretary of State William Rogers clung to the parameters established by the previous administration. An Arab–Israeli settlement continued to be perceived as a necessary basis for the pursuit of evenhanded and flexible diplomacy on behalf of U.S. interests throughout the Middle East. Ties with Israel, an Israel returned more or less to its pre-war boundaries, would continue to be a major, though not overriding, U.S. interest. Through the four-power and two-power talks, continuing efforts were made to establish grounds for a joint approach with the Soviet Union. The Palestinian question remained fixed in the administration's outlook as a refugee issue.

Following the final collapse of the Rogers Plan of 1969, and of the Rogers Initiative of 1971, a competing U.S. vision gained ascendancy. Under Henry Kissinger's direction, the new perspective dominated the U.S. approach to peacemaking throughout Nixon's remaining years in the White House and during the presidency of Gerald Ford. Washington now rejected the notion that the Arab–Israeli conflict was in itself harmful to U.S. interests in the Middle East. On the contrary, it was held that so long as U.S. power ensured a regional balance of forces decisively tipped in Israel's favor, the frustration engendered in the Arab world could only undercut Moscow's position. Thus, a settlement was not valued as removing an obstacle to the successful pursuit of U.S. objectives in the Arab world. Instead, the prospect of peace was seen as a lever to effect the Soviets' eventual expulsion from the region. The lever would be activated only once major steps toward this end were assured.

In this light, the purpose of a Middle East settlement was not to enhance U.S. political competitiveness but to consolidate Washington's anticipated victory over its superpower rival—in short, to inaugurate a true Middle East "Pax Americana" resting on unchallenged U.S. regional predominance.

As an instrument in this project, Israel was accorded far greater stature as a regional ally than had been the case under the Johnson–Rogers concept of peace. The Palestinians were not considered necessary participants in the peace process, and the Soviet Union was, of course, to be marginalized so far as possible from the dynamics of peacemaking.

Following the 1973 Arab–Israeli war, this scenario was partly played out in the drive toward an Egyptian–Israeli accommodation. However, with the conclusion of Sinai II, the hope of securing a purely U.S.-sponsored overall peace dimmed. Egypt was reluctant to break fully with the Arab world, and Israel was equally loath to negotiate a withdrawal from the territories taken from Syria and Jordan.

In large measure, the Carter administration reverted to the earlier Johnson–Rogers view of a Middle East settlement. Seeing no benefit to be derived from the prolonged conflict between Israel and the Arab world, the administration turned Washington's attention to peacemaking with a renewed sense of urgency. Israel, while still strongly supported, was expected to return to an approximation of its pre–1967 boundaries as part of an overall settlement. The Soviet Union was seen as a necessary participant in the drive toward comprehensive peace.

However, the Palestinian factor was the focus of an original departure. Jimmy Carter was the first U.S. president to imply that Palestinian nationalism was a legitimate force that had to be somehow satisfied in any equitable and stable settlement. His administration stands out among its counterparts for having made the strongest and most sustained effort to find a formula that would permit direct contact with the organizational manifestation of Palestinian nationalism, the PLO, in keeping with guidelines adopted at the peak of Kissinger's influence.

The failure of those efforts and the demise in late 1977 of Carter's hopes for collaborative peacemaking with the Soviet Union, combined with Anwar Sadat's direct appeal to Jerusalem, led to a renewed focus on an Israeli–Egyptian peace. After success was achieved on that front in 1979, the administration had little time or inclination to consider how peace might be extended to other areas of the Arab–Israeli conflict.

Ronald Reagan took office at a moment when this question had been placed in abeyance. His administration initially counted on it remaining in the background. Egypt's novel relationship with Israel had produced a tripartite stalemate in the Arab world that left Cairo facing the impotent wrath of Syria, Libya, the PLO, and other dissident forces while Jordan, Saudi Arabia, and the conservative Gulf states sat immobile, hesitating to commit themselves unambiguously to one side or the other.

Believing the Arab–Israeli problem to be frozen into inconsequence, the Reagan administration opted to neglect it, giving priority to creating an anti-Soviet Middle Eastern bloc. When the warnings of the Arab leaders it approached in this venture proved correct and the Palestine issue impinged violently on Washington's gaze, the administration was left confronting the same vacuum faced by all American policymakers in the wake of Sinai II.

However, it did so within a firmly held framework of objectives. The Soviet Union was to be excluded from the search for Mideast peace, and, if possible, from the region itself. Palestinian nationalism was also to be barred from effective participation in the arrangement of a settlement. Israel was to remain the United States' primary ally in the Middle East.

Israeli concepts of how best to meet these desiderata soon filled the vacuum in Washington. There ensued the Israeli–PLO war in Lebanon and the ill-fated U.S. attempt to restructure that country.

The end of the intervention in Lebanon in 1984 did not alter the administration's vision of the requirements of a Middle East settlement. Frustrated by its failure to mold conditions in the region through force (largely that of local surrogates), Washington again relegated the search for peace to the far backburners of its attention. The rather desultory interest it subsequently exhibited in a possible Jordan–Israel settlement and an international peace conference gave no indication of any substantial modification in the Reagan administration's opposition to both Palestinian full self-determination and a significant Soviet role in settling the Arab–Israeli conflict.

Even a superficial overview reveals several significant elements that helped mold the course of Washington's search for Mideast peace. For example, it is obvious that the personalities of key figures significantly affected U.S. decisions. Henry Kissinger's intellectual brilliance, crafty sense of timing, physical energy, and supreme self-confidence added up to a potent political force, particularly, it would seem, when he interacted with the complex personality of Richard Nixon. In a similar vein, Jimmy Carter's personal bent toward what he conceived of as humane politics based on reasonable dialogue and universal values, Alexander Haig's penchant for his own vision of hard-headed *real politik*, and Ronald Reagan's tendency to see radical forces as Soviet instruments all appear to have been important factors in major policy steps.

It also seems clear that historical accident played a considerable role in shaping the American approach. There was, for example, nothing inevitable in the coincidence that the U.S. search for peace was launched—and long remained—under the shadow of the Vietnam War. That conflict led Lyndon Johnson to decide against seeking a second term and preoccupied Richard Nixon during his first term. Both outcomes indirectly influenced Washington's efforts to deal with the Middle East. The same is true of the Watergate scandal as well as of the fall of Pahlavi Iran, each of which helped undermine an incumbent president.

A further feature of the overall U.S. approach to Mideast peacemaking is underscored by any perusal of the historical record. It can, for want of a better term, perhaps be best described as a form of intellectual rigidity that has long been a general characteristic of both U.S. public opinion and U.S. decision makers in matters related to the Palestine issue. For over forty years a notably consistent pattern has marked the American public's reaction to the clash between Arabs and Zionists. On the one hand, the majority of U.S. citizens have been largely uninformed about, and at best only slightly interested in, the question. On the other, among those who actively follow U.S. policy toward the issue, the balance of opinion has generally been strongly supportive of Israel.[4]

This helps explain why no serious outcry has arisen in the United States over the years during which Israel's steady entrenchment in the occupied territories progressively threatened the original—and still proclaimed—U.S. goal of an equitable peace based on the return of occupied lands. It also underlies the absence of sustained questioning of a U.S. approach that has come to single out the Palestinian people as a group to whom the basic right of political self-determination must be denied.

A form of intellectual rigidity has also long obtained among U.S. decision makers. For nearly half a century, whether in Congress, the White House, or the major national bureaucracies, formulators of U.S. policy have generally neither perceived nor reacted to the Arab–Zionist conflict in terms of its central issue: whether the Arabs and Jews in Palestine, or somehow both, will rule politically. Instead, they have responded to the question on the basis of its presumed implications for broader foreign policy problems or in light of domestic political considerations. This pattern, visible as early as 1939, has proved exceedingly resilient.[5] Despite the consistent intensity of the Palestinians' post–1967 struggle to reassert their status as a primordial participant in the Middle East conflict, Washington's acknowledgment that Palestinian nationalism must be coped with in the context of any political settlement has been slow, tentative, and incomplete.

The refusal to see the Palestine issue in its elemental form underlies the glaring contradiction between the Reagan administration's declared belief that Palestinians are entitled to "self-government" and its inflexible opposition to Palestinian sovereignty. Official explanations of this curious stand have entailed only vague assertions to the effect that a Palestinian state will destabilize the Middle East. This overlooks the obvious fact that the frustration of Palestinian nationalism has so far been one of the great destabilizers in the region. It also ignores various scenarios that for years have been put forth by Palestinian as well as Israeli analysts suggesting plausible specific conditions that might render the satisfaction of Palestinian demands for a sovereign state compatible with Israel's security.[6]

Fifty years ago, official American intellectual rigidity was largely a product of inexperience. In 1939, Franklin Delano Roosevelt knew little of the Middle East and less of the Arab–Zionist problem. Six years later, his stint as wartime president had given him a much broader understanding of the region's importance in global politics, while contacts with prominent Zionists had left him with a far better appreciation of the aspirations and problems surrounding their movement. Yet the depth of Arab opposition to Zionist plans for Palestine startled him when he had his first direct encounter with a major Arab leader.[7]

Today, the failure of U.S. policy to reflect an unambiguous understanding that the Arab–Israeli problem is still rooted in the core clash between Jewish and Palestinian nationalisms cannot be attributed to simple ignorance. Too much time has passed, and too much contact—both direct and indirect—has occurred between Washington and the protagonists for that explanation to be satisfactory. One must conclude that the operative dynamic has to a great extent been an act of will. The formulators of U.S. policy have insisted on perceiving the Palestine struggle as either a tool for attaining objectives not directly related to the Arab–Israeli conflict, or as an obstacle to those same ends. They have treated it accordingly.

It is at this point that obvious conclusions yielded by superficial surveys become unsatisfactory. The consistency with which U.S. policy has ignored the essential nature of the Palestine issue militates against placing any great reliance on the explanatory powers of such variables as personality, historical accident, or intellectual rigidity. As important as these may be in explaining particular decisions taken at particular moments, they cannot—individually or collectively—sustain a satisfactory analysis of the course of U.S. involvement with the Arab–Israeli problem. The real question is why different individuals working under different circumstances, and possessed of differing levels of intellectual capacity, have all habitually failed to guide U.S. peacemaking into a sustained and direct confrontation with the core element of the Palestine issue.

The answer must begin by frankly facing the nature of international relations. It is neither surprising nor reprehensible that Washington has defined the Arab–Israeli problem, not in terms of the intrinsic points of contention between Palestinians and Israelis, but rather in light of the clash's implications for broader U.S. goals. International politics is the pursuit of self-interest, and to expect altruism to underlie U.S. peacemaking efforts in the Middle East would be folly. Inevitably, the conflict between two small groups claiming the same relatively poor land in the eastern Mediterranean could be defined as a policy issue in Washington only after having been refracted through the prism of established U.S. objectives.

Inherent as it is in the nature of politics, the assignment of particularistic definitions to issues cannot in itself be decried. What is open to criticism is the determination to cling to, and act upon, such definitions when by doing so, policy becomes self-defeating. If U.S. policy is indeed helping to propel the Middle East toward further, and perhaps greater, Arab–Israeli tensions, it is open to this charge.

THE DYNAMICS OF U.S. POLICYMAKING

An effort to understand the U.S. search for Mideast peace must focus ultimately on the underlying sources of Washington's definitions of the Palestine issue. While it is clear enough that U.S. foreign policy formulation is a complex affair, involving inputs from a variety of sources, it is nonetheless true that the final product—policy decisions—may be taken as directed toward the composite image that in Washington defines the nature of the issue at stake.

Such operational definitions seem to arise from interaction among three factors: *perceptions* held by key actors of connections between the immediate issue and established U.S. interests; the *context*, formed of major regional and global political circumstances, in which the issue must be addressed; and the U.S. political *structure*—the domestic framework in which possible courses of action must be evaluated as realistic policy options.

Applying this to U.S. peacemaking efforts in the Middle East, it is evident that American perceptions of the Palestine issue have been fundamentally shaped by conclusions regarding the nexus between the Arab–Israeli conflict and U.S.–USSR competition, for in the hierarchy of established U.S. objectives in the Middle East that of besting the Soviet Union is first.

Although that goal has not been challenged by those charged with the conduct of U.S. foreign policy, judgments of its significance for U.S. responses to the Palestine issue have led to two competing perspectives, each of which, despite basic differences between them, accepts as unquestionable the American commitment to Israel's security. Both outlooks have also come to be based on the premise that a Palestinian state is unacceptable. In principle at least, both further hold that an eventual Middle East settlement must rest on the exchange of some degree of occupied territory for political concessions.

The first perspective, which might be termed "optimizing," views regional competition with the Soviet Union as a political fact of life that will be ongoing and implies that incremental gains will probably not lead to an overriding U.S. preponderance of influence in the Middle East vis-à-vis Moscow. This perspective therefore sees Arab–Israeli tensions as threatening—the equation, at its essence, being that so long as Arab–Israeli tensions exist, Washington's ties with Israel will inevitably hamper its ability to compete with the Soviet Union in the Arab world.

This outlook not only gives high priority to resolving the Arab–Israeli conflict but is also prone to explore possibilities of utilizing Moscow's influence to bring about that result. By the same token, it is relatively open to exploring prospects for accommodation with Soviet-supported regional actors within a framework guaranteeing Israel's existence.

The second major U.S. perspective, here labeled "maximalist," holds that it is realistic to aim at virtually, if not totally, eliminating Soviet influence in the Middle East and thereby securing for the United States a long-term position of unquestionable regional dominance. Seen from this vantage point, the Arab–Israeli conflict is perceived not so much as a threat as an opportunity. So long, goes the argument, as U.S. power is directly or indirectly effective in frustrating the demands of local forces who look to the Soviets for material and political support, there can only result the progressive erosion of Moscow's standing in the region. A major corollary to this is that Israel must be kept militarily strong not only on behalf of its own security interests but also (and at least equally) on grounds of U.S. strategic interests. In its determination to discredit the Soviet Union and radical local forces, the maximalist perspective is prepared to accept an enduring status quo upheld by force and to defer seriously exploring avenues toward political accommodation until Arab actors first abandon positions that are deemed unacceptable. Interest in searching for means to facilitate compromise, therefore, tends to be placed in abeyance pending initial concessions from the other side.

For over twenty years these perspectives have competed in Washington. Neither has yet held unchallenged sway, though at each point one or the other has been predominant. Yet it is obvious that neither singly nor in combination have these visions of the link between the Arab–Israeli problem and the overriding goal of besting the Soviet Union in competition for the Middle East been the sole sources of Washington's views on the requirements of peacemaking. This is most strikingly borne out by the fact that official adherents of both outlooks have come to hold firmly that under no circumstances can a Palestinian state form part of any eventual Middle East settlement.

Since there is nothing inherently contradictory in the idea of a pro-American Palestinian state, there is no logical necessity for this stand even under the maximalist perspective, although the logical gap is rather more visible in its optimizing counterpart. For if maximalists can try to rationalize their resistance to logic on the circuitous grounds that today's Palestinian nationalism opposes American opposition to itself and therefore must be absolutely rejected lest any compromise with it redound to Soviet benefit, adherents of the optimizing perspective cannot. Predicated as it is on an openness in principle to limited tradeoffs, the latter should logically lead to efforts to determine under what conditions Palestinian nationalism might, in return for a solution that does not require it to self-destruct, agree to a settlement upholding both Israel's security and U.S. interests in the Middle East. That this perspective does not lead to such efforts cannot even remotely be attributed to anything derived from the inherent logic of the perspective itself.

It becomes apparent that the full nature of U.S. peacemaking policy can be understood only by taking into account the interplay among, on the one hand, views of the intrinsic connection between the Arab–Israeli conflict and the U.S.–Soviet rivalry and, on the other, the context and structure within which policy decisions are made.

Context—the major regional and global circumstances obtaining at the moment of decision—inevitably affects existing appraisals of the Arab–Israeli struggle's relevance for U.S.–Soviet competition in the Middle East. Even strongly held perceptions do not exist in isolation from changing political currents. Thus, alterations in the international context have exerted visible influence over the years on the relative impact of the two basic perspectives informing Washington's approach to peacemaking.

However, the roles of perceptual and contextual factors in policy formulation are also affected by the structure of the U.S. decision-making system. Above all, the making of U.S. policy is a competitive enterprise. The system, with the White House both constitutionally and in practice at its apex, is pyramidal, embracing, in addition to the president and his advisers, the relevant bureaucracies, congress, political parties, organized interest groups, and—at its base—the great mass of the voting public. The structure inevitably invites participation and just as inevitably receives it from opposing views. The final outcome is often a compromise, or several compromises, among distinct preferences.

Faced with controversial questions, such a structure lends itself to short-term steps, and in the process frequently burnishes to high gloss the maxim that politics is "the art of the possible." Over an extended period of time, the compromises, the short-term steps, and the "art of the possible" tend to produce contradictions and reversals in the handling of any given issue.

This, however, does not imply either the absence of identifiable long-term policy trends or that opposing views are necessarily more or less equally supported within the U.S. system. Thus, American Zionists and supporters of Israel have worked effectively and efficiently within the competitive U.S. framework. Both their success in exercising significant influence on Washington's decisions at critical junctures and the overall trend toward greater U.S. support for Israel over the past two decades must be attributed at least partly to the lack of countervailing grassroots interest in the Arab–Israeli conflict.

The dynamic interaction among perspectives, context, and structure explains both the consistencies and inconsistencies that have characterized the American search for Mideast peace from the Johnson to the Reagan administrations.

It was not strange that the former took up the challenge in 1967 guided predominantly by an optimizing outlook. That orientation had in any case been the base upon which the United States had long sought to compartmentalize its approach to the Middle East through the "territorial integrity formula." Despite the rocky course of U.S. relations with Egypt, Syria, and Iraq in the 1950s and 1960s, Washington never saw Soviet gains in those countries as sufficient reason to replace generally active efforts to cultivate their political friendship with sustained, distant frigidity, which promised not to be removed until those governments were solidly in the U.S. camp.

The context in which the Johnson administration set out to promote an end to the Arab–Israeli conflict both reinforced and helped undermine Washington's commitment to an optimizing approach. On the one hand, the administration's preoccupation with the Vietnam War led it to hope for a quick resolution, effected through the exchange of occupied territory for political concessions. At the same time, the rudimentary state of the Palestinian resistance movement and indications of Arab governments' willingness to bargain for the recovery of their lost lands, encouraged the belief that such an exchange could be executed strictly within the confines of the existing Middle East state system. President Johnson's insistence that peace could not "reflect the weight of conquest," his dismissal of Israel's demand for direct negotiations by calling instead for the clarification of bargaining positions through "some agreed procedure," and his effort to force compliance with the latter point by delaying approval of Israel's requests for Phantom airplanes were highly visible manifestations of his optimizing approach.

On the other hand, Israel's steadfast refusal to consider indirect dealings with the Arabs, the very ambiguity of Arab willingness to accept the legitimacy of Israel's existence, and—most of all—Soviet refusal to agree to arms limitations in the Middle East underscored the prospect that the search for a compromise could irrevocably undercut the U.S. position in the Arab world.

These doubts were reinforced by the impact of the structural element in policy formulation. Although Johnson may have been personally freed from domestic political considerations by deciding within months of the June War against seeking re-election, efforts to pressure Israel out of its diplomatic inertia were opposed not only by Israel's domestic allies but also by those who believed that to do so would only strengthen Soviet prestige in the Arab world.

In the end, the administration tried to satisfy domestic opponents while simultaneously attempting to establish grounds for an accommodation with the Soviet Union in the Middle East. In the closing months of his term, Johnson's acquiescence on the supply of Phantom warplanes to Israel was paralleled by efforts to explore possibilities for a formula that could be advanced jointly with the Soviets in the Middle East. In a way, it was almost a startling move, for it openly acknowledged the Soviet

Union as a power with some degree of acceptable interests in the region. In another sense, however, it simply formalized what had in practice come to be accepted by U.S. policymakers.

The optimizing torch that passed to the Nixon administration in 1969 came in for more complex handling. Nixon's perspective on the relevance of the Arab–Israel issue to U.S.–Soviet competition in the Middle East remains a mystery. Evidence indicates that he vacillated, at different times holding strongly contradictory views on the merits of the optimizing and maximalist perspectives.

However, there is no doubt that during the early part of his first administration the inherited optimizing approach prevailed. Despite Henry Kissinger's ongoing opposition, Secretary of State William Rogers pursued the opening to the Soviets bequeathed by Johnson. The Rogers Plan remains not only the most specific statement of what the United States would view as an acceptable overall Middle East settlement but also the clearest proposal (on record) for which it has sought to win Soviet support.

But if Rogers had no reservations regarding the demarche, the president did. Nixon's ambivalence was shown by his own discreet efforts to distance himself from the proposal. It is likely that his doubts affected the credibility of the administration's commitment to the Rogers Plan in the eyes of the Soviet Union and Arab actors.

In this early Nixonian period, the influence of contextual and structural factors was again visible. At the outset of his presidency, Nixon was, if anything, even more preoccupied by Vietnam than his predecessor. He had, moreover, determined that China, Europe, and the overall global balance of U.S.–Soviet relations demanded priority. The State Department, rather than the White House, would deal with the Middle East. In that region itself, Israel was still opposed to anything less than direct negotiations with Arab states and, by now, was clearly in the grip of an internal struggle over the future of the occupied lands that minimized chances of imaginative diplomacy on its part. In the Arab world, the Palestinian Resistance was a growing force that, while still apparently marginal, opposed any signs of moderation by other Arab actors. Nasser's Egypt and Hussein's Jordan would still not clearly commit themselves to accepting Israel's legitimacy in the framework of a political settlement. The ambiguity of both—and particularly that of the latter—incurred the wrath of less flexible elements in the Arab world. The Soviet Union, while continuing to express interest in a political settlement, was solidly entrenched as the Arabs' chief political supporter and arms supplier.

These contextual circumstances partly explain Nixon's de facto undermining of the Rogers Plan, virtually the last hurrah of the optimizing approach to peacemaking under his stewardship. Again, what must be added to the equation is the impact of realities imposed by the structure within which foreign policy unfolds.

As had Johnson, Nixon faced a strongly pro-Israel congress. Capitalizing on this, the American president sought to inculcate flexibility in Israeli policymakers by making payoffs in the form of financial and military aid. Yet, when flexibility failed to result, the administration still confronted major domestic resistance to the Rogers Plan. In addition to Congress, Nixon found his National Security Adviser opposing Rogers' optimizing ethos and arguing a maximalist perspective: that by forgoing a coordinated approach with the Soviet Union, the United States could, if rigidity were backed by increased commitments to Israel, emerge as the sole arbiter of peace in the region.

The rise of maximalism was bolstered by contextual developments and crowned by the growing influence of maximalist spokesmen within the policymaking structure. Israel indirectly contributed to the 1970/71 defeat of the PLO in Jordan, and its role in the affair was highlighted by Henry Kissinger as a blow against Moscow. In 1971 Kissinger took charge of the administration's strategy toward the Middle East and in 1973 replaced William Rogers as Secretary of State while retaining his post as National Security Adviser.

Kissinger's view guided U.S. policy until early 1977. In the meantime significant steps were taken to ensure stringent limits on future efforts to deal with the Middle East on an optimizing basis.

Apart from that unblemished achievement, the Kissinger era produced mixed results. The context of Middle East peacemaking changed in important ways shortly after Nasser's death in 1970. Anwar Sadat became Egypt's leader and immediately projected an image of being more amenable than his predecessor to U.S. peacemaking efforts. More importantly, he took a series of well publicized steps to distance his regime from the Soviets. At the same time, Jordan's defeat of the PLO seemed to have marked the crest of that organization's influence in regional affairs.

Still preoccupied by Southeast Asia, China, and global relations with the Soviet Union, the Nixon administration continued to accord low priority to the Middle East. Kissingerian maximalism, noting that Egypt not only still relied on Soviet support but also demanded the return of all occupied lands in the framework of a settlement, was not modified by Sadat's overtures. U.S. diplomatic quiescence in the Middle East occasioned little alarm in the American foreign policy system, where eagerness to support Israel, distrust of the Soviets, and satisfaction with the torpid stability in the area continued to prevail.

The October War of 1973 together with the ensuing oil boycott galvanized U.S. peacemaking diplomacy. Nixon's original impulse to give free rein to his optimizing inclinations by seeking an immediate agreement with the Soviet Union on what would have amounted to an imposed regional settlement flared and quickly came to nothing. The futility of the president's initial reaction can be explained both by the context of ongoing crisis in which it arose and by Nixon's rapidly dwindling powers as a decision maker in the face of the Watergate scandal.

The context in which Kissinger set about peacemaking in the aftermath of the 1973 war proved amenable to his fundamental objectives of marginalizing the Soviet Union and local radical forces from the mainstream of regional politics, making the United States unquestionably the key outside power in the area, and strengthening Israel's security. Sadat, the Arab oil producers, and Syria were willing to support U.S. diplomatic efforts aimed at partial agreements rather than comprehensive peace. The Soviets, having been unable to help the Arabs in the final stages of the war, seemed equally incapable of stemming their own diplomatic decline, accepting with apparent resignation a purely formalistic role at the Geneva Conference and thereafter watching impotently as Washington pursued step-by-step diplomacy. The PLO, although it gained wide recognition after 1974 as the sole voice of the Palestinian people and began to amass a series of diplomatic and public relations victories on the international scene, was excluded—with the acquiescence of leading Arab governments—from what became known as the U.S.-sponsored "peace process." By the Ford administration's final year in office, the PLO's troubled relations with Arab governments would be severely complicated by its fight against Syrian and rightist forces in Lebanon.

Israel responded grudgingly to the peace process, disturbed by Sadat's effort to create his own special relationship with the United States and by the precedent of relinquishing part of the land it occupied in 1967. Kissinger's eventual success in persuading Israeli leaders to accept Sinai II can be mainly attributed to their recognition of the strength of Washington's desire to bring Egypt under its umbrella, the attraction of effectively severing Cairo from the rest of the Arab world, the range of American commitments they extracted—including, particularly, the conditional bar on U.S. contacts with the PLO—and Washington's careful avoidance of any linkage between the limited accord with Egypt and outstanding political and territorial questions dividing Israel from its remaining Arab enemies.

In general, the U.S. foreign policy structure strongly supported the post–1973 approach to Middle East peacemaking. Kissinger's step-by-step rationale was accepted with few questions raised about its implications for Washington's eventual ability to deal with fundamental points of contention between Israel and the Arab world. No serious domestic opposition developed at any point to the political and material commitments that induced Israeli progress along the road to Sinai II. On the other hand, the Ford administration's attempts to encourage Israeli flexibility by its touted policy "reassessment" sparked considerable resistance within the American system.

The combined impact of Kissinger's maximalist ethos, the context of policy formulation, and the U.S. decision-making structure also explains the suspension of active American peacemaking efforts after the signing of Sinai II in 1975. Maximalism, of course, limited the field of potential Arab participants in the peace process to Egypt and Jordan, the only two Arab actors who appeared possibly ready to cast their lot entirely with the United States as a prelude to a settlement. However, contextual and structural factors blocked sustained U.S. diplomatic initiatives in these directions.

Having already pushed against the bounds of political propriety in the Arab world by signing Sinai II, Egypt was not yet prepared to break fully with its Arab brothers. Although King Hussein was eager to sample step-by-step peacemaking, several considerations dissuaded Washington from responding positively. On the one hand, although Arab opponents of the U.S. peace process might carp incessantly, they seemed incapable of threatening the gains Washington had already achieved. Moreover, Syria and the PLO were plunging into open conflict in Lebanon, embarrassing the Soviet Union and even further reducing the effectiveness of their shared hostility to growing U.S. influence in the region. The situation left U.S. policymakers with little sense of urgency about extending the peace process and a great deal of satisfaction over the frentic impotence into which Middle East radicals had fallen.

On the other hand, Israel could be counted on to resist any effort to reduce its control of the West Bank. It was equally predictable that an attempt by the Ford administration to pressure Jerusalem in this direction would encounter stiff domestic opposition. Conversely, a retreat from energetic peacemaking would cause no outcry at home.

The result was that Jimmy Carter entered the White House after a hiatus of almost eighteen months in the U.S. search for peace. A committed optimizer, Carter firmly believed that U.S. interests were jeopardized by a prolongation of Arab–Israeli tensions. He was eager to explore possibilities for a comprehensive settlement that would somehow satisfy Palestinian nationalism, and he was convinced that progress toward that objective required Soviet involvement.

While his administration's effort to promote an international peace conference sprang from this basic outlook, Carter's policy was ultimately shaped more by contextual and structural realities.

By 1977, contextual factors reinforced the maximalist arguments of those who focused on immediate conditions in the Middle East: the area, though divided, seemed stable enough, and the Soviets had been thrust to the sidelines of regional diplomacy. To invite their return was seen not only as unnecessary but also as tantamount to throwing away earlier American gains. Such views were reinforced by alarm over Soviet moves on the Middle East's periphery, particularly in South Yemen and East Africa.

Moreover, the willingness of Arab actors, apart from Egypt and Jordan, but most certainly including the PLO, to accept Israel's right to exist, remained doubtful. Then too, Israel not only adamantly rejected the PLO's inclusion in peace negotiations under any circumstances but was also continuing to fall steadily under the sway of explicitly expansionist political sentiments.

In the Carter administration's judgment, the potentially detrimental impact of these conditions was counterbalanced by more positive indications. The very ambiguity that marked radical Arab postures, particularly those of the PLO and Syria, held hope for a resolution in keeping with U.S. interests and Israeli security. Egypt, having pioneered Arab involvement in substantive peacemaking under American auspices, had a strong interest in encouraging others to follow suit. The Soviet Union, its presence in the Middle East severely restricted, seemed to have an interest in reaching some accommodation over the region with the United States.

Carter's effort to test these conclusions failed, partly because of contextual realities and largely because of structural obstacles that prevented the pursuit of his overall design. Throughout 1977, the administration was unable to enlist the wholehearted support of either Syria or the PLO for its planned international peace conference. When the crowning point of departure for the projected conference—the U.S.–Soviet declaration on principles for a Middle East peace—was reached in late 1977, it quickly evaporated under the joint assault of anti-Soviet and pro-Israel domestic forces. The alacrity of the administration's retreat from this cornerstone of its policy helped unravel the fragile fabric of tentative moderation it had woven in the Middle East.

Egypt administered the coup de grace to Carter's initiative by embarking openly on the path to a separate peace with Israel. Faced with overwhelming obstacles to its original plans, Washington midwived the Camp David Agreements and the 1979 Egyptian–Israeli peace treaty. Yet the administration remained uncomfortable over having acted under the influence of contextual and structural pressures. Its long-term misgivings surfaced in Brzezinski's doubts as to the wisdom of pressing so hard for an Egyptian–Israeli agreement divorced from broader Arab–Israeli questions.

No such worries troubled the Reagan administration when it assumed office in 1981. Committed to roll back perceived Soviet gains throughout the world, it clung with profound conviction to a maximalist perception of the Middle East. Taking the Egyptian–Israeli treaty as a central reality that rendered existing tensions between Israel and the Arab world ephemeral, Reagan and his colleagues relegated Palestine to the borders of their attention and gave priority to consolidating U.S. supremacy in the Middle East. Alexander Haig's rallying cry—"This is America's moment in the Middle East"—was the underlying slogan of the new search for strategic consensus.

If Jimmy Carter misread contextual indications in light of an optimizing bias, the Reagan administration committed a similar fault swayed by maximalist ambitions. Neither warnings from Jordanian and Saudi leaders that the Arab world was seriously concerned with the Palestinians' fate, nor Anwar Sadat's assassination, jarred the administration's conviction that Arab and Israeli anti-communism offered the true material from which to construct an American-dominated anti-Soviet bastion in the Middle East. On the contrary, the urgency of this quest seemed reinforced by the 1979 Soviet invasion of Afghanistan and the fall of the Pahlavi regime.

A partial revision of this outlook was soon forced by local clashes in the Middle East that threatened to develop into a crisis. There followed Philip Habib's mission to negotiate a renewed cease-fire between Israel and the PLO. However, when the administration was finally convinced that the Arab–Israeli quarrel would continue obstructing the pursuit of U.S. interests in the Middle East; it reacted fully in keeping with its maximalist logic: countenancing Israel's 1982 attempt to destroy the PLO and, ultimately, allowing the United States to become a direct participant in Lebanon's civil chaos.

The Reagan administration's maximalist tendencies were initially encouraged by contextual and structural factors that appeared to override the cautionary advice offered by Jordanian and Saudi leaders. Haig's early tour of the Arab world found most of his interlocuters uneasy over the region's possible radicalization, a concern that saw Islamic fundamentalism and Palestinian activism as worrisome. Syria's stand on the Iran–Iraq War had undermined Damascus' influence in other Arab capitals.

Once it was clear that the Arab–Israeli problem could not be ignored, a crashing blow against Syria and the PLO (and therefore indirectly against the Soviet Union) seemed a viable way of extending the Egyptian–Israeli peace within the Camp David framework. Lebanon, cleansed of the Palestinian resistance, would set the tone and Jordan would follow. In the wake of Beirut's devastation, Washington sought to cloak the bitter prescription it had countenanced, and to shore up its credibility as the Middle East's "peacemaker," by donning the Reagan Plan's more conciliatory gown. The new costume's utter inadequacy was steadily revealed as the United States made no move to overcome the proposal's total rejection by Israel.

Sabra and Shatila altered the tactics but not the overall strategy. U.S. troops, first employed to ensure order, soon became tools to install a pliable Lebanese government. When local forces proved resistant to this approach, Washington withdrew—leaving behind the "Reagan Plan," and its tip-of-the-hat to limited Palestinian self-government but taking no action to pursue that restricted concept of a political settlement.

Again, contextual and structural factors help explain the course of U.S. policy. If the willingness of some Arab governments to undermine radicalism in the Middle East contributed to the Israeli–U.S. incursion into Lebanon, the unwillingness of others, and the popular appeal of the Palestinian cause in the Arab world, helped save the Palestinians from political extinction. On the other hand, while the U.S. foreign policy system supported the administration's initial indirect, and then direct, involvement in Lebanon, the specter of an open-ended commitment to rearrange Middle East politics caused it to balk. The "redeployment" of U.S. forces out of Lebanon was therefore effected with little domestic opposition.

While the 1984 withdrawal from Lebanon signalled an end to direct American efforts to construct an environment more conducive to a maximalist vision of regional peace, the Reagan administration had not—by the winter of 1988—substantially changed its outlook. In the intervening years, its policies continued to aim at strengthening ties between the United States and Israel, encouraging Jordan to enter into an agreement with Israel that would at least challenge, if not destroy, the territorial claims of Palestinian nationalism, and, finally, keeping regional and international competitors (particularly Syria and the Soviet Union) excluded from the theoretically ongoing search for peace.

Structural and contextual factors have so far tended to support these objectives. Despite growing concern with budgetary outlays, congress has not reacted against the yearly cost of the static peace between Egypt and Israel. Nor has the Reagan administration come under strong questioning from any quarter in the United States regarding the long-term implications of upholding an expensive and festering situation in the Middle East. On the other hand, the Soviet Union continues to stand outside the main currents of Middle East politics; the Egyptian government, although beset by economic and possibly rising political problems, shows no sign of altering its basic policies; the PLO, now seemingly recovered from its post–1982 debility, suggests that it pursues minimal nationalist objectives and seems powerless to do anything about their consistent rejection; Syria reinforces its own ties with the Soviet Union but seems unable to effect any major change in the Middle East environment; although King Hussein suddenly renounced his claim to the West Bank in the summer of 1988, the extent to which this fundamentally alters Jordan's traditional ambivalence towards its role in the peace process remains uncertain.

If there is a harbinger of fundamental change in the U.S. approach on the horizon, it is likely to be the spontaneous explosion of Palestinian anger that began to sweep the West Bank and Gaza in December 1987 and continues unabated as of this writing. Frustrated beyond endurance by their unrelieved condemnation to Israeli occupation and control, stone-throwing youths and demonstrators of all ages daily confront the occupier's well-armed troops—frequently paying with physical injury or death for the encounter. Shocking scenes of mayhem, including instances of personalized barbarity such as Israeli soldiers wielding rocks to break the bones of bound civilian prisoners, are transmitted globally by television cameras.

The images embarrass all Arab regimes, and at the popular level provoke mixed currents of pride, anger, and shame. The urge to express solidarity with the Palestinians' struggle and dismay over their own governments' inaction has brought students into the streets of Egypt, Jordan, and Syria. It cannot be doubted that the protests reveal only part of the concern and tension generated throughout the region by the ongoing plight of the Palestinians.

In Israel, the "Intifada" fuels controversy over whether compromise or increased repression is the adequate response. Mostly, however, it so far generates confusion. Few Israelis currently tolerate the idea that Palestinian sovereignty over the West Bank and Gaza may legitimately fall within the sphere of compromise. Shimon Peres' Labor followers appear amenable to some undefined arrangement with Jordan that will reduce, although not eliminate, Israel's hold on occupied lands. Prime Minister Yitzhak Shamir's Likud also hopes, in principle, for a Jordanian arrangement, though clearly loath to base it on territorial return. Farther to the right of Israel's political spectrum, the uprising is taken to validate calls for even more repressive measures than those that have already produced the deaths of so many unarmed Palestinians. The crisis, in short, highlights Israel's lack of readiness to act on any option but the maintenance of the smoldering status quo in the occupied lands.

Palestinian rage has also underlined the failure of the U.S. search for Mideast peace. That all was not well on the peace front has long been evident to anyone who cared to look. Evidence of Israel's inability to quell sustained rioting in Gaza and the West Bank has now forced the Reagan administration to acknowledge the point. However, it appears that Egyptian President Hosni Mubarak's 1988 public branding of the Camp David framework as no longer viable for building peace between Israel and the Arab world finally galvanized Washington into action.

By early March 1988, the administration was loudly proclaiming its renewed commitment to "comprehensive peace." So far, however, it seems that little has changed in Washington's approach. Secretary of State Shultz engaged in bouts of shuttle diplomacy, carrying a much advertised new peace plan to Israel, Egypt, Syria, and Jordan. On inspection, it proved, as one commentator noted, "a ... pot-pourri of ideas which have made no progress in the past."[8] The plan called for an early international conclave to launch negotiations between Israel and a Jordanian non-PLO Palestinian team; the establishment of Palestinian "autonomy" in the West Bank and Gaza by the fall of 1988; and finalization of those areas' status within three years. It came to nothing.

Not surprisingly, initial responses from all parties were essentially negative. It is open to question whether Washington will fulfill its current promises to continue working energetically for a peace formula that will be acceptable to major Arab states, Israel, and the Palestinian people. Arabs may be pardoned for skepticism. They have heard the same pledges before—most notably those associated with the 1982 Reagan Plan. With both Israel and the United States scheduled to hold national elections later in 1988, suspicions that current diplomatic promises may be aimed at momentarily defusing the crisis in the occupied territories cannot be dismissed.

On the other hand, precisely because it is evident that the dynamics behind Washington's current demarche parallel earlier ones, it is not totally inconceivable that the present upheaval may be a positive catalyst.

The history of the past twenty years seems to reveal patterns in the interplay among perceptual, contextual, and structural factors that have shaped the American search for Mideast peace. Among these, three seem particularly relevant.

The first is that *maximalist orientations tend to weaken in the face of crisis.* This pattern was followed when the Nixon administration confronted the crisis of the 1973 Arab–Israeli war. It was repeated by the Reagan administration when Philip Habib was sent to the Middle East in 1981. It was again tentatively repeated by the same administration following Israel's 1982 invasion of Lebanon, and it may have surfaced once more in 1988.

The second is that *optimizing orientations tend to be undercut by ambiguity and disunity on the part of Israel's adversaries.* This syndrome contributed to the downfall of Lyndon Johnson's effort to pressure Israel into indirect negotiations with Arab governments in 1968, the collapse of the Rogers Plan in 1969/70, and the failure of Jimmy Carter's strategy for comprehensive peace in 1977.

The third pattern is that *the impact of structural factors on U.S. decision making is heavily inclined in favor of maximalist policies in the Middle East.* This has been evident in many cases, including the circumstances sur-

rounding Lyndon Johnson's effort to pressure Israel into indirect negotiations, domestic reaction to the Rogers Plan, Richard Nixon's
reluctance to come out openly in support of an imposed peace, Gerald
Ford's policy "reassessment," and the fate of the Carter administration's
agreement on principles with the Soviet Union.

If it is accepted as given that current Middle East realities (the positions
of the PLO and Syria in particular) are sufficient to frustrate the maximalist hope of constructing a peace that precludes any significant contribution by the Soviet Union, these patterns currently offer only two
avenues toward eventual Arab–Israeli peace.

The first is a crisis of a magnitude that so threatens the U.S. position
in the Middle East that maximalists will be tempted to abandon their
outlook and rush to embrace a more conciliatory position. This theoretical possibility seems ominously unpromising. For, on the one hand,
it appears far more probable that a crisis of such proportions would lead
maximalists to rely on indirect or direct military means to cope with the
perceived threat. On the other hand, pursuing optimizing policies under
the threat of crisis—one is reminded of Nixon's short-lived attempt to
reach an arrangement with the Soviets during the 1973 war—is hardly
a formula for fruitful diplomacy. The bottom line, were such a situation
confronted within a maximalist framework, might be war—fought either
indirectly through Israel or directly—or, alternatively, an unduly costly
negotiating position.

The second avenue to Middle East peace under existing circumstances
therefore seems to depend overwhelmingly on the cultivation of an effective optimizing orientation in Washington that can shape policy without acting under the spur of explosive circumstances. Given the history
of the past two decades, it appears beyond question that this will not
result simply from the installation of an administration committed to an
optimizing ethos in the Middle East. Nor does there seem much hope
that the impact of structural influences on policy formulation will be
swayed by the logic of optimizers, even if these include those officials
most directly charged within the American system with the conduct of
foreign policy.

There is, then, very little left upon which to rely for a successful U.S.
role in Middle East peacemaking other than what have been termed here
"contextual factors." This—be it noted—reflects the fact that U.S. policy,
despite the assumption of the role of "peacemaker" by the United States,
has long been essentially reactive—responding to, rather than initiating,
developments in the search for Mideast peace.

The danger is that all parties recognize this and are tempted to pursue
their own maximalist demands in the hope of creating new circumstances
that will cause Washington's policies to shift in their favor. However,

Israelis encouraging unlimited U.S. support of maximalist territorial ambitions are actually likely to be promoting circumstances that will ultimately confront them, and perhaps Americans as well, with far greater dangers than currently exist. By the same token, Arabs who see Washington's vacillation as a doorway that may be pushed against until it opens onto the path to Israel's destruction further a perilous dynamic that in the end may engulf the Middle East as well as vastly larger portions of the world in flames.

If it is true that contextual factors are required to cultivate and sustain an optimizing orientation in Washington, the American role of peacemaker will be fulfilled only through the support of regional actors. It is, then, not so much the peacemaker who must lead the protagonists to peace as it is they who must now lead the peacemaker to an effective posture. This is not really a startling proposition, for it boils down to the prescription that Arab and Israeli moderates must give political sustenance to their counterparts in the United States.

Accepting, as has been done throughout this study, that the core of the Middle East conflict is the struggle between Israeli Jews and Palestinian Arabs for sovereign control of Palestine, the tactical onus of peacemaking must then be strongly assigned to these communities. In a word, uncertainty and ambiguity on the part of both sides undermine Washington's ability to project its resources purposefully toward a final resolution that will simultaneously uphold Israel's existence and the Palestinian's right to self-determination.

However, the events of the past two decades indicate that the heavier share of the burden has come to lie on the Palestinians. In the supreme paradox of a struggle that has seen Palestinians repeatedly victimized by a variety of parties, it is now they, the victims, who must offer hope for a peace from which all may benefit.

That this is so stems from the importance to U.S. policy of developments in the Arab world and Israel since 1967. While the former, including the Palestinians, have largely moved toward a reduction of pre–1967 demands, Israel has steadily gravitated toward maximum claims. To put things mildly, it is highly unlikely that Israel will provide the opportunity for the United States to exercise its considerable potential influence on behalf of a stable settlement—that is, one guaranteeing Israel's security and reconciling the Arab world, including a Palestinian state, with the Jewish state on the basis of territory-for-peace. It therefore seems necessary for Palestinians to spearhead a decisive change in contextual factors that will provide optimizing tendencies in the United States with the political strength to prevail in policymaking circles.

In concrete terms, this would call for the PLO, allying itself with all the support it could obtain in the Arab world, to declare specifically its willingness to accept Israel as a legitimate sovereign state within pre–1967 boundaries while reserving Palestinian claims to sovereignty in the remnant of Palestine.

It remains an open question whether current or future pressures and possible opportunities will lead the PLO to accept such an option. Even if it does—and herein lies a grave danger to the Palestinian cause—there is no guarantee that Washington will sooner or later cast its lot with the goal of Palestinian sovereignty over part of what was once Palestine.

For those hoping to see the Middle East escape the expansion of horrors that a continuation of the Arab–Israeli conflict will almost surely entail, this is the risk circumstances indicate Palestinians should take. The problem, of course, is that for a people whose daily life at the tender mercies of others has for so long been the very antithesis of peace, such logic may understandably be quite meaningless. Perhaps the most that can be hoped for from the foreseeable future is that it may lead to a direct dialogue between the PLO and Washington that will enhance this option's respectability in Palestinian eyes.

In the meantime, the Reagan administration faces the same question that is likely to continue presenting itself not only to the next U.S. president in Washington but also to Arab and Israeli protagonists: What next?

PROSPECTS

That few things are certain in politics is perhaps the most certain statement that can be made about the Middle East. Time and again the region confounds those with the temerity to predict its future. Still, it must be said that available evidence gives little reason for optimism regarding prospects for a definitive settlement of the Arab–Israeli problem.

Fundamental elements in the current positions of key governments seem to ensure that a peaceful settlement will remain elusive. In this regard, Israeli and U.S. opposition to the very concept of Palestinian sovereignty, together with the former's rejection of full withdrawal from all territories occupied in 1967, are basic. The same is true of the de facto encouragement that Cairo and Amman give to hopes that peace can be constructed on some basis that falls short of satisfying Palestinian cries for full self-determination. These mutually reinforcing trends promise to swirl in a futile circle that offers little chance of altering the basic positions of other key actors, particularly Syria and the Palestinian people, which rest on demands for territory and sovereignty.

Even should coming events once again belie analysis and somehow yield peace treaties between Israel and other states of the Arab world, it is very probable that the final product would be far removed from

Washington's original vision of peace—and indeed, perhaps from any recognizable definition of "peace" at all.

In short, there is little reason at present to suspect that any such arrangement, including one limited to Israel and Jordan, would closely resemble the early U.S. concept of an equitable peace based on minimal territorial modification of the pre–1967 territorial status quo. This seems assured by the combination of Israel's progressive consolidation of its position in the occupied territories, including Jerusalem, Washington's acquiescence in that development, and the deep-rooted nature of Palestinian nationalism. This last factor would very probably mean that any "imposed peace" that denied the minimal claims of Palestinian nationalism would merely prolong the Middle East struggle indefinitely.

However, barring some unexpected turn of events that increases present chances of another Arab state formalizing peace with Israel, it is more probable that the policies of major actors will not undergo profound change in the near future. If so, the dangerous dynamics gripping the Middle East will grind on, bringing recurrent crises and continuing instability.

A large part of this unpleasant scenario is apt to unfold in the occupied territories. It was obvious well before the end of 1987 that—without lessening their support of the PLO—Palestinians under occupation had increasingly come to see themselves as being on the front lines of the struggle for a Palestinian state.[9] It is likely that this trend will continue, and in doing so contribute to the Middle East's unenviable future.

As suggested above, the logic of circumstances indicates that if the United States is to move toward altering its approach to peacemaking in ways that may decisively stem the dismal course of things in the Middle East, it will probably be necessary for the Palestinians—through the PLO—to accept openly and unambiguously Israel's legitimacy as a sovereign state within its pre–1967 boundaries, while reserving their own nationalist claims on the remnant of mandated Palestine. Realistically, however, there is small chance of this. Nor—given the present high risk that Washington would not respond to such an overture by casting its weight behind Palestinian nationalism—there is no compelling political argument to persuade even the most moderate PLO leaders to adopt a course that many in their movement would see as a gratuitous concession, if not treason.

In fact, it seems all too sadly true that any argument capable of bringing Palestinians to unequivocal acceptance of Israel's legitimacy would have to be rooted in what is now patently nonexistent: mutual confidence between the PLO and the United States. If the current crisis in the West Bank and Gaza, or if one in the coming series of crises that probably lies ahead in the Middle East, brings Washington to abandon its sterile rejection of direct contact with the PLO, then a small, but significant, step will have been taken toward enhancing possibilities for effective American peacemaking.

In the meantime, the area can be expected to continue drifting toward possible multiple disasters. While the events of the past few years indicate that the occupied lands may well become the most frequent setting for Arab–Israeli clashes in the near future, it seems unrealistic to hope that the conflict can be indefinitely confined to that theater.

It is all too easy to find evidence that Arab regimes have repeatedly given empty lip service to the Palestinian cause; that in practice most Arab governments have not only maintained a clear distinction between their own interests and those of Palestinian nationalism, but also a quick readiness to sacrifice the latter whenever this seemed expedient. However, it is risky to conclude from this record that the Palestinian cause is politically irrelevant in the Arab world. The argument can be made that if Arab regimes have made empty bows to Palestinian nationalism, it is precisely because that movement's frustration evokes a deep response at the popular level in the Arab world; that if Arab leaders have sought to manipulate the Palestinian cause for their own ends, it is because they have recognized it as a vibrant emotional banner capable of unleashing enormous amounts of energy and sacrifice; and that if they have sought to limit or crush it, they have been motivated by fearful recognition that the Palestinian cause has independent potential to elicit powerful responses throughout the Middle East.

In short, while the immediate future may see the occupied territories become increasingly important as the most visible sphere of Israeli–Arab tension, it should not be assumed that the issue will not reappear as a central concern in the wider Arab world. In this context, it is hardly comforting to note that in politics, "current conditions" are not eternal.

Riddled by various crises and deep divisions, the Middle East now witnesses its major actors fighting against a variety of pressing problems, as well as against each other. Iraq has not yet made peace with Iran; Syria plods on in Lebanon, alternately contributing to chaos and a modicum of order in that country; Egypt must cope with grim and growing economic problems and a population that produces an additional one million mouths to feed every ten months; Jordan confronts mounting economic pressures. To one degree or another, all existing regimes find their legitimacy challenged internally. Divisions between rich and poor grow. Most regimes are also charged in one way or another with having corrupted essential national and cultural values. Whether in Beirut, Baghdad, Cairo, Amman, Damascus, or Riyadh, Arab leaders carefully watch the burgeoning popular appeal of reformist currents, particularly those characterized by fundamentalist Islamic orientations.

It is impossible to know how long this state of affairs may last, or what will replace it. All that is certain is that someday, in some way, it will change.

If the Palestine issue has not been resolved by then, part and parcel of the change may well be the renewal of major tensions, if not hostilities, between Israel and the Arab world. In the meantime, the Middle East remains poised in a tense stalemate that rests largely on the divisions among Arab governments, the Palestinians' demand for true self-determination, Israeli leaders' determined certainty that no compromise with Palestinian nationalism need be considered, and Washington's inability and unwillingness to challenge that Israeli premise.

POSTSCRIPT: PRELUDE TO PEACE?

While this book awaited its turn at the press, events injected new hope for a fruitful U.S. contribution to Middle East peace. Propelled by the *intifada*, which by December 1988 had cost the deaths of over three hundred Palestinians, moderate Arab forces launched a sustained peace drive. Strongly seconded by Egyptian President Hosni Mubarak and Jordan's King Hussein (who stuck by his renunciation of legal and administrative ties to the West Bank), Yassir Arafat mustered overwhelming support within the PLO for a determined public peace offensive.

By the fall of 1988, even the staunchest Arab rejectionists had muted their criticism of the demarche—influenced, apparently, by their own inability to suggest another alternative for building on the daily struggle of the *intifada*.

The Arab peace drive culminated in mid-November, with the Palestine National Council roundly approving Arafat's program and proclaiming the existence of a Palestinian state. The PNC stand amounted to an acceptance of Israel's right to exist and a rejection of terrorism and acceptance of Security Council Resolutions 242 and 338. It also seemed to accept limiting the declared Palestinian state to the West Bank and Gaza as well as to look favorably on a confederal arrangement on that basis with Jordan. This, at least, is how virtually all the world—including most of Washington's closest European allies—saw it.

The United States reacted in keeping with the analysis presented above. While the international context progressively generated pressures for a fundamental change in U.S. policy, personality and sructural factors generated strenuous resistance. Speaking for the Reagan administration, Secretary of State George Shultz denied Arafat a visa to the United States, and thereby prevented him from elaborating on the PLO's new posture at UN headquarters in New York. The General Assembly responded by accusing Washington of violating its legal obligations as host to the United Nations and deciding to hear Arafat in Geneva. Only the United States and Israel voted against the move, with Great Britain abstaining.

During the following weeks, Washington became even more politically isolated as various PLO spokesmen reiterated their movement's new position and over sixty members of the international community recognized or acknowledged the still theoretical state proclaimed by the PNC. Yet, when Arafat once more repeated the PLO's novel departure at the General Assembly's special Geneva meeting in December, the Reagan administration tightened its grip on increasingly fragile verbal straws and insisted that there were still no grounds for direct contact with the Palestinian organization. By this time, however, even the British had taken the opposite view.

Twenty-four hours after addressing the General Assembly, Arafat reiterated the PLO's position at a press conference and finally tipped the balance. Washington, though rejecting the Palestinians' declaration of statehood, agreed to a direct dialogue with the PLO for the first time since 1975.

Though this may mark a historic turning point in the fortunes of the Middle East, it is still only a fragile beginning. Nonetheless, the growing international legitimacy of Palestinian nationalism suggests that if a U.S.–PLO dialogue is sustained, the United States may come to formulate policy toward the Palestine issued by giving priority to the core clash between Jewish and Palestinian nationalisms, rather than—as has so far been the case—to assumptions regarding ramifications of that primordial conflict. If so, there is a respectable chance that Washington's prevailing myopic assumption that Palestinian nationalism is necessarily a hostile force may be tempered by a clearer vision of possibilities for putting U.S. power and traditional American principles to the service of a settlement that will not only ensure Israel's security but also the Palestinians' right to true self-determination.

Forces beyond American control will continue to play a vital role in determining whether this prospect can be realized. If Washington has suffered from progressive myopia in appraising Palestinian nationalism, dominant forces in Israel have long since fallen into blindness. Yet, these are by no means the only forces in the Israeli body politic, and it is not inconceivable that a purposeful U.S. commitment to equitable peace between Israelis and Palestinians may not only nurture but benefit from the development of moderate Israeli opinion.

At the same time, of course, Palestinians and other Arab actors will face their own challenges. The activist moderate cohesiveness that has recently characterized the bulk of the Arab world will in all probability have to be sustained over a fairly long period, and in the face of various internal and external threats, if it is to culminate in the sort of moderate solution now proposed by the PLO. Then too, international actors beyond the Middle East's borders will have to tread lightly in seeking advantage in the new situation, lest abrupt eagerness to capitalize on the new context undermine what seems to be an opportunity for fluid creativity in the search for peace.

Still, while Israelis, Arabs, and others will each have a hand in shaping future U.S. policy, the potential initiative now seems firmly in U.S. hands. Time will reveal whether this new stage in the search for Mideast peace will see the United States formulate its own policies and influence those of others in ways leading to a successful conclusion. The history of U.S. involvement in the Palestine problem warns against optimism. At the moment, however, it seems likely that future historians will someday look back at the period between 1967 and 1989 as a prelude. The question now is whether it will be described as a prelude to requiem for hopes of Mideast peace or to a celebration of the attainment of that goal.

APPENDIX A

JOINT COMMUNIQUÉ BY THE GOVERNMENTS OF THE UNITED STATES AND THE UNION OF SOVIET SOCIALIST REPUBLICS, OCTOBER 1, 1977

Having exchanged views regarding the unsafe situation which remains in the Middle East, U.S. Secretary of State Cyrus Vance and Member of the Politbureau of the Central Committee of the CPSU, Minister for Foreign Affairs of the U.S.S.R. A. A. Gromyko have the following statement to make on behalf of their countries, which are cochairmen of the Geneva Peace Conference on the Middle East:

1. Both governments are convinced that vital interests of the peoples of this area, as well as the interests of strengthening peace and international security in general, urgently dictate the necessity of achieving, as soon as possible, a just and lasting settlement of the Arab–Israeli conflict. This settlement should be comprehensive, incorporating all parties concerned and all questions.

The United States and the Soviet Union believe that, within the framework of a comprehensive settlement of the Middle East problem, all specific questions of the settlement should be resolved, including such key issues as withdrawal of Israeli Armed Forces from territories occupied in the 1967 conflict; the resolution of the Palestinian question, including insuring the legitimate rights of the Palestinian people; termination of the state of war and establishment of normal peaceful relations on the basis of mutual recognition of the principles of sovereignty, territorial integrity, and political independence.

The two governments believe that, in addition to such measures for insuring the security of the borders between Israel and the neighboring Arab states as the establishment of demilitarized zones and the agreed stationing in them of U.N. troops or observers, international guarantees of such borders as well as of the observance of the terms of the settlement can also be established should the contracting parties so desire. The United States and the Soviet Union are ready to participate in these guarantees, subject to their constitutional processes.

2. The United States and the Soviet Union believe that the only right and effective way for achieving a fundamental solution to all aspects of the Middle East problem in its entirety is negotiations within the framework of the Geneva peace conference, specially convened for these purposes, with the participation in its work of the representatives of all the parties involved in the conflict including those of the Palestinian people, and legal and contractual formalization of the decisions reached at the conference.

In their capacity as cochairmen of the Geneva conference, the United States and the U.S.S.R. affirm their intention, through joint efforts and in their contacts with the parties concerned, to facilitate in every way the resumption of the work of the conference not later than December 1977. The cochairmen note that there still exist several questions of a procedural and organizational nature which remain to be agreed upon by the participants to the conference.

3. Guided by the goal of achieving a just political settlement in the Middle East and of eliminating the explosive situation in this area of the world, the United States and the U.S.S.R. appeal to all the parties in the conflict to understand the necessity for careful consideration of each other's legitimate rights and interests and to demonstrate mutual readiness to act accordingly.

APPENDIX B

EXCERPTS FROM THE CAIRO DECLARATION ON THE PLO AND TERRORISM, NOVEMBER 7, 1985

The Palestinian people has and continues to struggle to liberate its occupied land, to exercise its right to self-determination, and to establish a state as a necessary condition for achieving a just and lasting peace in the region in which all peoples would coexist, free from acts of terrorism or subjugation. . . .

. . . And in the framework of pursuing a just and peaceful solution, and given the PLO's struggle by all legitimate means to regain the established national rights of the Palestinians as well as their political freedom, the PLO condemns all violations of human rights, especially the rights to life and security without discrimination on the basis of creed, gender, or color.

As an impetus to the efforts which have been exerted to convene an international peace conference, the PLO announces its criticism and condemnation of all acts of terrorism, whether they be those in which states become involved or those committed by individuals or groups against innocent and defenseless, wherever they may be.

The PLO reaffirms its declaration issued in 1974 which condemned all operations outside [Palestine] and all forms of terrorism. And it restates the adherence of all its groups and institutions to that declaration. Beginning today, the PLO will take all measures to deter violators.

In view of the fact that this adherence cannot be achieved unilaterally, it is up to the international community to force Israel to stop all its acts of terrorism both inside and outside [Palestine].

In this context, the PLO stresses its insistence upon the right of the Palestinian people to resist the Israeli occupation of its land by all available means, with the goal of achieving withdrawal from its land. . . .

Events underline the certainty that terrorist operations committed outside [Palestine] hurt the cause of the Palestinian people and distort its legitimate struggle for freedom. From another perspective, these events deepen our conviction that terminating the occupation and putting limits on its policies is the one way to achieve peace and security in the region. . . .

APPENDIX C

THREE PROPOSED DECLARATIONS SUBMITTED TO KING HUSSEIN OF JORDAN BY THE PALESTINE LIBERATION ORGANIZATION, FEBRUARY, 1986

Proposal One

If an invitation is extended to the Palestine Liberation Organization to attend an international conference with effective powers to find a peaceful solution to the Palestinian question and to resolve the Middle East conflict in which the permanent members in the Security Council participate and which is attended by the concerned Arab parties, the Palestine Liberation Organization accepts to participate on an equal footing in this conference within a joint Jordanian–Palestinian delegation on the basis of ensuring the legitimate rights of the Palestinian people, including their right to self-determination through a confederation with the Hashemite Kingdom of Jordan as stated in the Jordanian–Palestinian Accord signed in February 1985, and on the basis of the United Nations and Security Council resolutions relevant to the Palestinian question, including Resolutions 242 and 338.

In this context, the Palestine Liberation Organization reaffirms its denunciation and rejection of terrorism, which it had confirmed in the Cairo Declaration.

Proposal Two

The Palestine Liberation Organization (PLO), the sole legitimate representative of the Palestinian people, holds the strong belief that the peace process should lead to a just, comprehensive, and durable peace in the Middle East and should secure the legitimate rights of the Palestinian people, including their right of self-determination within the context of a Jordanian–Palestinian confederation.

On the basis of the Jordanian–PLO Accord of 11 February 1985, and in view of our genuine desire for peace, we are ready to negotiate within the context of an international conference with the participation of the permanent members of the Security Council, with the participation of all concerned Arab parties, and the Israeli government, a peaceful settlement of the Palestinian problem on the basis of the pertinent United Nations resolutions, including Security Council Resolutions 242 and 338.

The PLO declares its rejection and denunciation of terrorism, as had been assured in the Cairo Declaration of November, 1985.

Proposal Three

The invitation to convene an international conference to resolve the conflict in the Middle East and to solve the Palestinian question should be under the aegis of the United Nations because it is the international organization which was established after World War II to put an end to the sufferings of the peoples, to prevent aggression, and to maintain justice and respect for human rights. The Preamble of the United Nations Charter adopted in 1945 calls for the realization of international cooperation to resolve international problems, the realization of basic human rights, and the rights of peoples to self-determination.

Since the Palestinian question is the quintessence of the Middle East problem, the call to convene an international conference to resolve the conflict and to establish peace in the region should ensure the execution of resolutions and measures and should include the participation in the conference of the permanent members of the Security Council and be attended by all concerned Arab parties, including the Palestine Liberation Organization on an equal footing within a joint Jordanian–Palestinian delegation.

In accordance with the United Nations Charter, which reaffirms and confirms respect for basic human rights and the right of peoples to self-determination, and on the basis of United Nations resolutions relevant to the Palestinian question and the Arab region, including Resolutions 242 and 338, the PLO will participate in the international peace conference in its capacity as the sole legitimate representative of the Palestinian people, which is recognized on the Arab and international levels and has an observer membership status in the United Nations since the year 1974.

The participation of the PLO in the international conference will be on the basis of safeguarding the legitimate rights of the Palestinian people, including their rights to self-determination through a confederation with the Hashemite Kingdom of Jordan as stated in the Jordanian–Palestinian Accord signed in February 1985.

In this context, the PLO reaffirms its denunciation and rejection of terrorism, which is confirmed in the Cairo Declaration.

APPENDIX D

REPLY BY JAMES DYER, DEPARTMENT OF STATE, REGARDING THE U.S. POSITION ON THREE PLO PROPOSALS SUBMITTED TO KING HUSSEIN OF JORDAN IN FEBRUARY 1986*

Dear Mr. Chairman:

Your letter of 14 May contains a set of questions concerning three proposals presented by PLO Chairman Arafat to King Hussein in February 1986. I trust the following responses will clarify to your satisfaction the various points you have raised.

It should be noted that the texts contained in your letter are not identical to those provided to us by King Hussein, in that the proposals we received contained an additional section entitled "steps." This section, identical in each case, outlines the actions whereby the PLO would make a "conditional" acceptance of 242 in return for a U.S. "affirmation" of Palestinian self-determination. A copy of this statement is attached.

For the record, the U.S. expects a clear PLO acceptance of 242, not one conditioned on simultaneous U.S. acceptance of self-determination for the Palestinians.

When did the United States receive knowledge of any or all of these three documents? What knowledge did the United States have of them prior to King Hussein's speech of 19 February 1986?

While we were aware of drafts similar to the second proposal, we were shown the three as they are worded for the first time by King Hussein on 6 February, after they had been rejected by him.

*Letter of May 14, 1986, from Mr. James W. Dyer, Acting Assistant Secretary, Legislative and Intergovernmental Affairs, Department of State to Congressman Lee H. Hamilton, Chairman of the Subcommittee on Europe and the Middle East, Committee on Foreign Affairs, House of Representatives

Precisely, what is the United States position on these documents and how do you characterize them?

We were not asked to take and have taken no formal position on these proposals as worded. They were presented to and rejected by King Hussein. We share the king's conclusion that, as received by him, they did not meet his requirement for a clear, unequivocal response to his demand that the PLO accept Resolution 242, endorse negotiations with the state of Israel, and renounce the use of violence.

In what respects are they consistent with, or contrary to, U.S. policy?

How close do these statements come to meeting the U.S. conditions for dealing with the PLO?

They do not meet the long-standing requirements of U.S. policy regarding the PLO: they do not contain unequivocal acceptance of UN Security Council Resolutions 242 and 338 and Israel's right to exist.

In all three cases, acceptance of 242 and 338 is in the context of "relevant" or "pertinent" United Nations resolutions.

Only in the second proposal is Israel even mentioned, as a prospective participant at an international conference.

Finally, reference to the Cairo Declaration, given its publicly stated interpretation by the PLO, is deficient as a renunciation of violence.

Are they in any respect an advance or a retrogression on previous PLO positions and statements?

Explicit references to 242 and 338 and to Israel (in the second proposal) are new. Overall, however, they still do not represent acceptance of either the king's challenge or U.S. conditions.

What can you support in them and what can you not support?

Specifically, how could they be made more acceptable?

These statements do not unconditionally accept 242 and 338 and Israel's right to exist; therefore, we cannot accept them as a basis for U.S. recognition of, or negotiations with, the PLO.

Also, they do not contain a clear renunciation of the use of violence. This was one of King Hussein's demands. Another was that the PLO endorse negotiations with the state of Israel. The king's third demand was clear acceptance of Resolution 242 as the basis for negotiations. If the proposals had been amended so as to meet these conditions, we assume they would have been acceptable to King Hussein.

For our part, we would not object if the PLO wished to state its own positions, as long as its doing so did not impose conditions on or dilute the statement as a whole.

Which of them do you consider the best?

The second proposal comes closest to meeting our and King Hussein's needs.

Is the reference to the renunciation of terrorism within the context of the Cairo Accords unacceptable to the United States? If so, why?

As authoritatively and publicly interpreted by senior PLO officials, the Cairo Declaration does not rule out acts of violence in Israel and in the West Bank and Gaza. Such selective renunciation of violence is inadequate.

Is the reference to all pertinent UN documents, but specifying UN Resolutions 242 and 338, unacceptable? If so, why?

Resolutions 242 and 338 must be accepted on their own, without reference to other UN resolutions, as the basis for negotiations. The phrase "all pertinent UN resolutions" encompasses a very mixed bag of documents, some objectionable to the U.S. and to Israel. The PLO may cite its preferred resolutions but not in such a way as to place them on a par with 242 and 338 or to dilute its acceptance of these resolutions.

Is the reference to [the] Palestinian right to self-determination within the context of a Jordanian/Palestinian confederation consistent with U.S. policy or not?

The term "self-determination" has in the Middle East context come to connote the establishment of a Palestinian state. (Reference to a "Jordanian/Palestinian confederation" in no way changes this fact, given that the 11 February agreement between Jordan and the PLO refers to a confederation of two states.) The United States does not support the establishment of an independent Palestinian state. Therefore, such a reference is not consistent with U.S. policy.

Secretary Shultz has called for the need for creative ambiguity in the Middle East if a peace process is to be advanced: in what ways do the documents meet that criterion or fall short of it?

Creative ambiguity can indeed be usefully applied to Middle East peacemaking, with all its complexities, code words, and historical precedents. However, we are addressing here a very specific U.S. assurance to Israel. Its terms are either clearly and unequivocally met, or they are not; there is no room here for ambiguity.

Could any of them form the basis for further efforts to resolve procedural problems should the Jordanian government seek to revive the process, or are these proposals dead?

Were the Jordanian government to decide to revive political coordination with the PLO, it is not clear that the process would simply pick up from where it left off in February. For in the end, the issue is not whether this or that ingenious text can be crafted; it is one of political will and intent.

Sincerely,

James W. Dyer
Acting Assistant Secretary
Legislative and Intergovernmental Affairs
U.S. Department of State

Enclosure: Final Section of PLO Drafts

Final Section of PLO Drafts

Steps:
A. This plan is to be delivered to His Majesty the King:
B. The PLO will request from [His] Majesty the King that he obtain a pledge

from the United States of America to support the right of self-determination as provided for in the Jordanian–Palestinian Accord; and

C. Simultaneous statements will be issued by the PLO of its conditional acceptance of 242 and by the U.S. government of its pledge to affirm the right of self-determination of the Palestinian people.

NOTES

CHAPTER ONE

1. Dan Tschirgi, *The Politics of Indecision: Origins and Implications of American Involvement With the Palestine Problem* (New York: Praeger, 1983), passim. See also Cordell Hull, *Memoirs*, Vol. II (New York: Macmillan, 1948), p. 15–36.

2. Nadev Safran, *The United States and Israel* (Cambridge, MA: Harvard University Press, 1963), p. 42.

3. Tschirgi, pp. 268–69. See also Kenneth Ray Bain, *The March to Zion: United States Policy and the Creation of Israel* (College Station, TX: Texas A&M University Press, 1979); Evan M. Wilson, *Decision on Palestine: How the U.S. Came to Recognize Israel* (Stanford, CA: Hoover Institution Press, 1979).

4. J. C. Hurewitz, *The Struggle for Palestine* (New York: W. W. Norton, 1950), passim. See also Yehoshua Porath, *The Emergence of the Palestinian Arab Nationalist Movement* (London: Frank Cass, 1974) and *The Palestinian Arab Nationalist Movement, 1929–1939* (London: Frank Cass, 1977); Ann M. Lesch, *Arab Politics in Palestine, 1917–1939: The Frustration of a National Movement* (Ithaca, NY: Cornell University Press, 1979).

5. The United States provided over half ($27.4 million of $54 million) of the initial budget allocated to the United Nations agency established in 1950, the United Nations Relief and Works Agency to aid Palestinian Refugees. In the years since, it has remained the largest supporter of UNRWA. See Mohammed K. Shadid, *The United States and the Palestinians* (New York: St. Martins, 1981), p. 60.

6. Paul Jabber, *Not by War Alone: Security and Arms Control in the Middle East* (Berkeley: University of California Press, 1981), pp. 63–95.

7. The Tripartite Declarations's provisions related to the territorial integrity of the states of the Middle East are these:

The three governments take this opportunity of declaring their deep interest in and their desire to promote the establishment and maintenance of peace and stability in the area and their unalterable opposition to the use of force or the threat of force between any of the states in the area. The three governments, should they find that any of these states was preparing to violate frontiers or armistice lines, would, consistently with their obligations as members of the United Nations, immediately take action, both within and without the United Nations, to prevent such violation.

For the Declaration's complete text, see United States Department of State, *Department of State Bulletin* (Washington, D.C.: U.S. Government Printing Office [GPO]), Vol. 28, June 5, 1950, p. 886. Cited hereafter as *Department of State Bulletin*.

8. *New York Times*, February 6, 1966.

9. Margaret Arakie, *The Broken Sword of Justice: America, Israel and the Palestine Tragedy* (London: Quartet Books, 1973), p. 135.

10. For example, President Eisenhower's special representative, Eric Johnston, discussed with Arab and Israeli representatives a proposal for functional cooperation among Israel, Lebanon, Syria, and Jordan in the distribution and use of Jordan River waters. After nearly two years, his efforts ended in failure in 1955. Robert Anderson, another special emissary of the U.S. government, conducted an ultimately fruitless mission in 1955/56 to promote a meeting between David Ben Gurion and Gamal Abdel Nasser. In 1961, Joseph B. Johnson headed an unsuccessful American initiative to interest Israel and Arab states in simultaneous repatriation and resettlement measures to solve the Palestinian refugee problem.

11. Lyndon B. Johnson, *The Vantage Point* (New York: Holt, Rinehart and Winston, 1971), pp. 287–88.

12. Peter Mansfield, *The Arabs* (Middlesex: Penguin Books, 1979), p. 303.

13. Syrian Prime Minister Youssef Zeayen's statement of October 11, 1966 was typical:

We are not protectors of Israel's security. . . . We shall never restrain the revolution of the Palestinian people who are seeking to liberate their homeland.

Keesing's Contemporary Archives, 1967, p. 21,817. Hereafter cited as *Keesing's*.

14. *Arab Report and Record*, 16–30 November, 1966.

15. *Keesing's*, 1967, pp. 21,821, 22,063; Arakie, p. 139.

16. Cited by Arakie, p. 140.

17. Dan Hofstadter (ed.), *Egypt and Nasser*, Vol. 3 (New York: Facts on File, Inc., 1973), p. 27.

18. See p. 11–13.

19. " 'United States Opposition to Aggression by Any Nation in the Near East,' Address by President Johnson to the Nation, May 23, 1967," in United States Department of State, *American Foreign Policy: Current Documents, 1967* (Washington, D.C.: U.S. GPO, 1969), pp. 494–95.

20. Johnson, *The Vantage Point*, p. 291.

21. Ibid.

22. Hofstadter, *Egypt and Nasser*, p. 17.

23. Cited in Mansfield, *The Arabs*, pp. 336–7.

24. Stephen Green, *Taking Sides* (New York: William Morrow, 1984), pp. 204–11.

25. Israeli analysts estimated total Arab casualties at some 15,000 dead and over 50,000 wounded. Edgar O'Ballance, *The Third Arab–Israeli War* (London: Faber and Faber, 1972), p. 272.

26. *Department of State Bulletin* LVII, no. 1463, July 10, 1967, pp. 33–34.

27. Walter Z. Laqueur, *The Soviet Union and the Middle East* (New York: Praeger, 1959), pp. 341–42. See also, Roman Kolkowicz, "The Soviet Policy in the Middle East," in Michael Confino and Shimon Shamir (eds.) *The U.S.S.R. and the Middle East* (Tel Aviv: Israel Universities Press, 1973), p. 82.

28. George Lenczowski, *Soviet Advances in the Middle East* (Washington, D.C.: The American Enterprise Institute, 1972), pp. 101–04; 129.

29. Gur Ofer, "Economic Aspects of Soviet Involvement in the Middle East," in Yaacov Ro'i (ed.), *The Limits of Power: Soviet Policy in the Middle East* (London: Croom Helm, 1979), pp. 67–93.

30. See Aryeh Yodfat, *Arab Politics in the Soviet Mirror* (Jerusalem: Israel Universities Press, 1973), pp. 262–301. See also Oded Eran, "Soviet Perception of Arab Communism and Its Political Role," in Confino and Shamir, pp. 109–19. See also Lenczowski, p. 162. Lenczowski notes:

Had the West been more responsive to Arab aspirations and free from entanglements which soured its relations with the Arabs ... Arab governments would normally have chosen to purchase Western goods and acquire Western technology.... Students preferred to seek knowledge in the West rather than the East.... No Arab cabinet minister up to 1971 obtained his degree in the Soviet Union or Eastern Europe; by contrast, even in the most radically inclined regimes, a number of ministers held American or West European Ph.D. degrees. Similarly, preferences could be observed in Arab consumers' tastes for Western goods, fashions, motion pictures and vacation places...."

31. *New York Times*, June 20, 1967. (Cited hereafter as *NYT*.) From the start, however, Moscow took pains to express its support for Israel's right to exist. See Arthur Jay Klinghoffer with Judith Apter, *Israel and the Soviet Union* (Boulder, CO: Westview, 1985), pp. 60–63.

32. Peter Mangold, *Superpower Intervention in the Middle East* (New York: St. Martin's Press, 1978), pp. 119–20; Lenczowski, pp. 150–53.

33. P. J. Vatikiotis, "Notes for an Assessment of the Soviet Impact on Egypt," in Confino and Shamir, pp. 287–88.

34. It must be noted that in this sense Soviet arms transfer policy after 1967 was a continuation—with higher class weaponry—of Soviet practices prior to 1967. Soviet arming of the Arabs has never been designed to create an offensive capability against Israel. Amnon Sella's list of self-imposed restrictions on Soviet arms policy after 1973 could just as validly be applied to earlier years:

(a) not to allow any one Arab country to become so strong that it could go to war against Israel alone; (b) not to allow the Arab countries a configuration of their armed forces that might tempt them to go for an all-out offensive war; and (c) to maintain a measure of control over the supply of arms to the Middle East that would allow the USSR at least some leverage in its bargaining with the Arab countries. Amnon Sella, "Changes in Soviet Political-Military Policy in the Middle East After 1973," in Ro'i, *The Limits of Power*, p. 46.

35. See pp. 20–29.

36. Mohammed Hassanein Heikal, "USSR Now Aware of US Strategy," *Egyptian Mail*, August 26, 1967.

37. See Mohammed Hassanein Heikal's weekly column in *Al Ahram*: "Who is Responsible" ("Man Al-Masul"), June 16, 1972; "America's Role and Respon-

sibility" (Amrika wa Masuliyatiha") June 23, 1972; and, particularly, "... And the Soviet Union," ("Wal Itihad al-Sovyeti"), June 23, 1972.

38. Klinghoffer notes that a 1981 public opinion poll in Israel revealed that over 50 percent of the respondents felt the Soviet threat to Israel was "greater or equal to" that posed by the Arabs. Klinghoffer and Apter, p. 4. Israeli scholar Yaacov Ro'i argues that the Soviet Union has not answered for itself the question of whether it should be fully committed to Israel's sovereign existence or "actually further its annihilation." Yaacov Ro'i, "The Soviet Attitude to the Existence of Israel," in Ro'i, *The Limits of Power*, pp. 248–49.

For a discussion of developments in Soviet–Israel contacts since the breaking of diplomatic relations between the two states in 1967, see Klinghoffer and Apter, passim and particularly pp. 233–46.

39. Bernard Reich, *Quest for Peace* (New Brunswick, NJ: Transaction Books, 1977), p. 98.

40. R. Craig Nation, "The Sources of Soviet Involvement in the Middle East: Threat or Opportunity?" in Mark V. Kauppi and R. Craig Nation (eds.), *The Soviet Union and the Middle East in the 1980's* (Lexington, MA: Lexington Books, 1983), p. 43.

41. Walter Lacqueur, "The Middle East, the United States, the USSR, and Europe," in A. L. Udovitch (ed.), *The Middle East: Oil, Conflict & Hope* (Lexington, MA: Lexington Books, 1976), p. 262. (Emphasis added.)

42. Seth P. Tillman, *The United States in the Middle East* (Bloomington: Indiana University Press, 1982), p. 253.

43. *Keessing's*, 1967, p. 22,158.

44. *Arab Report and Record*, 1–15 July, 1967, p. 231; 16–31 July, 1967, p. 254; 16–31 August, 1967, p. 270.

45. For the text of the resolutions adopted at the Khartoum Conference, see ibid., 1–15 September, 1967, p. 286. Basing himself on discussions with leading Egyptian personalities on the eve of the Khartoum Conference, Eric Rouleau reported that Nasser went to the meeting determined to obtain approval for this approach, or, failing that, "to go it alone." *Le Monde*, August 19, 1967. See also, *Arab Report and Record*, 1–15 September, 1967.

46. See William Quandt, "Political and Military Dimensions of Contemporary Palestinian Nationalism," in William B. Quandt, Fuad Jabber, and Ann Mosely Lesch, *The Politics of Palestinian Nationalism* (Berkeley and Los Angeles: University of California Press, 1973), pp. 47–53. See Jabber's essay, "The Palestinian Resistance and Inter-Arab Politics," in the same work, pp. 158–59. See also Helena Cobban, *The Palestinian Liberation Organization* (Cambridge: Cambridge University Press, 1984).

47. Quandt places the first military operation undertaken by the Vengeance Youth as occurring in May 1967. Quandt, Jabber, Lesch, pp. 59–60.

48. Walid Kazziha, *Revolutionary Transformation in the Arab World: Habash and His Comrades From Nationalism to Marxism* (London: Charles Knight & Co., 1975), pp. 65–101.

49. Cobban, pp. 41–42. For an eye-witness account of the battle of Karameh, see Abdullah Schleifer, *The Fall of Jerusalem* (New York: Monthly Review Press, 1972), pp. 226–33.

50. Michael C. Hudson, "Developments and Setbacks in the Palestinian Resistance Movement," *Journal of Palestine Studies* I, no. 3 (Spring 1972), p. 70.

51. Helena Cobban offers a critical view of analyses tending to exaggerate the inability of Fateh to lead the PLO. As she also notes, "the national authority concept was [a] new departure, for it allowed, for the first time ever in the history of the Palestinian national movement, of the possibility of dividing the land of Palestine." Cobban, p. 17.

52. After having privately supported the concept of a Palestinian state since late 1973, Soviet officials publicly adopted this stance in September 1974. Klinghoffer and Apter, *Israel and the Soviet Union*, pp. 131–32; 151.

53. Jabber, "The Palestinian Resistance," in Quandt, et al., *Politics*, p. 214.

54. As discussed in following chapters, reference is made here to the Nixon administration's support of unspecified Palestinian "legitimate interests," the Carter administration's acknowledgment of "Palestinian rights" and its support of "full autonomy" for the Palestinian population of the West Bank and Gaza, and the Reagan administration's call for Palestinian "self-government."

55. Henry Kissinger, *Years of Upheaval* (Boston: Little, Brown, 1982), pp. 628–29.

56. Article VI of the Palestinian National Charter:

VI. The Jews who had normally resided in Palestine until the beginning of the Zionist invasion will be considered Palestinians.

The text of the Charter is available in John Norton Moore (ed.), *The Arab–Israeli Conflict*, Vol. III, "Documents" (Princeton: Princeton University Press, 1974), pp. 706–11.

57. *Arab Report and Record*, 1–15 June, 1967, p. 166.

58. An even smaller minority on the extreme left of Israel's political spectrum favored the return of all occupied Arab territories. See Baruch Kimmerling, *Zionism and Territory: The Socio-Territorial Dimensions of Zionist Politics* (Berkeley: Institute of International Studies University of California, Berkeley, 1983), pp. 147–82; Don Peretz, *The West Bank: History, Politics, Society and Economics* (Boulder, CO: Westview Press, 1986), p. 70.

59. Cited in Samuel Halperin, *The Political World of American Zionism* (Detroit: Wayne State University Press, 1961), pp. 50–51.

60. Akiva Orr, *The Un-Jewish State: The Politics of Jewish Identity in Israel* (London: Ithaca Press, 1983), pp. 1–65; Kimmerling, pp. 204–08; David M. Zohar, *Political Parties in Israel: The Evolution of Israeli Democracy* (New York: Praeger, 1974), pp. 10ff.; 34–48.

61. Lilly Weissbrod, "Core Values and Revolutionary Change," in David Newman (ed.) *The Impact of Gush Emunim: Politics and Settlement in the West Bank* (London: Droom Helm, 1985), pp. 70–90. See also, Peretz, *The West Bank*, pp. 49–51.

62. For distinct views on Jabotinski, see Walter Lacqueur, *A History of Zionism* (New York: Holt, Rinehart and Winston, 1972), pp. 338–83; and Lenni Brenner, *The Iron Wall: Zionist Revisionism From Jabotinski to Shamir* (London: Zed Books, 1984), pp. 72–110; 170. On mystic-nationalism see Weisbrod, pp. 70–90. See also Peretz, pp. 49–51.

63. Jean Rael Isaac, *Israel Divided: Ideological Politics in the Jewish State* (Bal-

timore: The Johns Hopkins University Press, 1976), pp. 45–72; Julien Bauer, "A New Approach to Religious-Secular Relationship?" in Newman, pp. 91–110. See also Weissbrod, "Core Values and Revolutionary Change," ibid., pp. 70–90.

64. Ehud Sprinlzak, "The Iceberg Model of Political Extremism," in Newman, p. 29.

65. Ibid., p. 30.

66. Bauer, in Newman, pp. 100–104.

67. Kimmerling, pp. 170–74; Weissbrod, in Newman, p. 72.

68. Eshkol was initially urged to relinquish the prime ministry to his arch-rival, David Ben Gurion. See Michael Brecher, *Decisions in Israel's Foreign Policy* (Oxford: Oxford University Press, 1974), pp. 381–416.

69. Ibid., pp. 37–38. On the National Religious Party see Zohar, pp. 48–50, and Peretz, pp. 46, 50.

70. Brecher, pp. 516–17; Isaac, pp. 57–60; 200, n. 32.

71. Brecher, pp. 460–63.

72. Ibid.

73. Brecher, p. 447.

74. *Deadline Data*, Israel, Domestic, 1967, p. 22.

75. Cited by Israel Mehlman, "There is an Alternative," *New Outlook* 13, no. 1 (January 1970), p. 42.

76. *BBC Summary of World Broadcasts*, Israel, July 13, 1967.

77. *Arab Report and Record*, 16–31 October, 1968; *Jerusalem Post*, October 15, 1969.

78. Zohar, *Political Parties*, p. 109. Gahal joined with the following groups to form the Likud: the State List, the Free Centre, and the Land of Israel Movement.

79. Ann M. Lesch, "Israeli Settlements in the Occupied Territories," *Journal of Palestine Studies* 8, no. 1 (Autumn 1978), p. 119; Meron Benvenisti, *The West Bank Data Project: A Survey of Israel's Policies* (Washington, D.C.: American Enterprise Institute, 1984), pp. 49–55.

80. All, that is, but the small area of Taba at the Gulf of Aqaba's northern shore. As of this writing (spring, 1988) Egypt and Israel are still involved in international arbitration to resolve their contradictory claims as to whether Taba falls on the Egyptian or Palestinian side of the international boundary between Egypt and mandated Palestine.

81. See pp. 161–162; 190.

82. Russell A. Stone, *Social Change in Israel: Attitudes and Events* (New York: Praeger, 1982), p. 41.

83. "Statement by Assistant Secretary of State Richard W. Murphy Before the Subcommittee on Europe and the Middle East of the House Foreign Affairs Committee," October 13, 1988. See also Murphy's earlier statement in *America–Arab Affairs* 18 (Fall 1986), pp. 162–66.

84. *Deadline Data*, Israel: Foreign Relations, 1967, p. 136.

85. Klinghoffer and Apter, *Israel and the Soviet Union*, pp. 61–62; Johnson, *The Vantage Point*, p. 484.

86. William B. Quandt, *Decade of Decisions: American Policy Toward the Arab–Israeli Conflict, 1967–1976* (Berkeley: University of California Press, 1977), p. 65.

87. George J. Tomeh (ed.) *United Nations Resolutions on Palestine and the Arab–Israeli Conflict, 1947–1974* (Beirut: Institute for Palestine Studies, 1975), p. 143.

88. For a well reasoned argument upholding this stance, see the editorial in the *Jerusalem Post*, November 24, 1967. See also *U.N. Monthly Chronicle* IV, no. 11 (December 1967), p. 8. For an overview of the Jarring Mission, see Ishaq I. Ghanayem and Alden H. Voth, *The Kissinger Legacy* (New York: Praeger, 1984), pp. 67–81.

89. *Jerusalem Post*, January 10, 1978; *NYT*, January 9, 1968; *The Israel Digest* XI, no. 2 (January 26, 1968), p. 1.

90. *The Israel Digest*, XI, no. 1 (January 12, 1968), p. 3; *NYT*, January 9, 1968.

91. *NYT*, February 22, 1968; *Jerusalem Post*, February 22, 1968.

92. See, for example, the replies of potential presidential candidates to the Israel Public Affairs Committee, *NYT*, May 16, 1968; Eugene McCarthy's statement on the necessity of supplying arms to Israel, ibid., May 18, 1968; and Robert Kennedy's call for the sale of Phantoms to Israel, ibid., May 27, 1968. See also *Jerusalem Post*, July 21, 1968.

93. *Jerusalem Post*, May 21; May 30, 1968. Israel's proposal, given to Jarring on May 29, contained the following points: 1) the parties to the conflict would meet face to face; 2) they would then proceed to work out agreements on all matters mentioned in Security Council Resolution 242; 3) the agreements would be incorporated in a peace treaty signed by the Arab states and Israel; 4) the provisions of the treaty would be implemented.

94. U.S. arms, in the form of an unspecified number of anti-aircraft HAWK missiles, were, however, supplied to Israel in July. Paradoxically, given the defensive nature of the weapon and Israel's reliance on an offensive-defensive strategy, even this may have been seen in Jerusalem as a subtle form of pressure—in the sense that the HAWK transfer provided a potential excuse for further delay on the outstanding Phantoms request.

95. U.S. Office of the Federal Register, *Weekly Compilation of Presidential Documents* IV, no. 37 (September 16, 1968), p. 1342.

96. Quandt, *Decisions*, p. 67.

97. *BBC Summary of World Broadcasts*, Israel, September 6, 1968.

98. See, for example, *Jerusalem Post*, October 1, 1968; *Jewish Observer*, October 4, 1968; *NYT*, October 9, 1968.

99. *Jerusalem Post*, October 18, 1968; *BBC Summary of World Broadcasts*, Israel, November 11, 1968.

100. *Jerusalem Post*, October 10, 1968.

101. Johnson's authorization led to an agreement, concluded in December, for Israel's purchase of fifty F–4 Phantoms.

102. See, for example: statements by Richard Nixon in an address to B'nai B'rith, *NYT*, September 9, 1968; Hubert Humphrey's message to the Zionist Organization of America supporting the sale of Phantoms to Israel, ibid., September 15, 1968; George Wallace's comments on the question of supplying arms to Israel, ibid., October 8, 1968.

103. Quandt, *Decisions*, p. 67, n. 58.

104. *Arab Report and Record*, December 1–15, 1968.

105. The Soviet Union reportedly suggested a peace plan to the United States in early September. See *NYT*, September 26, 1968. Accounts of the U.S. peace

plan may be found in the *Jerusalem Post*, January 6, 1969; *Near East Report* XII, no. 25 (December 10, 1968); and ibid., XIII, no. 12 (January 21, 1969).

106. *Jerusalem Post*, January 24, 1969; Reich, *Quest for Peace*, pp. 95–96.

107. Saadia Touval, *The Peace Brokers: Mediators in the Arab–Israeli Conflict, 1948–1979* (Princeton, NJ: Princeton University Press, 1982), p. 151.

CHAPTER TWO

1. Cited by William R. Brown, *The Last Crusade: A Negotiator's Middle East Handbook* (Chicago: Nelson-Hall, 1980), p. 303.

2. *NYT*, December 30, 1969.

3. The full text of Nasser's remarks are available in "President Nasser's Inaugural Speech, January 20," *Record of Political Opinions and Events in the Arab World* (Beirut: The Research and Publishing House, 1969), pp. 18–25.

4. Ibid., "Press Conference," p. 33.

5. Ibid, pp. 28, 33.

6. *Department of State Bulletin*, February 17, 1969, pp. 142–43.

7. Ghanayem and Voth, *The Kissinger Legacy*, p. 4; Stephen A. Garrett, "Nixonian Foreign Policy: A New Balance of Power or a Revised Concert," *Polity* VII (Spring 1976).

8. Henry Kissinger, *White House Years* (Boston: Little, Brown, 1979), p. 372; *Years of Upheaval*, p. 202.

9. Kissinger, *White House Years*, pp. 348, 369, 371–72; *Years of Upheaval*, p. 202; Ismail Fahmy, *Negotiating for Peace in the Middle East* (London: Croom Helm, 1983), pp. 49–52. See pp. 79–81.

10. For a contradictory, and to my mind utterly unsupportable view, see Ghanayem and Voth.

11. Kissinger, *White House Years*, p. 357.

12. Ibid., p. 26.

13. Ibid., p. 354. Original emphasis.

14. Kissinger, *Years of Upheaval*, p. 202.

15. See pp. 79–81.

16. " 'U.S. Foreign Policy: Some Major Issues,' Statement by the Secretary of State," *Department of State Bulletin* LX, no. 1555 (April 14, 1969), pp. 305–06.

17. Quandt, *Decisions*, p. 85.

18. *Deadline Data*, Israel: Foreign Relations, p. 169.

19. *Jerusalem Post*, March 7, 1969.

20. Ibid., March 19, 1969.

21. *Near East Report* 13, no. 9, April 30, 1969.

22. Egyptian Foreign Minister Mahmoud Riyad castigated Israel in late September for not accepting Security Council Resolution 242 since "that would mean withdrawing." In contrast, he said, Egypt accepted the resolution fully. "It's a package deal," he said, "and we want all of it implemented . . . how to implement it is Dr. Jarring's job. It is up to him to suggest a timetable." These remarks were widely interpreted as indicating that Egypt "had apparently abandoned the old demand that Israel withdraw from occupied territories before firm agreement on other items in the peace agenda." *NYT*, September 28, 1969.

23. Quandt, *Decisions*, pp. 84–88.

24. Ghanayem and Voth, pp. 36–45; Quandt, *Decisions*, p. 89; Kissinger, *White House Years*, pp. 363–67.

25. Ibid., p. 372.

26. Mangold, *Superpower Intervention*, p. 121.

27. Quandt, *Decisions*, p. 89.

28. *NYT*, September 28, 1969.

29. Kissinger, *White House Years*, pp. 371, 377.

30. *Deadline Data*, Israel: Domestic, 1969, p. 36; *Jerusalem Post*, October 15, 1969; *Arab Report and Record*, October 16–31, 1969.

31. *NYT*, October 30, 1969; *Le Monde*, November 5, 1969. See also Misha Louvish, "After the Elections," *Jewish Frontier* XXXVI, no. 10 (November 1969), p. 3.

32. Kissinger, *White House Years*, pp. 371–72.

33. *NYT*, December 14, 1969; *Arab Report and Record*, December 1–15, 1969; Quandt, *Decisions*, pp. 89–90.

34. *NYT*, December 22, 1969.

35. *NYT*, December 23, 1969.

36. *NYT*, December 12, 1969. See, for similar announcements by New York Senator Jacob Javits and New York City Mayor John V. Lindsay, *NYT*, December 16, 1969.

37. *NYT*, January 13, 1970.

38. *Facts on File*, 1970 (July 23–29), p. 529.

39. Kissinger, *White House Years*, p. 377.

40. Ibid.

41. Quandt, *Decisions*, p. 93.

42. Ibid.

43. For example, as late as September 27, Soviet Ambassador Anatoly Dobrynin called on Kissinger "with the perennial Soviet suggestion of a joint U.S.–Soviet position, this time to provide guidelines for Jarring...." Kissinger's account of the outcome is as follows:

I rejected the overture with the argument that as long as the Soviets were so unhelpful on Vietnam, joint action elsewhere would be "difficult." I had no intention to act jointly with the Soviet Union when the Soviets clearly expected to get a free ride on our exertions. But my rebuff merely sent Dobrynin back into other channels. He continued intensive talks with Sisco in September and October. (*White House Years*, p. 371.)

44. Mohammed H. Heikal, *The Road to Ramadan* (New York: Quadrangle Books, 1975). Noting that "few officials in Washington were prepared to accept the Israeli version," William Quandt points out that Israeli sources have generally maintained that the Soviet decision to increase military support to Egypt was taken prior to a trip Nasser took to Moscow in early 1970, an interpretation which "relieves Israel of the responsibility for provoking the Soviet response by engaging in deep-bombing raids near Cairo in early January...." *Decisions*, p. 95, n. 28.

45. *NYT*, February 4; 19, 1970.

46. Kissinger, *White House Years*, pp. 558; 569–75.

47. Ibid., p. 569.

48. On May 21, Nixon assured Israeli Foreign Minister Abba Eban that the

United States would continue to supply Israel with arms, though he urged that the commitment not be publicized. The president refrained from taking a final decision on Israel's request for Phantoms and Skyhawks, but assured his Israeli visitor that existing commitments would be met. Quandt, *Decisions*, p. 99.

49. Mangold, *Superpower Interventions*, p. 123.

50. Quandt, *Decisions*, p. 93.

51. Touval, *Peace Brokers*, p. 168.

52. Quandt, *Decisions*, p. 99.

53. On June 26, Kissinger generated a public commotion when he described the U.S. initiative during a not-for-attribution background press briefing as follows:

We are trying to get a settlement in such a way that the moderate Arab regimes are strengthened, and not the radical regimes. We are trying to expel the Soviet military presence, not so much the advisors, but the combat pilots and the combat personnel, before they become so firmly established.

Several days later, Kissinger reiterated his earlier remarks. Secretary of State Rogers' protests that such comments tended to undermine the ongoing U.S. initiative did not dissuade Nixon from speaking out publicly on July 1 in terms that were taken to support Kissinger's argument that U.S. policy toward the Arab–Israel conflict was determined more in light of U.S. ambitions to erode the Soviet Union's position in the Middle East than by the goal of promoting a negotiated regional peace. Kissinger, *White House Years*, pp. 579–81; *NYT*, July 2; 3, 1970.

54. Since the 1967 cease-fire on the Israeli–Jordanian front was still in effect, the relevance to Jordan of the 1970 Rogers Initiative's call for a cease-fire has been interpreted as an attempt to formalize the Hashemite Kingdom's responsibility for curtailing Palestinian guerrilla activities. Quandt, *Decisions*, p. 101, n. 47.

55. *NYT*, June 27, 1970.

56. At the beginning of July, Nixon explained U.S. policy in this way:

...the Middle East is terribly dangerous ... like the Balkans before World War I. ... Now what should the U.S. role be? I will summarize it in a word. One, our interest is in peace and the integrity of every country in the area. Two, we recognize that Israel is not desirous of driving any of the other countries into the sea. The other countries want to drive Israel into the sea. Three, then once the balance of power shifts where Israel is weaker than its neighbors, there will be a war. ... We will do what is necessary to maintain Israel's strength vis-à-vis its neighbors. ...

At the end of the month, Nixon told a press conference that Israel should enter into the negotiations proposed by the Rogers Initiative "without fear that by her negotiations her position may be compromised or jeopardized in that period." See, "A Conversation With the President," *Department of State Bulletin* LXIII, no. 1622 (July 27, 1970), pp. 112–13; Kissinger, *White House Years*, p. 584.

57. This account is drawn from Nadev Safran, *Israel: The Embattled Ally* (Cambridge, MA: Belknap Press, 1978), p. 446; Quandt, *Decisions*, pp. 101–02; Brecher, *Decisions in Crisis*, p. 493; Touval, *Peace Brokers*, pp. 173–74.

58. Kissinger, *White House Years*, p. 584.

59. The text of the Suez Canal Cease-Fire Agreement may be found in *Facts On File, 1970*, p. 587. See also Kissinger, *White House Years*, pp. 585–86.

60. Safran, *Israel*, p. 441; Heikal, *Ramadan*, p. 95.

61. "Ambassador Jarring's *Aide Memoir* to Israel and the United Arab Republic, February 8, 1971"; "The United Arab Republic Reply to Ambassador Jarring's *Aide Memoir*, February 15, 1971"; "Document Transmitted by the Israel Ambassador to the United Nations, Mr. Joseph Tekoah, to Ambassador Gunnar Jarring, February 26, 1971"; "Further Report by the Secretary-General on the Activities of the Special Representative to the Middle East, November 30, 1971," in Moore, *Arab–Israeli Conflict*, pp. 1106–1125.

62. *Facts on File, 1970*, August 27-September 2, p. 622.

63. See, for example, John B. Wolf, "The Palestinian Resistance Movement," *Current History* 60, no. 353 (January 1971), pp. 26–31; 49–50. For a personal account of the struggle between the PLO and the Jordanian government see John K. Cooley, *Green March, Black September* (London: Frank Cass, 1973).

64. Quandt, *Decisions*, p. 106.

65. Ibid., p. 131; U.S. Agency for International Development, *Fiscal Year 1975 Submission to the Congress: Middle East Peace and Security Assistance Programs*; see also ibid., *Fiscal Year 1976*.

66. *NYT*, October 21, 197 .

67. In the final analysis Malcolm Kerr's assessment of the U.S. "interim agreement" plan was correct: " . . . it all came to nothing, not simply because Egypt and Israel failed to agree on terms but because . . . Nixon and Rogers had no intention of going beyond the instrument of friendly persuasion." Malcolm Kerr, "Nixon's Second Term: Policy Prospects in the Middle East," *Journal of Palestine Studies* II, no. 3 (Spring 1973), p. 17.

68. A secret "tentative agreement" on principles for a Middle East peace was reached—at Soviet initiative—during the summit by Kissinger and Foreign Minister Gromyko. Kissinger's record of this occurrence clearly indicates that he had no interest or intention of seeking any serious cooperation with the Soviet Union in the search for Mideast peace. *White House Years*, pp. 1246–48; 1494, n. 4.

69. Anwar Sadat, *In Search of Identity: An Autobiography* (New York: Harper and Row, 1978), p. 274.

70. See, for example: "General Assembly Resolution 2851 (XXVI) Concerning the Report of the Special Committee to Investigate Israeli Practices affecting the Human Rights of the Population of the Occupied Territories, December 20, 1967," Moore, *Arab-Israeli Conflict*, pp. 944–46; George Dib and Fuad Jabber, *Israel's Violation of Human Rights in the Occupied Territories: A Documented Report* (Beirut: Institute for Palestine Studies, 1970), passim.

71. Lesch, "Israeli Settlements in the Occupied Areas."

72. Richard Nixon, *RN: The Memoirs of Richard Nixon* (New York: Warner Books, 1978), p. 307.

73. Ibid.

74. Kissinger, *Years of Upheaval*, pp. 295–300; Nixon, p. 430.

75. Safran, *Israel*, p. 593.

76. In a discourse to the United Nations General Assembly, Kissinger explained the core of his view of step-by-step diplomacy:

Each step forward modifies old perceptions and brings about a new situation that improves the chances of comprehensive diplomacy....

Cited in William Zartman, "Explaining Disengagement," in Jeffrey Z. Rubin (ed.), *Dynamics of Third Party Intervention: Kissinger and the Middle East* (New York: Praeger, 1981), p. 159.

77. By the end of October, all Arab oil producers but Iraq had joined the embargo.

78. Kissinger, *Years of Upheaval*, p. 481.

79. John Waterbury, "Egypt: The Wages of Dependency," in Udovitch, *The Middle East*. See particularly pp. 291–328. See also Ali Hillal Dessouki, "The Primacy of Economics in the Foreign Policy of Egypt," in Bahgat Korany and Ali E. Hillal Dessouki, *The Foreign Policy of Arab States* (Boulder, CO: Westview Press, 1984), pp. 119–46.

80. Quandt, *Decisions*, p. 176. Controversy surrounded the relatively slow pace of initial U.S. efforts to resupply Israel with arms during the war. Kissinger was accused by some observers of trying to pressure Jerusalem into accepting a cease-fire by delaying arms transfers while laying the blame on bureaucratic bungling in the Defense Department, a charge he has consistently denied. It is, at least, clear that during the war's early stages, U.S. officials confidently assumed that Israel would win a decisive and quick victory. Moreover, as those hopes faded, Washington was divided over the actual military losses suffered by Israel and the degree of resupply that should be extended. See Edward N. Luttak and Walter Laqueur, "Kissinger and the Yom Kippur War," *Commentary* 58, no. 3 (September 1974); Marvin and Bernard Kalb, *Kissinger* (Boston: Little, Brown, 1974), pp. 465–66; Kissinger, *Years of Upheaval*, pp. 491–507.

81. Sadat, *Search*, p. 258.

82. William Quandt's description of the American resupply effort is worth quoting in full:

From October 14 until the October 25 cease-fire, the United States resupply effort delivered approximately 11,000 tons of equipment, forty F–4 Phantoms, thirty-six A–4 Skyhawks, and twelve C–130 transports. Included were only four tanks on the early C–5 flights and fewer than twenty were sent during the entire airlift. From October 26 until the airlift ended on November 15, another 11,000 tons of equipment was delivered. In all, 147 sorties were flown by C–5s, with 10,800 tons aboard, and 421 sorties by C–141s with 11,500 tons. During the same period, El Al aircraft carried about 11,000 tons of military supplies to Israel in over 200 sorties. (*Decisions*, p. 185, n. 46.)

83. Safran, *Israel*, pp. 286–316.

84. Kissinger, *Years of Upheaval*, p. 551. Original emphasis.

85. Nixon, *RN*, 494.

86. Kissinger, *Years of Upheaval*, p. 552.

87. UN Security Council Resolution 338, text available in Tomeh, *United Nations Resolutions on Palestine*.

88. Kissinger, *Years of Upheaval*, pp. 558–89.

89. Ibid. Kissinger believed the Israelis were responsible.

90. Ibid., p. 583.

91. Ibid., p. 588.

92. Edward R. F. Sheehan, *The Arabs, Israelis and Kissinger: A Secret History*

of American Diplomacy in the Middle East (New York: Reader's Digest Press, 1976), p. 38.

93. Fahmy, *Negotiating*, p. 36; Kissinger, *Years of Upheaval*, p. 616.

94. Fahmy, p. 46; Kissinger, *Years of Upheaval*, p. 618.

95. Fahmy states he received written assurances from Nixon on the question of Israeli attacks. Quandt states that the assurances came from Kissinger. Fahmy, pp. 51, 54; Quandt, *Decisions*, p. 215.

96. Kissinger, *Years of Upheaval*, pp. 622–23; Nixon, *RN*, p. 503.

97. Kissinger, *Years of Upheaval*, pp. 655–56.

98. Ibid., p. 747.

99. "Memorandum To the President, December 19, 1973," reprinted in full in ibid., pp. 1249–50.

100. Quandt, *Decisions*, p. 227; Touval, *Peace Brokers*, p. 242; Sheehan, *The Arabs*, pp. 80–88; Kissinger, *Years of Upheaval*, pp. 799–800.

101. Sheehan, pp. 111–12.

102. Quandt, *Decisions*, p. 235.

103. Kissinger, *Years of Upheaval*, pp. 879; 978.

104. Sheehan, *The Arabs*, pp. 133–34; Quandt, *Decisions*, pp. 247–48; Fahmy, *Negotiating*, pp. 154–56.

105. Nixon, *RN*, p. 674.

106. Kissinger, *Years of Upheaval*, pp. 1138–42.

107. Nixon referred to the Palestinians' "legitimate interests" first in a message to Congress in May 1973 and again in June of that year in a U.S.–Soviet communique following his meeting with Leonid Brezhnev. Quandt, *Decisions*, pp. 157–60.

108. Sheehan, *The Arabs*, p. 155; Safran, *Israel*, p. 540.

109. Sheehan, pp. 155–56; Quandt, *Decisions*, p. 262.

110. Touval, *Peace Brokers*, pp. 263–64; 268–70.

111. Sheehan, p. 160.

112. A third option—that of a quasi-total settlement—between Israel and Egypt—that is, a further major Israeli pullback that would not be total in return for Egyptian nonbelligerence. In the end, of course, it was this option that Kissinger followed. Ibid., pp. 165–68; Quandt, *Decisions*, pp. 269–70.

113. Sheehan, *The Arabs*, p. 174.

114. *NYT*, May 22, 1975.

115. For the texts of the Sinai II agreements, see Sheehan, 'Appendix Eight': "Agreement Between Egypt and Israel" [and Annexes], pp. 245–57. See also *Arab Report and Record*, September 1–15, 1975, pp. 517–19.

116. Israel later dropped its request for Pershing missiles when the ease with which the weapon could be fitted with a nuclear warhead threatened to provoke congressional controversy.

117. Although that interpretation has prevailed, Harold Saunders, who served as Assistant Secretary of State for Near Eastern and South Asian Affairs between 1978 and 1981, describes the agreement not to recognize or negotiate with the PLO as "the most misunderstood and distorted commitment that I've ever had anything to do with." Saunders argues that "the agreement itself was

never intended to prevent our talking to the PLO." "Interview With Harold Saunders," *American–Arab Affairs* 15 (Winter 1985/86), pp. 15–16.

118. Touval, pp. 265–66; Safran, p. 554; Sheehan, pp. 190, 194.

119. Cited by Sheehan, p. 192.

120. *Arab Report and Record*, 1975, September 1–15, pp. 501–12.

121. Sheehan, passim; Safran, p. 559.

122. For U.S. aid to Israel, see Reich, *The United States and Israel*, Table 4.2, "U.S. Assistance to Israel, 1948–83," pp. 148–49. Figures regarding U.S. aid to Egypt are based on: Program Office, U.S. Agency for International Development, Cairo, "U.S. Economic Assistance to Egypt: Yearly Obligations, 1975–1987," April, 1987 (unpublished); U.S. Agency for International Development, *Fiscal Year 1977 Submission to the Congress Security Assistance Programs and Middle East Special Requirements Fund*, February 1976.

CHAPTER THREE

1. Reich, *The United States and Israel: Influence in the Special Relationship* (New York: Praeger, 1984), Table 4.2, 148–49.

2. Jimmy Carter, *The Blood of Abraham* (Boston: Houghton Mifflin, 1985), pp. 10–19.

3. *NYT*, January 4, 1977; *Keesing's*, 1977, p. 28,382.

4. *NYT*, January 3, 4, February 3, 1977. The mysterious PLO figure was Issam Sartawi. The story of Sartawi's contacts with Israeli leftists can be found in Uri Avinery, *My Friend, The Enemy* (London: Zed Books, 1986), pp. 153–64. In April 1983 Sartawi was assassinated by agents of the anti-PLO Palestinian terrorist, Abu Nidal.

5. For the text of the program passed by the 13th PNC Session, see *Keesing's*, 1977, pp. 28,384–86.

6. Ibid., p. 28,386.

7. Zbigniew Brzezinski, *Power and Principle: Memoirs of the National Security Adviser, 1977–1981* (New York: Farrar, Straus, Giroux, 1983), p. 88.

8. *Toward Peace in the Middle East: Report of a Study Group* (Washington, D.C.: The Brookings Institution, 1975).

9. Brzezinski, pp. 85–87; Jimmy Carter, *Keeping Faith* (New York: Bantam Books, 1982), pp. 280, 290–91; Harvey Sicherman, *Broker or Advocate: The U.S. Role in the Arab–Israeli Dispute, 1973–1978* (Philadelphia: Foreign Policy Research Institute, 1978), p. 34; *NYT*, March 15, 1977.

10. Brzezinski, pp. 87, 88 (original emphasis).

11. Cyrus Vance, *Hard Choices: Critical Years in America's Foreign Policy* (New York: Simon and Schuster, 1983), p. 169.

12. *NYT*, February 16; 17; 18; 20; 21; and 25, 1977.

13. Ibid., February 22, 1977.

14. Brzezinski, p. 90.

15. Ibid., p. 91; Carter, *Keeping Faith*, p. 280; *NYT*, March 9, 1977.

16. Carter, *Keeping Faith*, pp. 282–84; Brzezinski, pp. 93–94; *NYT*, April 5; 7, 1977. Toward the end of April, Carter authorized limited military aid to Egypt as a signal that moderation would be rewarded.

17. Carter, *Keeping Faith*, pp. 285–87; *Blood of Abraham*, pp. 70–74; Brzezinski, p. 95; *NYT*, May 10, 1977.

18. *NYT*, March 8; 10, 1977.

19. "President Carter's Remarks at Clinton, Mass., Town Meeting," *State Department Bulletin*, April 11, 1977, p. 335; Brzezinski, p. 91.

Actually, the Balfour Declaration referred to the establishment in Palestine of "a national home for the Jewish people." In years subsequent to the issuance of the Declaration, Zionists frequently referred to their program as the building in Palestine of a Jewish "homeland."

20. *NYT*, April 5; 27; May 10; 13; 17, 1977. Cobban, *PLO*, p. 85.

21. *Keesing's*, 1977, p. 28, 534.

22. *NYT*, June 18, 1977.

23. Brzezinski, *Power and Principle*, p. 96.

24. Among senators speaking out immediately in support of Javits were Edward Brooke, Bob Packwood, Richard Schwiker, S. I. Hayakawa, Pete Domenici, Richard Stone, and John Sparkman. *NYT*, June 27, 1977.

25. Throughout the spring Israel's supporters had attacked the administration largely on grounds of various decisions related to arms transfers to Israel. Among these were Carter's refusal to sell Israel sophisticated concussion bombs (CBU's), his rejection of Israel's request for permission to conclude a deal with Ecuador for the sale of Kfir fighter planes (which although designed and produced in Israel, carried U.S.-made engines and therefore required Washington's consent for transferral to other parties). Noting that despite these steps, the Carter administration had undertaken a range of commitments to strengthen Israel militarily, Anthony Lewis concluded that it was not Washington's arms policy but rather its framework for Middle East peace that was the real target of the sustained barrage of condemnation. *NYT*, May 1, 1977; Reich, *The United States and Israel*, p. 50.

26. Brzezinski, *Power and Principle*, p. 97.

27. *NYT*, June 17; 26; July 1; 23, 1977.

28. Brzezinski, p. 97.

29. Carter, *Keeping Faith*, pp. 290–91.

30. Brzezinski, pp. 101–02.

31. Ibid.; Vance, *Hard Choice*, pp. 185–90. Vance carried three other options as well: 1) Palestinian representation on a Jordanian delegation; 2) deferring the question of Palestinian representation until the beginning of the conference; 3) deferring it until some later point in the conference.

32. *NYT*, August 10; 11, 1977; Brzezinski, pp. 102–03.

33. *NYT*, August 21; 29; September 29, 1977; Carter, *Keeping Faith*, p. 292; *Blood of Abraham*, pp. 73–74.

34. The administration was indirectly in contact with PLO leaders through the efforts of Saudi Arabia during this period. The public dialogue culminated in Carter's August 8 declaration that "if the Palestinians say, 'we recognize UN Resolution 242 in its entirety, but we think Palestinians have additional status other than refugees,' that would suit us okay." See: *NYT*, August 8; 9; 10; 15; 16; 27; September 13; 15; 25; 30, 1977. See also Brzezinski, p. 105; Tillman, *United States*, pp. 224–25.

35. *NYT*, August 10, 1977.

36. *NYT*, September 13, 1977. For an analysis concluding that Israel was not really disposed to compromise on the question of PLO representation at Geneva, see Sicherman, *Broker or Advocate*, p. 55. In the spring, Israeli Prime Minister Yitzhak Rabin had told Cyrus Vance that "Israel would not seek to inspect the credentials of the Jordanian delegation" at any peace conference that might convene. The Carter administration took this to imply a willingness on Israel's part to accept the presence of low level PLO members at a conference. However, in their first encounter with Menachem Begin, Carter and Vance learned that Israel's government remained unmovingly opposed to PLO participation in any guise. See Vance, *Hard Choice*, pp. 171; 183.

37. Fahmy, *Negotiating*, p. 194.

38. Ibid., p. 203.

39. Ibid., p. 204.

40. Ibid., pp. 202; 211. According to Fahmy, the president elaborated this point in a private conversation held shortly after he met the Egyptian delegation: "President Sadat repeatedly asks me to exercise pressure on Israel, but I want you to know that I simply cannot do it because it would be personal political suicide for me." Ibid., pp. 196–98.

41. *NYT*, September 30, 1977.

42. Vance, pp. 188–89.

43. *NYT*, October 3; 4; 1977.

44. See Appendix A; U.S.–Soviet Declaration on the Middle East.

45. Walid Khalidi, *Conflict and Violence in Lebanon: Confrontation in the Middle East* (Cambridge, MA: Center for International Affairs, Harvard University, 1981), p. 127.

46. See, for example: *NYT*, October 3; 4; 5; 6; 15, 1977. See also Reich, *The United States and Israel*, pp. 53–55; Sicherman, *Broker or Advocate*, pp. 59–60.

47. *NYT*, October 5, 1977.

48. Brzezinski, *Power and Principle*, pp. 108–09.

49. Ibid.

50. *NYT*, October 6, 1977.

51. *NYT*, October 14, 1977. The first comparison of the original U.S. Working Paper draft and the document finally agreed upon by the United States and Israel appeared a day earlier in the *Jerusalem Post* in an article filed by that newspaper's Washington correspondent, Wolf Blitzer.

52. Carter, *Keeping Faith*, p. 295.

53. Brzezinski, p. 111.

54. The text of Sadat's speech is reproduced as Appendix V in *Search for Identity*.

55. *NYT*, November 28, 1977. Earlier, however, Sadat remarked in another interview that he first began to consider dealing directly with Israel in April 1977, when he was asked by an Israeli journalist in Washington why Israelis were allowed to cover his activities in the United States but not in Egypt. Ibid., November 20, 1977.

56. Fahmy, pp. 252–84; Sicherman, pp. 65–66, 114; Klinghoffer and Apter, *Israel and the Soviet Union*, p. 175–76. Moshe Dayan, *Breakthrough: A Personal Account of the Egypt–Israel Peace Negotiations* (New York: Alfred A. Knopf, 1981), pp. 38–54.

57. "U.S. Economic Assistance to Egypt, Yearly Obligation: 1975–1987," USAID/Cairo, Program Office, April 1987 (unpublished). The $2.5 billion total includes grants and loans but not military aid. Of the total, $1.9 billion took the form of loans and slightly over $.5 billion was in the form of grants.

58. The strongest evidence Sadat had of this was a by-product of Cyrus Vance's trip to the Middle East in August. At Washington's behest, the states involved directly in the Arab–Israeli quarrel had undertaken the exercise of submitting draft peace treaties for American perusal. Egypt's called for an Israeli withdrawal to the international frontier. Israel's vision of a settlement differed markedly on this point. A compromise text was suggested by Washington. It supported the Egyptian territorial clause. See Fahmy, pp. 228–32.

59. See William B. Quandt, *Camp David: Peacemaking and Politics* (Washington, D.C.: The Brookings Institution, 1986), pp. 152–58.

The text of the Israeli plan as announced in the Knesset on December 28, 1977, "Self Rule for Palestinian Arabs, Residents of Judea, Samaria and the Gaza District, Which Will be Instituted Upon the Establishment of Peace," is reprinted as Appendix 4 in Dayan, *Breakthrough*, pp. 359–61.

60. Brzezinski, pp. 110–12. *NYT*, December 29, 1977.

61. Brzezinski, p. 112.

62. Touval, p. 291.

63. Brzezinski, p. 236.

64. Cited by Sheehan, pp. 193–94.

Israel has consistently challenged the contention that the Fourth Geneva Convention for the Protection of Civilian Populations in Times of War is applicable de jure to the occupied areas. For a sympathetic discussion of the Israeli position, see Allan Gerson, *Israel, the West Bank and International Law* (London: Frank Cass, 1978), pp. 110–15. It should be noted that Gerson, while conceding that Israel's settlement and land acquisition practices are "against the grain of the Geneva Convention, assuming its applicability" (p. 237), concludes that Israeli policies are not "unlawful" (p. 173). The basis of this view is Gerson's contention that Israeli "settlement and land acquisition were more in the nature of incipient ad hoc populist trends than the outgrowth of established government policies" (pp. 173–74).

That argument, painfully weak when published in 1978, has been demolished by more recent studies. See, for example, Benvenisti, op. cit.; Peretz, op. cit. See also Sally V. Mallison and Thomas Mallison, "Israeli Settlements in Occupied Territories: Appraisal Under International Law," unpublished paper, forthcoming in: League of Arab States, *International Symposium on Israeli Settlements in Occupied Arab Land, 1985: Proceedings.* See also Ann M. Lesch, "The Gaza Strip: Heading Toward a Deadend," *UFSI Report*, No. 11 (Hannover, NH: Universities Field Staff International, 1984).

65. *NYT*, September 4, 1977.

66. Lesch, "Israeli Settlements in the Occupied Territories," op. cit.

67. Benvenisti; see particularly Table 28, p. 61.

68. Ibid., pp. 49–63.

69. Brzezinski, pp. 105–06.

70. United Nations Security Council Resolution 452 (1979). For an interesting account of the background to this resolution, see *Yearbook of the United*

Nations (New York: United Nations Department of Public Information, 1982), pp. 380–91.

71. *NYT*, March 17; 18; 19; 20; April 6; 8; June 14, 1978.

72. Tillman, pp. 98–106; Ghassan Bishara, "The Middle East Arms Package," *Journal of Palestine Studies* (Summer, 1978), pp. 67–78.

73. *NYT*, January 5, 1978.

74. Tillman, p. 221.

75. Brzezinski, pp. 239–47; Touval, pp. 292–97.

76. Carter, *Keeping Faith*, pp. 311–12; Brzezinski, p. 246.

77. " . . . I was prepared," recalls Carter, "to withdraw from the Middle East issue altogether. It would be a great relief to me and I certainly had my hands full with other responsibilities."

By late spring, Carter's strained relations with Israel led to the cancellation of Democratic fund-raising dinners in New York and Los Angeles, and various Democratic congressmen and party officials were urging the administration to "back out of the situation and repair the damage they claimed I had already done to the Democratic party and to United States–Israel relations." Carter, *Keeping Faith*, pp. 312–16.

78. Touval, pp. 313–14.

79. Brzezinski, p. 253.

80. Quandt, *Camp David*, chapters 9 and 10; Brzezinski, pp. 252–73; Carter, *Keeping Faith*, pp. 319–403.

81. U.S. Department of State, *The Camp David Summit* (Washington, D.C.: Department of State Office of Communication, Bureau of Public Affairs, September, 1978).

The Knesset approved the measure at the end of September.

82. Fayez A. Sayegh, "The Camp David Agreement and the Palestine Problem," *Journal of Palestine Studies* VIII, no. 2 (Winter 1979), p. 6.

83. "Framework for Peace in the Middle East," emphasis added.

84. Carter referred to statements made respectively on July 14, 1967 and July 1, 1969 by Ambassadors Arthur Goldberg and Charles Yost. For the relevant portions of these statements, see "Excerpts from a Statement by United States Representative Arthur J. Goldberg at the Fifth General Assembly Concerning the United States Position on Jerusalem, July 14, 1967," in Moore, pp. 962–67, and "Statement by Ambassador Charles W. Yost, United States Representative to the United Nations, in the Security Council, On the Situation in Jerusalem, July 1, 1969," ibid., pp. 992–95. For an account of Menachem Begin's reaction to Carter's letter on Jerusalem, see Quandt, *Camp David*, p. 252.

85. Department of State, *Camp David Summit*.

86. Brzezinski, p. 273.

87. Vance, p. 228; Brzezinski, p. 274; Carter *Keeping Faith*, pp. 405–07.

88. Carter, *Blood of Abraham*, p. 45.

89. Vance, pp. 223–40; Moshe Dayan, *Breakthrough: A Personal Account of the Egypt-Israel Peace Negotiations* (New York: Alfred A. Knopf, 1981), pp. 211–43; Ezer Weizman, *The Battle for Peace* (New York: Bantam Books, 1981), pp. 378–82; Quandt, *Camp David*, pp. 271–81; Carter, *Keeping Faith*, pp. 404–10.

90. The text of Hussein's questions and the answers they elicited is available in Quandt, *Camp David*, Appendix H, pp. 388–96.

91. Dayan, p. 202.
92. Vance, p. 241.
93. Ibid., pp. 241–42.
94. Brzezinski, p. 279.
95. See note 101 below.
96. Vance, p. 245.
97. Ibid.
98. Brzezinski, p. 282.
99. Ibid., p. 283.
100. Ibid., p. 285.
101. It is worthwhile noting the full text of the agreed minute relevant to the priority of obligations of the Egyptian–Israel Peace Treaty.

Article VI (2)

The provisions of Article VI shall not be construed in contradiction to the provisions of the framework for peace in the Middle East agreed at Camp David. The foregoing is not to be construed as contravening the provisions of Article VI (2) of the Treaty, which reads as follows:

> The Parties undertake to fulfill in good faith their obligations under this Treaty, without regard to action or inaction of any other Party and independently of any instrument external to this Treaty.

Article VI (5)

It is agreed by the Parties that there is no assertion that this Treaty prevails over other Treaties or agreements or that other Treaties or agreements prevail over this Treaty. The foregoing is not to be construed as contravening the provisions of Article VI (5), which reads as follows:

> Subject to Article 103 of the United Nations Charter, in the event of a conflict between the obligations of the parties under the present Treaty and any of their other obligations, the obligations under this Treaty will be binding and implemented.

See: Arab Republic of Egypt, *White Paper on Treaty for Peace Between Egypt and Israel* (Cairo: Government Printing Offices, 1983), pp. 95–96. Hereafter cited as *White Paper*.

102. At Israel's insistence the mention of the self-governing authority was qualified by a parenthetical reference to an "administrative council." The same had been true of the Camp David Accords.

103. Carter to Sadat, March 26, 1979, *White Paper*, p. 117. In the end, a multinational force was deployed in the Sinai. See p. 156.

104. "U.S.–Israel Memorandum of Agreement, 26 March, 1979"; "Memorandum of Oil Agreement Between U.S. and Israel, 26 March, 1979," *White Paper*, pp. 183, 187.

105. Khalil to Vance, March 25, 1979, *White Paper*, p. 171.

106. Khalil to Vance, March 26, 1979, *White Paper*, pp. 175–77.

107. "Draft of a Proposed Report: 'U.S. Assistance to the State of Israel' Prepared by the Staff of the U.S. General Accounting Office," in Mohammed El-Khawas and Samir Abed Rabbo, *American Aid to Israel: Nature and Impact* (Brattleboro, VT: Amana Books, 1984), p. 168; Quandt, *Camp David*, pp. 313–14.

108. Ali E. Hillal Dessouki, "The Primacy of Economics: The Foreign Policy

of Egypt," in Bahgat Korany and Ali E. Hillal Dessouki (eds.), *The Foreign Policies of Arab States* (Boulder: Westview Press, 1984), pp. 142–43, and Paul C. Noble, "The Arab System: Opportunities, Constraints and Pressures," Ibid., pp. 47–71.

109. Carter, *Blood of Abraham*, p. 208.

110. Ibid.

111. Ibid.

112. Brzezinski, pp. 276; Carter, *Keeping Faith*, pp. 426–27, 491.

113. Brzezinski, p. 276.

114. For an elaboration of this point and an effort to speculate on its more general implications, see R. D. Tschirgi, "Modernization and Foreign Policy," *ACIS Working Paper*, No. 29 (Los Angeles: Center for International and Strategic Affairs, University of California, Los Angeles, 1980).

115. U.S. Congress, Senate, 94th Cong., 2nd Sess., "Prospects for Peace in the Middle East," *Hearings Before the Subcommittee on Near Eastern and South Asian Affairs of the Committee on Foreign Relations* (Washington, D.C.: U.S. GPO, 1976), p. 247.

116. Quandt, *Decisions*, p. 283.

117. Khalidi, p. 87.

118. Nonetheless, true to its desire to see the broadening chaos quelled lest its step-by-step strategy come to grief, the United States looked favorably on a highly qualified French offer—made in May 1976—to help restore tranquility to Lebanon. Even before this development, the United States briefly tried its own hand at peacemaking, dispatching a high ranking emissary, Ambassador L. Dean Brown, on a futile mission to reconcile the warring factions. U.S. Congress, Senate, "Prospects for Peace in the Middle East," pp. 124–27.

119. Dan Tschirgi, with Georges Irani, "The United States, Syria, and the Lebanese Crisis," *CISA Research Notes*, No. 8 (Los Angeles: Center for International and Strategic Affairs, University of California, Los Angeles, 1982).

120. For an interesting analysis that stresses domestic determinants of Syria's intervention in Lebanon without, however, offering a view that is incompatible with explanations based on Syrian foreign policy concerns, see Fred H. Lawson, "Syria's Intervention in the Lebanese Civil War; A Domestic Conflict Explanation," *International Organization* (Summer 1984), pp. 451–80.

121. U.S. President, *Public Papers of the President: Gerald R. Ford, 1976–1977* (Washington, D.C.: U.S. GPO, 1978), pp. 1067, 1885.

122. U.S. President, *Public Papers of the Presidents: Jimmy Carter, 1977* (Washington, D.C.: U.S. GPO, 1978), p. 845.

123. U.S. Congress, Senate, 96th Cong., 1st Sess., "Fiscal Year 1980 International Security Assistance Authorization," *Hearings Before the Committee on Foreign Relations* (Washington, D.C.: U.S. GPO, 1979), pp. 162–64.

124. See Tschirgi and Irani, p. 9.

125. Ibid., p. 3, 22, n. 3. See also U.S. Congress, House, 96th Cong., 1st Sess., "Proposed Arms Sales for Countries in the Middle East," *Hearings Before the Subcommittee on Europe and the Middle East of the Committee on Foreign Relations"* (Washington, D.C.: U.S. GPO, 1979), Appendix 3.

126. *NYT*, June 17, 1980.

127. *State Department Bulletin* 80, no. 2037 (April 1980), p. 51–53.

128. See, for example, the statement of J. R. Abinader, Executive Director of

the National Association of Arab Americans, to members of congress. U.S. Congress, House, 96th Cong., 2nd Sess., *Hearings Before a Subcommittee of the Committee on Appropriations*, Part 5 (Washington, D.C.: U.S. GPO, 1980), p. 214.

129. Ibid., pp. 13–30. See statements by Toby Moffet, Mary Oakar, Paul McClosky, and Nick Joe Rahall.

CHAPTER FOUR

1. *NYT*, November 7, 1980.

2. Ibid., March 24, 1980. One of Reagan's first presidential pronouncements reiterated, in slightly modified form, his pre-election stand on Israeli settlements. "I disagree," said Reagan on February 2, 1981, "when the previous administration referred to [settlements] as illegal, they're not illegal." He added that under the circumstances then prevailing, he considered the settlements to be "ill-advised." Cited by Tillman, p. 170.

3. *NYT*, March 24, 1980.

4. *NYT*, September 4, 1980.

5. Richard B. Strauss, "U.S. Policy of Mideast has Altered," *International Herald Tribune*, April 30, 1986.

6. Alexander Haig, *Caveat: Realism, Reagan, and Foreign Policy* (London: Weidenfelt and Nicolson, 1984), p. 169.

7. For a discussion of Begin's approach to the concept of Palestinian autonomy, see Shlomo Avineri, "Beyond Camp David," *Foreign Policy*, no. 46 (Spring 1982), pp. 22–25.

8. *NYT*, March 3; 12, 1981.

9. Alexander M. Haig, *Caveat*, p. 169.

10. *NYT*, March 8; April 9, 1981.

11. Haig, pp. 169–70.

12. Ibid.

13. Ibid., p. 173.

14. Ibid., pp. 172–79.

15. *Keesing's*, 1983, p. 31,912; Tillman, *United States*, pp. 118–22.

16. Haig, pp. 167–91.

17. *NYT*, October 20, 1981.

18. *NYT*, October 29, 1981.

19. Stephen S. Rosenfield, "Dateline Washington: Anti-Semitism and U.S. Foreign Policy," *Foreign Policy*, no. 47 (Summer 1982), pp. 172–73; Haig, pp. 167–93; Reich, *The United States and Israel*, pp. 192–94; Tillman, pp. 118–22.

20. Tillman, p. 38; Reich, *The United States and Israel*, p. 38.

21. Haig, p. 184.

22. Ibid.

23. Ball, *Error and Betrayal*, p. 33; Reich, *The United States and Israel*, pp. 99–103; *Keesing's*, 1983, p. 31,909.

24. *NYT*, July 21, 1981; see also Reich *The United States and Israel*, pp. 100–30; *Keesing's*, 1983, p. 31,908. Tensions rose in the wake of the Beirut bombing as PLO forces in south Lebanon retaliated by launching multiple rocket attacks on Israeli targets across the border.

25. *NYT*, August 9, 1981.

26. *NYT*, August 6, 1981.

27. *NYT*, September 11, 1981.

28. *NYT*, September 12, 1981.

29. Adverse Arab reaction to the U.S. agreement on strategic cooperation was widespread, even among regimes that were generally well disposed toward Washington. Egyptian President Mubarak termed it "a major obstacle on the road to peace." Jordan's King Hussein described the agreement as "completely terrible." *Cairo Press Review*, December 3, 1983, p. 3; ibid., December 4, 1983, p. 8.

30. Haig, p. 327.

31. Reich, *The United States and Israel*, pp. 101–03; Haig, p. 338; *Keesing's*, 1983, pp. 31,911–12.

32. The Knesset measure extended Israeli law, jurisdiction, and administration over the Golan Heights. It did not use the term "annexation," although at the time, and since, the decision was generally taken both in Israel and abroad as amounting to annexation.

33. Haig, p. 329.

34. *NYT*, December 21, 1981.

35. With strong U.S. encouragement, an Egyptian–Israeli agreement on the MFO's deployment was signed in early August, 1981. However, the problem of the projected force's composition remained a thorny issue for several months. Annoyed by the European Community's 1980 "Venice Declaration," which inter alia called for recognition of the Palestinians' "legitimate rights" and for PLO involvement in the peace process, Israel was reluctant to see members of that body participate in the MFO. By the end of January, Washington had successfully negotiated an arrangement under which Israel, France, Italy, The Netherlands, and Great Britain agreed that the Camp David Accords would serve as the basis for European participation in the MFO. In addition to these countries and the United States, Australia, Colombia, Fiji, New Zealand, Norway, and Uruguay were also scheduled to provide contingents for the MFO.

36. Yoram Peri, *Between Battles and Ballots: The Israeli Military in Politics* (Cambridge: Cambridge University Press, 1983), p. 261. Original emphasis. See also Shlomo Aronson and Nathan Yanai, "Critical Aspects of the Elections and Their Implications," in Dan Caspi, Abraham Diskin, and Emanuel Gutmann (eds.), *The Roots of Begin's Success: The 1981 Israeli Elections* (London: Croom Helm, 1984), pp. 11–42.

37. Yoram Peri, "Coexistence or Hegemony Shifts in the Israeli Security Concept," in Caspi, et al., *The Roots*, p. 194.

38. Ibid., p. 202.

39. See Ball, p. 29; Ze'ev Schiff and Ehud Ya'ari, *Israel's Lebanon War* (London: George Allen & Unwin, 1985), p. 71.

40. The possibility of establishing a friendly Christian regime in Lebanon was not attractive only to Revisionist Zionists. Among other mainstream Zionists, David Ben Gurion had been tantalized by the prospect. In 1948 he described Lebanon as "the weak link in the Arab coalition" and noted:

Moslem rule is easy to undermine. A Christian state must be established whose southern border will be the Litani. We shall sign a treaty with it.

Cited by George Ball, *Error and Betrayal in Lebanon: An Analysis of Israel's Invasion of Lebanon and the Implications for U.S.–Israeli Relations* (Washington, D.C.: Foundation for Middle Peace, 1984), p. 27.

41. *NYT*, April 19; 22, 1982.

42. "Peace and Security in the Middle East," *Department of State Bulletin* 82, no. 2064 (July 1982), pp. 44–47.

43. Haig, *Caveat*, pp. 334–35.

44. The Lebanese government subsequently placed the total dead, including Palestinian and Syrian military personnel, at 17,825, while claiming that over 30,000 persons were wounded during the war. Israel disputed these figures, particularly the claimed number of civilian deaths. See *Keesing's*, 1983, pp. 31,919–20.

On the other hand, the Lebanese police reported that between June 4 and August 31, 1982 a total of 19,805 persons were killed in Lebanon and 30,302 were wounded. The figure of 12,000 dead, including combatants as well as civilians, was at one point offered by official Israeli spokesmen. See Ball, p. 47.

45. *NYT* June 14, 1982; *Facts on File*, 1982, p. 431.

46. *Facts on File*, 1982, p. 474. Yariv spoke on June 29.

47. Cited by Ball, p. 27.

48. See Herbert Kelman, "Talk With Arafat," *Foreign Policy*, no. 49 (Winter 1983); Larry Fabian, "The Red Light," *Foreign Policy*, no. 50 (Spring 1983); Ball, pp. 26–28.

49. Confidential source.

50. Ball, pp. 27–29; Schiff and Ya'ari, *Israel's Lebanon War*, pp. 45–61.

51. *International Herald Tribune*, May 25–26, 1985.

52. See Oriana Fallaci's interview with Ariel Sharon, *The Washington Post*, August 29, 1982; Haig, pp. 332–33.

53. *International Herald Tribune*, May 25–26, 1985; Haig, pp. 332–33.

54. Ibid., p. 327.

55. Ibid., p. 332.

56. Ze'ev Schiff, "The Green Light," *Foreign Policy* 50 (Spring 1983), pp. 80–81.

57. Ibid., p. 82.

58. Ibid.

59. Haig, p. 342.

60. Ibid.

61. Ibid., p. 318.

62. Ibid., p. 347.

63. Ibid., pp. 351–52.

64. On June 7, the State Department issued a statement declaring that "Israel will have to withdraw its forces from Lebanon and the Palestinians will have to stop using Lebanon as a launching pad for attacks on Israel." *Keesing's*, 1983, p. 31,915.

65. Haig, p. 344.

66. *NYT*, June 22, 1982.

67. *NYT*, July 26, 1982.

68. *NYT*, June 22, 1982.

69. Ibid.

70. *Keesing's*, 1983, p. 31,918.

71. *NYT*, July 17, 1982.

72. *The Times*, August 5, 1982.

73. Robin Wright, David Blundy, Henry Brandon, Mark Hosenbail, and Phil Finnigan, "Beirut: The Liquidation of a City," *The Sunday Times*, August 8, 1982.

74. "Press Clips," *The Village Voice*, September 22, 1982. See also Roger Morris, "Beirut—And the Press—Under Siege," *Columbia Journalism Review*, November/December, 1982; See also *The Israeli Invasion of Lebanon: Part II* (New York: Claremont Research Publications, 1983).

75. Wright, Blundy, et al.

76. *NYT*, August 13, 1982.

77. These figures refer to the approximate numbers of PLO fighters who had been killed or captured by mid-August. *Keesing's*, 1983, p. 32,040.

78. Ball, p. 55–56.

79. Schiff and Ya'ari, pp. 247–49.

80. *Keesing's*, 1983, p. 32,040; Carol Collins, "Chronology of the War in Lebanon: September–December, 1982," *Journal of Palestine Studies* XII, no. 2 (Winter 1983), p. 102.

81. *The Beirut Massacre: The Complete Kahan Commission Report*, (Karz-Cohl: Princeton, 1983.)

82. *Newsweek*, February 4, 1985.

83. Schiff and Ya'ari, pp. 230–33.

84. " 'United States Policy for Peace in the Middle East,' Address to the Nation, September 1, 1982," *Weekly Compilation of Presidential Documents: Administration of Ronald Reagan* (Washington, D.C.: U.S. GPO, September 6, 1982, pp. 1081–85.

85. Emphasis added.

86. " 'Middle East Peace Initiative,' Secretary Shultz's Statement Before the Senate Foreign Relations Committee on September 10, 1982," *Department of State Bulletin*, 82, no. 2067 (October 1982), pp. 5–7.

87. *NYT*, September 6, 1982; *Keesing's*, 1983, p. 32,036.

88. *NYT*, September 3; 6, 1982.

89. *Keesing's*, 1983, pp. 32,036–37.

90. The main features of the eight-point Fez Plan were as follows:

1. Israeli withdrawal from all lands, including East Jerusalem, occupied during the 1967 war.
2. Dismantling of Jewish settlements in occupied territories.
3. Guarantee of freedom of worship for all religions at Holy Places.
4. Reaffirmation of Palestinian People's right to self-determination and the exercise of its national rights under the leadership of the PLO and the indemnification of all those Palestinians not wishing to return to their land.
5. The placing of the West Bank and Gaza under UN control during a transitional period not to exceed six months.
6. The establishment of a Palestinian state with East Jerusalem as its capital.
7. Security Council guarantees of peace among all states of the region.
8. Security Council guarantees of the above principles.

See *NYT*, September 10, 1981.

91. *Keesing's*, 1983, p. 32,038.

92. Ibid.

93. See *Facts on File*, 1982, p. 414.

94. *Keesing's*, 1983, p. 32,039.

95. *Christian Science Monitor*, October 13, 1982.

96. *NYT*, October 13, 1982.

97. *Christian Science Monitor*, October 13, 1982.

98. Ibid.; *NYT*, October 14, 1982.

99. Cobban, *PLO*, p. 132.

100. "Final Resolutions Adopted by the Palestine National Council at its Sixteenth Session," *Journal of Palestine Studies* (Spring 1983), pp. 250–54.

101. Cited by Cobban, p. 134.

102. "Final Resolutions Adopted by the Palestine National Council at its Sixteenth Session," op. cit.

103. *Keesing's*, 1983, p. 32,232; Cobban, pp. 134–35; *Christian Science Monitor*, January 18; March 3, 8, 1983.

104. See "The Reagan Plan Killers," *The Economist* 287, no. 7285 (April 16, 1983), pp. 25–29.

105. "The P.L.O.: Stuck in a Time Warp," *The Economist* 287, no. 7284 (April 9, 1983), p. 52.

106. "The Reagan Plan Killers," op. cit., p. 26.

107. *NYT*, April 11, 1983.

108. For an eye-witness account of Syrian involvement, see Joseph B. Treaster, "Arafat's Soldiers Lose Stronghold," *NYT*, November 7, 1983.

109. *Christian Science Monitor*, June 29, 1983.

110. See George Ball's discussion of this point. Ball, pp. 75–79.

111. James McCartney, "The 'Limited' U.S. Mission in Lebanon is Deepening," *Philadelphia Inquirer*, October 21, 1982.

112. Elmo Zumwalt, Jr., "Israel and the U.S. Gained in Lebanon," *NYT*, May 18, 1983; Ball, p. 66.

113. Ball, p. 27; Schiff and Ya'ari, pp. 233–34.

114. Ibid., p. 234.

115. Ibid., pp. 236–37. Confidential source.

116. A small British unit was sent to Lebanon in early 1983.

117. Cited by Ball, p. 62.

118. Schiff and Ya'ari, p. 287.

119. David Ignatius, "U.S. Risk in Lebanon Seen Escalating," *Wall Street Journal*, October 11, 1982; Rowland Evans and Robert Novak, "Bashir Gemayel's Last Bequest," *Washington Post*, October 6, 1982.

120. Cited by Schiff and Ya'ari, p. 290.

121. *Keesing's*, 1983, p. 32,047.

122. See *Facts on File*, 1982, p. 756; Schiff and Ya'ari, p. 293; Ball, p. 67.

123. *Keesing's*, 1983, p. 32,163–64.

124. *NYT*, February 4, 1984.

125. Oswald Johnson, "Sustained Effort by Shultz Led to Lebanon Pact," *Los Angeles Times*, May 11, 1983; Ball, pp. 65–68; Schiff and Ya'ari, pp. 295–97.

126. *NYT*, May 18, 1983; Ball, p. 66.

127. "Syria Grounds the Shuttle," *Newsweek*, May 16, 1983, p. 34.

128. Ibid.; see also Ball, p. 66; Nahum Barnea, "Why We Signed the Agree-

ment," *Koterit Rashit*, in Claremont Research Publications, *The Invasion of Lebanon: Part II*, op. cit., p. 352.

129. "Interview: Walid Jumblatt," *Newsweek*, May 30, 1983, p. 76.

130. *Keesing's*, 1984, pp. 32,645–46.

131. "Question-and-Answer Session with Reporters, December 14, 1983," *Weekly Compilation of Presidential Documents: Administration of Ronald Reagan* (Washington, D.C.: U.S. GPO), December 19, 1983, pp. 1688–89.

132. Ball, p. 83.

133. Ball, p. 83; Anthony Cordesman, "The Middle East and the Cost of the Politics of Force," *The Middle East Journal* 40, no. 1 (Winter 1986), pp. 13–15.

134. Stephen Green, "Strategic Asset, Soviet Opportunity," *American–Arab Affairs*, No. 9 (Summer 1984), pp. 49–54.

135. See Cheryl A. Rubenberg, "The Conduct of U.S. Foreign Policy in the Middle East in the 1983/84 Presidential Election Season," *American–Arab Affairs*, No. 9 (Summer 1984), pp. 22–45.

Among a multitude of articles detailing efforts of presidential and vice-presidential aspirants to attract Jewish voters on the basis of pro–Israel policy stands, see those describing the activities of Gary Hart, Walter Mondale, and Geraldine Ferraro: *Philadelphia Inquirer*, April 8, 1984; *Washington Post*, October 27, 1984; *The Daily Telegraph*, October 30, 1984.

Late in the campaign season, Ronald Reagan had a bitter experience demonstrating that candidates could inadvertently offend potential Jewish voters by overeager campaigning. Appearing at a Long Island synagogue in a red, white, and blue yarmulke, Reagan, in the words of an outraged *Boston Globe* editorial, sought to justify his administration's earlier intervention in Lebanon in words calculated "to make Jewish souls vibrate with emotion." "Anyone who remembers the lesson of the Holocaust," declared the president, "must understand that we have a fundamental moral obligation to assure: never again."

The implication that U.S. troops had been in Lebanon to protect Israel caused considerable concern to American Jewish leaders. Sympathizing with their concern, the *Boston Globe* opined that "the lie Reagan told . . . is dangerous to Jews and should be repulsive to all Americans." American Jewish leader Rabbi Alexander Schindler strongly condemned the president's remarks for suggesting that Israel required the U.S. military to defend it as well as for demeaning the memory of the Holocaust. See, *The Boston Globe*, October 30, 1984, and *Jewish Telegraphic Agency*, October 30, 1984.

136. *Washington Post*, April 11, 1984; *NYT*, July 9, 13, 16, 1984.

137. See "Political Report Presented by PLO Executive Committee to the 17th Session of the Palestine National Council," *Journal of Palestine Studies* XV, no. 2 (Winter 1985), pp. 249–53.

138. "Text of Jordanian–Palestinian Accord Released February 23, 1985," *Journal of Palestine Studies* XIV, no. 3 (Spring 1985), p. 206.

139. See the text of King Hussein's address on the Middle East of February 19, 1986, in *Journal of Palestine Studies* XV, no. 4 (Summer 1986), pp. 206–32.

140. Ibid.

141. "Address by King Hussein of Jordan at the American Enterprise Institute," *American–Arab Affairs*, No. 13 (Summer 1985), pp. 135–41; *Time Magazine*, June 17, 1985.

142. Dan Tschirgi, "U.S. Must Define Stance to be Mideast Mediator," *The Middle East Times*, 22–29 June, 1985.

143. Israel immediately rejected the list of suggested Palestinian representatives. See *NYT*, July 18, 1985.

144. *NYT*, July 19, 1985. See also, "Address By King Hussein of Jordan at the American Enterprise Institute," op. cit., and *NYT*, June 16; July 31; August 4, 11, 14, 1985.

145. King Hussein's February 19, 1986 address, op. cit.

146. Ibid.

147. See above, Appendix B, "Excerpts From The Cairo Declaration."

148. Jonathan C. Randal, "Hussein Reveals Talks With PLO Have Failed," *International Herald Tribune*, February 20, 1986; "Failure in the Middle East," *International Herald Tribune*, February 22–23, 1986; Charles P. Wallace, "Hussein–Arafat Talks Reported to Have Collapsed," *International Herald Tribune*, February 10, 1986.

149. "Hussein Address on the Middle East of February 19, 1986," op. cit.

150. Only months after informing King Hussein of its conditional willingness to see an invitation to a peace conference sent to the PLO, the administration had an opportunity to elaborate its view of what would constitute an acceptable recognition of Security Council Resolutions 242 and 338. Responding to a query from Congressman Lee H. Hamilton, the State Department's Acting Secretary for Legislative and Intergovernmental Affairs, James W. Dyer, wrote as follows:

Resolutions 242 and 338 must be accepted on their own, without reference to other UN resolutions, as the basis for negotiations.

See above, Appendix D for excerpts from the text of Dyer's letter. See also *Journal of Palestine Studies* XVI, no. 1 (Autumn 1986), pp. 236–38.

151. King Hussein's address of February 19, 1986, op. cit.

152. *Congressional Record*, Extensions of Remarks on "Jordanian–PLO Negotiations and Middle East Peace Efforts," submitted by Representative Lee H. Hamilton, Chairman of the Subcommittee on Europe and the Middle East of the House Committee on Foreign Affairs, Washington, D.C., 5 June 1986, *Journal of Palestine Studies* XVI, no. 1 (Autumn 1986), pp. 234–35. See Appendix C above.

153. Response to Representative Lee H. Hamilton from Mr. James W. Dyer, Acting Assistant Secretary, *Journal of Palestine Studies* XVI, no. 1 (Autumn 1986), pp. 236–38. See Appendix D above.

154. "PLO Executive Committee Statement, Tunis, 7 March, 1986," *Journal of Palestine Studies* XV, no. 4 (Summer 1986), pp. 232–41.

155. *NYT*, February 23, 1986.

156. *NYT*, April 9; July 8, 1986.

157. "U.S. Says PLO Failed 'Challenge' of Peace Efforts," *International Herald Tribune*, February 21, 1986.

158. Randal, "Hussein Reveals Talks With PLO Have Failed," op. cit.

159. The text of the Five Year Plan announced by Jordan's Ministry of Planning is reproduced in *Journal of Palestine Studies* XVI, no. 1 (Autumn 1986), pp. 205–12.

160. *Facts on File*, 1986, p. 972.

161. John Kifner, "Anti-Arafat Position by Jordan's Hussein Appears to Back-fire," *International Herald Tribune*, March 6, 1986; Jonathan C. Randal, "Jordan and PLO Hold First Talks Since February '86," ibid., February 16, 1986.

In August 1986, Dr. Mohammed Shadid, of Al-Najah University in the West Bank town of Nablus, led a team that surveyed West Bank public opinion. The project was supported by the Palestinian West Bank newspaper *Al Fajr*, the Australian Broadcasting Company, and New York *Newsday*. Shadid's study, which was based on answers obtained from a random sample of 1,024 respondents, concluded that over 90 percent of Palestinians on the West Bank believed the PLO to be their sole legitimate representative; that over 70 percent saw Yassir Arafat as their leader. The next favored leader was King Hussein of Jordan, identified as such by 3.4 percent of the sample.

See "The *Al-Fajr* Public Opinion Survey," *Journal of Palestine Studies* XVI, no. 62 (Winter 1987), pp. 196–207.

162. UPI Dispatch, *The Egyptian Gazette*, February 22, 1987.

CHAPTER FIVE

1. See, West Bank Data Project, *Survey of Settlers and Settlements*, "Summary" (Jerusalem: West Bank Data Project, 1987), (Hebrew). M. S. Agnawi, "Goals Means, and Patterns of Settlements in the Occupied Territories," unpublished paper; forthcoming in League of Arab States, *International Symposium on Israeli Territories in Occupied Arab Lands, 1985: Proceedings*. Cited hereafter as *International Symposium*. See also, Ann M. Lesch, "The Gaza Strip: Heading for a Dead End," *UFSI Report*, No. 11 (Hanover, NH: Universities Field Staff International, 1984).

2. See: *Washington Post*, April 1, 1985, cited by Sally V. Mallison and Thomas Mallison, "Israeli Settlements in Occupied Territories: Appraisal Under International Law," unpublished paper; forthcoming in League of Arab States, *International Symposium*. Don Peretz, *The West Bank: History, Politics, Society and Economy* (Boulder, CO: Westview Press, 1986), p. 59. See also Lesch, "The Gaza Strip."

3. Meron Benvenisti, *The West Bank Data Project: A Survey of Israel's Policies* (Washington, D.C.: American Enterprise Institute for Public Policy Research, 1984), p. 55.

4. See Connie de Boer, "The Polls: Attitudes Toward the Arab–Israel Conflict," *Public Opinion Quarterly* 47, no. 1 (Spring 1983); Hazel Gaudet Erskine, "The Polls: Exposure to International Information," *Public Opinion Quarterly* 27, no. 4 (Winter 1963).

5. Tschirgi, *Politics of Indecision*, pp. 263–70.

6. Among the most tightly argued examples of these are Walid Khalidi, "Thinking the Unthinkable," *Foreign Affairs* 56, no. 4 (July 1978), pp. 695–713; and Mark Heller, *A Palestinian State: The Implications for Israel* (Cambridge, MA: Harvard University Press, 1983).

7. *NYT*, March 2, 1945.

8. "This Month in the Middle East," *The Middle East*, No. 161 (March 1988), p. 5.

9. For a more extended discussion of this point based on events in the occupied territories in the spring of 1987, see Dan Tschirgi, "High Hope, Bad News," *The Los Angeles Times*, June 28, 1987; and Dan Tschirgi, "A Bleak Year on the West Bank," *The Middle East*, No. 154 (August, 1987), pp. 11–16.

SELECTED BIBLIOGRAPHY

Ajami, Fouad. *The Arab Predicament: Arab Political Thought and Practice Since 1967*. Cambridge: Cambridge University Press, 1981.

Allen, Richard. *Imperialism and Nationalism in the Fertile Crescent: Sources and Prospects of the Arab–Israeli Conflict*. New York: Oxford University Press, 1974.

Arakie, Margaret. *The Broken Sword of Justice: America, Israel, and the Palestine Tragedy*. London: Quartet Books, 1973.

Avinery, Uri. *My Friend, The Enemy*. London: Zed Books, 1986.

Bain, Kenneth Ray. *The March to Zion: United States Policy and the Founding of Israel*. College Station, TX: Texas A&M University Press, 1979.

Ball, George. *Error and Betrayal in Lebanon: An Analysis of Israel's Invasion of Lebanon and the Implications for U.S.–Israeli Relations*. Washington, D.C.: Foundation for Middle East Peace, 1984.

Benvenisti, Meron. *The West Bank Data Project: A Survey of Israel's Policies*. Washington, D.C.: American Enterprise Institute, 1984.

Brecher, Michael. *Decisions in Israel's Foreign Policy*. Oxford: Oxford University Press, 1974.

———. *Decisions in Crisis: Israel, 1967 and 1973*. Berkeley: University of California Press, 1980.

Brenner, Lenni. *The Iron Wall: Zionist Revisionism From Jabotinski to Shamir*. London: Zed Books, 1984.

Brown, William R. *The Last Crusade: A Negotiator's Middle East Handbook*. Chicago: Nelson-Hall, 1980.

Brzezinski, Zbigniew. *Power and Principle: Memoires of the National Security Adviser*. New York: Farrar, Straus, Giroux, 1983.

Carter, Jimmy. *The Blood of Abraham*. Boston: Houghton Mifflin Co., 1985.

———. *Keeping Faith*. New York: Bantam Books, 1982.

Caspi, Dan, Abraham Disckin and Emannuel Gutmann (eds.). *The Roots of Begin's Success: The 1981 Israeli Elections*. London: Croom Helm, 1984.

Cobban, Helena. *The Palestinian Liberation Organization*. Cambridge: Cambridge University Press, 1984.

Confino, Michael, and Shimon Shamir (eds.). *The U.S.S.R. and the Middle East.* Tel Aviv: Israel Universities Press, 1973.

Cooley, John K. *Green March, Black September.* London: Frank Cass, 1973.

Dayan, Moshe. *Breakthrough: A Personal Account of the Egypt–Israel Peace Negotiations.* New York: Alfred A. Knopf, 1981.

Dib, George, and Fuad Jabber (eds.) *Israel's Violation of Human Rights in the Occupied Territories: A Documented Report.* Beirut: Institute for Palestine Studies, 1970.

El-Khawas, Mohammed, and Rabbo Samir Abed. *American Aid to Israel: Nature and Impact.* Brattleboro, VT: Amana Books, 1984.

Fahmy, Ismail. *Negotiating for Peace in the Middle East.* London: Croom Helm, 1983.

Gerson, Allan. *Israel, the West Bank and International Law.* London: Frank Cass, 1978.

Ghanayem, Ishaq I., and Alden H. Voth. *The Kissinger Legacy.* New York: Praeger, 1984.

Golan, Galia. *The Soviet Union and the Palestine Liberation Organization.* New York: Praeger, 1980.

Green, Stephen. *Taking Sides.* New York: William Morrow, 1984.

Haig, Alexander. *Caveat: Realism, Reagan, and Foreign Policy.* London: Weidenfelt and Nicolson, 1984.

Halperin, Samuel. *The Political World of American Zionism.* Detroit: Wayne State University Press, 1961.

Heikal, Mohammed Hassanein. *The Road to Ramadan.* New York: Quandrangle Books, 1975.

Heller, Mark. *A Palestinian State: The Implications for Israel.* Cambridge, MA: Harvard University Press, 1983.

Hofstadter, Dan (ed.). *Egypt and Nasser.* Vol. 3. New York: Facts on File, Inc., 1973.

Hudson, Michael. *The Precarious Republic: Modernization in Lebanon.* Boulder, CO: Westview, 1985.

Hurewitz, J. C. *The Struggle for Palestine.* New York: W. W. Norton, 1950.

Isaac, Jean Rael. *Israel Divided: Ideological Politics in the Jewish State.* Baltimore: The Johns Hopkins University Press, 1976.

Jabber, Paul. *Not by War Alone: Security and Arms Control in the Middle East.* Berkeley: University of California Press, 1981.

Johnson, Lyndon Baines. *The Vantage Point.* New York: Holt, Rinehart and Winston, 1971.

Kalb, Marvin, and Bernard Kalb. *Kissinger.* Boston: Little, Brown and Co., 1974.

Kass, Ilana. *Soviet Involvement in the Middle East: Policy Formulation, 1966–1973.* Boulder, CO: Westview, 1978.

Kauppi, Mark V., and Craig R. Nation (eds.). *The Soviet Union and the Middle East in the 1980s.* Lexington, MA: Lexington Books, 1983.

Kazziha, Walid. *Revolutionary Transformation in the Arab World: Habash and His Comrades From Nationalism to Marxism.* London: Charles Knight and Co., 1975.

Kenen, Isaiah L. *Israel's Defense Line: Her Friends and Enemies.* Buffalo, NY: Prometheus Books, 1981.

Khalidi, Walid. *Conflict and Violence in Lebanon: Confrontation in the Middle East.* Cambridge, MA: Center for International Affairs, Harvard University, 1981.

Kimmerling, Baruch. *Zionism and Territory: The Socio-Territorial Dimensions of Zionist Politics.* Berkeley: Institute of National Studies, University of California, Berkeley, 1983.

Kissinger, Henry A. *The White House Years.* Boston: Little, Brown and Co., 1979.

————. *Years of Upheaval.* Boston: Little, Brown and Co., 1982.

Klinghoffer, Arthur, and Judith Apter. *Israel and the Soviet Union.* Boulder, CO: Westview Press, 1985.

Korany, Bahgat, and Ali E. Hillal Dessouki. *The Foreign Policy of Arab States.* Boulder, CO: Westview Press, 1984.

Lacqueur, Walter Z. *A History of Zionism.* New York: Holt, Rinehart and Winston, 1972.

Lenczowski, George. *Soviet Advances in the Middle East.* Washington, D.C.: The American Enterprise Institute, 1972.

Lesch, Ann M. *Arab Politics in Palestine, 1917–1939: The Frustration of a Nationalist Movement.* Ithaca: Cornell University Press, 1979.

Lustik, Ian. *Arabs in the Jewish State: Israel's Control of a National Minority.* Austin: University of Texas Press, 1980.

Mangold, Peter. *Superpower Intervention in the Middle East.* New York: St. Martins Press, 1978.

Mansfield, Peter. *The Arabs.* Middlesex: Penguin Books, 1979.

Moore, John Norton (ed.). *The Arab–Israeli Conflict.* Vol. III, *Documents.* Princeton: Princeton University Press, 1974.

Newman, David (ed.). *The Impact of Gush Emunim: Politics and Settlement in the West Bank.* London: Croom Helm, 1985.

Nixon, Richard M. *RN: The Memoirs of Richard Nixon.* New York: Warner Books, 1978.

O'Ballance, Edgar. *The Third Arab–Israeli War.* London: Faber and Faber, 1972.

Orr, Akiva. *The Un-Jewish State: The Politics of Jewish Identity in Israel.* London: Ithaca Press, 1983.

Peretz, Don. *The West Bank: History, Politics, Society and Economics.* Boulder, CO: Westview Press, 1986.

Peri, Yoram. *Between Battles and Ballots: The Israeli Military in Politics.* Cambridge: Cambridge University Press, 1983.

Porath, Yehoshua. *The Emergence of the Palestinian Arab Nationalist Movement.* London: Frank Cass, 1974.

————. *The Palestinian Nationalist Movement, 1929–1939.* London: Frank Cass, 1977.

Quandt, William B., Fuad Jabber, and Ann M. Lesch. *The Politics of Palestinian Nationalism.* Berkeley and Los Angeles: University of California Press, 1973.

Quandt, William B. *Decade of Decisions: American Policy Toward the Arab–Israeli Conflict, 1967–1976.* Berkeley: University of California Press, 1977.

————. *Camp David: Peacemaking and Politics.* Washington, D.C.: The Brookings Institution, 1986.

Rafael, Gideon. *Destination Peace: Three Decades of Israeli Foreign Policy, A Personal Memoir*. London: Weidenfeld and Nicolson, 1981.

Reich, Bernard. *Quest for Peace*. New Brunswick, NJ: Transaction Books, 1977.

————. *The United States and Israel: Influence in the Special Relationship*. New York: Praeger, 1984.

Ro'i, Yaacov (ed.). *The Limits of Power: Soviet Policy in the Middle East*. London: Croom Helm, 1979.

Rubin, Jeffrey Z. (ed.). *Dynamics of Third Party Intervention: Kissinger and the Middle East*. New York: Praeger, 1981.

Sadat, Anwar. *In Search of Identity: An Autobiography*. New York: Harper and Row, 1978.

Safran, Nadev. *The United States and Israel*. Cambridge, MA: Harvard University Press, 1963.

————. *Israel: The Embattled Ally*. Cambridge, MA: Belknap Press, 1978.

Saunders, Harold H. *The Other Walls: The Politics of the Arab–Israeli Peace Process*. Washington, D.C.: American Enterprises Institute for Policy Research, 1985.

Schiff, Ze'ev, and Ehud Ya'ari. *Israel's Lebanon War*. London: George Allen and Unwin, 1985.

Schleifer, Abdullah. *The Fall of Jerusalem*. New York: Monthly Review Press, 1972.

Shadid, Mohammed K. *The United States and the Palestinians*. New York: St. Martins, 1981.

Sheehan, Edward R. F. *The Arabs, Israelis and Kissinger: A Secret History of American Diplomacy in the Middle East*. New York: Reader's Digest Press, 1976.

Sicherman, Harvey. *Broker or Advocate: The U.S. Role in the Arab–Israeli Dispute, 1973–1978*. Philadelphia: Foreign Policy Research Institute, 1978.

Stone, Russell A. *Social Change in Israel: Attitudes and Events*. New York: Praeger, 1982.

Tillman, Seth P. *The United States in the Middle East*. Bloomington: Indiana University Press, 1982.

Tomeh, George J. (ed.). *United Nations Resolutions on Palestine and the Arab–Israeli Conflict, 1947–1974*. Beirut: Institute for Palestine Studies, 1975.

Touval, Sadia. *The Peace Brokers: Mediators in the Arab–Israeli Conflict, 1948–1979*. Princeton: Princeton University Press, 1982.

Tschirgi, Dan. *The Politics of Indecision: Origins and Implications of American Involvement With the Palestine Problem*. New York: Praeger, 1983.

Udovitch, A. L. (ed.). *The Middle East: Oil, Conflict and Hope*. Lexington, MA: Lexington Books, 1976.

Vance, Cyrus. *Hard Choices: Critical Years in America's Foreign Policy*. New York: Simon and Schuster, 1983.

Vital, David. *The Origins of Zionism*. London: Oxford University Press, 1975.

Weizman, Ezer. *The Battle for Peace*. New York: Bantam Books, 1981.

Wilson, Evan M. *Decision in Palestine: How the U.S. Came to Recognize Israel*. Stanford: Hoover Institution Press, 1979.

Yodfat, Aryeh. *Arab Politics in the Soviet Mirror*. Jerusalem: Israel Universities Press, 1973.

Zohar, David M. *Political Parties in Israel: The Evolution of Israeli Democracy*. New York: Praeger, 1974.

INDEX

ABOUT THE AUTHOR

DAN TSCHIRGI specializes in U.S. relations with the Middle East and in Middle East politics. He is an Associate Professor of Political Science at the American University in Cairo. He has published various articles in his fields of interest and is the author of *The Politics of Indecision: Origins and Implications of American Involvement with the Palestine Problem.*

Dr. Tschirgi holds a B.A. and an M.A. from the American University in Beirut and a Ph.D. from the University of Toronto.